W9-DGL-410

Designing the Perfect Résumé

Second Edition

by

Pat Criscito, CPRW

President and Founder
ProType, Ltd.
Colorado Springs

Author of Barron's
Résumés in Cyberspace and
Guide to Distance Learning

BARRON'S

The résumés in this book are real résumés used by real people to get real jobs.
The names and contact information have been changed to protect their privacy.
Thank you to all my clients for their inspiration and permission to use their résumés.

All inquiries should be addressed to:
Barron's Educational Series, Inc.
250 Wireless Boulevard
Hauppauge, New York 11788
http://www.barronseduc.com

Library of Congress Catalog Card No. 99-86610

International Standard Book No. 0-7641-1268-6

Library of Congress Cataloging-in-Publication Data

Criscito, Pat, 1953–
     Designing the perfect résumé / by Pat Criscito — 2nd ed.
          p. cm.
     Includes index.
     ISBN 0-7641-1268-6
      1. Résumés (Employment) I. Title.

HF5383.C74 2000
808'.06665—IC21

99-86610

PRINTED IN THE UNITED STATES OF AMERICA
9 8

Contents

1 The Perfect Résumé?

The only *perfect* résumé is the one that fits the personality of its owner, tempered of course by the expectations of the industry. That means there are as many "perfect résumés" as there are kinds of people and kinds of jobs! Well, you won't find millions of résumés in *this* book, but you should find at least one that is a good match with your personality and industry. The ideas in this book can be used in your personal résumé or, if you are a professional résumé designer or career consultant, in your work with other people's résumés.

Even though Chapter 2 is devoted to writing the words in your résumé, the rest of this book is intended to help you express yourself visually in the design of your résumé. The choice of overall style, type font, graphics, and even paper color says something about your personality. If you consider yourself to be more conservative and if you are in a traditional job in senior management, banking, or accounting, you will probably be drawn to the résumés in the first half of this book. Later in the book, in Chapters 12 and 17, you will find résumés for more creative types, like actors, graphic designers, artists, and advertising professionals.

Remember, a résumé is just a way to get your foot in the door. It is a marketing tool—an advertisement. The *perfect* résumé will stand out in a two-inch stack of résumés on a busy executive's desk and help you get that all-important interview by making a strong first impression.

Even though content is important, many times well-qualified people aren't considered for positions because a poorly designed résumé didn't grab the reader's attention long enough to make sure the words were read. Just the opposite can be true as well. Even if your qualifications aren't the greatest, a well-designed résumé improves your chances of getting an interview because it stands out in a crowd of poorly designed ones.

Because I feel strongly that a résumé should reflect the personality of the person it represents, I respect my clients' wishes when it comes to the actual design of their résumés. This means that, even though my staff and I write and design more than a thousand résumés every year for clients in 42 countries, no two are exactly alike. You won't like every résumé in this book, and you shouldn't. Each one is designed and written to reflect an individual's personal career goals, industry, and personality.

Choose elements from various résumés that create a personalized look just for you, but keep in mind where you will be sending your résumé. Today, many mid-sized companies, large companies, and recruiters who receive a lot of résumés are now scanning résumés into electronic databases. Because of this trend, certain design elements are not appropriate for scanning. For those of you who know you will be sending résumés to Fortune 1000 and large high-tech companies, read Chapter 3 closely and pay attention to the bottom space under certain résumés in the book where you will find the word "Scannable." When a résumé doesn't have that word at the bottom, there is something about the design that makes it difficult for scanners to read. It simply might be the font used for the name or some other small element of the résumé, or it might be the entire design. Use Chapter 3 to guide you through your design choices.

This book is *not* devoted strictly to scannable résumés, however. Only about 30 percent of jobs openings today require a résumé that is scannable. The remaining 70 percent can be designed with your personality and industry in mind without a second thought to scannability. For those of you who will mix sending your résumé to companies that scan résumés and those who don't, it is possible to create a perfectly scannable ASCII text résumé (see page 30) that can be printed and sent along with a handsomely designed résumé that may not be scannable. Then your recipient has a choice of which résumé to scan.

Just because this book focuses on design doesn't mean you should neglect the words on your résumé. Chapter 2 will guide you through an award-winning twelve-step writing process that will help you get your experience and accomplishments down on paper. Remember, once your résumé design has grabbed your reader's attention, the words must then keep that attention.

About half of the book is devoted to the various design elements of a résumé with full-page samples: name, address, headings, dates, geographic locations, fonts, bullets, graphic lines, and other graphic design elements. Chapter 13 will show you the visual difference between laying out your résumé with bulleted short lines and paragraphs. Chapter 14 will provide you with samples of functional résumés and functional/chronological combinations. Curriculum vitae and executive/professional résumés have unique needs addressed in Chapters 15 and 16. Then we get to have some fun with creative résumés for artists, advertising professionals, actors, dancers, models, and other artistic people. In Chapter 18, you will find sample cover letters on various letterhead styles and a discussion of paper color, type, and size.

You have a wealth of designs and job descriptions in this book from which to choose, more than in any other résumé book on the market today. If you find wording that works for you, please feel free to use it as a foundation for the words on your own résumé. The index at the end of this book will help you find specific job titles that might help you to describe your experience. Every job title from every résumé in the book has been pulled out in alphabetical order to make it easier for you to locate specific job descriptions.

Now that you know what this book offers, let's get started writing your résumé!

2 How to Write the Perfect Résumé

Writing your résumé is often one of the most difficult things you will ever do! Think about it . . . you must turn your life history into a one-page advertisement that highlights a lifetime of experience, accomplishments, and education. Since we have been taught all of our lives not to brag, most people find this ultimate brag piece difficult to write.

Before you can begin to design your résumé on paper, you need to have the words. Use the following twelve-step writing process to help you clarify your experience, accomplishments, skills, education, and other background information, which will make the job of condensing your life onto a sheet of paper a little easier.

❑ Step One: Focus

Decide what type of job you will be applying for and then write it at the top of a piece of paper. This can become your objective statement, should you decide to use one, or be used in the first line of the profile section of your résumé to give your reader a general idea of your area of expertise.

Objectives are not required on a résumé, and often the cover letter is the best place to personalize your objective for each job opening. There is nothing wrong with using an objective statement on a résumé, however, provided it doesn't limit your job choices. As an alternative, you can alter individual résumés with personalized objectives that reflect the actual job title for which you are applying. Just make sure that the rest of your information is still relevant to the new objective, though.

Never write an objective statement that is not precise. You should name the position you want so specifically that, if a janitor came by and knocked over all the stacks of sorted résumés on a hiring manager's desk, he could put yours back in its right stack without even thinking about it. That means saying, "A marketing management position with an aggressive international consumer goods manufacturer" instead of "A position which utilizes my education and experience to mutual benefit."

❑ Step Two: Education

Under the objective on the first piece of paper, list any education or training that might relate. If you are a recent college graduate and have little relevant experience, then your education section will be placed at the top of your résumé. As you gain more experience, your education almost always gravitates to the bottom.

If you participated in college activities or received any honors or completed any notable projects that relate directly to your target job, this is the place to list them.

Showing high school education and activities on a résumé is only appropriate when you are under 20 and have no education or training beyond high school. Once you have completed either college courses or specialized technical training, drop your high school information altogether.

Continuing education shows that you care about life-long learning and self-development, so think about any relevant training since your formal education was completed. *Relevant* is the key word here. Always look at your résumé from the perspective of a potential employer. Don't waste space by listing training that is not directly or indirectly related to your target job.

❑ Step Three: Job Descriptions

Get your hands on a written description of the job you wish to obtain and for any jobs you have held in the past. If you are presently employed, your human resource department is the first place to look. If not, then go to your local library and ask for a copy of *The Dictionary of Occupational Titles* or the *Occupational Outlook Handbook*. These industry standard reference guides offer volumes of occupational titles and job descriptions for everything from Abalone Divers to Zoo Veterinarians (and thousands in between).

Another resource available at your local library or college career center is *Job Scribe*, a computer software program with more than 3,000 job descriptions. Other places to look for job descriptions include your local government job service agencies, professional and technical organizations, headhunters (i.e., recruiters), associates who work in the same field, newspaper advertisements for similar jobs, or online job postings (which tend to have longer job descriptions than print ads).

This book will provide you with hundreds of job descriptions taken from all of the résumé samples. Simply check the index at the back of the book for relevant job titles and turn to the appropriate page.

Now, make a copy of the applicable descriptions and then highlight the sentences that describe anything you have done in your past or present jobs. These job descriptions are important sources of keywords, so pay particular attention to nouns and phrases that you can incorporate into your own résumé.

❑ Step Four: Keywords

In today's world of e-mailed and scannable résumés, make sure you know the buzzwords of your industry and incorporate them into the sentences you are about to write. Keywords are the nouns or short phrases that describe your experience and education that might be used to find your résumé in a keyword search of a résumé database. They are the essential knowledge, abilities, and skills required to do your job. They are concrete descriptions like: C++, UNIX, fiber optic cable, network, project management, etc. Even well-known company names (AT&T, IBM, Hewlett-Packard, MCI) and universities (Harvard, Yale, SMU, SUNY, USC, Stanford, Tulane, Thunderbird) are sometimes used as keywords, especially when it is necessary to narrow down an initial search that calls up hundreds of résumés from a résumé database.

Acronyms and abbreviations here can either hurt you or help you, depending on how you use them. One example given to me by an engineer at Resumix was the abbreviation "IN." Think about it. "IN" could stand for *intelligent networks*, *Indiana*, or the word *in*. It is better to spell out the abbreviation if there could be any possible confusion. However, if a series of initials is so well known that it would be recognized by nearly everyone in your industry and would not likely be confused with a real word, then the keyword search will probably use those initials (i.e., IBM, CPA, UNIX). When in doubt, always spell it out at least one time on your résumé. A computer only needs to see the combination one time for it to be considered a "hit" in a keyword search.

Soft skills are often not included in search criteria, especially for very technical positions, although I have interviewed some companies that use them extensively for the initial selection of résumés for management positions. For instance, "communicate effectively," "self-motivated," "team player," and so on, are great for describing your abilities and are fine to include in your profile, but concentrate more on your hard skills, especially if you are in a high-tech field.

At the end of the chapter, you will find more examples of keywords for specific industries, although there is no such thing as a comprehensive listing of keywords for any single job. The computerized applicant tracking programs used by most companies allow the recruiter or hiring manager to personalize his or her list for each job opening, so it is an evolving process. You will never know whether you have listed absolutely every keyword possible, so focus instead on getting on paper as many related skills as possible, remembering to be absolutely honest and accurate.

The job descriptions you found in step three are some of the most important sources for keywords. You can also be certain that nearly every noun and some adjectives in a job posting or advertisement will be keywords, so make sure you use those words somewhere in your résumé, using synonyms wherever you can. Make a list of the keywords you have determined are important for your particular job search and then list synonyms for those words. As you incorporate these words into the sentences of your résumé, check them off.

One caution. Always tell the truth. The minute a hiring manager speaks with you on the telephone or begins an interview, any exaggeration of the truth will become immediately apparent. It is a bad idea to say, "I don't have experience with MS Word computer software" just to get the words *MS Word* or *computer software* on paper so your résumé will pop up in a keyword search. In a cover letter, it might be appropriate to say that you "don't have five years of experience in marketing but can add two years of university training in the subject to three years of in-depth experience as a marketing assistant with Hewlett-Packard." That is legitimate reasoning, but anything more manipulative can be hazardous to your job search.

❑ Step Five: Your Jobs

Starting with your present position, list the title of every job you have held on a separate sheet of paper, along with the name of the company, the city and state, and the years you worked there. You don't need to list addresses and zip codes, although you will need to know that information when it comes time to fill out an application.

You can list years only (1996–present) or months and years (May 1996–present), depending on your personality. People who are detail oriented are usually more comfortable with a full accounting of their time. Listing years alone covers some gaps if you have worked in a position for less than a full year while the time period spans more than one calendar year. For instance, if you worked from September 1996 through May 1997, saying 1996–1997 certainly looks better.

From the perspective of recruiters and hiring managers, most don't care whether you list the months and years or list the years only. However, regardless of which method you choose, be consistent throughout your résumé, especially within sections. For instance, don't use months some of the time and years alone within the same section. Consistency of style is important on a résumé, since it is that consistency that makes your résumé neat, clean, and easy to read.

❑ Step Six: Duties

Under each job, make a list of your duties, incorporating phrases from the job descriptions wherever they apply. You don't have to worry about making great sentences yet or narrowing down your list.

❑ Step Seven: Accomplishments

When you are finished, go back to each job and think about what you might have done above and beyond the call of duty. What did you contribute to each of your jobs?

- Did you exceed sales quotas by 150 percent each month?
- Did you save the company $100,000 by developing a new procedure?
- Did you generate new product publicity in trade press?
- Did you control expenses or make work easier?

6

- Did you expand business or attract/retain customers?
- Did you improve the company's image or build new relationships?
- Did you improve the quality of a product?
- Did you solve a problem?
- Did you do something that made the company more competitive?

Write down any accomplishments that show potential employers what you have done in the past, which translates into what you might be able to do for them. Quantify whenever possible. Numbers are always impressive. Remember, you are trying to motivate the potential employer to buy . . . you! Convince your reader that you will be able to generate a significant return on their investment in you.

❏ Step Eight: Delete

Now that you have the words on paper, go back to each list and think about which items are relevant to your target job. Cross out those things that don't relate, including entire jobs (like flipping hamburgers back in high school if you are now an electrical engineer with ten years of experience). Remember, your résumé is just an enticer, a way to get your foot in the door. It isn't intended to be all-inclusive. You can choose to go back only as far as your jobs relate to your present objective. Be careful not to delete sentences that contain the keywords you identified in step four.

❏ Step Nine: Sentences

Make sentences of the duties you have listed under each job, combining related items to avoid short, choppy phrases. Never use personal pronouns in your résumé (I, my, me). Instead of saying, *"I planned, organized, and directed the timely and accurate production of code products with estimated annual revenues of $1 million,"* say, *"Planned, organized, and directed. . . ."* Writing in the third person makes your sentences more powerful and attention grabbing.

Make your sentences positive, brief, and accurate. Since your ultimate goal is to get a human being to read your résumé, remember to structure the sentences so they are interesting to read. Use verbs at the beginning of each sentence (designed, supervised, managed, developed, formulated, and so on) to make them more powerful (see the list at the end of this chapter). Make certain each word means something and contributes to the quality of the sentence. If you find it difficult to write clear, concise sentences, take the information you have just written to a professional writer who can help you turn it into a winning résumé. Choose someone who is a Nationally Certified Résumé Writer (NCRW) or Certified Professional Résumé Writer (CPRW). That way you can be assured that the person has passed the strictest tests of résumé writing and design in the country, including peer review, administered by the National Résumé Writers Association (NRWA) and Professional Association of Résumé Writers (PARW).

❑ Step Ten: Rearrange

You are almost done! Now, go back to the sentences you have written and think about their order of presentation. Put a number 1 by the most important description of what you did for each job. Then place a number 2 by the next most important duty or accomplishment, and so on until you have numbered each sentence. Again, think logically and from the perspective of a potential employer. Keep related items together so the reader doesn't jump from one concept to another. Make the thoughts flow smoothly.

❑ Step Eleven: Related Qualifications

At the bottom of your résumé, think about anything else that might qualify you for your job objective. This includes licenses, certifications, affiliations, and sometimes even interests if they truly relate. For instance, if you want a job in sports marketing, stating on your résumé that you play tennis or are a triathlete would be an asset.

❑ Step Twelve: Profile

Last but not least, write four or five sentences that give an overview of your qualifications. This profile, or qualifications summary, should be placed at the beginning of your résumé. You can include some of your personal traits or special skills that might have been difficult to get across in your job descriptions. Here is a sample profile section for a computer systems technician:

- Experienced systems/network technician with significant communications and technical control experience.
- Focused and hard working; willing to go the extra mile for the customer.
- Skilled in troubleshooting complex problems by thinking outside the box.
- Possesses a high degree of professionalism and dedication to exceptional quality.
- Effective team player with outstanding communication and interpersonal skills.
- Current Top Secret/Sensitive Compartmentalized Information security clearance.

It is also acceptable to use a keyword summary like the one below to give a "quick and dirty" look at your qualifications:

- **Hardware:** IBM 360/370, S/390, 303X, 308X, ES-9000, Amdahl V6-II, V7, V8, 3705/3725, Honeywell 6000, PDP II, NOVA, Eclipse, Interdata 8/32, Wang OIS 115, 140, VS-80, VS-100, HP 3000, 9000, Vectra, IBM PC-AT, XT, and numerous other computers and mainframes.

- **Languages:** FORTRAN, PL/1, COBOL, BASIC, BAL (ALC), JCL, APL, DL/1, SQL, DS-2, HP-UX, and various PC-oriented software and support packages.

- **Systems:** DOS, OS, CICS, VSI/II, MVS, SVS, VM/CMS, IMS, MVT-II, MFT, POWER, TOTAL, DATANET-30, JES-2, JES-3, BTAM, QTAM, TCAM, VTAM, TSO, ACF, NCP, SNA, SAA, ESCON, SDLC, X-25, TCP/IP, UNIX, and TELNET.

This type of "laundry list" isn't very interesting for a human being to read, but a few recruiters in high-tech industries like this list of terms because it gives them a quick overview of an applicant's skills. You can use whichever style you prefer.

Busy recruiters spend as little as ten seconds deciding whether to read a résumé from top to bottom. You will be lucky if the first third of your résumé gets read, so make sure the information at the top entices the reader to read it all.

This profile section must be relevant to the type of job for which you are applying. It might be true that you are "compassionate," but will it help you get a job as a high-pressure salesperson? Write this profile from the perspective of a potential employer. What will convince this person to call you instead of someone else?

❑ You're Done: Well, Almost

Now you must typeset your information in a style that reflects your personality, which is what you will learn in the rest of this book. There is a science behind laying out a résumé just like there is a science behind designing advertisements, and you need to feel comfortable with your word processing software before you even start. If you are not, then you should call in a professional typesetter, designer, or résumé writer for this part. Make sure you take your copy of this book with you so you can choose your own design.

At this point, you have just finished the hardest part of a résumé—the writing of it—so you may be able to save some money by shopping around when getting it typeset. If you determine in the next chapter that you need a scannable résumé, make sure the designer knows you need a résumé that will scan perfectly and that you need a copy of the file on a computer disk so you can create an e-mailable version.

An experienced résumé writer and designer can take the work you have done and enhance it with a wealth of seasoned knowledge, turning it into a finely tuned marketing instrument that truly reflects who you are. The finished résumé will entice a reader to learn more about you in an interview, which is the whole purpose of your résumé anyway.

Whether you typeset your résumé yourself or hire someone else to do it for you, the ultimate responsibility for the accuracy of your résumé is *yours*. Make sure every word is spelled correctly and that your grammar is perfect. Double proofread your dates, address, phone number, and any other numbers that might appear in your résumé. Make sure punctuation is consistent and that you haven't used the ampersand (& sign) in place of the word *and* (except in the case of a company name when the company uses it that way). When you are absolutely certain it is perfect, then have someone else read it again just to make sure!

❑ Power Verbs

Just because a computer might screen your résumé in the beginning and look for keywords is no excuse for poor writing. Your ultimate goal is to entice a human being to read your résumé, so keep the sentences interesting by using positive power verbs. Here are some great power verbs to use at the beginning of your sentences:

A

abated
abbreviated
abolished
abridged
absolved
absorbed
accelerated
accentuated
accommodated
accomplished
accounted for
accrued
accumulated
achieved
acquired
acted
adapted
adopted
added
addressed
adjusted
administered
advanced
advertised
advised
advocated
affirmed
aided
alerted
aligned
allayed
alleviated
allocated
allotted
altered
amassed
amended
analyzed
answered
anticipated

appeased
applied
appointed
appraised
approached
appropriated
approved
arbitrated
aroused
arranged
articulated
ascertained
aspired
assembled
assessed
assigned
assimilated
assisted
assured
attained
attended
audited
augmented
authored
authorized
automated
averted
avoided
awarded

B

balanced
began
benchmarked
benefited
bid
billed
blended
blocked
bolstered
boosted

bought
branded
bridged
broadened
brought
budgeted
built

C

calculated
calibrated
capitalized
captured
cared for
carried
carved
categorized
catalogued
caught
cautioned
cemented
certified
chaired
challenged
championed
changed
charged
charted
checked
chose
chronicled
circulated
circumvented
cited
clarified
classified
cleaned
cleared
closed
coached
coded

collaborated
collated
collected
combined
commanded
commended
commenced
commissioned
communicated
compared
compiled
complemented
completed
complied
composed
compounded
computed
conceived
concentrated
conceptualized
condensed
conducted
conferred
configured
confirmed
confronted
connected
conserved
considered
consolidated
constructed
consulted
consummated
contacted
continued
contracted
contributed
controlled
converted
conveyed
convinced
cooperated

coordinated
copied
corrected
corresponded
counseled
created
critiqued
cultivated
customized
cut

D

dealt
debated
debugged
decided
decoded
decreased
dedicated
defined
delegated
delineated
delivered
demonstrated
deployed
derived
described
designated
designed
detailed
detected
determined
developed
devised
diagnosed
differentiated
diffused
directed
disbursed
discovered
discussed
dispatched
dispensed
displayed
disposed
disproved
dissected
disseminated
dissolved
distinguished

distributed
diversified
diverted
divested
divided
documented
doubled
drafted
dramatized
drew up
drove

E

earned
eased
economized
edited
educated
effected
elaborated
elected
elevated
elicited
eliminated
embraced
emphasized
empowered
enabled
encouraged
ended
enforced
engaged
engineered
enhanced
enlisted
enriched
enrolled
ensured
entered
entertained
enticed
equipped
established
estimated
evaluated
examined
exceeded
executed
exercised
exhibited

expanded
expedited
experienced
experimented
explained
explored
expressed
extended
extracted

F

fabricated
facilitated
factored
familiarized
fashioned
fielded
filed
filled
finalized
financed
fine tuned
finished
fixed
focused
followed
forecasted
forged
formalized
formed
formulated
fortified
forwarded
fostered
fought
found
founded
framed
fulfilled
functioned as
funded
furnished
furthered

G

gained
garnered
gathered
gauged

gave
generated
governed
graduated
grasped
greeted
grew
grouped
guaranteed
guided

H

halted
halved
handled
headed
heightened
held
helped
hired
honed
hosted
hypnotized
hypothesized

I

identified
ignited
illustrated
implemented
imported
improved
improvised
incited
included
incorporated
increased
indicated
individualized
indoctrinated
induced
influenced
informed
infused
initiated
innovated
inspected
inspired
installed

instilled
instituted
instructed
insured
integrated
intensified
interacted
interceded
interpreted
intervened
interviewed
introduced
invented
inventoried
invested
investigated
invigorated
invited
involved
isolated
issued
itemized

J

joined
judged
justified

L

launched
learned
lectured
led
lessened
leveraged
licensed
lifted
limited
linked
liquidated
listened
litigated
loaded
located
logged

M

made
maintained

managed
mandated
maneuvered
manipulated
manufactured
mapped
marked
marketed
mastered
maximized
measured
mediated
memorized
mentored
merged
merited
met
minimized
mobilized
modeled
moderated
modified
molded
monitored
monopolized
motivated
mounted
moved
multiplied

N

named
narrated
navigated
negotiated
netted
neutralized
nominated
normalized
notified
nurtured

O

observed
obtained
offered
officiated
offset
opened
operated

optimized
orchestrated
ordered
organized
oriented
originated
outdistanced
outlined
outperformed
overcame
overhauled
oversaw
owned

P

paced
packaged
packed
pared
participated
partnered
passed
penetrated
perceived
perfected
performed
persuaded
photographed
piloted
pinpointed
pioneered
placed
planned
played
praised
predicted
prepared
prescribed
presented
preserved
presided
prevailed
prevented
printed
prioritized
processed
procured
produced
profiled
programmed
progressed

projected
promoted
proofread
proposed
protected
proved
provided
pruned
publicized
purchased
pursued

Q

quadrupled
qualified
quantified
queried
questioned
quoted

R

raised
rallied
ranked
rated
reached
read
realigned
realized
rearranged
reasoned
rebuilt
received
recognized
recommended
reconciled
reconstructed
recorded
recovered
recruited
rectified
redesigned
redirected
reduced
re-engineered
referred
refocused
registered
regulated
rehabilitated

reinforced
reiterated
related
released
relied
relieved
remained
remodeled
rendered
renegotiated
renewed
reorganized
repaired
replaced
replied
replicated
reported
represented
reproduced
requested
researched
reserved
resolved
responded
restored
restructured
retained
retooled
retrieved
returned
revamped
reversed
reviewed
revised
revitalized
revolutionized
rewarded
risked
rotated
routed

S

safeguarded
salvaged
saved
scanned
scheduled

screened
sculptured
searched
secured
seized
selected
sent
separated
sequenced
served
serviced
set up
settled
shaped
shared
sharpened
shipped
shortened
showed
signed
simplified
simulated
sketched
slashed
smoothed
solicited
sold
solidified
solved
sorted
sourced
sparked
spearheaded
specialized
specified
speculated
spent
spoke
sponsored
spurred
staffed
standardized
started
steered
stimulated
streamlined
strengthened
stretched

structured
studied
submitted
succeeded
suggested
summarized
supervised
supplied
supported
surpassed
surveyed
swayed
swept
symbolized
synthesized
systemized

T

tabulated
tackled
talked
tallied
targeted
tasted
taught
teamed
tempered
tended
terminated
tested
testified
tied
took
topped
totaled
traced
tracked
trained
transcribed
transformed
transitioned
translated
transmitted
traveled
treated
trimmed
tripled

troubleshot
turned
tutored
typed

U

uncovered
underlined
underscored
undertook
underwrote
unearthed
unified
united
updated
upgraded
upheld
urged
used
utilized

V

validated
valued
vaulted
verbalized
verified
viewed
visualized
voiced
volunteered

W

weathered
weighed
widened
withstood
won
worked
wove
wrote

Y

yielded

❑ **Keywords**

As discussed in step four of the résumé writing process, using the right keywords for your particular experience and education is critical to the success of your résumé if it is ever scanned or e-mailed into an electronic résumé database. Without the right keywords, your résumé will float in cyberspace forever waiting for a hiring manager to find it. If your résumé contains all of the right keywords, then you will be among the first candidates whose résumés are reviewed. If you lack only one of the keywords, then your résumé will be next in line after résumés that have them all, and so on.

Remember, your keywords are the experience and skills that come from the specific terminology used in your job. For instance, *operating room* and *ICU* immediately classify the experience of a nurse, but *pediatric ICU* narrows it down even further. Don't try to limit your résumé by using fewer words. Recall, however, that you only need to use a word one time for it to be considered a "hit" in a keyword search. Try to use synonyms wherever possible to broaden your chances of being selected.

You should also understand the difference between a simple keyword search and a "concept" search. When a recruiter opens an electronic résumé file in MS Word and sends the computer on a search for a single word like *marketing*—which you can do in any word processing program with a few clicks of a mouse or function key—he or she is performing a keyword search. You are also performing a keyword search when you type a word or combination of words into the command line of a search engine like Yahoo or Excite.

A concept search, on the other hand, can bridge the gap between words by reading entire phrases and then using sophisticated artificial intelligence to interpret what is being said, translating the phrase into a single word, like *network*, or a combination of words, like *project management*.

The software that allows scanners to read your paper résumé and turn it into an electronic résumé is able to do just that. Resumix, one of the most widely used applicant tracking systems, reads the grammar of noun, verb, and adjective combinations and extracts the information for placement on the form that will become your entry in a résumé database. Its expert system extraction engine uses a knowledge base of more than 120,000 rules and over ten million résumé terms. It even knows the difference between *Harvard Graphics* (a computer software program) and *Harvard* (the university) by its placement on the page and its relationship to the header that precedes it *(Computer Skills* or *Education)*. Aren't computers amazing?

Because of this complicated logic, and because companies and hiring managers have the ability to personalize the search criteria for each job opening, it is impossible to give you a concrete list of the thousands of possible keywords that could be used to search for any one job. For instance, in one high-tech company I interviewed, a keyword search included the following criteria from two different hiring managers for the same job title:

Financial Analyst/Senior Accountant:

REQUIRED:
- BS in finance or accounting with 4 years of experience or
- MBA in related field with 2 years of relevant experience
- certified public accountant
- forecasting

DESIRED:
- accounting
- financial
- trend analysis
- financial statement
- results analysis
- trends
- strategic planning
- develop trends
- financial modeling
- personal computer
- microcomputers
- DCF
- presentation skills
- team player

REQUIRED:
- BS in finance or accounting with 4 years of experience or
- MBA in related field with 2 years of relevant experience
- accounting
- financial reporting
- financial statement
- Excel

DESIRED:
- ability
- customer
- new business
- financial analysis
- financial
- forecasting
- process improvement
- policy development
- business policies
- PowerPoint
- Microsoft Word
- analytical ability

You can see why it is so difficult to give definitive lists of keywords and concepts. However, it is possible to give you samples of actual keyword searches used by recruiters I have interviewed to give you some ideas. Let me emphasize again that you should list only experience you actually have gained. Do not include these keywords in your résumé just because they are listed here.

Business Manager (Central Archive Management):

REQUIRED:
- BS in engineering or computer science
- 10 years of related engineering and/or manufacturing experience
- strategic planning
- network
- product management
- program management

DESIRED:
- business plan
- line management
- pricing
- team player
- CAM
- marketing
- product strategy
- vendor
- general management
- OEM
- profit and loss

Business Operations Specialist:

REQUIRED:
- bachelor's degree
- 4 years of related experience
- production schedule
- project planning

DESIRED:
- ability to implement
- CList
- data analysis
- off-shift
- team player
- automation
- ability to plan
- customer interaction
- VM, CMS, JCL
- REXX, UNIX
- MVS
- analytical ability
- customer interface
- network
- skills analysis
- automatic tools

Senior Software Engineer:

REQUIRED:
- BS/MS in engineering, computer science or closely related field
- 8 to 9 years of experience

DESIRED:
- C++
- customer
- hiring/firing
- prototype
- structured design
- code development
- DASD
- methodology
- real time
- supervision
- communication skills
- experiment design
- problem solving
- software design
- testing

Secretary III:

REQUIRED:
- high school education or equivalent
- 5 years of experience
- typing skill of 55–60 wpm
- interpersonal skills
- oral communication

DESIRED:
- administrative assistance
- clerical
- data analysis
- file maintenance
- material repair
- PowerPoint
- project planning
- reports
- screen calls
- troubleshoot
- answer phones
- communication skills
- document distribution
- mail sorting
- Microsoft Word
- presentation
- publication
- schedule calendar
- secretarial
- appointments
- confidential
- edit
- material
- policies and procedures
- problem solving
- records management
- schedule conference
- telephone interview

3 Designing the Perfect Scannable Résumé

What happens when you create a beautiful paper résumé and mail or fax it to a company that scans résumés into a computerized database instead of forwarding it to a hiring manager for review? It ends up in cyberspace instead of on someone's desk. This automated process requires some special design considerations in order to make your résumé scanner friendly, which is what this chapter addresses.

According to *U.S. News & World Report*, more than 1,000 unsolicited résumés arrive every week at most Fortune 500 companies, and before the days of applicant tracking systems and résumé scanning, 80 percent were thrown out after a quick review. It was simply impossible to keep track of that much paper. As companies downsize and human resource departments become smaller, it is even more important to manage the job application and screening processes in an efficient manner.

Today, nearly half of all mid-sized companies and almost all large companies are scanning résumés and using computerized applicant tracking systems (still just 30 percent of all job openings, though). Some smaller companies turn to service bureaus to manage their scanning or to recruiters who scan résumés because of the volume of résumés they receive every day. If you are sending your résumé to one of these companies and your paper résumé is not formatted in such a way that a scanner can read it, the words won't be spelled right. And, if the words aren't spelled right, a keyword search will never turn up your résumé.

This chapter is devoted to helping you avoid the pitfalls that commonly cause a résumé to scan poorly. This includes choosing the right fonts, laying out the text of your résumé in such a way that it is scanner friendly, selecting the right paper color, etc. With these guidelines, your résumé will be ready for a hiring manager's computerized keyword search.

In the sample résumés throughout this book, not just in this chapter, you will find the word *Scannable* in the bottom inside corner of every résumé that meets the criteria set forth in this chapter. Recall, however, that the résumés not marked as such may only be unscannable because of one element (like a font or creative name). Use the rules found in this chapter to decide how to combine elements from various résumés to create a scannable one.

If you would rather not worry about whether your résumé is scannable, then simply send your formatted résumé (styled any way you like) along with an unformatted (ASCII text) résumé like the one on page 33. Your recipient will then have a choice whether to scan the "ugly" one or to send the formatted one to the hiring manager for review. You can never go wrong when you send both styles.

For complete instructions on how to format and use an ASCII text file, both on paper and on the Internet, you should obtain a copy of Barron's *Résumés in Cyberspace*. In it you will learn everything you need to know to take full advantage of the Internet and the three types of electronic résumés—scannable, e-mailable, and home page.

❑ Understanding the Technology

When your paper résumé is received by a human resource department that uses a computerized applicant tracking system, your résumé must first be transferred from paper into binary information that a computer can read before it can be stored in the résumé database. This is accomplished with a scanner that is connected to a computer running a special kind of software that can examine the dots of ink on your printed page and determine by their shapes which letters they represent. This is called optical character recognition, or OCR for short.

This software matches patterns with sets of characters stored in its memory, which is one of the reasons why it is important to choose a type style (or font) for your résumé that conforms to normal letter shapes. If you use a highly decorative type style, the OCR software will have difficulty making matches and will misinterpret letters. This means your words won't be spelled correctly, which of course means that a keyword search for the word *bookkeeping* will never turn up your résumé if the OCR thought you typed *bmkkeepmg*.

For now, let's assume that you have designed a résumé that the scanner can read. First, depending on the company's procedures, your résumé will be received directly by the recruiter assigned to fill a certain position (if the job was advertised) or by the human resource department in general (if you have sent your résumé unsolicited).

When the recruiter has finished reviewing your information, your résumé is added to the stacks of résumés to be processed by the computer that day. A clerk will then put your résumé into the automatic feeder bin of a flatbed scanner, separating your résumé from the one above and below it with a blank piece of paper. Within seconds, the scanner has passed its light over your pieces of paper and the software interprets the black dots of ink as letters of the alphabet. The computer then begins extracting information to fill in its electronic form, which will become part of your résumé in cyberspace.

❑ Your Name

Let's start at the top of your résumé and work our way down to examine the various elements that make a résumé scannable. What is the first thing you see on a résumé? The name, of course. The size and boldness of the type of your name should be larger than the largest font used in your text, but for a scannable résumé it should be no larger than 20-point type. You may use all capital letters, a combination of upper and lower case, or a combination of capitals with small capitals (LIKE THIS). Following is an example of a Times Roman Bold font in a few good point sizes for the name on a scannable résumé:

- **14 POINT NAME**
- **16 POINT NAME**
- **18 POINT NAME**
- **20 POINT NAME**

Avoid using decorative fonts like these for either your name or your text:

- **Bodini**
- Crazed
- BROADWAY ENGRAVED
- *Freestyle Script*
- Bullwinkle
- Kashmir
- *Commercial Script*
- *Kaufmann*
- COTTONWOOD
- Linotext

Using reverse boxes to print white type on a black (or gray shaded) background is another mistake. Scanners can't read them and your name will be missing from your résumé! Here is a sample of a reverse boxed name:

PAT CRISCITO

Lastly, make certain your name is at the top of each page of your résumé. The clerks who scan résumés are often dealing with hundreds of pieces of paper a week—if not every day. It is very easy for the pages of your résumé to become separated from each other, especially since it is not a good idea to staple a scannable résumé.

❑ Address

Next comes your contact information. It isn't always necessary to put your address at the top of your scannable résumé. Today's sophisticated applicant tracking systems know by more than position on the résumé whether the text is an address or phone number. It is six of one, half a dozen of another whether you put your contact information at the top or bottom of your résumé. Choose based on your personal preference. However, always list your e-mail address in addition to your phone/fax numbers and postal mailing information. It shows you are comfortable with today's technology.

❏ Fonts

Use popular fonts that are not overly decorative in order to ensure optimum scannability.

This sentence is typeset in a decorative font that is known to cause problems with résumé scannability (Sanvito).

This font is also a problem for scanners because of its unconventional shapes (Joulliard Italic).

Following are some samples of good fonts for a scannable résumé:

Serif Fonts (traditional fonts with little "feet" on the edges of the letters)

Bookman . . . . The quick brown fox jumps over a lazy dog
THE QUICK BROWN FOX JUMPS OVER A LAZY DOG

Clearface . . . . The quick brown fox jumps over a lazy dog
THE QUICK BROWN FOX JUMPS OVER A LAZY DOG

Garamond . . . . The quick brown fox jumps over a lazy dog
THE QUICK BROWN FOX JUMPS OVER A LAZY DOG

Minion Condensed . . . . The quick brown fox jumps over a lazy dog
THE QUICK BROWN FOX JUMPS OVER A LAZY DOG

New Century Schoolbook . . . . The quick brown fox jumps over a lazy dog
THE QUICK BROWN FOX JUMPS OVER A LAZY DOG

Palatino . . . . The quick brown fox jumps over a lazy dog
THE QUICK BROWN FOX JUMPS OVER A LAZY DOG

Times Roman . . . . The quick brown fox jumps over a lazy dog
THE QUICK BROWN FOX JUMPS OVER A LAZY DOG

Utopia . . . . The quick brown fox jumps over a lazy dog
THE QUICK BROWN FOX JUMPS OVER A LAZY DOG

Sans Serif Fonts (contemporary fonts with no decorative "feet")

Arial . . . . The quick brown fox jumps over a lazy dog
THE QUICK BROWN FOX JUMPS OVER A LAZY DOG

Arial Narrow . . . . The quick brown fox jumps over a lazy dog
THE QUICK BROWN FOX JUMPS OVER A LAZY DOG

Avant Garde . . . . The quick brown fox jumps over a lazy dog
THE QUICK BROWN FOX JUMPS OVER A LAZY DOG

Eurostile	The quick brown fox jumps over a lazy dog
	THE QUICK BROWN FOX JUMPS OVER A LAZY DOG
Helvetica Condensed	The quick brown fox jumps over a lazy dog
	THE QUICK BROWN FOX JUMPS OVER A LAZY DOG
Myriad	The quick brown fox jumps over a lazy dog
	THE QUICK BROWN FOX JUMPS OVER A LAZY DOG
Optima	The quick brown fox jumps over a lazy dog
	THE QUICK BROWN FOX JUMPS OVER A LAZY DOG

It doesn't make any difference whether you choose a serif or a sans serif font, but the font size should be no smaller than 9 points and no larger than 12 points for the text. Having said that, you will notice that the fonts in the examples above are all slightly different in size even though they are exactly the same point size (11 point). Every font has its own designer and its own personality, which means that no two typefaces are exactly the same. Look at the difference between the 9 point Avant Garde and the 9 point Times Roman fonts below:

- Times Roman—9 point

- Avant Garde—9 point

You will notice that the Times Roman appears considerably smaller and could potentially cause problems with a scanner, while the 9 point Avant Garde scanned fine in all of our tests.

The key to choosing a font for a scannable résumé is that none of the letters touch one another at any time. This can be caused by poor font design, by adjusting the kerning (the spacing between letters) in your word processor, or by printing your résumé with a low-quality printer (i.e., some dot matrix printers). Even some inkjet printers can cause the ink to run together between letters with the wrong kind of paper.

Any time one letter touches another, a scanner will have a difficult time distinguishing the shapes of the letters and you will end up with misspellings on your résumé. A keyword search looks for words that are spelled correctly, so a misspelled word is as good as no word.

This is the same reason you don't want to use underlining on your résumé. Underlines touch the descenders on letters like g, j, p, q, and y and make it difficult for an OCR program to interpret their shapes. Take a look at these words and see if you can tell where a scanner would have trouble:

- The quick brown fox jumps over a lazy dog

- *The quick brown fox jumps over a lazy dog*

- **The quick brown fox jumps over a lazy dog**

- <u>The quick brown fox jumps over a lazy dog</u>

Related to fonts are bullets—special characters used at the beginning of indented short sentences to call attention to individual items on a résumé. These characters should be solid (•, ▸, ▪) for a scannable résumé. Scanners interpret hollow bullets (○) as the letter "o." Avoid any unusually shaped bullets (□ , ❖, ✛) that a scanner might interpret as a letter.

While we are on the topic of special characters, the % and & signs in some fonts cause problems for OCR software because they look like letters of the alphabet, so always spell out the words *percent* and *and*. Foreign accents and letters that are not part of the English alphabet will also be misinterpreted by optical character recognition.

Even though you have probably heard that italics are a no-no on a scannable résumé, today's more sophisticated optical character recognition software can usually read italics without difficulty (provided the letters don't touch one another!). The experts at Resumix and SmartSearch2 all state that their software has no problem reading italics, and my staff has confirmed that with tests. We have even scanned résumés typeset in all italics without a problem, although I don't recommend serif italics simply from a readability standpoint. The exception, of course, are those italic fonts where one letter touches another. The key is to choose a font that is easy to read and not overly decorative.

❏ Format

Rely on white space to define sections. Scanners like white space. They use it to determine when one section has ended and the next has begun. Horizontal lines can also be used to define sections since they are usually ignored by more sophisticated scanning software, provided they do not touch any of the letters on the page. However, avoid the use of short, vertical lines since scanners try to interpret these as letters.

Don't use columns (like a newspaper) on your résumé (like the résumés on pages 44, 47, 57, 168, among others). Scanners read from left to right and often have difficulty determining how to relate text to headings when the columns are the same width or when there are more than two columns. Although the keywords will be intact, your résumé may end up looking like garbage in the ASCII text version created during the OCR process. Using a narrow column of headings on the left followed by the text on the right doesn't seem to cause the same problem, however.

Dot leaders (like this . . . .) can cause major headaches for the scanner, so avoid them.

One nice thing about electronic résumés is that they don't have to be limited to one page. The more keywords and synonyms you are able to use, the better your chances of being selected in a keyword search. Therefore, it is better to have a two-page résumé with all of your skills and qualifications listed than to have a one-page résumé with information missing because you tried to conserve space. The general rule for an electronic résumé today is:

- New graduates—one page
- Most people—one or two pages
- Senior executives—two or three pages

One caution, however. The reader may decide to stop reading after the first page if something doesn't entice him or her to read on. Therefore, you should make certain that the meat of your résumé is on the first half of the first page.

Remember to keep your sentences powerful and interesting to read. Cyberspace doesn't negate the need for good writing. You still want a human being to read your résumé sooner or later!

❏ Paper

Print your résumé on a high-quality, light-colored paper (white, off-white, or *very* light gray). Never use papers with a background (pictures, marble shades, or speckles). The scanner tries to interpret the patterns and dots as letters. This is a good rule to follow even for paper résumés that will never be scanned. Often companies will photocopy your résumé to hand to a hiring manager, and dark colors or patterns will simply turn into dark masses that make your résumé difficult to read. If a company has multiple locations, the original résumé may even get faxed from one site to another and the same thing happens.

Avoid using photocopies of your résumé. Original laser printed masters are best, although a high-quality inkjet printer is acceptable. Do not use a dot matrix printer since the letters sometimes touch each other or are not solid.

Print on only one side of the page and use standard-size, 8½ × 11 paper. The scanner cannot turn your page over, so the reverse side might be missed when the clerk puts your résumé into the automatic document feeder. That same process is the reason why you should not use 11 × 17 size paper. The pages would have to be cut into 8½ × 11 sheets and the printing on the reverse side would not get scanned.

Don't fold your résumé since the creases make it harder to scan. It is much better to invest in flat, 9 × 12 envelopes and an extra two bits of postage to make a good first impression. Laser print and copier toner tend to crack off the page when creased, making the letters on the fold line less than solid, which a scanner could easily misinterpret. Staple holes can cause pages to stick together, so never put a staple in a résumé you know will be scanned.

Now that you know all the secrets for designing a résumé that will pass the scannability test, let's look at some sample résumés that scanned well.

ALVIN E. BLUMBERG, JR.

123 Pluto Drive ‣ Colorado Springs, Colorado 80906 ‣ (719) 555-1234 ‣ E-mail: criscito@aol.com

PROFILE

Seasoned financial services professional with recognized expertise in trust management, integrated asset management, benefits administration, insurance, business processes, project management, and employee training. Results-oriented team leader with exceptional communication skills and a creative problem-solving approach. Proven strategist who establishes a motivational climate and fosters organizational and individual achievements. Holds a current Series 6 NASD license; previously carried Series 7.

PROFESSIONAL EXPERIENCE

DISTRICT LIFE MANAGER, Farmers Insurance Group, Colorado Springs, Colorado (1997 – present)
Managed and motivated 25 agents in the sale of nonproperty and casualty insurance products (life, disability, long-term care, and annuities) to businesses and individuals in the Colorado Springs metropolitan area. Collaborated with agents in the design and presentation of complex, multi-million-dollar cases to prospective clients. Trained agents in two new product lines.
- Ranked the number two district in the state in only twelve months.
- Increased sales production by 40 percent over previous year.

PRINCIPAL, Colorado Financial Group, Inc., Colorado Springs, Colorado (1996 – 1997)
Chief operating officer of a successful business succession and estate planning firm providing financial services to businesses and nonprofit organizations with from 5 to 500 employees and sales of up to $25 million. Hired and supervised three direct reports. Selected and supervised the implementation of a new computer system that streamlined financial reporting.
- Used extensive experience in advanced case design, investments, tax-qualified retirement plans, trusts, deferred compensation, and supplemental retirement plans to expand the target market.
- Re-engineered management processes and developed marketing strategies that doubled sales.
- Developed a new profit center in retirement consulting with fees of more than $50,000 per year.
- Analyzed existing and new client portfolios for sales opportunities and made recommendations that significantly increased revenue.

VICE PRESIDENT, INSTITUTIONAL TRUST, US Bank, Colorado Springs, Colorado (1995 – 1996)
Administered all institutional trust accounts for the Southern Colorado area. Responsible for plan design, investment management, new business development, marketing, and customer service. Supervised and evaluated two employees. Created and implemented training programs for both internal and client staff on new product lines and their uses.
- Implemented a new daily valuation retirement plan product line that resulted in more than 20 major client upgrades to the plan.
- Successfully transitioned all existing clients to a new product line, increasing fees by more than $25,000 as a result of personal expertise in plan management, documentation, and tax compliance.
- Key officer in several civic and professional organizations, resulting in a marked increase in public awareness and positive image for the bank.

Scannable

ADJUNCT PROFESSOR, University of Phoenix, Colorado Springs, Colorado (1994 – 1996)
Taught organizational communication and fundamentals of executive management to both graduate and undergraduate students enrolled in the MBA and Masters of Organizational Management programs.

SENIOR TRUST OFFICER, Bank One, Colorado Springs, Colorado (1990 – 1995)
Responsible for all employee benefit accounts of a multi-billion-dollar trust department. Designed plans and administered self-directed and bank-managed IRAs, defined contribution, and defined benefit profit sharing and pension plans, including 401K and Keogh plans. Monitored plans for tax and regulatory compliance, and coordinated all plan cash transactions. Hired, supervised, and evaluated a staff of ten. Created and implemented training programs for staff members in outlying offices. When Bank One was bought out by Affiliated Bancshares, the department was downsized.

- ▸ Succeeded in growing market share even during the reorganization by transition from an administrative to sales orientation; increased new business by an average of $75,000 per year.
- ▸ Participated in and led several department and statewide teams charged with implementing new product lines and procedures.
- ▸ Developed and delivered in-depth presentations to local professional groups to increase awareness of qualified plan and management concerns.

PRESIDENT, Dimensions Financial Services, Colorado Springs, Colorado (1984 – 1990)
Founded a financial consulting firm that provided integrated financial and business planning. Responsible for providing coordinated asset and business process management emphasizing current concepts in tax, income, estate, and retirement planning. Sold life, disability, and health insurance plans.

EDUCATION

MASTER OF BUSINESS ADMINISTRATION
University of Utah, Salt Lake City, Utah

BACHELOR OF SCIENCE IN INTERNATIONAL AFFAIRS
United States Air Force Academy, Colorado Springs, Colorado

CHARTERED LIFE UNDERWRITER (CLU)
CHARTERED FINANCIAL CONSULTANT (ChFC)
American College, Bryn Mawr, Pennsylvania

AFFILIATIONS

President, Colorado Springs Estate Planning Council (1993 – 1994)
National Director, U.S. Air Force Academy Association of Graduates (1979 – 1987, 1993 – present)

Scannable

Nick A. Dayton

1234 Harlan Court • Lake Forest, Illinois 60045 • (847) 555-1234 • E-mail: criscito@aol.com

PROFILE

- Dynamic leader with proven quality assurance and operations management experience, including:
  - Strategic Planning
  - Supervision and Training
  - Production Management
  - Quality Engineering
  - FDA Good Manufacturing Practices
  - Design Control Requirements
  - ISO 9000 Certification
  - Process Improvements
- Able to use a strong technical background to analyze complex processes and develop innovative solutions to challenges.
- Track record of gaining greater efficiencies from existing resources.
- Especially adept at increasing profitability without negatively impacting the organization.
- Strong communication and interpersonal skills; skilled in building effective teams to maximize results.

EXPERIENCE

ABBOTT LABORATORIES (1982 – present)
Director, Quality Assurance (1996 – present)
Hospital Products Division, Abbott Park, Illinois
- Managed quality engineering, label control, specifications and documentation, vendor/supplier quality assurance, compliance auditing, complaint handling, and clinical affairs quality assurance for this manufacturer of drugs, solutions, and medical devices with division sales of $2 billion.
- Developed and supervised the implementation of the division's quality assurance guidelines and policies to maintain ISO 9000 certification.
- Ensured that third-party vendors and customers met quality standards.
- Collaborated with plant quality assurance managers from 12 plants to develop corrective actions in response to FDA Good Manufacturing Practice (GMP) observations by internal auditors and external regulatory inspectors.
- Developed 21 CFR Part 11, compliance methodologies to improve the audit trail, system security, and system self-check.
- Successfully implemented an advanced electronic documentation management system to improve the accuracy of product databases and to permit a systems approach to complaint handling.
- Hired, supervised, and evaluated 5 department managers responsible for a staff of 85.
- Developed and administered a $10 million budget with no overruns.
- Served as the division trainer for the Situational Leadership II management development program.

Site Quality Assurance Manager, Hematology Business Unit (1993 – 1996)
Diagnostics Division, Santa Clara, California
- Selected to manage all quality and regulatory compliance functions for this Abbott acquisition, including quality assurance for manufacturing, vendors, software, and research and development.
- Managed GMP compliance, label control and specifications, and 501(k) submittals.
- Passed FDA audits with no citations in spite of a very complex operation and the introduction of 3 new products (advanced hematology analyzers).
- Achieved ISO 9000 certification for product design, software development, and manufacturing operations in only 12 months.
- Responsible for hiring and supervising 55 direct reports; grew the operation from 300 to 500 employees.
- Succeeded in increasing the number of products offered and substantially reducing the product development-to-market time.
- Increased revenues from $12 million to $300 million in less than 3 years.

Plant Quality Assurance Manager, Critical Care/Electronic Drug Delivery Systems (1989 – 1993)
Hospital Products Division, Mountain View, California
- Directed plant quality assurance program for this new Abbott acquisition with 600 employees and $100 million in annual sales.
- Achieved ISO 9000 certification for the manufacture of infusion pumps, cardiac output computers, and Opticaths.
- Increased throughput and investment in research and development while reducing costs.
- Created an ergonomics program with a multi-disciplinary team of specialists from quality assurance, industrial engineering, safety, and industrial hygiene departments that significantly reduced injuries.

26

EXPERIENCE **(continued)**	**Manufacturing Unit Manager** (1985 – 1989) **Hospital Products Division, Austin, Texas** • Supervised all wet-side manufacturing operations on four shifts operating seven days per week. • Recruited, hired, and supervised 30 production supervisors and 4 production managers. • Managed preparation, filling, sterilization, inspection/overwrap, packaging, and shipping of intravenous solutions. • Increased production volumes from 90 million to 300 million units per year while meeting an annual cost reduction of $3–9 million per year. **Production Manager** (1982 – 1985) **Hospital Products Division, Austin, Texas** • Built the production operations from the ground up for this start-up operation, including staffing the plant with 980 production workers, training, developing/validating production processes and procedures, and scheduling. • Selected, installed, and tested all production equipment and refined operating procedures. **TRACOR, INC., Aerospace Group, Austin, Texas** (1978 – 1982) **Product Line Manager** (1980 – 1982) **Manufacturing Manager** (1978 – 1980) • Managed the manufacturing operations and marketing of military countermeasures, teletypewriters, and digital systems.
TEACHING	**ADJUNCT PROFESSOR** (Fall Semester 1999) **DePaul University, Kellstadt Graduate School of Business**, Chicago, Illinois • Taught MBA courses in quality assurance and operations management **CERTIFICATIONS** • Situational Leadership II, Blanchard Training and Development • Quality Assurance Systems, Zenger-Miller • Frontline Leadership, Zenger-Miller
EDUCATION	**DOCTOR OF BUSINESS ADMINISTRATION** (1999) GPA 3.94/4.0 **The University of Sarasota**, Florida Emphasis in Health Care Administration Dissertation: *Critical Success Factors in Total Quality Management Systems: A Practitioner-Based Study of U.S. Quality Systems* **MASTER OF ARTS IN ORGANIZATIONAL MANAGEMENT** (1994) GPA 3.95/4.0 **University of Phoenix**, Northern California Campus, San Jose, California Thesis: *ISO 9000 Program Development and Implementation* **BACHELOR OF ARTS IN INDUSTRIAL MANAGEMENT** (1979) **St. Edward's University**, Austin, Texas
AFFILIATIONS	**Parenteral Drug Association (PDA)**: Core Team Member of the Task Group for Computer Validation and 21 CFR Part 11, Electronic Records/Signatures **American Society of Quality**, Illinois **American Society of Quality, Biomedical Division**, Santa Clara, California **American Electronics Association**, Santa Clara, California

KENNETH L. DAVIS
12345 Quiet Circle East
Colorado Springs, CO 80917-2009

SSN: 123-45-6789

Home: (719) 555-1234
Work: (303) 555-1234, ext. 33
E-mail Address: criscito@aol.com

This is the scannable format preferred by many government agencies. Often, it can be used instead of a Form SF-171 or Form OF-612.

SKILLS
More than twenty years of logistical management experience, including procurement, budgeting, supply sources, reconciliation, account tracking, forecasting, manpower, research, receiving, delivery, inventory management, stock levels, records, reports of survey, forklift operation, and military supply rules. Detail-oriented with a talent for developing innovative solutions to problems. Team player who is willing to work long hours to get the job done. Computer literate with experience in Windows 95, Alpha Five Database, MS Word, Excel, WordPerfect, Quattro Pro, and MAPCON.

WORK EXPERIENCE
March 1997 to Present. 40 hours per week. Property Administration Specialist, $31,000 per year. Antarctic Support Associates, 1234 Inverness Drive East, Englewood, CO 80112, Jane Doe, (303) 555-1234. Responsible for purchasing, receiving, and warehousing of $80 million in inventory. Conducted annual inventories in the Antarctic, New Zealand, and at three U.S. sites. Accountable for 9,500 line items of capital equipment.

September 1993 to March 1997. 56 hours per week. Senior Materialsperson, $27,560 per year. McMurdo Power and Water Plants, Antarctica, Antarctic Support Associates, 1234 Inverness Drive East, Englewood, CO 80112, John Doe, (303) 555-1234. Contracted to manage and account for supplies, parts, and equipment needed to maintain the operation of the power and water plants. Coordinated the requisitioning of parts and equipment through MAPCON Power "1000." Conducted aisle audits to ensure proper accounting and receipt of items issued from stock. Performed any other duties required by plant or logistics supervisor. Performed duties as Galley Pad Food Supervisor responsible for the unloading of McMurdo's year supply of food and proper storage of dry and frozen foods.

April 1993 to September 1993 (between contracts) and August 1991 to September 1992. 40 hours per week. Material Handler, WG-5. U.S. Army, Terminal Operations, DOL, Ft. Carson, CO 80913, James Doe, (719) 555-1234. Received supplies and equipment and moved items by forklift, handcart, conveyor, etc.

September 1992 to April 1993. 56 hours per week. Materialsperson, $25,500 per year. Palmer Station on the Peninsula, Antarctica, Antarctic Support Associates, 1234 Inverness Drive East, Englewood, CO 80112, Jane Doe, (303) 555-1234. Interfaced with laboratory supervisor to ensure timely requisition, receipt, and distribution of science cargo for various science groups. Automated Palmer Station's parts and supply inventory into MAPCON. Hazardous cargo packing/shipping for transport on commercial and DOD systems.

March 1991 to August 1992. 30 hours per week. Administrative Clerk, volunteer. University of Southern Colorado, Extended Studies, 229 East Pikes Peak Avenue, Colorado Springs, CO 80903, John Doe, (719) 555-1234. Counseled veterans regarding their education benefits part-time while attending the university.

Scannable

August 1966 to September 1989. 40 hours per week. Supply/Accounting Sergeant, E-7. U.S. Army, 4th Division Support Command, Ft. Carson, CO 80913, Natalia Armstrong. Twenty-four years of active duty military service, including fifteen years of logistical experience and nine years of aviation maintenance experience. Instrumental in managing three separate property book accounting teams for three different Army divisions made up of 27 combat units/companies each. Maintained document files and property records for equipment totaling $800 million to $2.5 billion. Supervised the Retail Supply operation for 52 units, including requisition, warehousing, and issue procedures for Army equipment and repair parts. Managed a multinational work force of 30 Korean nationals and 31 military personnel. Identified areas requiring change and specifically revised logistical practices and procedures, which streamlined property storage, distribution, and accountability. Conducted cyclic inventories and logistic operation inspections. Managed all capital and organizational equipment requisitioning. Coordinated retrograde procedures for unserviceable equipment. Assistant logistics manager for brigade-level supply operations, maintaining authorized levels of organizational equipment and repair parts. Successfully coordinated the deployment and fielding of two Patriot Missile Batteries to Germany, controlling and establishing accountable property records for $1.3 billion in equipment.

EDUCATION
Undergraduate studies toward a Bachelor of Science in Business Administration (March 1991 to August 1995), University of Southern Colorado, Extended Studies, 229 East Pikes Peak Avenue, Colorado Springs, CO 80903. Associate of General Studies (August 1988 to January 1991), Pikes Peak Community College, 5675 S. Academy Boulevard, Colorado Springs, CO 80906.

"I certify that, to the best of my knowledge and belief, all of my statements are true, correct, complete, and made in good faith." February 2, 2000

KENNETH L. DAVIS   SSN: 123-45-6789

LESLIE A. MARTIN
123 North Cascade Avenue #29
Colorado Springs, Colorado 80903
Phone: (719) 555-1234
E-mail: criscito@aol.com

If you would rather not worry about whether your résumé is scannable, simply save the file as a DOS text file and reformat it like this. Send it along with your formatted résumé.

PROFILE
~~~~~~~~~~~~~~~~~~~~~~~~~~~~~~~~~~
Goal-oriented sales and customer support professional with successful experience in account management, needs assessment, high-tech sales, promotion, training, and relationship building. Strong background in building new territories and using creative marketing approaches. Respected for problem solving skills; willing to go the extra mile to make the customer happy. Demonstrated ability to create client loyalty above and beyond the sales relationship. Self-motivated and flexible; comfortable working independently with little supervision. Computers: Solomon, MS Word, Excel, Access, Outlook, Lotus Notes, ACT!, Support Magic, Winzip, Windows 95, PC Anywhere, Passport, MS Explorer.

EXPERIENCE
~~~~~~~~~~~~~~~~~~~~~~~~~~~~~~~~~~
DEALER SALES AND MARKETING REPRESENTATIVE (1999 to present)
ARI Network Services, Inc., Colorado Springs, Colorado
Successfully sold software to the outdoor power industry for parts lookup, e-commerce, and warranty tracking. Formulated, designed, and conducted sales presentations to small engine dealers, repair centers, and ATV/snowmobile dealers. Established and developed a commercial account base throughout the United States. Successfully turned around customers who were unhappy with the merger through effective marketing, professional sales presentations, and follow-up. Won President's 100 Percent Club Award for meeting 100 percent of quota for the fiscal year 1998-1999.

LEVEL I TECHNICAL SUPPORT (1997 to 1999)
Powercom 2000, Colorado Springs, Colorado
Hand picked by the transition manager to demonstrate the business component of the software (invoicing, inventory, point-of-sale) to a potential buyer, a transaction ultimately worth several million dollars. Consistently exceeded sales quotas through cold calling and referrals. Effectively taught technophobic customers and made them feel comfortable with the technology. Began the position as a temp-to-hire, survived two downsizings, and was hired by the purchasing company in 1999.

ACADEMIC COUNSELOR (1993 to 1997)
National University, San Diego, California
Generated student enrollments for this private university for adult learners. Made biweekly presentations and recruited local community college students for the undergraduate degree programs. Enrolled and counseled potential students and provided financial aid advice. Regularly exceeded quotas, enrolling up to 52 students per month. Selected as one of the top three sales representatives. Supervised, trained, and motivated eight academic advisors. Translated academic transcripts and ensured the accuracy of credit transfers. Served as an intermediary between students and faculty and reported recurring problems with faculty to senior management.

ASSISTANT MANAGER (1991 to 1993)
Adventure Car Rentals, San Diego, California
Financed college education by managing a rental car agency specializing in high-end sports cars. Hired and supervised staff and resolved problems with insurance companies.

EDUCATION
~~~~~~~~~~~~~~~~~~~~~~~~~~~~~~~~~~
BACHELOR OF BEHAVIORAL SCIENCE (1996)
National University, San Diego, California
Graduated cum laude; maintained a 3.5 GPA while working full time.

Scannable

4 Stand-out Names

S ince your résumé is basically an advertisement for you and your skills, you should think about the design of your résumé from a marketing standpoint. When you see a well-designed ad, what is the first thing you notice (besides a picture of the product)? The product name, of course. Since *you* are the product, your name should be the first thing a reader sees and remembers. To accomplish that, there is really only one rule to remember: *Your name should be easy to read and it should stand out above the rest of the text.* That can be done by using:

A Larger Font in Upper/Lower Case

ALL CAPS

FIRST LETTER LARGER

A Creative Font

On the samples in this section, you will also notice the use of graphic elements and lines to help define the name and separate it from the rest of the text. Even scanned clip art letters or a signature can be used to enhance a résumé, but the latter only works when you have great handwriting. Your name, however, should not distract the reader from the message. Make it part of the overall design of your résumé but separate it from the body text with lines or spacing.

The most important thing is to make sure the style of your name reflects your personality, tempered by the expectations of your industry. If you are flamboyant and are looking for a job in the arts, then you have a license to be creative. Go for it! If, on the other hand, you work in a conservative industry or you feel uncomfortable with your name printed large, then it is important to tone it down.

Remember to look for the word *Scannable* if you are trying to design a résumé for a high-tech or large company. Designer fonts, names with graphic elements in the place of letters, reverse boxes, and script names will not scan.

MARIA SALAZAR

SELECTED EXPERIENCE

Retail System Administrator   1996 – Present
Salvatore Ferragamo   New York, New York
> Developed new position as operational liaison to retail stores.
> Train cashiers and shipping staff in all Ferragamo stores on new computerized system.
> Supervise staff in maintenance of large, dynamic database.
> Communicate frequently with computer programmers in Italy to recommend improvements and adjustments.
> Responsible for flow of information to accounting department, merchandise buyers, and company executives.
> Travel often to U.S. stores and headquarters in Italy.

Assistant to Director of Administration   1994 – 1996
The Americas Society   New York, New York
> Commended in writing by president of Society as outstanding employee in 1995.
> Assisted in all areas of personnel management, including administering benefits and interviewing prospective employees.
> Supervised Spanish-speaking maintenance staff.
> Purchased all supplies for organization.
> Coordinated high-level special events with caterers and internal program directors.

Customs Liaison   1992 – 1994
Esprit de Corp   San Francisco, California
> Served as a link between U.S. Customs, brokers, and production staff to ensure smooth importation of all goods and samples manufactured overseas.
> Made seasonal presentations of Esprit's entire line to U.S. Customs officials.
> Regularly persuaded Customs to reconsider tariffs on high-duty items by using knowledge of import laws and garment/fabric construction.
> Taught Italian to employees twice weekly through company-sponsored program.

EDUCATION

Master of International Management   May 1992
American Graduate School of International Management (AGSIM)
Thunderbird Campus   Glendale, Arizona   GPA 3.34

Bachelor of Arts in Political Science   May 1990
Bachelor of Arts in Italian Language
University of Arizona   Tucson, Arizona   GPA 3.15

LANGUAGES & COMPUTERS

Fluent in Italian   Highly proficient in Spanish
Working knowledge of German   Advanced knowledge of Lotus 1-2-3
Working knowledge of French   Knowledge of word processing software

OTHER EXPERIENCE

> Designed original artwork for displays in Ferragamo's Fifth Avenue show windows   1997
> Executive Board, AGSIM Alumni Chapter, New York   1995 – Present
> Passed Foreign Service Officer examination, including oral and written portions, and State Department security clearance   1995
> Variety of retail sales positions   1987 – 1995
> Studied and traveled extensively throughout Italy and Mexico   1989 – 1991
> Summer internship with Outdoor Advertising Association of America   1989

ADDRESS   123 East 99th Street #123, New York, New York 10017   (212) 555-1234

BERNADETTE D'EVES

EXPERIENCE

NISSAN NORTH AMERICA, Torrance, California (Dec. 1997 – Present)
Product and Market Strategy Analyst
- Explore and analyze needs and trends of American consumers to aid long-term corporate and product development
- Develop product concepts based on analysis of market viability and regulatory requirements, and coordinate with Nissan entities as lead analyst of electric vehicle program
- Coordinate and implement innovative primary research with aid of outside consultants
- Work as team member with product planners in vehicle development
- Determine future implications for Nissan in changing political and regulatory environment
- Act as voice of U.S. market for Japanese colleagues

SAATCHI & SAATCHI DFS/PACIFIC [Advertising], Torrance, California (Oct. 1986 – Nov. 1997)
Assistant Account Executive (10/90 – 11/97)
- Coordinated development and production of broadcast, print, and collateral national and regional advertising for Toyota Motor Sales
- Handled business-to-business advertising for Toyota Industrial Equipment
- Maintained working production budgets and coordinated print and broadcast media allocations
- Supervised Account Coordinator
- Acted as Account Executive on $4 million campaign

Print Traffic Assistant (11/88 – 9/90)
- Scheduled and coordinated the creation and production of print materials for accounts such as Toyota, Yamaha, MGM/UA, Physician's Formula Cosmetics
- Monitored project costs

Broadcast Traffic Forwarder (10/86 – 10/88)
- Coordinated broadcast allocations for airing on radio and television networks and spot stations throughout the country
- Restructured position, which improved operations and increased job responsibilities

DAILEY AND ASSOCIATES [Advertising], Los Angeles, California (Dec. 1985 – June 1986)
Business Coordinator
- Monitored cost control of estimates and invoices
- Assisted Account Management group

LE PHARE JEAN D'EVE, S.A., La Chaux-de-Fonds, Switzerland (June 1984 – Sep. 1985)
Marketing Intern
- Researched history of international Swiss watch company and proposed advertising, public relations, and promotional ideas for company's centennial celebration
- Conducted business entirely in French

LOS ANGELES OLYMPIC ORGANIZING COMMITTEE (May 1983 – Aug. 1984)
Customer Service Supervisor
- Supervised customer service staff at USC Olympic Village
- Arranged transportation for visiting athletes and delegates
- Wrote and implemented procedures plan for customer service operations

EDUCATION

MASTER OF INTERNATIONAL MANAGEMENT (Jan. 1991)
American Graduate School of International Management (Thunderbird), Glendale, Arizona
Marketing Director for Taco John's International, Inc. – InterAd Group Project

BACHELOR OF ARTS, ENGLISH (Dec. 1985)
University of California, Los Angeles (UCLA)
University of Paris, Sorbonne (Fall Semester 1984)

LANGUAGES

ENGLISH (Native), **SPANISH** (Proficient), **FRENCH** (Proficient)
Computers: **Canvas, Lotus 1-2-3, Microsoft Word, Excel, DeltaGraph, WordPerfect**

ADDRESS

1234 South Redford Drive, Apt. 1, Los Angeles, California 90035, Phone (310) 555-1234

 Scannable

33

ALLEN L. MARCOS

12345 E. Cache La Poudre • Colorado Springs, Colorado 80909 • 800-555-1234, ext. 3000

SKILLS
- Experienced professional with a strong background in banking/finance.
- Good understanding of basic accounting principles and financial analysis.
- Team player with exceptional communication and customer sales/services skills.
- Proficient in Windows, MS Word, Excel, Access, and MS-DOS applications.
- Knowledge of specialized LAN and general WAN applications.

EXPERIENCE

NORWEST DIRECT, Colorado Springs, Colorado
Quality Monitoring Associate (1/97 – Present)
- Identified road blocks to service delivery and customer satisfaction.
- Developed ways to avoid those road blocks in the future to ensure customer satisfaction.
- Ensured that all telephone calls were being handled according to company standards.
- Developed key quality indicators to measure and report processes and credit decisions.
- Provided constructive, skill building feedback to sales representatives and team leads.
- Coached and trained staff on consistent customer service quality guidelines.
- Identified trends and issues that impeded efficiency, quality, and customer satisfaction; developed action plans to improve the processes.
- Developed and maintained a tracking and reporting database system.

Customer Service/Loan Officer (6/96 – 1/97)
- Reviewed and processed loan requests; analyzed customer financial information.
- Promoted and recommended products and services, answered customer inquiries, and advised customers of approval or denial.
- Assisted customers in determining financial needs; recommended appropriate credit solutions.
- Assisted with affinity group conversion from Minneapolis location to Colorado.

BANKAMERICA, Mira Mesa, California
Telesales Representative (4/95 – 6/96)
- Provided customers with detailed product/pricing information and qualified sales leads using extensive telephone contacts.
- Initiated the application process, processed incoming loan applications, and produced weekly management reports.
- Provided verbal prequalification analysis and loan status reports.

OFFICE OF SUSAN CROUCH, Del Mar, California
Finance Manager/Bookkeeper (11/93 – 4/95)
- Managed the office and resolved customer service issues.
- Responsible for maintaining general ledger, accounts payable, and accounts receivable.

WELLS FARGO BANK, San Marcos, California
Business/Personal Loan Officer (1/91 – 10/93)
- Responsible for managing and developing a portfolio of business and consumer clients.
- Retained existing branch accounts and sourced new business, meeting or exceeding established branch business and consumer sales thresholds.
- Expanded individual account relationships by actively cross-selling bank products and services; ensured that customer commitments were met.
- Provided leadership as a "team player" in overall branch activity.

WELLS FARGO BANK, San Diego, California
Senior/Lead Mortgage Specialist, Sales Support (2/89 – 1/91)
Mortgage Expert/Sales Support
- Provided extensive telephone customer service with detailed product and pricing information; referred qualified sales leads to branches.
- Initiated application processes and provided verbal prequalification analysis and loan status.

EDUCATION

SAN DIEGO CITY COLLEGE, San Diego, California (1982 – 1984)
Classes in Telecommunications

CONTINUING EDUCATION
Completed Real Estate Principles Course and passed State of California Real Estate Exam   1994

Terri French

1234 Weather Vane Drive
Colorado Springs
Colorado 80920
(719) 555-1234

PROFILE
- Experienced retail sales professional with a background in customer service.
- Self-motivated manager with exceptional interpersonal and communication skills.
- Able to adapt to constant change and to manage multiple priorities with ease.
- Skilled in working effectively as a team member or alone with minimal supervision.
- Knowledge of Windows, WordPerfect, Lotus 1-2-3, and GDS (Global Distribution System).

EXPERIENCE

Sales/Customer Service
- Increased the average daily room rate by $12 through suggestive and up-selling techniques.
- Sold computer systems and taught computer/technology studies and careers to junior high and elementary school students.
- Successfully developed commercial markets for cellular telephones and pagers, serving as ambassador to the Chamber of Commerce.
- Investigated credit histories and preapproved auto loans, working closely with customers throughout the sales and closing process.
- Provided value-added service to customers by meeting or exceeding their expectations.
- Performed telemarketing and assisted the sales and marketing directors in blitzes and trade shows, exceeding established goals.

Retail/Merchandising
- Planned, opened, and managed a new store, including hiring and training all personnel, preparing payroll, balancing daily store sales, and designing advertisements.
- Directed fashion shows; suggested new designer lines that increased sales by 25 percent.
- As a retail buyer, increased department sales volume by 50 percent in three stores.
- Prepared visual merchandising displays using mannequins, alternatives, fabric drapes, suit/dress forms, lay down presentations, fixtures, gondolas, aisle tables, and build-ups.
- Assisted in the implementation of merchandising policies and programs, display publications, and merchandise calendars; arranged interior and window displays for a bridal shop.

Management/Administration
- Accurately received and processed customer reservations for an award-winning hotel.
- Maintained rate integrity through effective yield management, forecasting for rooms based on sales and expenses, parallelling inventory of heads and beds with corporate reservations.
- Worked with front office manager to determine rates based on seasonal and daily fluctuations.
- Evaluated and trained reservation agents through taping, group analysis, and evaluations.
- Performed competitive analyses through phone calls and evaluation of GDS system.
- Assisted in maintaining accurate room inventory control system and records for no-show billings.
- Trained in the management of sales representatives and incentive programs.
- Tracked patients in a study of pain during combat training; gathered, entered, and analyzed data.
- Used initiative to provide input and recommend procedural changes that affected the accuracy of the data collection, diagnosis, and treatment phases of the study.
- Selected and taught medical study participants to control muscle tension through the use of a variety of self-regulatory techniques.

HISTORY

Sales Representative, Phil Long Ford, Colorado Springs, Colorado	1999 – present
Customer Service Representative, Maharishi Ayur-Ved, Colorado Springs, Colorado	1998
Director of Corporate Sales, PC Brokers, Colorado Springs, Colorado	1997 – 1998
Reservationist/Manager Trainee, Radisson Hotel, Colorado Springs, Colorado	1997
Account Representative, DCC Solutions, Colorado Springs, Colorado	1996 – 1997
Account Representative, AirTouch Cellular, Colorado Springs, Colorado	1996
Visual Merchandiser, AAFES, USAF Academy, Colorado	1994 – 1995
Bio-Psycho-Physiological Technician, Fitzsimons, Aurora, Colorado	1993

EDUCATION

BACHELOR OF ARTS, PSYCHOLOGY   1993
University of Colorado, Colorado Springs, Colorado

CONTINUING EDUCATION: How to Create Reservation Sales Agents, Radisson Reservation Managers Training Program, Computer Classes, Biofeedback Training, Theater Production

Scannable

35

W. Craig Brown

123 Crawford Circle • Longmont, Colorado 80501
E-mail: criscito@aol.com • Phone: (303) 555-1234

PROFILE

- Self-motivated systems engineer with 23 years of experience in analysis, implementation/integration, automated data processing equipment, business development, and project management.
- Background in supervision, staffing, training, quality assurance, production scheduling and control, feasibility studies, standards analysis, cost control, and audio/video system design.
- Skilled in applying logical but creative approaches to problem resolution.
- Track record of completing projects on or ahead of schedule and on budget.
- Hold a current DoD Secret Security Clearance.

COMPUTERS

OVERVIEW: Experience in computer operations, scheduling, programming, language and hardware conversions, security engineering, systems analysis/design/specifications, hardware/software system testing, and Year 2000 analysis.

HARDWARE: IBM-PCs, Macintosh/Apple systems, Cray II, ELXSI, Rational, Honeywell 2000-6000, PRIME 550-9950, IBM 30XX, VAX 11/7xx, and 88xx systems.

COMMUNICATIONS: Apple Talk, Ethernet, STP, LANs, WANs, T1–T3, SATCOM, FDDI, HIPPI, Video Teleconferencing, Encryption Devices (both commercial and military).

SOFTWARE AND LANGUAGES: MS Word, Excel, McDraw, FoxPro, MS-DOS, OS JCL, Basic, Fortran, COBOL, CPL, CList, DCL, DataTrieve, DBQ, EasyTrieve, ED, EMACS, IDMS, IMS DB/DC, DLI, Info, MFS, OWL, OS/MVS, PL1, PanValet, RPG2, Runoff, TEXT, Total, TSO/ISPF, VAXII DBMSII, VSAM, ADA (lab and class training).

EXPERIENCE

1995 – 1997

NORTHERN NEF (SETEC, INC.), Colorado Springs, Colorado
Implementation and Integration Manager
- Assisted senior management in business startup, which included defining the company focus, developing a business plan, and establishing a customer base.
- Provided technical engineering leadership for marketing of systems analysis and integrated security systems to both government and commercial sectors.
- Project coordinator for the Defense Satellite Program technical order updates; surveyed all sites both in the United States and Australia.
- Senior systems analyst for Year 2000 analysis of all Cheyenne Mountain computer equipment.
- Analyzed and recommended solutions for seventeen key computer and communications systems.

1988 – 1995

MARTIN MARIETTA IT SERVICES, National Test Bed Program, Colorado Springs, Colorado
Project Manager, Cheyenne Mountain Training and Simulation Systems
- Responsible for five delivery order tasks and three primary tasks for integrating the Cheyenne Mountain Training and Simulation Systems into the National Test Facility structure.
- Directed the initial project evaluation and determined detailed mission requirements.
- Led startup, design, and build-out phases using proactive systems engineering methodology to complete design within three months.
- Managed staffing, budget preparation and administration, and requirement modifications.
- Successfully added more than $4 million in new business to the budget baseline based on the positive response of the customer to the contractor's outstanding effort.

ADPE Hardware Engineering Task Lead
- Maintained all the automated data processing equipment (ADPE) and audio/visual architecture for the National Test Facility.
- Responsible for review/approval of design solutions, baseline drawings, audio/visual productions, budgets, and staffing.
- Re-evaluated the ADPE architecture in order to define requirements for future use of supercomputers, high-speed network interfaces, mass archival system, high-end graphic workstations for simulations, analysis workstations, and program productivity tools.

36

Scannable

EXPERIENCE (continued)

MARTIN MARIETTA INFORMATION TECHNOLOGY SERVICES (continued)

Task Requirements Notice Directed Energy Manager
- Developed and managed a $1.5 million budget in the design and implementation effort for the Directed Energy Systems Center (completed two months ahead of schedule).
- Responsible for project staffing, requirements definition and design, management and customer reviews, planning, scheduling, and implementation.

Implementation and Integration Project Lead
- Designed, planned, budgeted, and staffed the integration of the SBIO National Test Bed simulation gaming center, which included combining several like centers at the National Test Facility, including ADPE, audio/visual, and software systems.
- Installed a mini-center at the Pentagon and directed the demonstration of the new capabilities to the Secretary of Defense.

1982 – 1988

MARTIN MARIETTA DATA SYSTEMS, Denver, Colorado

Acceptance Test Project Lead
- Primary Martin Marietta operation and maintenance customer interface during conversion and acceptance test phases.

Project Lead/Supervisor
- Responsible for the work package analysis team and word processing support group on a minerals management service conversion project.
- Consistently completed final products ahead of scheduled deadlines.

Principal Computer Systems Designer
- Responsible for the functional system design specifications for a PRIME-based data dictionary system.
- Lead analyst for the warehouse inventory management system maintenance.

1980 – 1982

GENERAL MOTORS, INC., Rochester Products Division, Rochester, New York

Senior Programmer Analyst
- Designed, created program specifications, coded online and batch programs, and created documentation for a 1,200 program production scheduling and inventory control system.

Team Lead
- Implemented an online project tracking system.

Programmer Analyst
- Designed and coded fifty percent of the online screens for GMAC's joint salary payroll system development effort.

EDUCATION

BACHELOR OF SCIENCE, COMPUTER SCIENCE

Regis University, Colorado Springs, Colorado
- Completed 100 credit hours

ASSOCIATE OF APPLIED SCIENCE, DATA PROCESSING

Genessee Community College, Batavia, New York
- Minor in business math

CONTINUING EDUCATION
- Total Quality Management (TQM) Training
- Electrostatic Discharge (ESD) Training with annual recertifications since 1990
- Data Processing Diploma, Harkness Vocational Center, Buffalo, New York

Scannable

PATRICIA S. SAATCHI

1234 Waddell Avenue
Colorado Springs, CO 80915

Telephone:
(719) 555-1234

QUALIFICATIONS
- Highly creative, self-motivated individual with nearly 15 years of insurance experience.
- Background in marketing and underwriting.
- Bachelor of Science degree in management of human resources.
- Team player with exceptional interpersonal and presentation skills.
- Achieved "Competent Toastmaster" with Toastmasters International.

EXPERIENCE

FARMERS INSURANCE GROUP, Colorado Springs, Colorado (1983 – Present)
Marketing Specialist
- Developed marketing programs to sell insurance agents on new products and productivity programs.
- Tracked results of marketing effectiveness and assisted division agency managers in implementing programs and problem solving for agency development.
- Designed and managed the publication of regional agency magazine and newsletters.
- Coordinated and supervised the Life Operations Desk, which included developing promotions for life insurance products and tracking sales results.
- Planned and organized large off-site conferences for district managers; responsible for facilities, food, publicity, registration, speakers, and entertainment.
- Arranged and appeared in public relations coverage for company events in print media.
- Traveled within a five-state region to implement new computer systems and train end users.

Senior Underwriter
- Reviewed insurance applications to evaluate, classify, and rate individuals for personal lines coverage.
- Accepted, bound risk, declined, or modified applications.
- Examined application forms, inspection reports, insurance maps, and medical reports to determine degree of risk.
- Evaluated applicant financial standing, age, occupation, accident experience, and value and condition of property.
- Maintained underwriting quality and proper rating classification.
- Coordinated work flow and personnel scheduling for the office.
- Developed auditing procedures.
- Performed audits and field activities to ensure quality of transactions.
- Conducted week-long customer service seminars for agency staff.
- Assisted in the training and development of new personal lines underwriters.
- Provided technical advice and assistance to other regional offices regarding coverage interpretation, policy, and endorsement provisions.
- Acted as consultant to individual personal line underwriters in matters of procedure and underwriting judgment.

EDUCATION

BACHELOR OF SCIENCE (1993)
Colorado Christian University, Colorado Springs, Colorado
- Major in Management of Human Resources
- Course work in human resource management, employment law, accounting, economics, statistics, among others
- Trained in interpreting and handling issues and claims involving EEOC and ADA laws and regulations

CONTINUING EDUCATION
- Certificate in General Insurance, Insurance Institute of America
- Colorado Licensed Insurance Producer in Property, Casualty, and Life

COMMUNITY SERVICE
- Junior Achievement Classroom Volunteer
- Safe Kids Coalition Board Member
- Western Insurance Information Speakers (WIIS)
- Toastmasters International
- Colorado Springs Women's Chamber of Commerce

Scannable

BRADLEY D. WAYZATA

PROFILE
- Self-motivated professional with four years of experience in Information Systems.
- Effective team player with strong interpersonal, communication, and presentation skills.
- Talent for penetrating new accounts, sourcing candidates, and satisfying clients.
- Skilled in organization, leadership, management, and problem solving.

EXPERIENCE

ACCOUNT EXECUTIVE, Interim Technology, Scottsdale, Arizona (1/97 – current)
- Perform sales functions, including prospecting, qualifying, and closing business.
- Negotiate contracts and respond to RFP's.
- Penetrated and developed new business with the following companies: Motorola, MicroAge, Mayo Clinic, Arizona Public Service, Wells Fargo, Anasazi, City of Phoenix, America West Airlines, Arizona Supreme Court, Arizona Department of Corrections, and Arizona Department of Economic Security.
- Personally responsible for generating $1.4M of collectible revenue in services and products.
- Maintain an excellent rapport with clients and provide consulting on their I.S. requirements.
- Develop and manage client relationships to ensure their needs are met and exceeded.
- Maintain excellent working relationships with employees to ensure expectations are met.
- Worked within clients' budgets and organizational structure to find qualified contract professionals.

TECHNICAL RECRUITER, Delta Professional Services, Phoenix, Arizona (6/96 – 12/96)
- Built a consulting firm from the ground up, breaking into four major accounts and turning a profit within six months.
- Developed and implemented recruiting systems, procedures, and a resume database.
- Conducted interviews of potential candidates to determine their technical capability, suitability, and experience; selected the most qualified and capable candidates to meet client needs.
- Sourced and recruited candidates via the Internet, Access Database.
- Recruited and interviewed key personnel, including systems analysts and database administrators, for placement with companies such as American Express, Arthur Andersen & Co., Federal Express, AT&T, National Semiconductor, and Lockheed.
- Trained and supervised other technical recruiters in effective methods of locating, screening, and qualifying candidates to meet client requirements.
- Coordinated Delta's involvement in job fairs.

TECHNICAL RECRUITER, Maxim Group, Denver, Colorado (9/94 – 5/96)
- First out of 100+ recruiters; consistently exceeded quotas by 200 percent, generating $1.8M.
- Successfully launched the Colorado Springs office for Maxim Group.
- Trained and mentored other technical recruiters in effective methods of locating, screening, and qualifying consultants to meet client requirements.
- Placed 47 consultants in one year by sourcing, recruiting, and interviewing candidates.
- Utilized a computerized resume retrieval system to pinpoint skills for client requirements.
- Served as liaison and resolved conflicts between clients and consultants.

EDUCATION

PURDUE UNIVERSITY, West Lafayette, Indiana (1994)
Bachelor of Science in IT

PROFESSIONAL DEVELOPMENT
- Solution Selling: Selling Practice Services, sponsored by Interim Technology.
- Software Quality Management Training in Products, Methodologies, and Services, sponsored by Interim Technology, San Francisco, California.
- Recruiting Procedures Program, sponsored by Interim Technology, Scottsdale, Arizona.
- Sales Training Program, sponsored by Professional Development Center, Baltimore, Maryland.

ADDRESS   1234 E. Thomas Road, Apt. 1234, Scottsdale, Arizona 85251   (602) 555-1234

39

ELAINE A. TAYLOR

1234 North Prospect Street • Colorado Springs, Colorado 80903 • (719) 555-1234

PROFILE

- Thirteen years of results-oriented experience in budget coordination, project management, organizational development, and office management, including:
  - Financial tracking
  - Credit analysis
  - Market research
  - Supervision
  - Training
  - Quality assurance
  - Meeting planning
  - Medical benefits management
  - Customer service
- Analytical self-starter with a strong attention to detail and the ability to bring order to chaos.
- Computer skills in Windows 95, MS Word, Excel, Access, Lotus 1-2-3, MultiMate, and other software.

EXPERIENCE

BUDGET COORDINATOR, MCI Worldcom, Colorado Springs, Colorado (1998 – present)

- Responsible for compiling financial data and assisting project managers in tracking financial information.
- Provide internal customer service and serve as point of contact for financial questions from 50 employees.
- Develop procedural guidelines for budget reporting processes.
- Member of the budget team responsible for developing capital models for budget projects using Excel.
- Assist budget managers and financial operations department in updating project financial information.
- Maintain staff reports, staffing assignments, and staff profiles for more than 50 employees.
- Resolve accounts payable and payroll problems and manage time sheets.
- Research, document, and provide accrual and reclassification information to the accounting department for incurred expenses.
- Train project managers to use MCI's Intranet to retrieve financial data.

PROJECT MANAGEMENT ASSISTANT, MCI Worldcom, Colorado Springs, Colorado (1997 – 1998)

- Served as liaison between the MIS, Data Account, and Project Management Departments.
- Developed the first financial spreadsheets to track actual versus budgeted expenses for department projects.
- Member of the Steering Committee charged with developing a new database to compile financial, historical, and project information.
- Helped to create initial project management and new hire guidelines.
- Researched, analyzed costs, and procured computer hardware and software for the department.
- Reduced downtime by troubleshooting computer problems and upgrading systems.
- Wrote job descriptions and flow charts; trained new administrative assistants.

PRODUCTION/STORAGE CLERK, Colorado Interstate Gas, Colorado Springs, Colorado (1995 – 1996)

- Provided administrative support for engineers and geologists.
- Input payroll into the accounting system and tracked vacation and sick time.
- Compiled data and prepared in-house and BLM gas production reports.

ADMINISTRATIVE ASSISTANT, Hechinger Company, Landover, Maryland (1993 – 1995)

- Assisted the Senior Vice President in creating an administrative procedural handbook.
- Prepared computerized payroll for more than 20 employees; assisted in preparing divisional salary/bonus reports; analyzed and reconciled monthly payroll reports.
- Coordinated U.S. and international travel; organized the departmental office move.

OFFICE MANAGER, Atlantic Cellular Company, L.P., Providence, Rhode Island (1990 – 1993)

- Managed office operations for a privately held cellular telephone company with more than 836,000 customers and assisted the company's President/CEO.
- Researched and co-authored the company's first employee handbook.
- Assisted in the design and layout of corporate offices; procured office equipment and furnishings.
- Compiled and calculated demographic data used in acquisition activities and special marketing projects.
- Worked closely with the Vice President of Operations in the formulation and revision of human resource procedural guidelines.

EDUCATION

ASSOCIATE OF ARTS, HUMAN SERVICES (1986)
Community College of Rhode Island, Warwick, Rhode Island

40

Scannable

Michael Williams

PROFILE
- Dedicated professional with more than 13 years of management and technical experience
- Strong background in system level testing and logistics analysis; top secret security clearance (TS/BI)
- Detail-oriented worker who can quickly grasp system operations
- Effective team player with strong interpersonal and communication skills

EXPERIENCE

MOORE BUSINESS SOLUTIONS, Sales Representative, Denver, Colorado (1995 – present)
- Sold and serviced accounts for NAPA Auto Parts distributors nationwide.
- Consistently exceeded sales quotas.

UNITED STATES AIR FORCE (1981 – 1995)

Lead Logistics Evaluator for Operational Test and Evaluation of DoD Military Satellite Communications Programs, Peterson Air Force Base, Colorado (1992 – 1995)
- Planned, conducted, evaluated, and reported the logistics aspects of the operational test of both the MILSTAR satellite communications program and the Air Force Satellite Communications Terminal Upgrade.
- Evaluated the entire spectrum of Integrated Logistics Support to include the reliability and maintainability, integrated diagnostics capabilities, and the overall logistics supportability of the MILSTAR terminal segment installed in airborne, fixed ground, and transportable configurations.
- Reviewed and rewrote MILSTAR technical orders; performed integrated logistics support management and logistics support analysis reviews; four years of experience analyzing logistics support records.
- Collected and analyzed logistics test data to support major acquisition milestones for the MILSTAR program.

Supervisor, MILSTAR Terminal Maintenance, Falcon Air Force Base, Colorado (1990 – 1992)
- Lead technician supporting all MILSTAR maintainability/testability demonstrations.
- Established and managed the MILSTAR satellite communications work center, including two AN/FRC-181(V2) extremely high frequency ground command post satellite terminals and two MILSTAR satellite mission control subsystems valued in excess of $5 million.
- Determined the requirement for personnel, materiel, and training; developed performance standards, ensured strict supply discipline and adherence to safety standards.

Space Communications Equipment Operations and Maintenance Technician, Falcon Air Force Base, Colorado (1987 – 1990)
- Supervised personnel in the operation and maintenance of dual AN/GSC-52 satellite communications terminals, AN/USC-28 spread spectrum multiple access modems, and a Digital communications satellite subsystem in support of the North American Aerospace Defense Agency missile warning and satellite command missions.
- Coordinated circuit activations and terminal downtime for operational or maintenance requirements, resulting in an outstanding three-year uptime reliability rate of 99.98 percent.

Aircraft Armament Systems Specialist and Instructor, Williams Air Force Base, Arizona (1981 – 1987)
- Selected as a Squadron Lead Crew Chief; conducted the load crew standardization and training program for 40 weapons load crews.
- Trained, evaluated, and certified/decertified load crews in standardized munitions loading procedures.
- Provided introductory training on fighter aircraft weapons release and gun systems maintenance.
- Conducted classroom academics training for 250 wing maintenance personnel.
- Produced lesson plans for five associated aircraft maintenance and support equipment courses.

EDUCATION

ASSOCIATE OF APPLIED SCIENCE, Electronic Systems Technology (May 1994)
Community College of the Air Force

TECHNICAL TRAINING: Satellite Communications Principles, Satellite Communications Terminal AN/GSC-52 Maintenance Course, MILSTAR Terminal Maintenance Course, MILSTAR Mission Control Element Maintenance Course, MILSTAR Mobile Constellation Control Station Maintenance Course, Air Force Satellite Communications Terminal Upgrade Operator/Maintenance Course, Test and Evaluation Management Course, Acquisition Logistics Fundamentals Course, Fundamentals of Integrated Logistics Support, Introduction to Acquisition Management, Non-Commissioned Officer Leadership School

ADDRESS

1234 Silver Torch Terrace, Colorado Springs, Colorado 80919   (719) 555-1234

John R. Franck, III

1234 Westview Drive • Deephaven, Minnesota 55391 • (612) 555-1234

PROFILE

- Dedicated manager with a strong background in the food and beverage industry.
- Experienced in operations management, budget development, staffing, and cost control.
- Results oriented; consistently achieve corporate objectives.
- Exceptional organizational and planning skills; adaptable; enjoy new challenges.
- Adept at communicating effectively with guests, vendors, and staff and motivating employees to perform to their maximum potential.

EXPERIENCE

Achievements

- Generated $1 million in annual revenue for an exclusive, 600,000 acre, Ted Turner hunting and fishing resort in northern New Mexico.
- Maintained expenses below budget through accurate planning, purchasing, and cost-effective operating procedures.
- Renovated and re-opened the New Sheridan Bar, achieving gross revenues of $475,000 in the first year.
- Achieved significant reductions in operating expenses for a 500-employee grape ranch through implementation of a three-phase program of planning, on-site management, and take-charge leadership.
- Developed an intensive training program for all staff that resulted in a 421 percent increase in wine sales.

Management/Supervision

- Successfully managed the food and beverage operations of an upscale resort with a budget of $350,000.
- Directed the food/beverage operations of resorts, restaurants, country clubs, and bars.
- Accountable for cost control, budgeting, profit and loss, payroll, and general accounting.
- Designed marketing campaigns and determined advertising placement.
- Recruited, hired, supervised, scheduled, and motivated a staff of up to 40 employees.
- Trained service staff to enhance customer service and increase profits through suggestive selling.
- Planned menus, estimated food and beverage costs, and purchased supplies.
- Investigated and resolved food/beverage quality and service complaints, ensuring customer satisfaction.
- Developed wine lists, wine tasting events, and special menus for banquets and private parties.

Enology/Viticulture

- Managed the operations of a grape ranch with more than $4 million in annual sales.
- Handled contract negotiations and labor relations for 500 employees.
- Managed a $3.5 million budget.

WORK HISTORY

Restaurant/Bar Manager, Vermejo Park Ranch, Raton, New Mexico	1996 – 1999
Beverage Manager, Julian's Restaurant, Santa Fe, New Mexico	1995 – 1996
Beverage Manager, Wayzata Country Club, Wayzata (Minneapolis), Minnesota	1992 – 1994
Supervisor, Big Powderhorn Mountain, Bessemer, Michigan	1991 – 1992
General Manager, New Sheridan Bar, Telluride, Colorado	1990 – 1991
Sales Representative, Western Wine Merchants, Denver, Colorado	1988 – 1989
Beverage Manager/Wine Steward, Julian's Restaurant, Telluride, Colorado	1985 – 1988
Food/Beverage/Catering Manager, Telluride Ski Area, Telluride, Colorado	1984 – 1985
General Manager, Ranch #2, Indio, California	1980 – 1984
Vineyard Manager/Assistant Winemaker, Reuter's Hill Vineyards, Forest Grove, Oregon	1977 – 1980

EDUCATION

MASTER OF SCIENCE, VITICULTURE/ENOLOGY (1977)
University of California, Davis, California

BACHELOR OF SCIENCE, WILDLIFE MANAGEMENT (1967)
University of Michigan, Ann Arbor, Michigan

1234 Westview Drive • Deephaven, Minnesota 55391 • (612) 555-1234

Scannable

E-mail: criscito@aol.com

June thru July: 1234 Metric Blvd., Apt. 1123, Austin, Texas 78727
After July: 1234 Memorial Drive, Apt. 1210, Cambridge, Massachusetts 02139

Phone: (512) 555-1234
Phone: (617) 555-1234

TEACHING EXPERIENCE

CLASSROOM TEACHER, FOURTH GRADE (1997 – 1999)
Otero Elementary School, Harrison School District, Colorado Springs, Colorado

SUBSTITUTE TEACHER (1997)
Harrison School District, Colorado Springs, Colorado
Fountain/Fort Carson School District, Colorado Springs, Colorado

CLASSROOM TEACHER, THIRD GRADE (1996 – 1997)
Campus Canyon Elementary School, Moorpark Unified School District, Moorpark, California

EXPERIENCE HIGHLIGHTS

+ Integrated Colorado Standard-Based Education into the curriculum.
+ Administered CSAP and Body of Evidence testing to measure the effectiveness of writing and reading instruction.
+ Implemented a new four-block literacy program, consisting of 70-minute blocks of guided reading, self-selected reading, writing, and word building.
+ Used Mimosa Math, Math Land, and Saxon Math in the classroom to help strengthen problem-solving skills.
+ Prepared and taught fourth grade Colorado history.
+ Taught gifted and talented students in an after-school program.
+ Tutored first grader in math and reading; set learning goals and developed lesson plans.
+ Planned, developed, and implemented third grade curriculum with the teaching team.
+ Used thematic units to incorporate social studies, reading, writing, and art.
+ Taught physical education during third grade rotation.
+ Established an active learning environment through positive feedback.
+ Effectively used cooperative learning strategies.
+ Implemented effective behavior management strategies for each student.
+ Provided students with individualized attention.
+ Established and maintained written and oral communication with parents.

EDUCATION

BACHELOR OF SCIENCE IN APPLIED LEARNING AND DEVELOPMENT (1996)
University of Texas, Austin, Texas
+ Area of specialization: Earth Science
+ Dean's List for 3 semesters
+ Recipient of the Fort Hood Military Family Member Scholarship
+ Colorado certificate issued 9/97, expires 9/99
+ Texas certificate issued 1996

CONTINUING EDUCATION
+ Standard-Based Education in-service training
+ Student Assessment Data Analysis
+ "Laying the Foundation" in-service presented by Steve Dunn
+ Gifted and Talented
+ Computer Technology in the Classroom
+ Disaster and First Aid
+ Conflict Management, Behavior Management
+ Six-Trait Writing Training
+ Teaching in a Multilingual District
+ Leadership Seminar, Department of the Army, Fort Benning, Georgia
+ Beginning Teacher Support and Assessment Program, Campus Canyon Elementary

AFFILIATIONS, ACTIVITIES, & HONORS

+ Association of American Educators
+ Member, Social Committee, Campus Canyon Elementary School
+ Certificate of Achievement for volunteer work at Fort Hood, Texas
+ Member of the Otero Elementary School Math Committee
+ Kennedy Center Imagination Celebration Volunteer and Participant
+ Study and Implementation of a Title I School-wide Restructuring Model

John S. DeOlden

PROFILE
- Self-motivated manager with a strong leadership and customer service background.
- Confident, professional communicator with outstanding listening and presentation skills.
- Well organized and resourceful; work well independently or as part of a team.
- Knowledge of Windows 95, MS Word, Excel, PowerPoint, and Lotus 1-2-3.
- Current Secret security clearance granted by Defense Investigative Services.

EDUCATION

BACHELOR OF SCIENCE IN BUSINESS ADMINISTRATION/MANAGEMENT December 1998
University of Southern Colorado, Pueblo, Colorado
- Courses in business management, production/operations management, strategy and policy, and finance.

EXPERIENCE

UNITED PARCEL SERVICE, Colorado Springs, Colorado 1996 – 2000
Preloader
- Sorted and loaded parcels for accurate delivery.
- Volunteer hazardous materials responder.

AAA ENGINEERING AND DRAFTING, Colorado Springs, Colorado 1996 – 1997
Assistant Contract Manager
- Managed a large government information management contract, including postal operations and courier services.
- Directed the operations of five mailrooms, a publications warehouse, secure e-mail server, and the distribution of top secret documents at Peterson, Falcon, and Cheyenne Mountain Air Force Bases.
- Established mail and courier distribution schedules to meet contract requirements.
- Managed a $1.7 million budget, accounted for purchases and expenditures, and tracked payroll and time records.
- Supervised, scheduled, and evaluated 27 team members; provided training in safety, government regulations, and security procedures.
- Re-engineered job descriptions, eliminating ten full-time positions and saving $200,000 per year.
- Coordinated the maintenance and scheduling of a three-vehicle operations fleet.

DATA MONITOR SYSTEMS, INC., Colorado Springs, Colorado 1990 – 1996
Mail Operations Technician, Courier/Driver/Messenger
- Delivered U.S. Mail, United Parcel Service, Federal Express, and U.S. Government documents and packages.
- Provided exceptional service to more than 12,000 customers.
- Determined postage requirements and implemented cost-saving measures whenever possible.
- Managed employee payroll, human resource development, and training programs.
- Operated mail room postage equipment and weighing scales.

GOVERNMENT SERVICES, INC., Colorado Springs, Colorado 1987 – 1990
Postal Service Center Mail Operations and Base Locator Technician
- Delivered all personal and official mail to mailbox patrons at Peterson, Falcon, and Cheyenne Mountain Air Force Bases.
- Directed base locator operations in support of 12,000 customers.
- Provided mail directory service to all military and civil service families arriving from global locations.
- Briefed new customers and found innovative ways to improve customer service.

1234 Sable Oaks Drive • Round Rock, Texas 78664 • (512) 555-1234

DAVID P. CORWIN, RN

OBJECTIVE	A position as a Staff Nurse

PROFILE

- Goal-directed professional with exceptional technical knowledge and skills.
- Specialized clinical training in medical/surgical and psychiatric nursing.
- Empathetic caregiver who is able to quickly establish and maintain rapport with patients.
- Detail oriented and thorough; dedicated to providing excellence in patient care.
- Adept at managing multiple, diverse tasks simultaneously; work well under pressure.

EDUCATION

ASSOCIATE OF APPLIED SCIENCE DEGREE, NURSING (May 1995)
Pikes Peak Community College, Colorado Springs, Colorado
- Specialized training in medical/surgical and psychiatric nursing.

NURSING EXPERIENCE

STAFF NURSE, *Pikes Peak Dialysis*, Colorado Springs, Colorado (1997 - present)
- Monitored and provided nursing care to up to 4 patients at a time on dialysis.
- Administered various medications.
- Supervised fluid intake and nutrition.

STAFF NURSE, *St. Mary Corwin Hospital*, Pueblo, Colorado (1997 – 1997)
- Provide post-operative nursing care to up to 8 patients per day on the orthopedic floor.
- Recover patients from surgery and support fracture, trauma, and back surgery patients.
- Take histories, perform physicals, and give patient discharge instructions.
- Administer medications, change dressings, adjust traction, and use other treatment modalities.

CHARGE NURSE, *Cheyenne Mesa*, Colorado Springs, Colorado (1995 – 1997)
- Assess physical and psychological health problems of adolescents and respond with appropriate interventions.
- Chart patient behavior and nursing care; distribute medications.
- Supervise two mental health workers on the night shift.

NURSING ASSISTANT, *Penrose Hospital*, Colorado Springs, Colorado (1994 – 1995)
- Provided support to doctors and nurses during medical procedures.
- Accurately took and recorded patient vital signs.
- Assisted patients with daily living activities.
- Transported patients to meals and various therapies.

STUDENT NURSE, *Memorial Hospital*, Colorado Springs, Colorado (1993 – 1995)
- Medical/surgical clinical rotation from 4 to 8 hours per day.

OTHER EXPERIENCE

DELIVERY PERSON, *The Gazette*, Colorado Springs, Colorado (1991 – 1993)
- Delivered newspaper to over 200 subscribers every morning.

NIGHT STORE CLERK, *Seven-Eleven Store*, Colorado Springs, Colorado (1991)
- Provided customer service and managed store operations.

MILITARY SERVICE
Colorado Air National Guard (1990 – Present)
United States Air Force (1982 – 1990)
- Cryogenic Fluid Production Operator: produced liquid and gaseous nitrogen/oxygen for hospital use.
- Weather Observer: briefed pilots and disseminated data.
- Refrigeration and Air Conditioning Specialist.

ADDRESS   1234 Dolphin Circle, Colorado Springs, Colorado 80918   (719) 555-1234

1234 Willow Bend Circle #1
Colorado Springs, CO 80918

E-mail: criscito@aol.com

Home Phone: (719) 555-1234
Work: (719) 555-1234, ext. 670

PROFILE

- Goal-oriented computer professional with a strong manufacturing background.
- Focused and hard working; able to troubleshoot complex problems and get the job done.
- Effective team player with exceptional communication and interpersonal skills.
- Committed to staying current on innovations in technology and computer science.

COMPUTERS

Certifications

- Microsoft Computer Systems Engineer (MCSE) to be completed September 1999.
- A+ Certification completed March 1999.

Networking

- Hands-on experience with TCP/IP configuration of Windows 95/98, networking in Windows NT, installation of Windows NT Server/Workstation, and installation of network interface cards (PCM-CIA).
- Trained in networking essentials, administering MS Windows NT Workstation 4.0, implementing and supporting NT Server 4.0, enterprise technologies, internetworking with TCP/IP, and creating/configuring a Web server using IIS 4.0.

Software/Hardware

- Installed and configured software for Macintosh and IBM-compatible computers.
- Partitioned hard drives, set up Windows 95/98, and backed up network servers.
- Proficient in Lotus 1-2-3, Claris Works, MS Works, and other business applications.
- Experienced in the installation and trouble shooting of hard disk drives, floppy disk drives, CD-ROM drives, and peripherals (printers, scanners, etc.).
- Trained in the C++ programming language; completed the course with a 4.0 GPA.

EDUCATION

MICROSOFT COMPUTER SYSTEM ENGINEER COURSE (1999)
Knowledge Alliance and Executrain, Colorado Springs, Colorado

UNDERGRADUATE STUDIES
Colorado Technical University, Colorado Springs, Colorado (1996 – 1997)
- Completed 16 credits toward a Bachelor of Computer Science
Maharishi International University, Fairfield, Iowa (1986 – 1988)
- Completed 18 credits of business and liberal arts studies
University of Negros Occidental, Recoletos, Philippines (1979 – 1981)
- Full-time accounting studies; completed 60 credits toward a bachelor's degree

EXPERIENCE

PRODUCTION ADMINISTRATOR/MANAGER (1993 – present)
Maharishi Ayur-Ved Products International, Inc., Colorado Springs, Colorado
- Managed the production of herbals and food supplements; implemented process efficiencies and line changes to increase assembly line speed.
- Hired, trained, and motivated a production team of 12 to exceed production goals.
- Responsible for cost containment, production scheduling, and machine maintenance.
- Made recommendations for the purchase of capital equipment.
- Helped to build a new computer and connected it to the network.
- Managed half a million dollars in raw materials and served as a liaison between the purchasing department and vendors to negotiate lower prices.
- Projected raw material usage and ensured that there was adequate material on hand to meet production goals.

PRODUCTION SUPERVISOR (1989 – 1993)
Purity Farms, Inc., Leominster, Massachusetts
- Supervised the manufacturing of clarified butter and solved customer problems.
- Responsible for cooking, bottling, labeling, packaging, and shipping.

46

TWILA VALENCIA

PROFILE

- Detail-oriented accounting clerk with experience in accounts payable, accounts receivable, general ledger, and check writing.
- Background in customer service, counseling, fund raising, transcription, and data entry.
- Effective team player with strong interpersonal and written communication skills.
- Computer literate in WordPerfect, Lotus 1-2-3, Reynolds and Reynolds accounting system.
- Typing 60 wpm, data entry 8,000 kph, automated check signer, and most office machines.

EXPERIENCE

ACCOUNTING CLERK   1996 – Present
Colorado Springs Jeep Eagle, Colorado Springs, Colorado
- Calculated, posted, and verified accounts payable and receivable.
- Compiled, sorted, and filed documents for substantiating transactions.
- Collected past-due accounts by calling customers directly.
- Called credit bureaus to verify reliability of customer credit.

ACCOUNTING CLERK   1996
Rocky Mountain Motorworks, Woodland Park, Colorado
- Temporary job through Accountemps to assist the company in catching up with statistical data entry.

ACCOUNTING CLERK   1989 – 1996
Liquid Sugars, Inc., Emeryville, California
- Accurately entered data for invoices, purchase orders, nonpurchase orders, and freight waybills.
- Processed up to $2.5 million in accounts payable weekly.
- Printed and disbursed 250–300 checks per week.
- Generated weekly, monthly, and year-end accounts payable reports.
- Researched past-due invoices, set up new vendors in system, and filed documents.
- Gained experience with general ledger procedures and Lotus 1-2-3.

VOLUNTEER COUNSELOR (part-time)   1990 – 1996
Crisis Pregnancy Services, Oakland, California
- Counseled women on pregnancy options, consequences, diseases, and prenatal care.
- Solicited sponsors and participated in annual charity walk-a-thon.

RECEPTIONIST (part-time)   1995
H&R Block, Oakland, California
- Greeted clients, answered telephones, arranged appointments, and filed.

PRINTER   1981 – 1989
Faulkner Color Lab, Inc., San Francisco, California
- Set up to print, rolled, and cut film.
- Ensured quality and packaged film and prints for distribution.
- Gained experience on Lucht package printers and S-5a/b machines.

EDUCATION

SHILOH BIBLE COLLEGE, Oakland, California   1993 – 1996
- Part-time evening classes in theology

HEALD BUSINESS COLLEGE, Oakland, California   1989 – 1990
Certificate of Secretarial Accounting
- One-year of comprehensive business studies

Joanne Osborne

PROFILE

- Experienced project manager with the ability to translate business needs into broad-based technology requirements for high-tech industries.
- Known for being able to see the big picture while focusing on project details.
- Decision maker who believes there is an answer to every challenge.
- Proficient in MS Word, MS Project, Excel, PowerPoint, ccMail, Timeline, WordPerfect, and propriety operational applications such as Pacer and FAST400.
- Experienced in the use of Prime, AS400, UNIX, IBM mainframe, and IBM PC systems and networks.

EXPERIENCE

GEOLOGISTICS AMERICAS INC. (formerly LEP Profit International), Marietta, Georgia (1980 – present)
GeoLogistics is a transportation management and freight forwarding company that provides logistics consulting services to large corporate clients such as Lucent Technologies, Silicon Graphics, and PepsiCo.

Director of Customer Solutions and Logistics Operations (1993 – present)

- Project manager responsible for the design and delivery of a $25 million transportation logistics solution for Lucent Technologies' transition from legacy systems to SAP systems.
- Manage a multi-disciplinary team in 100 locations for this re-engineering of distribution channels to support merged-in-transit product delivery.
- Interface at the director level of Lucent and report to the corporate Senior Vice President of Operations.
- Achieved a $3 million reduction in transportation costs in the first year in addition to a significant decrease in inventory.
- Led an intercompany team in the integration of discrete operating processes and systems data exchanges as the result of a merger of Bekins Van Lines with LEP.
- Analyzed payable processes and discovered overpayments to vendors of $2 million in 1998; anticipate the recovery of another $5 million in 1999.
- Coordinate the application design between multiple parties around the world for the mapping and managing of standard EDI transaction sets.
- Managed the project design, development, implementation, testing, and user training for a major internal computer application rewrite project with a budget of $3.5 million.
- Projected future trends, met with impacted internal staff, and translated their needs into technical solutions.
- Managed the design and implementation of an asset recovery project for CompuCom.
- Spearheaded the production of the user specifications for the internal computer applications required to support both the reconciliation of returned inventory and proper pricing metrics.

Director of Operations Training (1988 – 1993)

- Planned, created materials for, and implemented a new field training program for the operational units located throughout the U.S. and Puerto Rico.
- Trained, supervised, and evaluated seven training specialists based in six locations.
- Coordinated international training and support in selected European and Pacific Rim offices.
- Developed and conducted training classes for 80 new salespeople in a five-week product knowledge course designed to increase productivity.
- Certified as an ISO 9000 auditor through Georgia Tech and the British Standards Institute (BSI).

Manager, Transportation Services (1984 – 1988)

- Designed and implemented the hub-and-spoke surface transportation system that moved 100,000 pounds of freight per week through Columbus, Ohio.
- Ensured carrier compliance with transportation regulations at local, state, and national levels.

Domestic Operations Manager (1981 – 1984)

EDUCATION

BACHELOR OF BUSINESS ADMINISTRATION, Shorter College, Marietta, Georgia (1995)

ADDRESS

1234 Spicer's Lane • Woodstock, Georgia 30189 • (770) 555-1234 • criscito@aol.com

Scannable

Jason Paul

1234 Urbano Street ▸ Los Angeles, California 90066 ▸ Phone (310) 555-1234 ▸ Pager (800) 555-1234

PROFILE
- Creative designer with experience in film and theater
- Diverse background in the design and production of stop-motion animation, puppets, props, sound, sets, and lighting
- Graduate degree in fine arts from the California Institute of the Arts
- Self-motivated with strong problem solving and organization skills

EXPERIENCE

FILM:
- Formulated design concepts, selected locations, and directed and coordinated set design and construction
- Established budgets and schedules, estimated construction costs, and monitored expenses
- Designed concepts for costumes, makeup, photographic effects, titles, and related production items; created miniature production sets

Art Department
- Cartoon Network ID (animated), directed by Mark Osborne for Bad Clams Productions (1997)
- Frutopia "origami" (animated), animation directed by Mark Osborne for Shooting Ducks Production (1997)
- Production assistant for Vincent Jefferds, Production Designer, *The Phoney Perfector* (1993)

Swing Gang, *Boboli Commercial*
- Hallmark Commercial Series for Johnson Burnett Productions, Jim Wager, Decorator (1997)
- Scream LLC Productions, Jim Wager, Decorator (1996)

Thesis Project, *La Lune* (1996)
- Successfully wrote and produced an 8-minute stop-motion animation film, including story boards, set design and construction, timing, editing, and sound

Video Production Intern, Biomedical Communications, Tucson, Arizona (1993)

PUPPETS:
- Experienced in mold making, casting compounds, and foam latex construction

Puppet Builder, *Watt's Supa Sister Girl* (1996)
- Constructed "Kinks the Talking Afro-Pick" for Director John Gary

Artisan, The Character Shop (1995)
- Built a giant fiberglass hand mold for "Cong"
- Painted the feathers of the "Bud Light Vulture"

Intern, Tony Urbano Productions (1995)
- Carved and foam constructed "Grampa Nature"; created properties for *911*

THEATER:
- Designed properties and scenic effects
- Integrated requirements, interpretation, research, design concepts, and practical considerations (mobility, interchangeability, budget) with set design

Properties Artisan, California Institute of the Arts (1995)
- *Marisol, Oregon Gothic, The Nose, Hedda Gabler, Brave New World*

Scenic Artist, University of Arizona (1993)
- *The Mystery of Edwin Drood*

Properties Artisan, University of Arizona (1991 – 1992)
- *Lie of the Mind, The Rover*

EDUCATION

MASTER OF FINE ARTS, California Institute of the Arts, Valencia, California (1996)
BACHELOR OF FINE ARTS, University of Arizona, Tucson, Arizona (1994)

KIRSTAN GRAHAM

HIGHLIGHTS OF QUALIFICATIONS

Detail-oriented marketing and advertising professional with a strong background in research and media buying.
Well regarded for organizational, interpersonal, written, and oral communication abilities.
Willing and able to handle a wide variety of tasks simultaneously.
Able to acquire knowledge rapidly; creative and thorough in developing a project.
Computer Skills: Microsoft Office, ACT, MM+ Media Buying Software, Media Pro Research Software,
WordPerfect, Electronic Funds Transfer Software, Mac P&L, Internet, E-mail.

RELEVANT SKILLS AND EXPERIENCE

Marketing and Advertising

- Created and developed successful marketing strategies to increase sales and to improve customer service.
- Created media plans; researched and purchased television, newspaper, and radio space.
- Researched demographics and psychographics of various markets.
- Completed a three-month advertising internship with Praco, Ltd.; followed up press releases, updated membership list for the local Press Association, and developed media contacts.
- Collaborated on the planning and promotion of the 1997 Career Opportunities Fair with student government; corresponded weekly with equipment company and directed set-up; helped publicize event; assisted in the search for employers.
- Promoted community involvement with the university housing village through safe Halloween trick-or-treating program; obtained sponsorships and donations through written and oral presentations; managed all publicity; coordinated hall decorating contest.

Administration

- Managed accounts receivable, accounts payable, and payroll.
- Arranged files and analyzed performance of existing accounts for prospective clients.
- Developed, registered, and evaluated student support activities.
- Assisted in crisis management situations; advocate and mentor for high-risk children.

Leadership

- Represented student body on student government as a senator at large.
- Selected as representative to the Model Organization of American States, Washington, D.C.
- Member of the Programming Board, Health Advisory Board, Budget Committee, and Commencement Committee; Media Coordinator for Ski Club.

EMPLOYMENT HISTORY

Assistant Media Buyer (1998 – Present)
The Graham Group, Colorado Springs, Colorado

Advertising/Public Relations Intern (1997)
Praco, Ltd., Colorado Springs, Colorado

Administrative Assistant (1995 – 1997)
Rooney and Associates, Ltd., Colorado Springs, Colorado

Resident Advisor (1996 – 1997)
University of Colorado Housing Village, Colorado Springs, Colorado

EDUCATION

Bachelor of Arts in Psychology and Communications (1997)
Honors in Communications • Emphasis in Advertising, Marketing, and Public Relations
University of Colorado, Colorado Springs

JOANNE PETERSON

1234 Quarter Circle Drive
Colorado Springs, CO 80922
Telephone: (719) 555-1234

QUALIFICATIONS

- Dependable office worker with more than five years of hands-on experience.
- Able to thrive in a fast-paced environment that involves managing multiple tasks simultaneously.
- Versatile, quick learner who loves challenge and adapts well to new situations.
- Self-motivated; work well with little or no supervision.
- Knowledge of Windows 95, MS Word, and Excel computer software.
- Skills: typing, ten-key, and multiple phone lines.

EXPERIENCE

U.S. HANG GLIDING ASSOCIATION, Colorado Springs, Colorado   1998 – present
Membership Services Representative
- Answer questions from members over the telephone, receive membership dues and orders, and resolve problems through correspondence.
- Enter data into spreadsheets, reconcile balances, process credit cards, and make daily bank deposits.
- Enter special piloting skills into a rating database that is imported directly into the *Hang Gliding and Paragliding* magazine.

APG SECURITY, Vancouver, Washington   1995 – 1998
Switchboard Operator (under contract to Hewlett-Packard)
- Answered multi-line telephone where the accurate taking of detailed messages was essential.
- Provided customer service for emergency and nonemergency situations while trafficking an after-hours call center.
- Accountable for ensuring the security of computer and voice mail password requests.
- Implemented quick responses to assembly line accidents and other emergencies.
- Activated pagers, performed trouble shooting, and instructed customers in the use of cellular phones and voice mail.
- Edited and distributed in-house information to hearing impaired employees.
- Sorted, distributed, and redirected paper flow within office; filed and purged customer accounts.

PROTECTION ONE ALARM SERVICES, Portland, Oregon   1993 – 1995
Contract Administration Specialist
- Responsible for monitoring client account activity and for reconciling and activating/deactivating accounts.
- Updated cash receipts from branch transfers and prepared daily deposits.
- Performed monthly billing for entire customer base of 11 branches; calculated final billings and processed credit card accounts.
- Reviewed client contracts, wrote adjustment authorizations, and maintained existing accounts.
- Assisted technicians with new customer setup and testing during alarm monitoring activation.
- Answered multiple phone lines and provided exceptional customer service.
- Directed incoming and outgoing communications, both mailed and faxed.
- Performed data entry and general office duties.
- Achieved steady promotions from file clerk to receptionist to data entry clerk to contract administration specialist.

TRAINING
- Windows 95
- Safety Procedures
- Astoria Beauty College, 1989

Scannable

51

KELLIE A. McZENGER

1234 East Thomas Road, Apt. 2132
Scottsdale, Arizona 85251
Phone: (602) 555-1234

OBJECTIVE

A challenging opportunity in corporate or industrial training.

SUMMARY OF QUALIFICATIONS

- Six years of experience as a **trainer** in both the corporate and public sectors.
- Strong background in developing company training programs and computer-based instruction.
- Skilled in organization, leadership, management, and problem solving.
- Comfortable with IBM PCs, Windows, MS Word, Excel, PowerPoint, Lotus 1-2-3, MS Schedule, Paintbrush, Apple Deskscan, Photoshop, Corel Photo, networks, MES Fabtop, and telecommunications software.
- Certifications: Indiana Teaching Certificate, Certified Red Cross Instructor for CPR and First Aid, Certified Zenger Miller Instructor.

PROFESSIONAL EXPERIENCE

TRAINING MANAGER, Flip Chip Technologies, Phoenix, Arizona (1996 – Present)
- Coordinate internal and external training programs for operations and sales department (i.e., DOE, SPC, and sales training).
- Design and develop curriculums and instruct courses in orientation, safety, clean room protocols, problem solving, team building, wafer handling, chemical handling, and software for groups of up to 40 employees.
- Editor of monthly company newsletter distributed to 200 employees and clients.
- Create training manuals and course materials for all training programs.
- Coordinate open houses and event planning for customers and employee families.
- Act as liaison between managers, instructors, supervisors, and trainees.
- Devise evaluation instruments to analyze performance; institute program changes to meet training goals.

CORPORATE TRAINER, Confertech International, Westminister, Colorado (1994 – 1996)
- Administer professional development, supervisory, and software training programs in three locations.
- Conduct on-site visits to monitor operations and compliance with policies and procedures.
- Develop learning objectives for in-house computer training programs and devise instructional materials.
- Make presentations, including lectures, seminars, and orientations for groups of six to ten employees.
- Wrote and designed computer-based training manuals, user materials, and training publications.

OPERATIONS MANAGER, Confertech International, Westminister, Colorado (1993 – 1994)
- Managed the operations of a 300-employee department.
- Administered all policy and procedure documentation and ensured consistency with corporate objectives and training efforts.
- Created, implemented, and monitored personnel training programs.
- Developed new guidelines for the call center.

EDUCATION

BACHELOR OF SCIENCE, Indiana University, Bloomington, Indiana (1992)
- Major in Education

CONTINUING EDUCATION, University of Colorado, Denver, Colorado (1996)
- Studies toward a Master of Arts in Instructional Technology

AFFILIATIONS

- American Society of Training Development

52

5 Address Positions

People must be able to locate you, but your address and phone number are some of the least important marketing details on a résumé. Some managers spend only a few seconds perusing a résumé and might get through the first third of it, if you are lucky. The reader's eyes should be drawn immediately to the things that will motivate him or her to read all the way to the bottom.

However, you don't want to make the reader work too hard when it comes time to make that critical call for an interview! You should make the address section part of the overall design of the résumé so it doesn't detract from the text, much as you did with your name, but keep it in an easy-to-find location. That can be done by placing the address(es) either at the top or the bottom of the résumé.

Two addresses, a current and permanent, are often needed when a person is still in school or will be moving in a few months. Presenting them at the top sometimes creates design problems and requires a bit of imagination (pages 54, 57, 60, 64, 66, 69, and 73). Placing two addresses at the bottom is often easier.

An address at the top of the résumé should be made part of the design so that the reader's eyes easily skip over it to begin reading the text. Graphic lines are particularly useful in this case (pages 55, 56, 58, 61, 62, 65, 68, 71, and 76), and so is the judicious use of italics (pages 57, 74, and 77).

Matching lines at the bottom of a résumé sometimes help to create a sense of balance so the résumé is not top heavy (pages 72–74, 77, and 78). The address can be centered under or between the line(s) (pages 74 and 77), made to follow the same format as the text of the résumé (pages 72, 73, and 78), or tab aligned (page 72 and 78).

If you have an e-mail address, always include it on your résumé. The same goes for your Web page address if you have a portfolio online.

Leslie Neal Keogh

Dirección: Edificio San Remo • Calle Coronel Carlos Guerrero y Bosemediano • Quito, Ecuador • Teléfono: 123-456
Permanent Address: 1234 Sonata Street • New Orleans, Louisiana 70115 • (504) 555-1234

OBJECTIVE

A challenging entry-level position in marketing management that will allow growth into positions of broader responsibility

SUMMARY OF QUALIFICATIONS

- Master of International Management Degree with emphasis in marketing
- Seven years of experience in highly competitive markets
- Skilled in planning and organization; outstanding persuasive abilities
- Effective team player experienced in developing successful marketing/network teams
- Resourceful and articulate; results-oriented with high standards of job performance
- Proficient in Spanish

PROFESSIONAL EXPERIENCE

UNDERWRITER, April 1998 – December 1999
National Union Fire Insurance Company, New York, New York
(Subsidiary of American International Group, Inc.)
- Researched and analyzed documentation on companies to assess solvency and risk factors
- Reviewed financial reports, litigation history, and insurance history
- Exclusively handled accounts of $25 million and above

FINANCIAL COUNSELOR, June 1997 – April 1998
Integrated Resources Investment Center, Smithtown, New York
- Introduced financial services to customers in seven branch banks
- Conducted consultations and sold financial products
- Broadened client base through development of interbank referral network
- Educated bank personnel in financial services and built effective marketing teams

ACCOUNT EXECUTIVE, September 1994 – June 1997
Merrill Lynch Pierce Fenner & Smith, Inc., Melville, New York
- Established and developed client base through cold-calling
- Conducted seminars and coordinated direct mail marketing
- Provided investment advice and services to clients
- Hired as youngest broker in branch

ACCOUNT EXECUTIVE, December 1991 – August 1994
Dreyfus Service Corporation, Garden City, New York
- Provided information and assistance to clients regarding mutual fund activities
- Responsible for sales and servicing of IRA, Keogh, money markets, and other new bank products in the Specialty Sales Division
- Selected to participate in marketing task force for life insurance product

EDUCATION

MASTER OF INTERNATIONAL MANAGEMENT, December 1998
American Graduate School of International Management
Thunderbird Campus, Glendale, Arizona
Emphasis: Marketing

BACHELOR OF ARTS: PSYCHOLOGY, 1989
University of Florida at Gainesville
Minor: Business

INTERNATIONAL STUDIES
Guadalajara, Mexico, Summer 1998
Antigua, Guatemala, Winter 1997 – 1998
Quito, Ecuador, March – June 1997
University of Innsbruck, Austria, Summer 1987

54

Scannable

MARIE PYNE

12345 Daphne West • Mission Viejo, California 92691 • (303) 555-1234

PROFILE

- Experienced accounts payable manager with a diverse background in manufacturing, retail, health care, and pharmaceutical industries, including expertise in:
  - ▸ SAP systems integration/conversion
  - ▸ SAP ERP system implementation
  - ▸ International accounts payable system conversions
  - ▸ International currency regulations
  - ▸ Accounts payable site consolidations
  - ▸ Streamlining accounts payable processes
  - ▸ Eliminating non-value-added processes
  - ▸ Development of departmental budgets
  - ▸ Management and supervision
  - ▸ Mergers and acquisitions
- Enthusiastic team player with the ability to build a consensus within both large and small groups.
- Self-starter with exceptional organizational and problem solving abilities.
- Proficient with mainframe accounts payable manufacturing software, including SAP, Pansophic, D&B, BPCS, Praxa, and MaCola; skilled in Windows 95, MS Word, Excel, PowerPoint, Outlook, and Netscape.

EXPERIENCE

MANAGER OF ACCOUNTS PAYABLE SERVICES (1983 – present)
Allergan, Inc., North American Shared Service Center, Irvine, California
Managed all North American accounts payable services for this leading manufacturer of eye/skin care products and surgical equipment with annual revenues in excess of $1 billion. Supervised a staff of 17 direct reports, servicing 8 U.S. and 5 international locations. Answered to the Assistant Controller.

- Integral part of the team responsible for managing Allergan's finance re-engineering project that resulted in the successful implementation of a complex SAP enterprise resources planning system (ERP) in 13 locations in the United States, Mexico, Canada, and Puerto Rico.
- Seamlessly converted the system in less than 18 months through extensive on-site travel, integrated testing, training, process re-engineering, process consolidations, and employee empowerment.
- Maintained timely and accurate payables of $450 million annually while at the same time reducing the accounts payable team more than 56 percent over two years as a result of the re-engineering.
- Expanded the procurement credit card program from 3,500 to 7,000 transactions per month, which will result in a reduction of small dollar invoice processing by 80 percent and staffing by $60,000 in 1999.
- Participated in the selection and implementation of the iXOS imaging software to eliminate hard data storage and to manage invoice approval, invoice accruals, and direct vendor invoice imaging online, saving $48,000 per year and making the accounts payable process nearly paperless.
- Honored with five Outstanding Achievement and Impact Awards for successful implementation of cutting-edge technology solutions.

ACCOUNTS PAYABLE SUPERVISOR (1980 – 1983)
Advanced Health Center, Irvine, California
Supervised 9 staff members in the accounts payable support of 37 doctor's offices, 12 acute care hospitals, and 14 alcoholic treatment centers.

- Trained all employees for new acquisitions and streamlined the payables process, allowing a 20 percent decrease in payroll.

ACCOUNTS PAYABLE SUPERVISOR (1978 – 1980)
Builders Emporium Home Improvement Center, Irvine, California
Supervised a staff of 7 in the servicing of 52 California, Nevada, and Arizona locations of this retail home improvement outlet.

- Received the Employee of the Year Award for improving relationships, resolving outstanding problems, and implementing new processes to prevent recurrence of problems at a major vendor.

EDUCATION

PITTSBURGH UNIVERSITY and **PITTSBURGH ART ACADEMY**, Pittsburgh, Pennsylvania
CONTINUING EDUCATION: Managing a High-Performance Self-Directed Team, Philip Crosby Quality Improvement Program, Management, Leadership Challenges, Cost Accounting, Non-Exempt Performance Review Course, Managing New Employees, How to Interview, Negotiation Skills, Writing Skills

AFFILIATIONS

Member of International Accounts Payable Professionals; presenter at IAPP conferences
Member of the Institute of Management and Administration; presenter at IOMA conferences

Scannable

55

ERMINIO ANDERSON

1234 West Desert Cove • Phoenix, Arizona 85029 • Home: (602) 555-1234 • Work: (602) 555-1234

EXPERIENCE

CITY OF PHOENIX, ARIZONA (1986 – Present)

Equipment Maintenance Superintendent (1994 – Present)
- Direct the operation of automotive shops for the repair and maintenance of 5,000+ pieces of automotive, construction, and special duty equipment.
- Supervise more than 300 employees.
- Establish work policies, schedules, repair, and maintenance work standards.
- Supervise the presentations of monthly and annual maintenance cost reports, and prepare budget estimates for maintenance operations.
- Investigate personnel problems and submit reports and recommendations.
- Assisted in the design of an employee attitude survey.
- Coordinator for the Public Works Department Partnership Program (quality circle program).
- Served on the Supervisory Development Advisory Council to formulate criteria for the Phoenix Supervisor Academy.
- Member of Total Quality Management Task Force and Apprenticeship Program Committee (Chairman since 1994).

Equipment Shop Supervisor (1991 – 1994)
- Directed the maintenance performed on equipment management fleet at the satellite shops, police substations, landfills, and water treatment plants.
- Managed project for rebuilding landfill equipment, saving an average of $60,000 per vehicle.

Equipment Shop Foreman (1988 – 1991)
- Set priorities, planned, assigned, and coordinated all the work for the heavy duty, welding, tire, and battery shops.
- Played a role in setting a nationwide trend toward using mechanical lifting devices in refuse collection. Assisted in designing some of the first vehicles used for this purpose.
- Supervised building trucks from the ground up, reconditioning them in order to save the expense of purchasing new vehicles.
- Member of the Organization Development Steering Committee, which acted as a change agent in the assembly, marketing, and support of city-wide improvements.

Heavy Equipment Mechanic, Auto Mechanic, and Mechanic's Helper (1986 – 1988)

EDUCATION

PHOENIX COLLEGE, Phoenix, Arizona (1984 – 1988)
Associate of Arts Degree in Public Administration (82 hours)

TRAINING PROGRAMS

Equipment Maintenance/Management Conference (3 days)
Advanced Public Works Supervision for the 1990's (2 days)
Business Writing Skills (1 day)
Strategies of Effective Writing (1 day)
Introduction to Microcomputers
Introduction to Lotus 1-2-3
Assertive Management, ASU
Partnership Leader Training
Preventive Maintenance for Fleet Operations (1.4 CEU's)
Improving Management Skills for New Managers
Supervisor as Counselor
National Safety Council Key Man Development Program
Arc and Gas Welding Certificate (16 weeks)

PROFESSIONAL MEMBERSHIPS

- American Society for Public Administration
- Rocky Mountain Maintenance Association
- Phoenix Sister Cities Commission (Hermosillo Committee Chairman)
- ASPTEA – Administrative, Supervisory, Professional, and Technical Employees Association of the City of Phoenix, Arizona
- Institute for Equipment Services
- Arizona Fleet Maintenance Council
- Maricopa Technical Community College (Chairman)

56

Scannable

C. DAVID MAROUN

Current:
1234 W. Eugie Avenue, #1234
Glendale, Arizona 85304
Phone: (602) 555-1234
Fax: (602) 555-1234

Permanent:
123 Racquette River Dr., Box 123
Tupper Lake, New York 12986
Phone: (518) 555-1234
Fax: (518) 555-1234

EXPERIENCE

AMERICAN GRADUATE SCHOOL OF INTERNATIONAL MANAGEMENT
Thunderbird Campus, Glendale, Arizona
Graduate Assistant
June 1999 thru Dec. 1999
- Performed feasibility study of the Arab Gulf via primary research and data analysis to establish an international institute for technology transfer
- Developed teaching curriculum for an interactive computer program used in Arabic language classes

TEXAS INSTRUMENTS, Dallas, Texas
Educational Products Division
Marketing Research Consultant
Feb. 1998 through May 1998
- Determined market potential and formulated entry strategies for a new product line in the U.S. Hispanic market
- Designed and implemented qualitative and quantitative research methods to assess: 1) barriers to market entry, 2) channels of distribution, 3) product modifications, 4) product positioning, 5) key purchasers and influencers of purchase

XEROX CORPORATION, Rochester, New York
United States Marketing Group, Major Markets Contract Pricing Administration
Marketing Intern
Jan. 1997 through May 1997
- Generated reports needed for feasibility analyses and strategic pricing
- Created pricing matrices to reflect changes in major government contracts
- Expedited the authorization process for revisions to government contracts

CAMIL G. MAROUN, JR. INSURANCE AGENCY, Tupper Lake, New York
General Insurance Agency, Personal and Commercial Lines
General Office Assistant
Summers 1993–1997
- Generated new accounts and recommended appropriate coverages for clients
- Originated and designed procedural manuals for quotations and policy endorsements
- Prepared accounting data for monthly batch

EDUCATION

MASTER OF INTERNATIONAL MANAGEMENT
American Graduate School of International Management
Glendale, Arizona
Dec. 1997
- International Consumer Marketing Workshop
- Marketing to U.S. Hispanics Seminar
- Advanced Commercial Spanish
- International Insurance
- Co-Chair, Middle East Club

BACHELOR OF SCIENCE IN MANAGEMENT
St. John Fisher College, Rochester, New York
May 1996
Concentration: International Business   **Minor:** Spanish
- Business Manager for the Spanish Club   • Spanish Tutor

FOREIGN STUDY
Universidad de Salamanca, Salamanca, Spain
American Institute for Foreign Studies (AIFS)
Sep. 1994 through May 1995

LANGUAGES & SKILLS

English (native) • **Spanish** (fluent) • **Arabic** (proficient)
Computer: PowerPoint, Lotus 1-2-3, Macintosh, SPSSpc, MS Word, Excel

SCHOLARSHIPS & HONORS

R. K. Thomas Assistantship (1994) • Arabic Scholarship (1994) • Presidential Scholarship (1992–1994) • Dean's List (1992–1994) • Alpha Mu Gamma (National Collegiate Foreign Language Honor Society) (1992–Present) • Admissions Scholarship (1989–1991) • Thunderbird Honor Student

ADAM L. WASHINGTON

12345 N. 59th Avenue #123 • Glendale, Arizona 85306 • Phone/Fax: (602) 555-1234

QUANTITATIVE SKILLS

EXPERIENCE
- Research and analysis of U.S. economic data and the federal budget for U.S. senator
- Financial analysis and forecasting for commercial real estate properties
- Market research of commercial real estate markets
- Computer: designed spreadsheet models and constructed databases

EDUCATION
- Graduate level: Finance, Accounting, Statistics, Marketing Research, Economics

QUALITATIVE SKILLS

EXPERIENCE
- Drafted U.S. senator's positions on especially sensitive issues, including Political Action Committees, campaign finance reform, and congressional perquisites
- Responded in writing daily to political constituents on a range of important issues
- Designed marketing strategies for a nonprofit health association, an information company (with proprietary computer databases), and a real estate development company
- Project presentation experience
- Computer: utilized word-processing and database programs

EDUCATION
- Graduate: management, marketing, team-based work, project presentation, public speaking
- Undergraduate: liberal arts, political science, literature, extensive writing courses

INTERNATIONAL SKILLS

EDUCATION
- Master of International Management
- International Studies concentration: Western European Integration, Eastern Europe, Russia
- World Business concentration: International Marketing and Finance
- Countertrade and Offset Management: Certificate of Competency

LANGUAGES
- French: U.S. State Department Level 3
- English: Native speaker with exceptional writing abilities

EXPERIENCE
- Atlantic Treaty Association Conference, U.S. Delegate, Paris
- American Council of Young Political Leaders, Reception Host for Australian Delegation
- Friends of Costa Rica (Earthquake Relief Effort), Fund-raising Committee Member
- Institute for Comparative Political and Economic Systems, Alumni Board Member

EMPLOYMENT HISTORY

1999 – 2000	Market Analyst/Admin. Asst.	Carey Winston Company	Washington, DC
1999	Membership Director	National Assn. of Nonsmokers	Washington, DC
1998	Staff Assistant (concurrently)	GAC Oversight Subcommittee	Washington, DC
1997 – 1998	Legislative Assistant	U.S. Senator William S. Cohen	Washington, DC
1996	Administrative Assistant	Brick Landing Plantation	Isle Beach, NC

ACADEMIC DEGREES AND HONORS

MASTER OF INTERNATIONAL MANAGEMENT – May, 2000   GPA: 3.9
American Graduate School of International Management, Thunderbird Campus, Glendale, AZ
Thunderbird Scholar, American Graduate School of International Management, 1994

BACHELOR OF ARTS, GOVERNMENT – 1995
University of Virginia, Charlottesville, VA

INSTITUTE FOR COMPARATIVE POLITICAL AND ECONOMIC SYSTEMS, Graduate – 1993
Georgetown University, Washington, DC

58

 Scannable

CARROLL W. HATCH

1234 Eagle Trace #304 • Memphis, Tennessee 38125
Phone: (901) 555-1234 • E-mail: criscito@aol.com

PROFILE

- *Creative programmer and systems analyst with ten years of in-depth experience.*
- *Skilled in developing new products to save the company money.*
- *Able to simplify complex products for the end user.*
- *Knowledge of the pitfalls inherent in the design of infrastructures.*
- *Team player with strong communication and interpersonal skills.*
- *Fluent in Cambodian; working knowledge of French.*

COMPUTERS

Programming Languages: *Natural, Focus, SAS, COBOL, DB2/SQL, Visual Basic, C/C++, HTML, Java, Sybase, Fortran, Pascal, PL/I, IBM Clist/Panels, Syncsort, EZtrieve, UNIX shells/scripts*
Operating Systems: *MVS, VMS, UNIX, OS/2, Windows NT/Server, Windows 95*
Software: *MS Word, Access, PowerPoint, Excel, Informix, GPSS, Limdep, MicroFocus*

EXPERIENCE

FEDERAL EXPRESS, *Memphis, Tennessee (1998 to present)*
Project Lead, Comforce Contractor
- *Initiated a client-server project to re-host six major DEC VAX applications onto two UNIX Sun E4000 servers using MicroFocus COBOL and Sybase.*
- *Team leader responsible for acquiring the resources needed for the project and presenting the project plan to management.*
- *Managed the user requirements engineering phase and aligned cross-functional departments to collaborate on the project.*
- *Documented Sybase physical/logical data models and created development documents for programmers.*
- *Created the business process definition to help developers speed up the coding process.*
- *Completed a six-month contract according to plan.*

MCI TELECOMMUNICATIONS CORPORATION *(1991 to 1998)*
Senior Systems Analyst II, *Colorado Springs, Colorado (1997 to 1998)*
- *Developed a SAS GUI system on the DEC UNIX platform to provide analysts with access to the Traffic 2000 call processing system using C++ and Sybase.*
- *Returned revenue to MCI by allowing analysts to perform traffic recoveries and to further analyze problems in real-time situations.*
- *Developed a Web site to replace the SAS GUI system.*
- *Assisted management in projecting future problems and developing solutions.*

Senior Systems Analyst I, *Colorado Springs, Colorado (1994 to 1997)*
- *Provided third-level order entry and billing support for data products like TDS, DDS, HyperStream, among others.*
- *Resident expert for trouble shooting all billing system-related questions.*
- *Wrote Natural and COBOL codes to fix order entry/billing production problems.*
- *Helped form a committee to oversee the quality of MCI's billing accuracy.*
- *Used extensive understanding of data products to assist account teams and MCI's external customers in resolving issues and to educate them on data products.*
- *Achieved the MCI Rev Ops (Revenue Operations) award from the Vice President for key contributions to the billing quality initiative program.*

Systems Programmer/Analyst, *Dallas, Texas (1991 to 1994)*
- *Developed a forecasting tool for all of MCI's inbound call centers.*
- *Worked with a doctor of statistics to accumulate data using the mainframe call processing feeds.*
- *Developed SAS MVS/UNIX programs that predicted calls by half hour, program type, and center for the following month, achieving a 98.5 percent forecast accuracy rate.*
- *The program was so successful that it was used as a model for predicting traffic for all call centers.*

EDUCATION

MASTER OF SCIENCE, TELECOMMUNICATIONS *(1996 to present)*
University of Colorado, *Colorado Springs, Colorado*

BACHELOR OF SCIENCE, STATISTICS, *Virginia Tech (1988)*

Scannable

CARLOS J. MANUEL

OFFICE ADDRESS	123 Rivera Manuel Ave., Suite 1234, San Juan, PR 00918	Telephone: (809) 555-1234
HOME ADDRESS	P. O. Box 12345, Hato Rey, PR 00912	Telephone: (809) 555-1234

OBJECTIVE   A Challenging Position in **International Operations** leading to Senior Management Opportunities

SKILLS
- **ASSERTIVENESS** – Earned six promotions and four merit nominations in less than four years at Pepsi-Cola. Reached record sales and market shares within months.
- **FOCUS** – Consistent ability to identify and exploit major growth opportunities and effectively address the "real" issues – proven in both highly developed and underdeveloped markets.
- **LEADERSHIP** – Commitment, integrity, and dedication have allowed me to motivate and work effectively through bottlers, peers, and subordinates. Co-instructed a Dale Carnegie course on self-confidence, public speaking, and interpersonal skills at the age of 19.
- **SELF-STARTER** – Four years of entrepreneurial experience. Require minimal supervision. Have been able to materialize and implement key projects long delayed in the planning process. Self-financed 100 percent of graduate and 50 percent of undergraduate education.
- **LANGUAGES** – Fluent in English and Spanish. Working knowledge of Portuguese.
- **COMPUTERS** – Lotus 1-2-3, Excel, DW4, WordPerfect, Harvard Graphics, On Target, Windows, DOS

EXPERIENCE   **PEPSI-COLA CARIBBEAN**, San Juan, Puerto Rico   Jan. 1995 – Present
- P&L and market share responsibilities – primary link between company and bottlers
- Brand and Key Account Management, Market Development, Strategic Planning
- Also accountable for Packaging Innovation, Distribution, Merchandising, and Promotions

Operations → District Manager PUERTO RICO   **Oct. 1997 – Present**
- Manage four subordinates, a $9,000,000 budget, and 35% of regional volume
- Gained brand leadership for Pepsi-Cola in less than a year on the job
  (our main competitor had uninterruptedly been the #1 brand for over seven years)
- Reversed declining sales trends (-15% → +23%) amid a heavily taxed soft drink industry
- Instrumental in creating and implementing a three-year leadership plan with Bacardi

Operations Manager HISPANIOLA DISTRICT   **Jan. – Sep. 1997**
- Managed four countries, a $1,400,000 budget, and 26% of regional volume
- Reversed volume drops in Dominican Republic (-25% → +27%), Haiti (-20% → +26%), and Jamaica (-44% → -2%) amid worsening economic and political conditions
- Launched Sprite in the Dominican Republic, capturing 50% share of segment within six months
- Pioneered a Street Vendor Cooler project in Haiti, creating a new trade channel

Country → Operations Manager N.E. CARIBBEAN   **Jan. – Dec. 1996**
- Managed 14 territories, a $400,000 budget, and 12% of regional volume
- Achieved record growth in Bahamas (+24%) and USVI (+18%) with profits 10% above budget

Account Services Representative → Cold Drink Manager   **Jan. – Dec. 1995**
- Instrumental in gaining exclusivity-conversions in key fountain accounts in Puerto Rico

SELF-EMPLOYED, Austin, Texas   July 1989 – Aug. 1993
- Introduced CONTI designer apparel and test marketed Latin American products
- Founded the first ticket brokerage agency in Central Texas (Showtime Tickets, Inc.)

EDUCATION   **MASTER OF INTERNATIONAL MANAGEMENT**   Dec. 1995
American Graduate School of International Management, Glendale, Arizona
- Emphasis on Investments and Multinational Operations
- Worked as a Marketing Intern for Pepsi-Cola Caribbean (June–August 1988)
- First scholar to take majority of graduate courses at the most advanced level

BACHELOR OF BUSINESS ADMINISTRATION   May 1991
University of Texas, Austin, Texas   **Major:** Business/Electrical Engineering

SEMINARS AND WORKSHOPS   1996 – 1998
Customer Service, Key Account Management, High-Performance Organizations, Project Management, Pricing and Packaging, International Merchandising, Communications Skills

60

JEFFREY K. ENGLEWOOD

1234 Hollow Drive, Colorado Springs, Colorado 80920
(719) 555-1234

OBJECTIVE

A marketing management position with the opportunity to develop and implement marketing strategies that will promote innovative products and/or services

QUALIFICATIONS

- *Highly creative, self-motivated individual*
- *Team player with exceptional interpersonal skills*
- *Sixteen years of managerial and marketing experience*
- *Area representative with the Christian Booksellers Association*
- *B.A. degree in business administration with an emphasis in both management and marketing*

EXPERIENCE

VICE PRESIDENT AND GENERAL MANAGER *(1990 – Present)*
The Lord's Vineyard, Inc., *Colorado Springs, Colorado*
- *Responsible for consistent growth from start-up to $2.3 million, including management, inventory control, accounting, marketing, and customer service functions*
- *Hired, scheduled hours worked, and organized job descriptions for twenty store personnel*
- *Managed a diverse staff and succeeded in motivating employees to excellence*
- *Developed cash management, forecasting, and budgeting systems*
- *Supervised computer and information systems and assisted in developing computer programs*
- *Designed and managed inventory tracking systems and sales/shipping procedures*
- *Analyzed the market using various research methods to better determine customer desires*
- *Informed sales personnel of customer buying habits, buying motives, and likes and dislikes regarding products and services through weekly staff meetings*
- *Developed and facilitated strategic product promotions and in-store sales events*
- *Scripted and produced radio and television commercials with successful results*
- *Discovered customer wants that could only be satisfied by new or improved products and then provided product development ideas for the CBA industry*

ADVERTISING AND PROMOTION MANAGER *(1994 – 1997)*
Mustardseed Bible Bookstores, *Englewood, Colorado*
- *Entered into a partnership with two other individuals and purchased a chain of five bookstores in the Denver metropolitan area*
- *Directed the advertising, promotion, and product marketing strategies of these five retail stores in Denver, in addition to three store locations in Colorado Springs under The Lord's Vineyard*
- *Achieved a 50 percent increase in sales by the end of the three years*
- *Assisted in purchasing inventory and managing the inventory tracking systems*
- *Sold interest in the business in order to concentrate on the Colorado Springs stores*

GENERAL MANAGER *(1987 – 1990)*
Living Word Christian Supply, *Albuquerque, New Mexico*
- *Part owner responsible for managing, inventory control, and marketing of the business*
- *Doubled sales in three years*
- *Managed six employees and was directly involved in purchasing, sales, marketing of the store and its products, and customer service*
- *Sold business and moved to Colorado to start The Lord's Vineyard, Inc.*

RETAIL SALES MANAGER *(1986 – 1987)*
National Pen Corporation, *San Diego, California*
- *Responsible for product development and the implementation of distribution strategies*
- *Determined through market research which products to sell*
- *Designed products from start to finish and determined methods of distribution*
- *Learned the necessity of increased efficiency in reducing the costs of distribution*
- *Test marketed the products in the San Diego area and was about ready to head the hiring of a national sales force when I received a call to move to Albuquerque to become involved with the Living Word Christian Supply*

Scannable

RON CONDER

12345 River Oaks Drive
Colorado Springs, Colorado 80921

Telephone: (719) 555-1234
E-mail: criscito@aol.com

SUMMARY

♦ Demonstrated success in project management and customer support.
♦ Definitive abilities in leadership, planning, organization, decision making, and team building.
♦ Skilled in visualizing resourceful and enterprising solutions to problems.
♦ Team player with exceptional communication, interpersonal, and customer service skills.
♦ Effective and comfortable communicating and presenting to executive-level management.
♦ Computer skills: MS Project, MS Word, Excel, PowerPoint, Outlook, Access, FrontPage, HTML, AutoCAD, Crystal Reports, NETCOM/CMS/NET PRO databases, Aperature (CADFM), Visio, E-mail, Internet browsers, and wide area network equipment.
♦ Demonstrated talent for learning and utilizing new technologies, including client/server network systems.

EXPERIENCE

PROJECT MANAGER, MCI Worldcom, Colorado Springs, Colorado
1999–Present: Manage the entire process of Y2K readiness assessment and subsequent upgrades to customer premise equipment for 103 accounts valued at more than $100 billion in annual revenue.
♦ Worked closely with executive and technical customers to win their cooperation and participation.
♦ Developed and implemented process plans and creative solutions to unique Y2K problems.
♦ Led the on-site remediation team and made quick decisions to overcome obstacles encountered during the upgrade.
♦ Produced plans for Y2K upgrades of routers/hubs/switches/frame relays, etc.
♦ Tracked progress of the project to ensure that timelines and milestones were met.
♦ Served as liaison between internal and external customers and third-party vendors to manage the remediation process under tight deadlines.
♦ Researched and documented the equipment and activity on customer accounts in the database via web interface forms, Crystal Reports, and Access query tools.
♦ Developed requirements for enhancements to web-based interface used for database input, query, project tracking, and research.
♦ Provided direct input to developers relating to enhancements of database input/extraction forms that significantly improved the quality and ease of researching, updating, scheduling, tracking, and reporting.

PROJECT MANAGER, SYSTEM ADMINISTRATOR, MCI Worldcom, Colorado Springs, Colorado
1998–1999: System Administrator for the company-wide, web-based Conference Room Intranet Scheduler (CRIS), including the development, activation, and promotion of new web sites, training of new users, and maintenance of the Web server.
♦ Developed tracking and trending reports using multi-level Excel spreadsheets that were utilized by executive management to determine funding and cost savings of projects.
♦ Used PowerPoint to create presentations of new systems benefits for executive review.
♦ Analyzed the report writing functions of a proprietary SQL database (Aperature CADFM system) used by corporate space planners and created weekly, monthly, and quarterly reports.
♦ Saved $360,000 in productivity and outside consulting expenses per year.

FACILITY SERVICES SUPERVISOR, MCI Communications, Colorado Springs, Colorado
1993–1998: Managed 156,000 square feet in six software application development and sales facilities.
♦ Developed the concept for and implemented MCI's CRIS conference room intranet scheduler for online scheduling of conference rooms that saved MCI $150,000 per year.
♦ Researched and proposed a computer-aided facilities management system that was adopted corporate-wide and resulted in a Sudden Impact Award.
♦ Coordinated a project to set up a new facility and move 500 people, desktop PCs, and network equipment to the facility in less than four weeks (Spotlight Award).
♦ Brought this 100,000 square foot telecommunications facility on line from the ground up, including the coordination of the LAN, voice and data network, environmental systems, uninterruptible power sources, specialized cooling systems for the lab environment, security, space management, and facility services.

EXPERIENCE   **FACILITIES SERVICES MANAGER** (continued)
- Managed the allotment of space to users; created win-win situations to keep internal customers satisfied.
- Served as liaison to property management organization for outside maintenance, parking, etc.
- Solicited bids from contractors and negotiated and managed contracts for numerous services.
- Worked with contractors and municipal power company on the installation of a new UPS power system and electrical transformer to ensure continuous backup power during a six-hour planned outage.
- Saved MCI over $50,000 in the last year by reallocating underutilized resources and another $70,000 by negotiating lower bids from vendors.
- Interviewed, hired, supervised, and evaluated four supervisors and seven support staff.
- Focus on providing exceptional customer service; tenacious in solving problems for internal customers.

STAFF ARCHITECT/PROJECT MANAGER, Davis Partnership, P.C., Denver, Colorado
1990–1992: Supervised construction projects and developed contract documents.
- Project captain and designer on a new ambulatory suite for Swedish Hospital.
- Awarded First Prize in Professional Art Division of the AIA art show, 1991.

PROJECT MANAGER, The Providence Group, Inc., Colorado Springs, Colorado
1988–1990: Managed design development and construction documents. Supervised a staff of three.
- Produced construction drawings; primary CADD system operator for the firm.

PROJECT MANAGER, Glen Eyrie Conference Center, Colorado Springs, Colorado
1985–1988: Designed and managed various remodeling and construction projects involving numerous trades and consultants.
- Managed the process from design concepts to completed building requiring excellent communication, organizational, and presentation skills.

EDUCATION   **BACHELOR OF ARCHITECTURE**, 1981
University of Kentucky College of Architecture, Lexington
- Excellence in Design Award
- One semester of AutoCAD

CONTINUING EDUCATION
- Windows 98, Microsoft Office Suite (Access, Excel, Outlook, MS Word, MS Project, PowerPoint), FrontPage, Visio, and Crystal Reports
- Seven Habits of Highly Effective People, MCI Management Course on Conflict Resolution

JAMES P. JONES

Present Address: 1234 Aragon Drive, Colorado Springs, Colorado 80920 (303) 555-1234
After Nov. 1999: 1234 Silver Valley Lane, Georgetown, Texas 78626 (512) 555-1234

HIGHLIGHTS OF QUALIFICATIONS

Enthusiastic computer professional with more than six years of experience.
Background in project management, supervision, training, and quality control.
Analytical and detail-oriented problem solver with a strong work ethic.
Hold a current Top Secret SCI security clearance with special access program clearance.

EDUCATION

MASTER OF SCIENCE IN COMPUTER SCIENCE
Colorado Technical University, Colorado Springs, Colorado, September 1999
Major in Software Engineering • Minor in Software Component Engineering

BACHELOR OF SCIENCE IN SYSTEMS MANAGEMENT
Colorado Technical University, Colorado Springs, Colorado, 1997

RELEVANT EXPERIENCE

COMPUTER HARDWARE/SOFTWARE
- Programming Languages and Tools: C/C++, Visual C++, Visual J++, Java, HTML, Win 32 API, MFC, ActiveX, COM/ATL COM, CASE Tools, Rational Rose, UML, and OMT.
- Operating Systems: Windows 95/NT, Macintosh, VAX/VMS, MS-DOS.
- Software: MS Developer Studio, MS Word, Access, PowerPoint, Excel, Outlook, MS Project, Hot Dog 5, FrontPage 98, Paintshop Pro, Internet Explorer, Netscape, among others.
- Hardware: IBM compatible microcomputers, Macintosh, mainframes (VAX 4000/8000), and peripherals.
- Networks: WAN, LAN, IDNX switches, fiber optic modems, Cisco routers, cryptographic devices, etc.
- Completing course work in object-oriented programming/analysis/design, software requirements engineering, software verification/validation, software systems architectures, software design, systems engineering, and systems integration/testing.
- Supervised a massive communications upgrade for the US Space Command's sensitive C2 circuit, including relocation of comm racks, mainframe computers, and circuits worldwide.
- Served as senior government representative in negotiations with contractors and program managers in the development of key computer/communications systems.
- Created a new network surveillance system that increased performance and reduced error rates.

MANAGEMENT/ADMINISTRATION
- Supervised the Space Control and Information Operations Division, troubleshooting projects at the branch level and building effective teams from a staff of 50 officers and airmen.
- Participated in strategic planning for the division; developed and oversaw the operations budget.
- Managed the operations of seven operations centers worldwide operated by 450+ personnel.
- Identified and managed major configuration changes to the command's planning and decision aid system, saving more than 100 maintenance manhours and increasing system efficiency by 40 percent.
- Developed and implemented portions of national policy relating to control of classified space operations, reducing program costs to the government by 50 percent.
- Directed highly complex exercises involving 200+ personnel deployed worldwide.
- Developed requirements for and directed delivery of critical mission equipment worth over $50 million.

EMPLOYMENT HISTORY

UNITED STATES AIR FORCE, 1977 – 1997
Manager of Space Control and Information Operations Division;
Computer Network (WAN and LAN) Manager; Special Operations Manager (NORAD)

CATHERINE THOMPKINS

1234 South 8th Street, Monument, Colorado 80920   Telephone: (719) 555-1234

PROFILE
- Goal-oriented retail manager who enjoys a challenge and is committed to the highest quality standards.
- Background in human resource management, marketing, sales, staff development, inventory control, purchasing, and customer service.
- Effective team player with proven communication skills; skilled in creating staff loyalty and empowering employees to excel.

EXPERIENCE
Management
- Successfully managed the daily operations of a high-volume department store with annual sales of $12 million.
- Managed operating and payroll budgets, maintained control of expenses, and achieved production goals.
- Point of contact for all Mervyn stores in the district with budget and operations questions or concerns.
- Negotiated contracts for facility maintenance and oversaw housekeeping operations.

Accomplishments
- Increased gross annual sales by 10 percent through effective store management and by training sales staff to enhance customer service.
- Selected to represent the district in a San Francisco open forum meeting with executive management.
- Developed a reputation for building team spirit through active listening and proactive problem resolution.
- Trained and developed four associates who were promoted into management positions.
- Recognized by corporate headquarters for developing a school partnership with the local deaf and blind school, which helped to expand funding for academic programs.
- Increased sales for Silgo by effectively researching and negotiating with suppliers.
- Directly contributed to an overall sales increase of 38 percent in one year for Robinson's Department Store; increased special orders by building strong relationships with major manufacturers.

Human Resources
- Interviewed, hired, trained, and developed team leaders, area coordinators, and team members (up to 135 employees).
- Actively involved in the interview process for potential store manager candidates.
- Performed employee performance evaluations, and instituted HR policies and procedures.
- Scheduled team members to meet hourly productivity guidelines, maintaining flex production at 99–102 percent.
- Developed incentive programs to build effective teams, increase employee productivity, and ensure top-quality customer service.
- Facilitated continuing education classes for exempt managers.
- Administered OSHA, safety, compensation, and benefits programs; supervised payroll processes.

Purchasing and Merchandising
- Supervised inventory and shortage control, merchandise assortment, annual store inventory, and stockroom organization.
- Communicated with corporate headquarters regarding merchandise concerns for $5 million in inventory.
- Responsible for achieving maximum sales potential through timely execution of all company merchandising directives and strategies.
- Wrote, updated, and published the store's inventory procedures manual.
- Responsible for purchasing and account management for Silgo International, a private manufacturer of children's products selling to both domestic and international markets.
- Developed a successful special merchandise presentation and designed a 16-page catalog.

WORK HISTORY

Store Manager, Dillard's, Denver, Colorado	1995 – 2000
Store Operations Manager, Joslyn's, Boulder, Colorado	1994 – 1995
Team Leader, Joslyn's, Boulder, Colorado	1992 – 1994
National Sales Manager, Starbuck's, Seattle, Washington	1990 – 1992
Area Manager, Bon Marche, Boise, Idaho	1987 – 1990
Buyer, Bon Marche, Salt Lake City, Utah	1984 – 1987

EDUCATION   **BACHELOR OF SCIENCE IN BUSINESS**, University of Colorado, Boulder, Colorado

Michael C. Nobel

Permanent Address: 1234 Edgepark Road ♦ Vienna, Virginia 22182 ♦ Message: (703) 555-1234
Present Address: Jan Luykenstraat 44 ♦ 1234 CR Amsterdam ♦ The Netherlands
Home: (+31) 20-123-0575 ♦ Work: (+31) 20-123-6911 ♦ E-mail: criscito@aol.com

PROFESSIONAL BACKGROUND

- Highly motivated senior manager with more than ten years of experience in all facets of global telecommunications networking.
- Instrumental in several phases of the development of a new European telecommunications provider that competed with an entrenched monopoly for the first time on the continent; succeeded by working smarter and faster with limited resources.
- Background in business development, strategic planning, start-up processes, product marketing, sales, and contract negotiations in the global arena.
- Directed the design of managed voice and data networks that produced significant cost benefits.
- Developed and successfully sold value propositions for complex frame relay and Internet applications.

PERSONAL PROFILE

- Adept at building trust and turning around troubled client relationships.
- Able to simplify complex ideas and present them effectively at the highest executive level.
- Exceptional motivator who is able to build enlightened teams with a strong customer focus.
- Team player and approachable coach who leads by example.
- Comfortable working in cross-cultural environments; lived and worked in The Netherlands.

--- **Experience** ---

SENIOR MANAGER, CUSTOMER NETWORK DESIGN (8/97 to present)
Telfort Networks and Systems, Amsterdam, The Netherlands (on temporary assignment from MCI)

Developed a customer-focused design team to meet the needs of the sales group for this new European telecommunications provider. Recruited, trained, and managed a team of 14 technical sales support professionals responsible for advanced telecom design and application consulting in support of a $150 million account base. Uncovered high-end applications and found solutions that effectively focused on customer needs. Advised the CIO on the feasibility of designs, developed business plans, and made high-level executive presentations. Prepared and administered $200,000 capital budgets and $500,000 operating budgets.

Key Accomplishments
- Directed the integrated (voice/data) network design, proposal development, and implementation planning process that was instrumental in securing $10 million in annual new revenues from customers such as Shell, World On Line, and NLNet.
- Consulted with sales account teams and assisted them in presenting business application proposals to Philips and Akzo Nobel, securing managed data network contracts valued at $7 million in annual new revenues.
- Saved $5 million in network operating expenses by reorganizing the backbone network structure and consolidating third-party maintenance under one master contract.

SENIOR NATIONAL ACCOUNT MANAGER (5/95 to 8/97)
MCI National Accounts, San Francisco, California, and Atlanta, Georgia

Managed a team of six sales and technical support professionals responsible for business communication application development and consulting to a Fortune 500 global account base with an $18 million annual revenue quota.

Key Accomplishments
- Achieved exclusive vendor status with Fireman's Fund Insurance by executing a four-year, $20 million contract for MCI HyperStream frame relay, Vnet, toll free, and video conferencing services. Turned around a bad relationship, reinvigorating the staff and rebuilding trust at the highest client level before convincing the client of the compelling benefits of a managed data network.
- Implemented a fully managed, 200-node frame relay network for Fireman's Fund, including an alliance sale of $700,000 in Cisco routers, saving the client more than $300,000 through a multivendor partnership.

Scannable

- Negotiated a very complex and creative contract with Fujitsu that generated $10 million in revenue during a two-year period, taking the client from AT&T even though it had Fijitsu's business on price. Developed the plan for the global application of a Pacific Rim 45-megabit Internet backbone network.
- Received the Director's Chair Award for exceptional service; exceeded quotas by as much as 180 percent.

PARTNERSHIP DEVELOPMENT MANAGER, MCI Business Markets, Atlanta, Georgia (6/94 to 5/95)
Directed a team of three marketing and finance professionals responsible for developing reciprocal sales partnerships with retailers who sold to small and mid-sized customers. Negotiated with corporate executives in order to increase director-level support.

Key Accomplishments
- Saved the Staples sales partnership by redesigning the marketing plan and operating agreement, which produced a 100 percent increase in revenue and customer base.
- Designed and implemented a successful OfficeMax partnership centered around joint catalog mailings, newsletter delivery, and an in-store kiosk trial.

GLOBAL ACCOUNT MANAGER, MCI Global Accounts, Atlanta, Georgia (12/91 to 6/94)
Responsible for network design, implementation consulting, and strategic planning for a Fortune 500 global account base with a $14 million annual revenue quota. Managed a team of three sales and technical support professionals.

Key Accomplishments
- Replaced AT&T by selling Syncordia a three-year, $11 million contract covering a wide range of MCI services, including a 35-megabit global IDNX/Ericsson backbone network that ultimately produced more than $20 million in revenue.
- Secured a global MCI Vnet and toll free service network for Syncordia valued at $1.5 million annually.
- Established the first global financial broker network within Robinson Humphrey under a two-year, $1.5 million contract for MCI Vnet and toll free service.
- Achieved the Chairman's Inner Circle in 1993 for the top one percent of salespeople.

PRODUCT MARKETING MANAGER, MCI Global Marketing, McLean, Virginia (10/89 to 12/91)
Managed MCI's $50 million global leased line business, including service development, field support, and portfolio business management. Supervised a team of three marketing and finance professionals. Negotiated operating agreements with foreign carriers.

Key Accomplishments
- Developed and implemented MCI network service arrangements and MCI multiline service, which produced $7.5 million in incremental revenue between 1990 and 1991.
- Managed the business model development and product marketing strategy integration of MCI's $20 million acquisition of Overseas Telecom, a niche provider of satellite telecommunications services to South America.
- Directed the complete restructuring of MCI's leased line pricing format, simplifying the pricing structure by consolidating five tariffs into one and building models for the impact on the installed revenue base.
- Honored with the MCI Excellence in Service Award for the top one percent of MCI staffers.

———————————— **Education** ————————————

BACHELOR OF SCIENCE, TECHNOLOGY EDUCATION (1986)
Virginia Polytechnic Institute and State University

CONTINUING EDUCATION
Global Account Management (40 hours), Advanced Technical Marketing (80 hours), Executive Presentation Forum (24 hours), Simplifying LAN/WAN Interconnection (24 hours), Data Selling Skills (40 hours)

Scannable

KIMBERLY A. COLLINS

12 Bridgewater Court
Marlton, New Jersey 08053
(609) 555-1234

OBJECTIVE   A management position in banking or finance

QUALIFICATIONS
- Opened and managed two commercial bank branch offices
- Demonstrated managerial competence as evidenced by rapid promotions
- Experienced in training and development
- Excellent communication skills

EXPERIENCE

SENIOR COLLECTOR   11/94 – present
First Interstate Bank, Marlton, New Jersey
- Managed individual portfolio of delinquent accounts
- Negotiated and implemented repayment plans with customers and outside agencies
- Prepared, summarized, and recommended accounts for senior management and legal review
- Exceeded established departmental and individual delinquency goals

BANK OFFICER/BRANCH MANAGER   2/89 – 10/94
Jefferson Bank of New Jersey, Mt. Laurel, New Jersey
- Opened and managed $38 million branch
- Functioned as liaison between bank president and all other internal departments
- Designed and marketed branch's business development activities
- Administered all personnel decisions, including hiring and firing
- Developed and implemented training program for branch employees
- Performed all phases of consumer loan requests and participated in commercial loan analysis
- Maintained all internal policies, security procedures, and audit controls

BRANCH MANAGER/ASSISTANT BRANCH MANAGER   2/88 – 2/89
Chemical Bank of New Jersey, N.A., Marlton, New Jersey
- Managed daily operation of branch office
- Performed outside sales efforts and planned marketing strategies
- Directed all inside sales promotions
- Conducted cross-training for branch employees
- Approved consumer loan requests
- Supervised staff and produced monthly management reports

MANAGEMENT TRAINEE   5/86 – 2/88
Chemical Bank of New Jersey, N.A., Oaklyn, New Jersey
- Performed all assistant management duties, including joint sales calls
- Troubleshooter for various branch locations and departments

EDUCATION

B.A. BUSINESS ADMINISTRATION   1989
Rutgers University, Camden, New Jersey
- Course work concentrations in Management and Business Law
- Group leader, marketing project – developed, authored, and presented strategic marketing decisions for a national corporation

Stewart J. Lucas

Current Address
123 North 23rd Street
Colorado Springs, CO 80904
Phone: (719) 555-1234

Permanent Address
1234 Washington Road
Barrington, RI 02806
Phone: (401) 555-1234

EDUCATION	**VILLANOVA UNIVERSITY**, Villanova, Pennsylvania *Bachelor of Arts, General Arts* GPA 3.14 • Minor in Spanish • Service and Justice for Education: Theology/Peace and Justice course, which integrates classroom knowledge with community service, Fall 1995 • Study Abroad Program: Concepcion, Chile, Summer 1994	Spring 1996

VOLUNTEER EXPERIENCE	**HOLY CROSS ASSOCIATE PROGRAM**, Colorado Springs, Colorado
	Holy Cross Associate
	• Lived in community on a fixed income with shared financial responsibility.
	• Organized fund raising projects directed toward individuals and corporations,
	  including direct mail campaigns, cold calling, and raffles.
	• Served as a paraprofessional at the Cleo Wallace Center, a psychiatric treatment
	  center for children and adolescents.
	• Assisted in maintaining residential milieu and facilitating issues groups.
	• Assisted teachers and therapists in developing curriculum and making treatment
	  decisions for children.
		July 1996
		to July 1997

	HABITAT FOR HUMANITY, Villanova University, Villanova, Pennsylvania *Trip Coordinator* • Organized and coordinated arrangements with site supervisor for a trip to Meridian, Mississippi. • Selected 20 volunteers, delegated responsibilities, and led group meetings.	March 1996
	HABITAT FOR HUMANITY INTERNATIONAL, Guatemala *Volunteer* • Learned and shared cultures while living with a host family. • Studied Spanish and worked with the community to build homes.	May 1995 to June 1995

	DELTA GAMMA SORORITY, Villanova University, Villanova, Pennsylvania
	Vice President, Foundations
	• Organized philanthropic activities, sales, and events, including fund raisers for
	  Blind and Sight Conservation.
	• Coordinated *Anchor Splash*, a fund raiser in cooperation with twelve other
	  campus sororities and fraternities.
	• Facilitated Executive Board meetings; served as liaison to local businesses.
		Fall 1994
		to Spring 1996

PROFESSIONAL EXPERIENCE	**AUGUSTINIAN FRIARY**, Villanova, Pennsylvania *Assistant to the Director of Foreign Missions* • Responsible for contacting foundations and writing/submitting grant proposals for various projects in Peru.	January 1996 to May 1996
	UNIVERSITY ORTHOPEDICS, Providence, Rhode Island *Secretary* • Assisted therapists and doctors with scheduling appointments and answering client inquiries.	Summers 1991 to 1995

ACTIVITIES

Bijou House Tutor, 1996 – 1997	ACLAMO Hispanic Youth Center, 1995 – 1996
Faith and Light, 1996 – 1997	Amnesty International, 1995 – 1996
Friends in Transition, 1996 – 1997	Special Olympics, 1994 – 1995
Teach for America, 1995 – 1996	Bryn Mawr Hospital Volunteer, 1993 – 1994
Campus Ministry, 1995 – 1996	Project Sunshine, 1992 – 1993

PETER B. OSAKA

12345 Cavalry Drive
Fairfax, Virginia 22030
(703) 555-1234

JAPANESE-SPEAKING PRODUCT MANAGER with broad experience in planning and product management at Ford Motor Company and Inter-Tel, Inc., a software intensive telecommunications company. Highly experienced in Japan-U.S. new business coordination. Lived in Japan five years; reads, writes, speaks fluent Japanese. International M.B.A. Highly computer literate, familiar with voice/data communications, networking, UNIX, C.

EXPERIENCE

INTER-TEL, INC., Product Manager, Asian Region
Corporate Headquarters, Fairfax, Virginia (1999 – Present)
Inter-Tel, Japan, Tokyo, Japan (May – Oct. 1999)

- Responsible for start-up, sales, and support of $2,000,000 Japanese key telephone project for Teleway Japan and Canon
- Established Inter-Tel office in Tokyo, Japan
- Interfaced with Japanese customers and Inter-Tel's C and 68000 assembly language programmers for host computer download
- Investigated new markets for Inter-Tel IBM PC-based, 600 port ISDN PABX, key telephone systems, and voice mail
- Interfaced with management and engineering on international telecommunication market trends, system revisions, system approvals
- Trained by Inter-Tel in telecom sales, PABX/PC market trends, peripheral device sales, ISDN concepts

FORD MOTOR COMPANY, Product Engineer
Plastic Products Division (PPD), Dearborn, Michigan (1995 – 1997)
PPD Far East Office, Hiroshima, Japan (1994 – 1995)

- Worked directly with PPD top management on advanced planning, purchasing, sourcing, and engineering for first Mazda project
- Coordinated establishment of PPD tech office in Hiroshima
- Identified communication problems; saved engineering and tooling costs of $500,000
- Returned to U.S. in October 1985 to follow PPD JIT program supplying instrument panels and consoles to Mazda's Flat Rock, Michigan, assembly plant
- Trained by Ford in Total Quality Control, JIT, SPC, CAD

JAPAN LIFE PLAN ASSOCIATION, Tokyo, Japan, Salesman (1993)

- Marketed English tape systems to Japanese businesspeople. All sales and transactions in Japanese

TEIJIN INC., Osaka, Japan, Translator/Language Coordinator (1990 – 1993)

- Translated technical material from Japanese to English, including major translations in electronic product development

EDUCATION

MASTER OF INTERNATIONAL MANAGEMENT (1998)
American Graduate School of International Management
Thunderbird Campus, Glendale, Arizona

- Concentration in technical product marketing
- Major research papers on business computer systems, networking, and computer hardware/software

BACHELOR OF FINE ARTS (1990)
Parson's School of Design, New York City, New York

- Concentration in product design

Scannable

Criselle Bruce, MSN RN CNNP CFNP

1234 Gemstone Way • Colorado Springs, Colorado 80918 • (719) 555-1234

Qualifications

Dedicated Family Nurse Practitioner with more than 20 years of nursing experience.
Background in emergency, intensive care, internal medicine, critical care, neonatal, and in-flight nursing.
Flexible, quick learner who adapts easily to new situations and enjoys a challenge.
Self-motivated professional with a commitment to providing quality nursing care.
Strong organizational and communication skills.

Credentials

Registered Nurse (License #51436)
Nationally Certified Family Nurse Practitioner
Nationally Certified Neonatal Nurse Practitioner

Certifications

Basic Life Support
Advanced Cardiac Life Support
Pediatric Advanced Life Support
Neonatal Resuscitation Program Regional Instructor

Education

BSN, MSN, FNP, University of Colorado at Colorado Springs, May 1998
Neonatal Nurse Practitioner Certificate, Beth-El College of Nursing, Colorado Springs, Colorado, 1986
Associate Degree in Nursing, Mesa College, Grand Junction, Colorado, 1971 – 1973

Professional Experience

EMERGENCY DEPARTMENT STAFF NURSE, Memorial Hospital, Colorado Springs, CO .... 1999 – present

FAMILY NURSE PRACTITIONER, Dr. John Genrich, Colorado Springs, CO .... 1998 – present

NEONATAL NURSE PRACTITIONER, Memorial Hospital, Colorado Springs, CO .... 1986 – present
- Responsible for attending all deliveries and providing appropriate medical care, assessment, and case management in a Level III regional medical center.
- Member of the neonatal transport team; selected as a clinical resource person for the institution.

FLIGHT NURSE/ER NURSE, St. Mary's Medical Center, Grand Junction, CO .... 1983 – 1985
- Provided nursing care during helicopter transport of patients.

LEVEL II ICN STAFF NURSE, St. Mary's Medical Center, Grand Junction, CO .... 1982 – 1983
- Provided comprehensive nursing care to patients in a Level II ICN.

EMERGENCY DEPARTMENT STAFF NURSE, St. Anthony's Hospital, Denver, CO .... 1976 – 1982
- Served as a staff nurse in both the Emergency Room and Medical ICU.
- Hospital night supervisor.

Professional Affiliations, Research, and Publications

- Chairperson of NNP quality improvement committee, Memorial Hospital NICU
- Member of the American Academy of Nurse Practitioners
- Co-investigator. (1992). Conventional versus high-frequency oscillatory ventilation following exosurf administration in infants with respiratory distress syndrome, Memorial Hospital
- Lemmons, M. P., Bruce, C. E., Monaco, F. J., and Meredith, K. M. (1993). Conventional versus high-frequency oscillatory ventilation following exosurf administration in infants with respiratory distress syndrome: A preliminary retrospective review. Abstract published in *Pediatric Pulmonology*.

Scannable

71

SUSAN L. VISCON

QUALIFICATIONS

+ Experienced buyer with a background in corporate private label development and domestic resource coordination.
+ Self-motivated leader with a strong work ethic.
+ Proven problem-solving and decision-making abilities.
+ Exceptional interpersonal skills, including communication, presentation, management, negotiation, and training.
+ Able to discern workload priorities and manage multiple projects with divergent needs.

EXPERIENCE

REI, Kent, Washington (1997 – present)
Inventory Analyst
+ Managed inventory and forecasted sales of $48 million for retail and mail order stores.
+ Contributed to Outdoor Specialty Shop, achieving 1997 sales, turn, and gross margin goals.
+ Analyzed productivity to react to current trends and made strategic assortment decisions for future seasons.
+ Developed strong team relationships, displayed positive leadership, and inspired peer cooperation.

DILLARD'S DEPARTMENT STORES, Phoenix, Arizona (1991 – 1997)
Women's Sportswear Buyer (1995 – 1997)
+ Developed, coordinated, and evaluated a $42 million corporate private label sportswear program.
+ Created, executed, and evaluated merchandise inventory plans, including $12 million in sales, receipt flow, turnover, and profit for 28 stores.
+ Corporate coordinator responsible for vendor price negotiation, managing corporate advertising, and achieving buyer consensus for five buying divisions representing 250 stores.
+ Strengthened vendor relations through open, continuous communication.

Children's Sportswear Buyer (1994 – 1995)
+ Increased sales volume and gross profit 20 percent over prior year.
+ Earned Buyer of the Month for October 1994.
+ Top performing children's buyer for fiscal 1994.
+ Focused the direction and assortment of the children's area to reflect the updated market.
+ Maximized key vendor business to exceed corporate average by 60 percent.
+ Developed and coordinated successful private label program that performed 15 percent above profit plan.

Home Store Assistant Buyer (1993 – 1994)
+ Assertive in learning all aspects of the buying position.
+ Planned and purchased stock for the bath accessory department; achieved a 5 percent increase in sales and improved profit and turn.
+ Demonstrated professionalism, solid decision-making skills, and self-motivated goal achievements that led to promotion to buyer.

Home Store Area Sales Manager (1991 – 1993)
+ Hired, trained, scheduled, motivated, reviewed, and supervised 20 associates.
+ Responsible for $1.6 million in volume; consistently exceeded sales goals.
+ Merchandised home store products and created visual displays.
+ Managed stock through maintenance of points and levels, minimizing stock shortages, initiating markdowns, and reviewing best sellers with buyers.

EDUCATION

BACHELOR OF SCIENCE IN BUSINESS ADMINISTRATION (1991)
Northern Arizona University, Flagstaff, Arizona
+ Graduated summa cum laude (3.9 GPA).
+ Outstanding Marketing Senior Award.
+ Self-financed 70 percent of education through scholarships, resident assistant position, and part-time employment.

ADDRESS   1234 42nd Avenue, S.W., Seattle, Washington 98136   (206) 555-1234

Jaime Melissa Boyd

SUMMARY

- Friendly and giving speech therapist with a recent degree in speech language disorders.
- Proven leader with a strong work ethic and a deep commitment to helping others.
- Personable and articulate with excellent interpersonal and communication skills.
- Well organized, able to balance priorities and work independently.

EDUCATION

BACHELOR OF SCIENCE, SPEECH LANGUAGE PATHOLOGY (May 1998)
Abilene Christian University, Abilene, Texas
- Trained in language and speech disorders, with an emphasis on etiology, diagnosis, and clinical management of these disorders.
- Mastered the international phonetic alphabet and learned to identify the sounds of English and to transcribe and translate.
- Learned the components, stages, and differences between how human beings use and acquire language.
- Gained a comprehension of articulation and fluency disorders and treatments.
- Studied the theory and practice of rehabilitative audiology and hearing.
- Learned how to conduct basic hearing assessments on children and adults.
- Also studied Advanced Speech-Language Pathology, Sign Language I-II, Acoustics and Voice Science, Normal Language Development, Whole Language and Pragmaticism, Linguistics, Language and Learning Disabilities, and Anatomical and Physiological Processes of Communication.

EXPERIENCE

CLINICAL PRACTICUM, Abilene Christian University, Abilene, Texas (1998)
- Wrote lesson plans for the treatment of adults, children, and Down's syndrome clients in a two-semester practicum that provided hands-on experience in speech language pathology.
- Worked closely with three children with articulation, dysphonia, and language disorders.
- Set long-term and short-term goals and made recommendations for treatment and follow-up.
- Maintained reports for each patient that included evaluation, diagnosis, treatment plan, procedures, and methods.

YOUTH INTERN, Hillcrest Church of Christ, Abilene, Texas (1997 – 1998)
- Taught classes for middle school and high school students and provided counseling for members of the youth group.
- Attended weekly strategic planning meetings with the youth minister and other interns.
- Planned retreats, mission trips, and youth activities.

ACTIVITIES & HONORS

- Recipient of the Audra Cobb Memorial Scholarship, 1997.
- Member of the Texas Speech-Language Hearing Association.
- Member of the Speech Pathology Organization (1 year).
- Member of the Students' Association Senate; Co-chair of the Special Friends Committee (2 years), which planned activities to enable student interaction with mentally and physically handicapped adults.
- Member of the Freshman Orientation Steering Committee (2 years), composed of 40 students who planned and implemented activities for more than 1,000 new students to aid in their transition into college life.

ADDRESSES

Until May 1998: ACU Box 1234, Abilene, Texas 79699
Permanent: 1234 Ruidoso Drive, Fort Worth, Texas 76179

Phone: (915) 555-1234
Message: (817) 555-1234

JAMES J. KISH

OVERVIEW

Experienced Class A PGA Professional with a background in the management of private clubs, golf centers, and pro shops. Proven track record of increasing revenues and improving the delivery of service to members. Skilled in the resolution of complex problems, delegating responsibilities, and developing effective teams to accomplish organizational goals. Colbert/Ballard Certified Instructor with experience teaching golf to both adult and youth learners. Proficient in Windows, MS Word, Excel, PowerPoint.

CAREER HIGHLIGHTS

SITE MANAGER/HEAD GOLF PRO (1998 – present)
Colorado Springs Family Golf Center, Colorado Springs, Colorado
Successfully managed the operations of the driving range, miniature golf course, batting range, pro shop, and restaurant/cafe. Hired, supervised, and motivated a staff of 21 assistant pros, maintenance personnel, restaurant manager, and customer service representatives. Mentored assistant pros to head pro positions within the company. Used extensive knowledge of golf techniques, swing mechanics, and fundamentals of the game to teach students from 6 years old to adults.
- Improved the overall operations, making it the best practice facility in Colorado Springs.
- Added a pro shop, snack bar, two chipping greens, fairway, and greenside bunkers.
- Developed and implemented customer service training programs that dramatically improved service delivery.
- Achieved gross revenues of 63 percent over 1998.

DIRECTOR OF INSTRUCTION/HEAD GOLF PRO (1997 – 1998)
Kennedy Family Golf Center, Aurora, Colorado
Achieved a fast-track promotion from teaching professional to head golf professional for this 36-hole public golf course. Hired and supervised seven golf professionals. Coordinated group and private lessons, as well as free clinics for organizations like the American Cancer Society, American Arthritis Foundation, and Special Olympics. Provided golf instruction to players of all experience levels and ages.
- Expanded the teaching program and developed a full-scale junior golf program.
- Achieved $160,000 in gross revenues through lessons alone.

TEACHING PROFESSIONAL (1992 – 1996)
Taught beginning, intermediate, and advanced golf at the Lost Tracks Golf Club (Bend, Oregon) and the Catalina Golf Center (Tucson, Arizona). Helped clients achieve their goals through one-on-one instruction and motivation. Taught golf classes at the local community college (Bend, Oregon).

HEAD GOLF PROFESSIONAL, Tucson Country Club, Tucson, Arizona (1985 – 1990)
Provided professional services to 600 members of this exclusive, private country club. Managed driving range operations, pro shop, caddie, and club storage services. Hired, trained, scheduled, and supervised 8 support staff and 30–40 caddies.
- Member of the Board of Directors of the Southern Chapter of the Southwest Section PGA (1988 – 1990).
- Chairman of the Southwest Section Apprentice Interviews (1988 – 1990).
- Coordinated the Special Olympics golf clinic in conjunction with the 1986 Tucson Open.
- Selected as a finalist for the 1988 Merchandiser of the Year (Private Club), Southwest Section PGA.

EDUCATION

UNDERGRADUATE STUDIES, Indiana University, Bloomington, Indiana (1987 – 1988)

HONOR GRADUATE, San Diego Golf Academy, San Diego, California (1980)
Studied Pro Shop Management, Retail Sales and Merchandising, Human Resource Management, Tournament Operations, and Advanced Teaching Techniques

1234 Caribbean • Falcon, Colorado 80919 • (602) 555-1234

Scannable

JEFFREY B. WEST

1234 Cliff Point Circle
Colorado Springs, Colorado 80919
Home: (719) 555-1234 • Cellular: (719) 555-1234
E-mail: criscito@aol.com

PROFILE
- Confident leader with more than 19 years of successful management experience.
- Background in information technology, commercial, and government/military contracts.
- Self-motivated professional with strong problem solving and organizational abilities.
- Persuasive communicator with highly developed negotiation and presentation skills.
- Computers: MS Word, PowerPoint, Excel, Access, Windows 95/NT, Exchange.

EXPERIENCE

SSDS, Inc., Colorado Springs, Colorado (1996 – 1999)

Account Director (September 1998 – September 1999)
- Managed an $8.2 million cable plant and LAN/WAN installation contract for the largest school district in Colorado Springs.
- Plan, design, and install the data, voice, RF, and telephone cable plants in 51 individual school buildings.
- Hire and supervise subcontractors, technicians, and office staff to support the operation.
- Responsible for all materials management and budget requirements for this firm fixed-price contract.

Program Manager (March 1996 – September 1998)
- Managed a $21 million government contract for the operation of the administrative computer network for the U.S. Space Command.
- Supervised the design and implementation of local and wide area networks for 6,000 users in Colorado and for 15 remote sites worldwide.
- Set program scope and direction; balanced schedule, cost, and performance criteria.
- Prepared and managed a $5 million budget, allocating resources to achieve program goals.
- Monitored program status; identified and corrected technical and functional problems.
- Negotiated with and integrated the efforts of government liaisons, top management, functional support groups, consultants, and end users.
- Selected, organized, and placed divisional management teams for each project.
- Directly responsible for hiring, supervising, and evaluating 45 employees.
- Fostered enthusiasm, team spirit, confidence, and a reputation for excellence.

Key Accomplishments:
- Increased program value 100 percent from $9.8 million to more than $21 million.
- Achieved company's first-ever 99.02 percent cost-plus award fee and maintained for the last two years.
- Implemented improvements to the network, bringing reliability to near 100 percent.
- Developed state-of-the-art programs to ensure almost 100 percent network security.
- Established a formal two-week career development training program for individual employees that enhanced daily performance, morale, and sense of team participation.

UNITED STATES ARMY (1980 – 1996)

Chief, Plans and Operations
- Led a 35-man division responsible for planning and directing all operations of the U.S. Army in Japan and the western Pacific region.

Inspector General
- Investigated more than 250 personnel grievances and allegations of fraud/waste/abuse.

Operations Officer
- Planned and executed training activities for all infantry soldiers in the U.S. Army.

EDUCATION

MASTER OF ARTS, MANAGEMENT, Webster University, 3.97 GPA (1988)
BACHELOR OF ARTS, CRIMINAL LAW, Stephen F. Austin State University (1980)

Scannable

75

Susan Fitzpatrick

1234 Briarcliff Road
Colorado Springs, CO 80918
Telephone: (719) 555-1234

PROFILE
- Experienced administrative assistant and legal secretary.
- Background in human resources, claims handling, insurance, and medical areas.
- Self-starter with strong organization and communication skills.
- Personable, friendly, and loyal team player who is able to relate well to clients.
- Skilled in IBM PCs, WordPerfect, and Microsoft Word.
- Notary public in the state of Colorado.

EXPERIENCE

LEGAL ASSISTANT/OFFICE MANAGER (1988 – Present)
Gerlach & Weddell, P.C., Colorado Springs, Colorado
Administrative assistant for a law firm specializing in worker's compensation, personal injury, and social security claims.
- Prepare legal documents and correspondence, including briefs, summons, complaints, motions, and subpoenas.
- File claims with the Division of Labor and insurance companies.
- Prepare court exhibits, maintain law libraries, order office supplies.
- Prepare and execute settlement distributions.
- Work closely with clients to ensure satisfaction with services.
- Schedule hearings, depositions, attorney conferences, and client visits.
- Write and place advertisements for part-time help, interview prospective employees, and train secretarial staff.
- Process employment applications and assist in other employment activities.
- Examine employee files to answer inquiries of authorized persons.
- Transcribe dictation, process mail, answer telephone, and greet clients.

LEGAL SECRETARY (1986 – 1988)
Gradisar & Trechter, Pueblo, Colorado
Assistant to Charles Trechter, attorney who practiced general and domestic law.
- Prepared legal documents and correspondence from dictation.
- Ensured that pleading deadlines were met and documents were filed in a timely manner.
- Provided administrative assistance, greeted clients, and answered telephones.
- Performed client intake interviews.

RECEPTIONIST (1980 – 1985)
J.C. Penney Company, Burnsville, Minnesota
- Greeted prospective employees in the personnel office and answered telephone inquiries.
- Tallied time cards and maintained records.
- Compiled sales reports and typed documents.

SECRETARY/SALES REPRESENTATIVE (1980)
L.B. Foster Company, Burnsville, Minnesota
- Assisted with start-up of a new branch office.
- Recruited, interviewed, and hired a secretary.

EDUCATION

OHIO STATE UNIVERSITY, Columbus, Ohio
- Two years of study with a concentration in mathematics
- Earned approximately 45 credits toward a business degree

PIKES PEAK COMMUNITY COLLEGE, Colorado Springs, Colorado
- Legal research course

76

Scannable

JAN T. TRAXLER

SUMMARY OF QUALIFICATIONS

♦ Reliable and committed sales and marketing professional with 16 years of experience in the telecommunications industry.
♦ Proven track record of success in positions of increasing responsibility.
♦ Outstanding organizational and management skills; talent for seeing "the big picture."
♦ Adept at establishing effective working relationships with clients and colleagues.
♦ Highly motivated with a strong commitment to delivering quality service.
♦ Skilled in contract negotiations; articulate and persuasive in written and verbal presentations.

PROFESSIONAL EXPERIENCE

Sales/Marketing

Member of the sales team responsible for launching two cable television networks—Cable Health Network and Lifetime Television:

♦ Established network affiliates through analysis of the marketplace, cold calling, and exceptional after-sale service.
♦ Positioned niche network, negotiated contracts, and effected ongoing affiliate support with local ad sales, promotions, and community outreach programs.
♦ Consistently exceeded aggressive annual sales goals by 20 percent.

As Manager, Special Markets for Lifetime Television and Bravo Networks:

♦ Negotiated more than 200 new client agreements, expanding national distribution and revenue.
♦ Collaborated with marketing department to create targeted marketing campaigns for new distribution outlets, resulting in increased value, awareness, and sales.
♦ Organized and participated in regional and national industry trade shows.
♦ Developed and conducted product training seminars for client staff.

Management

Explored, analyzed, and developed alternate distribution opportunities in emerging technology markets, creating and implementing sales and marketing strategies to increase overall distribution and annual revenue for cable television networks ($10 million for Lifetime Television).

♦ Developed business plan, competitive analyses, budgets, and sales strategies for the division.
♦ Worked closely with legal department to create form agreements for five distinct technology markets and revised agreements based on changing demands of marketplace.
♦ Evaluated and acted as internal consultant on government rules and regulations affecting competitive markets.
♦ Made presentations and participated in panels at industry trade shows, increasing awareness and value of the network in the new marketplace.
♦ Directed trade association task forces to examine and resolve industry issues.

WORK HISTORY

1997 – present	Consultant/Special Markets Manager	Bravo Networks, Denver, Colorado
1988 – 1996	Special Markets Manager	Lifetime Television, Dallas, Texas
1985 – 1988	Regional Account Manager	Lifetime Television, Dallas, Texas
1984 – 1985	Marketing Coordinator	Lifetime Television, Dallas, Texas
1982 – 1984	Marketing Coordinator	Cable Health Network, Dallas, Texas
1980 – 1982	Sales/Marketing Assistant	Frito-Lay, Inc., Dallas, Texas

1234 Brixham Circle ♦ *Castle Rock, Colorado 80104* ♦ *(303) 555-1234* ♦ *E-mail: criscito@aol.com*

Scannable

77

JAMES A. DAVIS

SUMMARY

- Self-motivated sales professional with a successful track record in customer service, retail sales, and health/wellness fields.
- Proven ability to develop and maintain profitable client relationships.
- Effective team player with strong interpersonal, communication, and presentation skills.
- Known for the ability to defuse potentially volatile situations.

EXPERIENCE

SALES CONSULTANT (1998 – 1999)
Sofa Mart, Colorado Springs, Colorado

- Successfully sold furniture in a retail setting.
- Assisted customers in making merchandise selections and improved store profitability through effective suggestive sales techniques.
- Top salesperson in the store for three months.

MASSAGE THERAPIST (1995 – 1997)
Sedona Racquet Club, Sedona, Arizona

- Provided massage therapy services to an elite clientele in this upscale resort community.

PRIVATE CHEF FOR THE WRIGLEY FAMILY, Sedona, Arizona (1992 – 1995)

- Planned menus, prepared, and served vegetarian meals for special dinner parties.
- Responsible for the family's overall eating plan and health consciousness.

ROAD MANAGER, PERSONAL TRAINER, PRIVATE CHEF (1987 – 1992)
Shields and Yarnell, Sedona, Arizona

- Coordinated theatrical light and sound staff for comedy stage shows in the United States and abroad (England, Jamaica, cruise ships, etc.).
- Planned and prepared meals and supervised the fitness regimen for both entertainers.

ACTOR, Hollywood, California (1985 – 1987)

- Appeared in movies, commercials, and live theatrical performances.
- Played the part of the caretaker in *Psychocop*.
- Completed two television commercials, one for an automobile museum in Las Vegas and the other for Nexus hair products.
- Played the part of Young Siward in *Macbeth* at The Globe Theater in West Hollywood.
- Performed in the play *Career* in North Hollywood.

LAB TECHNICIAN (1982 – 1985)
UCLA Department of Kinesiology, Los Angeles, California

- Conducted connective tissue experiments by training and exercising animals.
- Published "Quantitative Histochemical Determination of Muscle Enzymes: Biochemical Verification," *Journal of Histochemistry and Cytochemistry*, Volume 33, Issue 10, pp. 53–39, October 1985.

DEPARTMENT MANAGER, Oshman's Sporting Goods, Garden Grove, California (1978 – 1982)

- Managed the fitness department of a large sporting goods store.
- Sold exercise equipment and supplies.

EDUCATION

BACHELOR OF SCIENCE IN HEALTH AND WELLNESS (May 1999)
Regis University, Colorado Springs, Colorado

- Course work in health and wellness, emergency care, physical health assessment, nutrition, health education, community health resources, death and dying, psychology, physiology, neuromuscular anatomy, biology, organic structures and reactions, statistics, speech communication, critical thinking, and others.
- Completed a senior capstone project with a clinical nutritionist.

ADDRESS

1234 Alicia Point, Apt. 201, Colorado Springs, Colorado 80919   (719) 555-1234

Scannable

6 Headings to Define the Sections

Headings are one of the major design elements of a résumé. How you choose to divide sections determines the readability of your résumé. Graphic lines and/or white space help define groups of similar information and draw the reader's eyes down the page.

One of the keys to a readable résumé is the judicious use of white space, and consistent spacing in critical. You will notice throughout the samples in this book that more white space is used between major sections than within sections. This breaks the résumé into easily digested chunks of information. The white space between these sections should be identical throughout the résumé. Likewise, the smaller white space within sections should be the same throughout.

There are two basic positions for your headings. One is centered (pages 82–85) with or without lines, and the other is left justified (pages 81, 86–96). Which style you choose depends on what you find pleasing to your eye. There is no right or wrong way. If you like the design, then it is a good fit with your personality. Some of your options include:

- All caps (page 83, 85, 86, 88, 89, 92, 93)
- First letter larger (pages 90, 91)
- Upper/lower case (pages 81, 82, 84, 95, 96)
- All lower case (page 94)
- Very large fonts (page 81, 82, 84)
- Underlines with all capital letters—don't use underlines with lower case lettering (pages 85)

Since people read from the top to the bottom and from left to right, begin your résumé with the most important information. Then work your way down to less important information. The top half of your résumé's first page should be packed with your strongest qualifications.

So, which section goes first? Should it be education or experience? Start with the section that contains your strongest qualifications for your target job. If you have had little experience in your prospective field but have a degree that qualifies you for a starting position in the industry, then by all means list your education first. Most people eventually move their education below their experience as they get further from their school days. If you change your career and go back to school, then the education will move to the top again and begin to gravitate to the bottom as you gain relevant experience.

The same idea goes for information within each section. For instance, if you went to an Ivy League school, you can list the school before the degree. Look at the difference in emphasis between these two methods:

HARVARD, Cambridge, Massachusetts
Master of Business Administration

MASTER OF BUSINESS ADMINISTRATION
Little Known College, Backwoods, Idaho

The same principle applies to your experience. If your job title is more impressive than where you worked, then list it first.

VICE PRESIDENT OF MARKETING
Little Known Company, Boulder, Colorado

IBM CORPORATION, Boulder, Colorado
Assistant Export Coordinator

Avoid the use of underlining since it cuts into the descenders in lower case letters. For example, notice the "p" in:

Assistant Export Coordinator

It is acceptable to use underlining when the letters are all capitalized since there are no descenders:

ASSISTANT EXPORT COORDINATOR

Italics, **bold**, ALL CAPITALS, FIRST LETTER LARGER, or any combination of the four are all good ways to make certain information stand out within the text. However, these styles can be overdone very easily. To make them more effective, use these type treatments sparingly.

Carol D. Friese

1234 Monitor Rock Lane ▸ Menlo Park, California 95153 ▸ Phone (908) 555-1234 ▸ Fax (908) 555-1235

Profile

Marketing . . . Administration . . . Public Relations . . . Customer Service . . . *Goal-oriented professional with successful experience in sales, marketing, and administration. A skilled communicator, persuasive and adaptable. Keen insight into customers' needs and views. Highly developed organizational, planning, and time management skills. Extensive business writing experience, including proposals, reviews, and marketing pieces. Self-motivated with initiative and focus. Articulate and professional in presentation. Computer literate with experience in Microsoft Windows, WordPerfect, Lotus, and Excel. Areas of skill include:*

- *Administration / Project Management*
- *Sales / Account Management*
- *Market Research / Analysis*

- *Public Relations / Customer Service*
- *Negotiation / Facilitation*
- *Creative Presentations / Promotions*

Experience / Accomplishments

Territory Manager*, VIVUS, Inc., Menlo Park, California (1996 – present)*
Launched first product offering for a small biotech company. Marketed to urology and endocrinology. Worked autonomously with little direct supervision in a young company with a flat organizational structure. Managed tight deadlines and an extensive travel schedule (four days per week).

- *Consistently exceeded sales goals by 118 percent; ended 1997 at 218 percent of goal.*
- *Achieved 78 percent of territory market share.*

Marketing / Sales Manager*, Daubes Bakery Incorporated, Rochester, Minnesota (1995 – 1996)*
Repositioned large-scale wholesale and retail bakery/cafe business in the maturity phase of its product life cycle. Developed and implemented programs to address customer perception, price/value issues, service, and salesmanship. Designed and implemented sales training program for staff.

- *Achieved 20 percent increase in sales dollars.*
- *Stabilized employee turnover problem.*
- *Evaluated entrepreneurial opportunity.*

Technical Sales Representative*, CytoDiagnostics Incorporated, Oklahoma City, Oklahoma (1994 – 1995)*
Marketed state-of-the-art laboratory services exclusively to urology in a five-state territory. Established accounts with private practice physicians and incorporated capabilities into clinic and contracted laboratory settings.

- *Increased new account sales by 79 percent and regained 66 percent of account sales (ranked 4th).*
- *Expanded new product sales by 37 percent and established base histology business with no previous usage in the five-state territory.*

Professional Sales Representative*, Takeda/Abbott Products, Deerfield, Illinois (1991 – 1994)*
Marketed highly specialized product line to urology, oncology, and gynecology practices. Territory included clinics, institutions, and private practices in northwestern Wisconsin and Minnesota.

- *Educated Mayo Clinic residents on product line through in-services and educational support materials.*
- *Served as reimbursement specialist to ensure third-party coverage for higher priced specialty product.*
- *Consistently exceeded sales goals; ranked 2nd of 10 for sales district and 61st of 259 for nation in 1993 (started 1993 7/10 and 189/259) and 14th in the nation for one product line; increased sales 30 percent during the first five months in territory; achieved 113 percent of first year's sales goal.*
- *Originally hired as a Customer Service Representative; promoted in June of 1992.*

Education / Training

Bachelor of Science Degree, Marketing*, Northern Illinois University (1992)*

- *Member of Golden Key National and Marketing Honor Societies.*
- *Recipient of Motorola Sales and Marketing Executive Scholarship.*
- *Awarded full University Honors upon graduation.*

81

Elisabetta M. Phillips, CPA

1234 Astronomy Court ▸ Colorado Springs, Colorado 80917 ▸ (719) 555-1234

Overview

Experienced manager with a background in the nonprofit and banking sectors.
Skilled in scheduling, coordination, team building, budgeting, and resource allocation.
Able to take the initiative, improve processes, and meet time-sensitive deadlines.
Diplomatic and persuasive; adept at communicating effectively with people of diverse interests and levels of authority.
Proficient in Windows 95, MS Word, Excel, PowerPoint, Lotus Notes, JDEdwards, Solomon, Quicken, and MS Explorer.
Bilingual in English and Italian; traveled throughout Europe and Japan.

Professional Experience

MANAGEMENT/ADMINISTRATION
- Managed multi-million-dollar projects and created Gantt charts for meeting project milestones.
- Allocated resources within budget guidelines and scheduled projects to ensure timely completion.
- Supervised a staff of five internal auditors in addition to multinational audit teams on site.
- Traveled to Japan and Germany when needed to analyze operational activities.
- Reduced management reporting time by 25 percent through implementation of Excel report templates.
- Managed the staff and daily operations of an insurance brokerage firm.
- Negotiated with division heads to recover $24,100 discovered through compliance auditing.
- Devised a spreadsheet to track commissions and issued monthly commission payroll for 60 clients.
- Created a work-in-process system to accurately monitor and track proposals within the system.
- Attracted and retained new clients through excellent customer service and rapid response.

KEY ACCOMPLISHMENTS
- Led team in the discovery of a $26 million reporting error.
- Conducted paperless audits of financial, operational, and regulatory activities worldwide for a bank with assets exceeding $180 billion and net income of $2 billion.
- Reduced division administrative expenses 40 percent by implementing template documents and converting files into a standard format.
- Authored audit program for division-wide use, ensuring consistency and compliance with management objectives.
- Reduced external audit costs by performing Defense Contractors Audit Agency programs in 50 percent less time than budgeted, eliminating the need for review for two years.

AUDITING
- Managed pre- and post-implementation reviews for a Department of Defense contract; discovered $44 million in unreconciled accounts.
- Lead auditor on the largest audit in USOC history; used team auditing concepts for more than 2,000 hours.
- Redesigned the audit process to include analysis of key indicator trends.
- Served as audit representative on special task forces and project teams.

Career Chronology

INTERNAL AUDITOR, United States Olympic Committee, Colorado Springs, Colorado, 1997 – present
SENIOR FINANCIAL AUDITOR, NationsBank of Texas, N.A., Dallas, Texas, 1994 – 1997
OFFICE MANAGER, C&C Insurance Services, Austin, Texas, 1990 – 1994

Education

BACHELOR OF BUSINESS ADMINISTRATION, ACCOUNTING, University of Texas, Austin, Texas, 1994
ASSOCIATE OF APPLIED SCIENCE, BUSINESS ADMINISTRATION, Central Texas College, Killeen, Texas, 1985

Affiliations

Institute of Internal Auditors, Advertising Chair (1995), American Institute of Certified Public Accountants

Scannable

JANE LAMME ACKERMAN

Phone: (719) 555-1234 ▪ Fax: (719) 555-1235 ▪ E-mail: criscito@aol.com
1234 Pejn Avenue ▪ Colorado Springs, Colorado 80904

QUALIFICATIONS
- Results-oriented sales and marketing professional with 17 years of experience.
- Highly motivated to surpass sales quotas and attain marketing objectives.
- Proven ability to generate new leads and substantially increase sales.
- Skilled at developing long-term relationships with clients, generating loyalty above and beyond the sales relationship.
- Enthusiastic, creative team player with strong problem solving and organizational skills.

EXPERIENCE

ACCOUNT EXECUTIVE

The Colorado Springs Business Journal, Colorado Springs, Colorado (1997 – present)
- Successfully sold advertising for two weekly newspapers that were considered the authority on local business news in Colorado Springs and Pueblo.
- Developed new corporate and small business accounts through effective marketing, cold calling, networking, professional sales presentations, and follow-up.
- Created a rapport with national advertising agencies to acquire large corporate accounts.
- Assisted companies in developing and maintaining effective advertising campaigns.
- Wrote print copy and assisted in the design and layout of advertisements.
- Built relationships with local contacts that provided leads for breaking news stories.
- Highest achiever for the *Book of Lists,* a tabloid-sized directory containing more than 75 top lists of the area's leading industries.
- Increased the number of new advertisers and consistently exceeded sales goals, doubling sales in two years.
- Created an ACT! computerized database of more than 2,500 key contacts.
- Designed sales tools for all sales staff, including promotion sheets, commission schedules, annual advertising time lines, and sales tracking systems.

SALES & INFORMATION DIRECTOR

Direct Marketing Specialists, Colorado Springs, Colorado (1993 – 1996)
- Directed the sales of Val-Pak direct mail services in a very competitive market.
- Developed quality, long-term business relationships with an exceptionally high percentage of repeat customers and a corresponding increase in sales.
- Recognized by the national corporate office for outstanding achievement, including multiple bonuses for high sales levels and marketing performance.
- Successfully generated new leads through active networking, professional memberships, and community service activities.
- Created and implemented a customized billing service and individual quality assurance programs to ensure customer satisfaction.
- Interviewed, selected, and trained sales representatives.

OWNER & MANAGER

Professional Relocation Services, Redondo Beach, California (1989 – 1993)
- Surveyed, previewed, and selected requested properties for relocating clients.
- Consistently identified customer needs and communicated realistic expectations.
- Marketed services through major corporations, property managers, realtors, and professional organizations.
- Developed and maintained business relationships with property owners to facilitate the location of suitable properties.

EDUCATION

BACHELOR OF SCIENCE IN SOCIOLOGY, Arizona State University, Tempe, Arizona
Graduated with honors

CONTINUING EDUCATION
Dale Carnegie, Zig Zigler, and Tony Robbins Sales Training

 Scannable

83

Joseph D. Wometeo

12345 North 11th Avenue   Phoenix, Arizona 85027   (602) 555-1234

. . . . Experience . . . .

SENIOR REFRIGERATION SHOP MECHANIC   April 1990 – Present
St. Joseph's Hospital and Medical Center
Responsible for maintenance and repair of all equipment associated with air conditioning, heating, and refrigeration. Responsible for ordering shop stock and repair parts. Involved in primary start-up of new air handling equipment.

FIELD REPRESENTATIVE   September 1989 – April 1990
Ramada Energy Systems
Ramada Energy Systems was involved in the research and development of a solar collector made of clear plastic materials. My responsibilities included the construction of mounting devices and related equipment for testing of the panels. Monitored the systems being tested and made modifications to the systems.

MAINTENANCE MECHANIC, CONSTRUCTION TECHNICIAN   June 1989 – September 1989
Universal Propulsion Corporation, Division of Talley Industries
Constructed new buildings and installed new machinery. Remodeled buildings to suit the needs of the growing company, including layout and construction of electrical power lines, pneumatic lines, and water lines. Maintained buildings, including carpentry, roofing, and painting. Constructed small building for experimental work. Installed and performed primary checkout of two-million-volt X-ray unit. Performed preventive maintenance on air compressors, A/C, hydraulic pumps, leak detector, and X-ray unit. Experienced in the use of hand tools, carpentry tools, A/C gauges, meters, power tools, ditch witch, jack hammer, forklift, and paint sprayer, among others.

REFRIGERATION SHOP MECHANIC   April 1988 – May 1989
St. Joseph's Hospital and Medical Center
Maintained and repaired hospital heating, A/C, and refrigeration equipment. Performed trouble shooting and repairs to ice machines, refrigerators, air conditioners, freezers, exhaust fans, air handlers, pneumatic and electric thermostats, water towers, and booster pumps. Preventively maintained thermal systems equipment, water treatment, wash down coils, and water towers.

ROUTE DRIVER, SALES REPRESENTATIVE   September 1985 – July 1987
Wometeo Coca-Cola Bottling Company of Northern Arizona
Started as route driver, which included delivery of sold product and stocking of space provided. Was promoted to sales representative, which included selling products, writing invoices, laying out truck loads, promoting product discounts, securing space for product, selling product and coolers, performing maintenance and making minor repairs to vendors and coolers, and collection of money.

SEAMAN ABOARD *USS HENRY CLAY* AND *USS DULUTH*   September 1982 – September 1985
United States Navy
Aboard the *USS Henry Clay:* helmsman, prepared the ship for going to sea, lookout until submerged, maintained steady course of ship while underway, assisted in galley. On the *USS Duluth:* Changed rating from seaman to fireman, performed preventative maintenance and repairs on boiler, evaporator, and supporting systems.

. . . . Training . . . .

2000	Staefa Building Controls – one week
1995	Honeywell Building Controls, Level Two Seminar – one week
1994	Honeywell Building Controls, Level One Seminar – one week
1/90 – 8/92	Maricopa Community College, successfully completed courses pertaining to solar energy and air conditioning and other courses required for an A.S. Degree
8/87 – 4/88	Universal Technical Institute – Extensive training in diagnosis, repair, installation, and maintenance of air conditioning units, heat pumps, gas furnaces, and refrigeration equipment and their controls
9/82 – 9/85	U.S. Navy Training – Basic Submarine (4 months), Basic Electrical (6 weeks), Demolition (2 weeks), Fire Fighting (2 weeks), Piping and Welding (3 weeks), Evaporator (6 weeks)

MARY JANE PRICE

12345 East Becker Lane
Phoenix, Arizona 85032
(602) 555-1234

SUMMARY

Certified Public Accountant with over five years of auditing experience with Price Waterhouse, in addition to six years of experience as controller for several interrelated small real estate investment companies. Honors graduate with exceptional mathematical talents. Strengths include perseverance, a very positive attitude, and good interpersonal skills.

EXPERIENCE

PRICE WATERHOUSE, Senior Auditor   December 1985 – October 1988, July 1995 – Present

EXTENSIVE TRAINING PROGRAM

Working as part of an efficient audit team gave me experience working under the pressure of deadlines and an invaluable knowledge of a wide variety of accounting systems. Industry experience includes Insurance, Retail, Manufacturing, Banking, and Health Care. PC skills include Lotus and WordPerfect.

SUPERVISORY SKILLS

Assignments supervising up to five staff. Experience in delegation, training, communication, and review. Responsible for planning engagements and evaluating staff.

SAC REAL ESTATE INVESTMENT COMPANY, Controller   October 1988 – June 1995

IBM PC EXPERIENCE

Responsible for all aspects of accounting, including cash management, monthly reports, general ledger (BPI Accounting software on IBM PC), financial statements, and consolidated statements. Developed great organizational and problem solving skills.

SELF-STARTER

Special projects included financial analysis of land sales, financing, construction spending, property taxes, insurance, and preparation of financial data as needed for marketing purposes.

MANAGEMENT CAPABILITIES

Assisted in interactions with lenders, attorneys, lessees, and subcontractors. Responsible for tax planning and coordination of work with tax specialists and external auditors.

EDUCATION

BACHELOR OF SCIENCE
Magna Cum Laude
Business Administration
Major: Accounting
Arizona State University
December 1985

4.0 Accounting GPA
3.78 Overall GPA

HONORS
Beta Alpha Psi
Beta Gamma Sigma
Phi Kappa Phi
Arizona Board of Regents'
Academic Scholarship

MINOR
Music: Classical Piano

Scannable

85

LARRY O. WIORA

12345 Capella Drive • Monument, CO 80132 • Phone: (719) 555-1234

EXPERIENCE

XEROX CORPORATION, Denver, Colorado   1986 – Present
Xerox Engineering Systems Division – Versatec Products

Engineering Systems/Major Account Marketing Executive (1993 – 1996, 1998 – Present)
Sold and marketed large format engineering printers, plotters, and document management systems, interfacing with SNA, IP, and IPX-based networks in a three-state region. Provided focused expertise and marketing sales support in complex sales cycles which include demonstrations, surveys, and presentations to the highest levels of corporate management. Delivered a plan of more than $1,000,000 in systems priced from $20,000 to $250,000. Responsible for maintaining dealer and rural agent channels, third-party software alliances, and close communication with service technicians to maintain market share and maximize customer satisfaction.
* Number 1 out of 150 worldwide and 90 nationally, 1998
* Number 1 in Western region sales, 1993, 1994, and 1995
* Number 2 out of 104 team members in sales nationally, 1995
* Number 2 out of 50 team members in sales nationally, 1994
* Number 3 out of 50 team members in sales nationally, 1993
* President's Club, 1993, 1994, 1995, and 1998
* Received the "Honorary Sales Support Quality Award" from Lucent Technologies, 1998

Systems Sales Executive (1997)
Ensure the achievement of the district's product and revenue objectives by providing system sales leadership, training, and support for seven sales representatives in a six-state region selling high-end engineering printers/plotters and electronic engineering document storage/retrieval systems. Conduct closing sales calls and plan/review sessions with the sales representatives to formulate and evaluate account management sales strategies and developmental action plans. Implement quarterly seminars and technology symposiums for the team to improve market penetration. Utilize and leverage key third-party alliance system solutions to meet customer requirements. Provide to top management accurate monthly, quarterly, and yearly business forecasts for the district's systems performance.
* Exceeded annual sales quota of $5.0 million
* Number 4 out of 14 system sales executives nationally, 1997

Engineering Document Management Specialist (1992)
Responsible for the marketing introduction in a seven-state region of Xerox Docuplex (a high-tech engineering document management system with an average price of $250,000 – $500,000). Developed a strong potential sales market with major presentations to top corporate managers on the advantages of moving their organization to electronic storage and retrieval of engineering documents.
* Installed the first major system in the United States marketplace

High-Volume Engineering Executive (1990 – 1991)
Supervised a team of seven territory sales representatives in a five-state region delivering a plan of more than $4.0 million in large-ticket products greater than $75,000. Responsibilities included resource management, account maintenance, sales training, prospect development, 90-day action plans, monthly plan and review sessions, major account calls, implementation of national marketing actions, and operation reviews to senior management.
* President's Club, 1990 (top 15 percent nationally)
* Number 2 of 6 in volume in Midwest region

(Scannable)

EXPERIENCE *(continued)*

XEROX CORPORATION (continued)

Marketing Executive, Pasadena, California and Denver, Colorado (1986 – 1989)
Responsible for account maintenance and new business penetration selling engineering products mostly priced in excess of $100,000.
- President's Club, 1986, 1987, 1988, and 1989 (top 15 percent nationally)
- Number 1 in sales Long Beach Team, 1986 and 1987
- Number 1 of 8 in sales Denver Team, 1988
- Number 2 of 8 in sales Denver Team, 1989
- Number 1 out of 180 people nationally for sales of aperture card printers, 1987

HUGHES AIRCRAFT, Fullerton/Irvine, California   1980 – 1985
Business Management Specialist (1980 – 1985)
Managed the business functions of the Advanced Systems Office in support of the Product Line Manager of a $20 million department. Directed and supervised administrators and financial analysts in developing and implementing financial planning and project controls. Organized, prepared, and presented department program reviews, budgets, and strategies to top divisional management. Interfaced with the product line and group support organizations in developing strategies and resolving business-related problems.

Project Control Administrator (1980 – 1983)
Established all necessary plans to organize, staff, direct, and control project manpower, materials, facilities, and budgets for multi-million dollar contracts for the project manager.

FORD AEROSPACE, Newport Beach, California   1977 – 1979
Financial Analyst
Prepared proposals and monitored critical elements of each assigned area, anticipating, investigating, and resolving unusual financial developments. Fulfilled customer and corporate reporting requirements, including budgets, estimates, proposal pricing, program reviews, performance analysis, and manpower planning.

EDUCATION

MASTER OF BUSINESS ADMINISTRATION   1977
University of Arizona, Tucson, Arizona
Major: Finance/Management
- GPA 3.8 (top 10 percent of MBA class)

BACHELOR OF SCIENCE IN ACCOUNTING   1976
University of Arizona, Tucson, Arizona
- GPA 3.6 (3.9 in Major)
- Dean's List throughout college, graduating with high honors

TRAINING

XEROX
Sales Training I, II, III
Quality Improvement Process
Facilitator Training
Management Studies

HUGHES AIRCRAFT
Management Skills Training
Negotiating Skills Training

(Scannable)

GERALD L. HOLLAND

PROFILE

- Demonstrated success in a wide range of teaching, technical, and administrative positions.
- Team player with outstanding interpersonal, communication, and presentation skills.
- Aggressive problem solver; able to conceptualize and implement innovative solutions.
- Top Secret SCI security clearance (renewed January 1994).
- Knowledge of Windows, WordPerfect, MS Word, and Excel.

EXPERIENCE

INSTRUCTION

- Established, administered, and conducted training and certification programs for USAF personnel in multinational combat operations centers.
- Wrote curricula materials for qualification, recurring, corrective, and refresher training.
- Instrumental in the research, development, and supervision of the modular control equipment student lab upgrade.
- Ensured that students received the most realistic training possible through creative methods of simulating operational scenarios and through innovative classroom instruction.
- Improved more than 1,300 classroom visual aids and corrected outdated testing items.
- Counseled students, administered critiques, and tested and measured student progress.

TECHNICAL

- Missile Warning Center crew chief responsible for monitoring worldwide satellite, radar, and computer operations in support of the NORAD warning mission.
- Recognized expert in missile warning training and operations.
- Played an integral role in the activation of the missile warning center theater cell, including training 15 personnel and spending off-duty hours administering pre-evaluations to meet deadlines.
- Ensured a smooth and orderly fighter flow through knowledge of airborne orders/scramble procedures and coordination with external agencies.
- Gathered critical operational data for visual presentation to the First Air Force Commander.
- Operated and inspected aircraft simulators and related equipment.

ADMINISTRATION

- Provided leadership and direction to subordinates; responsible for crew discipline and morale.
- Motivated crew to exceptional 100 percent accuracy in global missile event processing.
- Improved user satisfaction by serving as an effective liaison with NORAD customer base.
- Served as Safety NCO, Supply Custodian, Flight Safety NCO, Base Mobility Augmentee, Course Forms Representative, and member of the Quality Air Force Instructor Team.

WORK HISTORY

UNITED STATES AIR FORCE (1977 – 1997)
NCOIC Missile Warning Center Training Section, Technical Instructor, Airborne Aircraft Controller, Senior Director Technician, Air Defense Technician, Aircraft Pilot Simulator Technician

EDUCATION

COLORADO TECHNICAL UNIVERSITY, Colorado Springs, Colorado (1996)
70 credits toward a Bachelor of Science in Management Information Systems

ASSOCIATE OF SCIENCE IN INSTRUCTIONAL TECHNOLOGY AND MILITARY SCIENCE (1992)
Community College of the Air Force

MILITARY TRAINING
Instruction: Technical Training Instructor (216 hours), Interpreting Training Codes and Objectives (36 hours), Instructional Systems Development (40 hours), Technical Training Teaching Practicum (216 hours), Test and Measurement (40 hours), Academic Counseling (32 hours)
Management: USAF Supervisor's Course (53 hours), NCO Academy (220 hours)
Technical: Airborne Aircraft Controller (12 weeks), Water Survival (3 days), Combat Survival (17 days), Aerospace Control and Warning Systems Operator (180 hours)

ADDRESS

1234-D Tyndall Avenue
Colorado Springs, Colorado 80916

Telephone: (719) 555-1234
E-mail: criscito@aol.com

Scannable

John W. Chloe

12345 Bradshaw Road
Peyton, Colorado 80831

E-mail: criscito@aol.com

Home Phone: (719) 555-1234
Cell Phone: (719) 555-1234

PROFILE

- *High-energy real estate sales professional with proven success in resale and new home sales.*
- *Developed a personal sales philosophy that customers will buy if you give them a reason to buy.*
- *Especially adept at finding the need and taking advantage of the opportunity created by that need.*
- *Self-motivated and tenacious salesperson who gets more excited than the buyer.*
- *Skilled in MS-DOS, Windows 95, MS Word, Excel, PowerPoint, MLS, and the Internet.*

EXPERIENCE

COMMUNITY MANAGER *(1998 – present)*
Rocky Mountain Homes, *Colorado Springs, Colorado*

- *Demonstrated features and benefits of new homes in three subdivisions.*
- *Closed one out of every four deals on the first visit; closed two of the remaining three within 30 days through effective follow-up and exceptional customer service.*
- *Increased sales by 150 percent in only ten months over the previous year, selling more than $10 million in 1998 with projected growth of another 150 percent by year-end 1999.*
- *Accomplished more net profit than the sister company, Hallmark Builders, with half the staff.*
- *Built long-term working relationships with a local realtor base of 150 agents.*
- *Hired, supervised, trained, scheduled, and provided corrective/positive feedback for two sales assistants.*
- *Developed print, radio, and television marketing campaigns; managed a $60,000 annual advertising budget.*
- *Responsible for placement, negotiation of media pricing and terms, advertisement design, and evaluation of campaign effectiveness.*
- *Shopped the competition monthly to compare incentives, pricing, and sales volume.*
- *Ensured that model homes were always in top condition and ready for customer traffic.*

COMMUNITY MANAGER *(1997 – 1998)*
Richmond American Homes, *Colorado Springs, Colorado*

- *Assumed responsibility for the Colorado Center location—one of the slowest sales locations in the company—and grew sales in only six months to number one in Colorado Springs.*
- *Closed out the Gateway Vista subdivision three months early by selling more homes in three months than had been sold since construction began in that filing.*
- *Honored with the Homebuilders Association 1997 Silver Award for achieving $4.8 million in sales.*
- *Selected as top salesperson for three months.*

REALTOR *(1996 – 1997)*
McGinnis Better Homes and Gardens, *Colorado Springs, Colorado*

- *Sold $1 million in resale homes in the first year through effective marketing and promotion.*
- *Developed client contacts through farming, door-to-door, and mall kiosk sales.*

SALES SUPERVISOR *(1994 – 1996)*
MCI Worldcom, *Colorado Springs, Colorado*

- *Successfully sold cellular telephones, pagers, and accessories.*
- *Managed the Citadel Mall retail kiosk and ensured revenue goals were consistently exceeded.*
- *Recruited, hired, trained, and supervised three sales representatives.*
- *Set up merchant account and checking accounts; made initial marketing recommendations.*
- *Selected as top salesperson for the division every month.*
- *Hand picked to fly to the Memphis, Tennessee, and Springfield, Missouri, stores to train their salespeople, who subsequently achieved 150 percent increases in sales the month after training.*

EDUCATION

JONES REAL ESTATE SCHOOL, *Colorado Springs, Colorado*

- *Licensed real estate agent (1996); completed course work in real estate law, Colorado contract law and practices, real estate practices, multi-state closings, escrows, etc.*
- *Certified Managing Broker; completed broker administration training in 1999.*
- *Currently pursuing an Effective Buyer Representation (EBR) designation with courses that will end in November 1999.*

MARCUS BAYLOR

1234 Ilex Drive ▸ Colorado Springs, Colorado 80920
Phone: (719) 555-1234 ▸ E-mail: criscito@aol.com

PROFILE

- ▸ Effective information systems manager with twelve years of proven leadership experience.
- ▸ Demonstrated results in the management of high-dollar projects in multi-platform environments.
- ▸ Comprehensive experience in the acquisition of management information systems and software project management, including requirements analysis, design, systems-level integration, and test engineering.

EXPERIENCE

CITY OF COLORADO SPRINGS, POLICE DEPARTMENT, Colorado Springs, Colorado (1998 – present)
Information Technology Manager

- ▸ Manage the operations of large computer and telecommunication systems that are critical to public safety and the prosecution of criminal and civil offenses, including emergency 911, computer-aided dispatch, criminal justice information system, geographic information systems, geographically distributed substation support, and crime lab/analysis units.
- ▸ Direct the design, testing, implementation, subsystem interface, operation, and maintenance of information systems software.
- ▸ Develop strategic plans, long-range operating plans, and departmental policies.
- ▸ Manage all aspects of automation within the department, including telecommunications, two-way radio systems, mobile data computer components, and remote access security.
- ▸ Hire, supervise, motivate, and evaluate the performance of 15 software engineers, network administrators, web designers, Windows NT server administrators, and hardware technicians.
- ▸ Plan, prepare, and administer a $2 million departmental budget for all IT functions.
- ▸ Manage the Year 2000 program; accountable for risk management, remediation actions, and contingency planning.
- ▸ Demonstrate software and make program briefings to the police chief and city council.

Accomplishments:

- ▸ Re-engineered the Information Technology Section, improving communication and providing a structure for a previously informal process.
- ▸ Used information technology to enable process improvements and increase efficiency.
- ▸ Customized help desk software to allow users to visually track project priorities, increasing internal customer satisfaction.
- ▸ Managed the development of a new police records management system that allows patrol officers to create case reports on their laptops, ensuring faster access to information, improving executive information systems (DSS), and saving $500,000 over vendor bids.
- ▸ Developed a new system for digital mug shot processing, saving $60,000 by maximizing in-house resources.
- ▸ Completed a massive $250,000 hardware infrastructure upgrade using open system architecture.
- ▸ Implemented quality software processing standards program using Software Engineering Institute's Capability Maturity Model, UML, and CORBA.

REGIS UNIVERSITY, Colorado Springs, Colorado (1997 – present)
Associate Faculty Member

- ▸ Facilitate adult learning in the School of Professional Studies MBA and MSCIS programs.
- ▸ Teach classes in Process Management, Database Management, System Integration, Technical Management, and System Analysis, Design, and Implementation.
- ▸ Made recommendations to the university's steering committee to increase student participation in technology programs.

JOINT NATIONAL TEST FACILITY, Schreiver AFB, Colorado (1990 – 1998)
Systems Engineering Manager, Sparta Incorporated, Colorado Springs, Colorado (1997 – 1998)
IT Consulting/Project Manager, Vanguard Research, Inc., Colorado Springs, Colorado (1993 – 1997)
Systems Engineer/Project Manager, Mitre Corporation, Colorado Springs, Colorado (1990 – 1993)

- ▸ Managed system engineering, integration, and implementation of key projects, including:
  - – Cheyenne Mountain Training and Simulation System .... $8.0 million
  - – Ballistic Missile Defense Simulation Support Center Web Technologies .... $4.0 million
  - – Wintel Client-Server Upgrade (from Macintosh Computing Platform) .... $2.3 million
  - – Strategic Planning for Workstations and NT Servers .... $3.7 million
- ▸ Provided technical consulting and management oversight of contractor system engineering activities from requirements analysis/definition to design, development, integration, test, and system administration.
- ▸ Developed strategic plans to address competitive advantages, action plans, operational necessity for upgrades, and total estimated life cycle costs of integrating future technology.

JOINT NATIONAL TEST FACILITY (continued)
- Created budget databases, recommended project selection and implementation, generated monthly project status reports, and participated in the quarterly financial management review board.
- Serviced 900-clients with a FY97 budget of $18+ million, including software, hardware, and communications systems.
- Technical Lead for the National Test Bed simulation tool; managed this $2.5 million contract and ten software engineers.
- Lead Engineer for the National Test Bed resource management system; authored capacity analysis report that resulted in an additional allocation of $5 million for Cray 2 supercomputer and mainframe component upgrades.
- Provided departmental system administration support for a 28-user network of PCs at Mitre Corporation.

Accomplishments:
- Successful in planning and budgeting scalable information systems that accommodated a variety of customers.
- Effected positive changes and delivered high-quality software products.
- Developed the Multimedia Services Department Upgrade Seven-Year Budget Plan for fiscal years 1997 through 2003.
- Selected to co-chair the executive board of the ADPE integrated product team, which addressed the Macintosh to Windows 95/NT migration of 670 computer systems, including planning, budgeting, training, and establishment of standards.
- Provided the vision for integrating future information technology as a contributing member of the information systems architecture, resource management/planning and graphics media presentation integrated product team; responsible for strategic planning, budgeting, multimedia requirements analyses, and design of distributed MIS solutions.
- Developed a mobile computing strategy for system acquisition and remote access security.

PLANNING RESEARCH CORPORATION, Sierra Vista, Arizona (1987 – 1990)
Telecommunications Engineer
- Technical Lead for the integration studies of geographically distributed Army MIS and program offices.
- Performed numerical/statistical analysis of 60 management information systems to identify critical success factors and levels of interoperability.

Accomplishments:
- Developed system simulations and recommended alternatives that improved system performance by more than 50 percent.
- Promoted from Junior Programmer to Programmer Analyst and later to Communications Engineer in only three years.

EDUCATION

MASTER OF BUSINESS ADMINISTRATION, INFORMATION SYSTEMS (1996)
Regis University, Colorado Springs, Colorado

MASTER OF SCIENCE, OPERATIONS RESEARCH (1992)
University of Northern Colorado, Greeley, Colorado

BACHELOR OF SCIENCE, APPLIED MATHEMATICS (1987)
University of Houston, Texas

TECHNICAL

Computer/Networking Technology: Completed Microsoft Certified System Engineer courses for Windows 95/NT. Working knowledge of many distinct computer systems, ranging from large mainframes (DEC, IBM, Cray, Data General) to personal computers (IBM clones, Macintosh), utilizing various operating systems (VMS, MVS, UNIX, Windows 95/NT, MacOS, SunOS), programming languages (Visual Basic, SAS, Pascal, FORTRAN, Minitab, COBOL, HyperCard), database management systems (Access, MS SQL Server, DB2, dBASE), communication protocols (Ethernet, ATM, ISDN, TCP/IP, Frame Relay, X.25, AppleTalk), project management software (Microsoft Project), and Web page development (Microsoft FrontPage).

Mathematical Modeling: Designed engineering and cost models for NASA as an undergraduate at the University of Houston. Performed numerical/statistical analysis on deterministic and stochastic space station model results. Presented research at the Johnson Space Center, University of Houston, and Tarleton State University. Winner of Best Student Paper Award for *Statistical Analysis of Cost Estimates on the Space Station.* Developed queuing models for the Survivable Communication Information System.

Computer Network Simulation: Provided requirements analysis and definition support to the National Missile Defense High Fidelity System Simulation Project. Developed multi-fidelity computer network simulations of the Army Civilian Personnel System. Simulations were based on high-level conceptual models and detailed vendor-provided data. Presented briefings to management and incorporated summary results in a new system development plan.

Scannable

Damon R. Heath

1234 Smoketree ■ Colorado Springs, Colorado 80920 ■ (719) 555-1234

QUALIFICATIONS
- Proven sales leader with a positive attitude and commitment to integrity.
- Good speaker with exceptional communication/motivation skills and public relations experience.
- Able to see the entire picture, organized, and detail oriented.

SUMMARY OF EXPERIENCE

SALES/SPEAKING
- Successful sales experience in both retail and telemarketing environments.
- Dale Carnegie graduate; facilitate Dale Carnegie classes as a graduate assistant.
- Wrote and delivered motivational speeches to Rotary, Sertoma, and other community groups.
- Wrote and delivered a motivational speech to a group of 3,500 Harding students.

MANAGEMENT
- Coordinated orientation for 1,000+ students, reorganizing the program for increased efficiency.
- Arranged for speakers and conference rooms; wrote information letters and facilitated mailings.
- Formulated and executed travel plans for visits to Athens, Greece, and Florence, Italy.

LEADERSHIP
- Serve as Assistant Scout Master for a local Boy Scout troop of 30 young men.
- Achieved the highest rank in Boy Scouts (Eagle Scout).

OTHER SKILLS
- Developed public relations and manufacturing skills while learning to work with the diverse clientele of a small manufacturing company.
- Computer experience with WordPerfect, Quattro Pro, Lotus 1-2-3, Internet, and e-mail.
- Continually reading and improving sales and management skills.

EMPLOYMENT

SALES ASSOCIATE, The Home Depot, Colorado Springs, Colorado (1997 – present)
- Assisted customers with purchases of power tools, pointing out product features and benefits.
- Helped customers find the best tool for the job and increased profits through suggestive selling.
- Co-leader of the Kid's Clinic; developed projects and instructed training sessions for children.
- Honored with several service awards for outstanding customer service; Employee of the Month.

OPERATIONS MANAGER, Get Waxed, Colorado Springs, Colorado (1996 – 1997)
- Managed daily operations of two stores; opened and closed the stores; made deposits.
- Edited operations manual and created forms to improve operating procedures.

RELATIONSHIP MANAGER, Norwest Direct, Colorado Springs, Colorado (1995 – 1996)
- Sold home equity lines of credit and checking/savings accounts to existing customers.
- Consistently met or exceeded sales quotas.
- Made courtesy calls to existing customers to ensure satisfaction and customer retention.

GOLF AGENT, Broadmoor Hotel, Inc., Colorado Springs, Colorado (1995)
- Coordinated corporate billing and maintained a petty cash account.
- Opened and closed two clubhouses; registered golfers and resolved conflicts.
- Interfaced with high-end clientele daily, giving directions and arranging tee times.

DIRECTOR, STUDENT ORIENTATION, Harding University, Searcy, Arkansas (Summer 1994)
- Coordinated orientation for more than 1,000 students.

EDUCATION

BACHELOR OF BUSINESS ADMINISTRATION IN BUSINESS MANAGEMENT
Harding University, Searcy, Arkansas (May 1995)
- Appointed director of team efforts in Leadership course.
- Researched production methods and marketing strategies for children's lithographs as part of a Small Business Management course.
- Developed public speaking skills by making presentations.
- Attended motivational seminars outside of class requirements.
- Studied European culture in Florence, Italy, Spring 1993.

ALEXANDER THOMPSON

1234 E. Shea Boulevard, #2101
Scottsdale, Arizona 85254

Telephone: (480) 555-1234
E-mail: criscito@aol.com

PROFILE

Experienced sales and marketing professional with five years of demonstrated success in:
- Consultative selling and account management.
- Small business management from a corporate and entrepreneurial perspective.
- Relationship building and customer service.
- Classic and "grass root" product management.
- Formal market research, including questionnaire and focus group design.

EXPERIENCE

US WEST COMMUNICATIONS, Phoenix, Arizona (1998 – Present)
Account Manager
- Completed a comprehensive corporate management training program.
- Certification training in frame relay, digital private line, DS1, DS3, OC3, PRI, BRI, DSL, IP, and digital voice applications; knowledge of LAN and WAN topology, including CPE integration.
- Attained more than 100 percent of objective in the first year of sales activity, generating $1.5+ million in revenue.
- Proactively integrated the sales of voice and data solutions with long-term contractual agreements facilitating customer retention for more than 100 small business customers.
- Managed a "module" of 700 small business customers, employing a consultative sales approach to provide a total customer experience and to promote the concept of US WEST Communications as a full-service provider of voice, data, and Internet business solutions.

STONEPOINT INCORPORATED, Phoenix, Arizona (1996 – 1997)
National Sales Manager
- Established the "Triumph! Sport Energy" brand in the Western United States through special event participation, innovative cross-promotions, select advertising, and aggressive "up and down the street" sales activity.
- Trained and motivated area managers to form brand equity partnerships with distributors emphasizing "hands-on" sales management, event promotions, and aggressive sales incentive programs.
- Initiated West Coast distribution for "Triumph! Sport Energy" in eleven states.
- Created pricing and promotional programs emphasizing market penetration and price parity for the natural food, mass market, health club, and convenience markets.
- Established 400 retail accounts in the Southwest region for "Triumph! Sport Energy."

R.W. GARCIA COMPANY, San Jose, California (1995 – 1996)
Sales Representative – Grocery Division
- Coordinated the sales and merchandising efforts of a Direct Store Distribution team, facilitating chain-wide placement in 171 Lucky's grocery stores.
- Negotiated schematic design and product placement at the corporate and store management level.
- Developed and managed a database integrating all sales and promotional activity.

PRIVATE LABEL ADVANTAGE, Encino, California (1994 – 1995)
Marketing Manager
- Managed a private label distribution business from the conceptual stage to $500,000 in annual sales in less than one year of sales activity.
- Created a partnership with 50 individual natural food retail accounts through proactive customer service and relationship selling.
- Directed the manufacture, purchase, and timely distribution of a unique private label food program.

EDUCATION

MASTER OF INTERNATIONAL MANAGEMENT (1991)
American Graduate School of International Management – Thunderbird Campus, Glendale, Arizona
- Tripartite Emphasis: Marketing management, cross-cultural communications, and the Spanish language.
- Project leader for a corporate consulting team conducting business intelligence for a proposed new product introduction.

BACHELOR OF ARTS IN COMMUNICATION (1987)
William Paterson College, Wayne, New Jersey
- Concentration in interpersonal communications; minor in business administration.

Scannable

MARCELA WILLIAMS
12345 N. 59th Avenue, #123
Glendale, Arizona 85306
(602) 555-1234

education
1998 – 1999

AMERICAN GRADUATE SCHOOL OF INTERNATIONAL
MANAGEMENT (THUNDERBIRD CAMPUS)   PHOENIX, AZ
Candidate for Master of International Management degree, December 1999. International Management curriculum with emphasis on marketing. Selected by faculty to tutor foreign language students. Organized Thunderbird International Symposium with Latin American and Andean Clubs. Member of Marketing and Import/Export Clubs.

1991 – 1995

UNIVERSITY OF COLORADO   BOULDER, CO
Awarded Bachelor of Arts degree in Business Spanish for the Professions, an interdisciplinary program in business and the Spanish language and culture. Concentration in business development in Latin America. Awarded Regent Academic Scholarship and University Research Opportunities Scholarship. Published paper on sports injuries in children. Wrote senior thesis on the Spanish language and its problems in the United States after serving 10 months as volunteer Assistant Probation Officer for Hispanic offenders. Elected president and treasurer of Spanish Club. Overseas study in Madrid, Spain.

experience
1997 – 1998

CIBA-GEIGY PHARMACEUTICALS   BOGOTA, COLOMBIA
Product Manager, Cardiovascular Line
Responsible for enhancing profitability, sales, and market share of cardiovascular products through the development and implementation of strategic and tactical marketing plans, encompassing all traditional brand management activities.
- Devised marketing strategy for product launch of new ACE-Inhibitor in Colombia.
- Developed advertising campaign for national product launch.
- Led focus groups and conducted interviews with physicians, pharmacists, and distributors.
- Conducted all prelaunch financial analyses and feasibility studies.
- Developed and expanded market share by an average of 13 percent for three products.
- Presented market share analysis and recommendations to International Product Management.
- Designed and supervised physician and prescription market research program.
- Trained 80 sales representatives on the cardiovascular system and its corresponding product line.

1996 – 1997

Assistant to Marketing Manager
- Implemented Resource Allocation Model for optimal utilization of funds in the Marketing Division at all levels.
- Monitored and presented monthly spending and cost applications per product.
- Acted as liaison between product managers and advertising agency.

1995 – 1996

BANCO POPULAR   BOGOTA, COLOMBIA
International Development Manager
- Evaluated branch viabilities in Miami and the Cayman Islands.
- Prepared and presented official applications for first branch office in the United States to the Central Banking Authority of Colombia as well as the Federal Reserve of the United States.
- Designed and recommended office structure and job descriptions for new office in Miami; handled all administrative procedures.
- Negotiated investment terms and analyzed legal documentation for a personal money transfer system from the United States to Colombia.
- Aided in the creation of a five-year business plan. Developed financial model to generate and control monthly income statements, balance sheets, and cash flows for the distinct international divisions in 60 regional offices.

personal

United States/Colombian/Bolivian citizenships
Fluent in **Spanish** • Fluent in **English** • Knowledge of **French**

94

Scannable

Mary Ann Whitman
12345 North 71st Avenue
Glendale, Arizona 85308
(602) 555-1234

Objective	To provide elementary students with a stimulating learning environment oriented to many learning styles. It is very important to enhance this environment with encouragement, kindness, and feelings of success.

Certificates

• Arizona Elementary Certificate K-8
• Oregon Basic Elementary Certificate K-8

Experience

SUBSTITUTE TEACHER . . . . 9/98 – Present
Deer Valley and **Peoria Unified School Districts**, Phoenix, Arizona
Long-term assignments at Village Meadows School and Greenbrier School.

TEACHER, KINDERGARTEN . . . . 9/96 – 6/98
Ainsworth Elementary School, Portland, Oregon
Successfully provided full curriculum, including language arts (i.e., phonics, *Success in Reading* program, journal writing, literature-based and language-experience-based reading program using a whole language approach, drama), *Math Their Way* program, science, health, social studies, music, art, and italic printing. Many lessons planned using ITIP formula. Successfully worked with special education children mainstreamed into the kindergarten class. Utilized parent helpers when appropriate to provide lower student/adult ratio.

SUBSTITUTE TEACHER . . . . 2/96 – 6/98
Portland Public Schools, Portland, Oregon
Substituted at grade levels K-8. During this period, became familiar with many styles of teaching and many programs.

STUDENT TEACHING, FIRST GRADE . . . . 9/95 – 12/95
Whitman Elementary School, 1234 S.E. Flavour, Portland, Oregon
A successful and delightful experience with first grade—a great opportunity for growth.

Education

B.S. ELEMENTARY EDUCATION, Portland State University, 1995

Staff Development and Continuing Education

• Spanish foreign language experience
• Higher level thinking skills
• Early childhood education seminars
• *Math Their Way* classes
• Art projects for elementary children
• Multicultural education – African American history
• Nellie Edge seminars, whole language (musical)
• Valerie Welk seminar, whole language (enrichment)

Other Experience with Children

• FIELD EXPERIENCE with Portland State University classes, providing a variety of experiences with children in grades K-4. Worked with *Writing to Read* programs and prepared many art/social studies projects.
• Camp Fire leader with second grade Bluebird group
• Child care co-op volunteer, N.E. YMCA, Portland, Oregon

Margaret Erin Fielding

Qualifications

- Masters degree in International Management with emphasis on International Insurance
- Proven leadership and communication skills
- Three years experience in the insurance industry
- Computer literacy with multiple operating systems and applications

Professional Experience

Chubb Group of Insurance Companies, *International Underwriter*, 1998 – Present
- Solicit and service international accounts
- Demonstrate Chubb global expertise in the marketplace
- Analyze and strengthen current global insurance programs
- Educate clients on the complexities and necessity of international insurance
- Prospect current domestic clients with probable international exposures
- Specialized training includes nine intensive weeks in Warren, New Jersey, at the Chubb Commercial Lines School of Insurance

SAFECO Insurance Company, *Underwriter*, 1994 – 1998
- Managed a field of 30 independent insurance agencies
- Analyzed applications, claims, and other data to select insurance risks
- Communicated underwriting accept or reject decisions to the independent agency force in the field

Special projects included:
- Selected as department coordinator to work with the home office to launch an automated computer decision system
- Planned and organized a full-day seminar for company Vice Presidents and local branch staff
- Conducted informational seminars for the independent agency field and newly appointed SAFECO agents
- Analyzed agency loss ratio data and provided recommendations to increase agency growth and profitability

Tektronix, Inc., *Summer Employment*, 1990 – 1993
- Increased responsibilities from an hourly Technical Typist to a salaried Technical Writer. Final project was the documentation set for a major software product
- Organized large amounts of information and presented it in a concise format
- Worked closely with the marketing and engineering departments
- Participated on the product launch team

Education

Master of International Management, 1997 (GPA 3.7)
American Graduate School of International Management,
Thunderbird Campus, Glendale, Arizona
- Focus on Insurance/Risk Management and Finance
- Participated in International Insurance and Risk Management Conference
- Recipient – Hugh M. Blake International Insurance Scholarship
- Recipient – Mavis Voris Partial Assistantship

Bachelor of Arts, International Studies, 1994 (GPA 3.33)
University of Oregon, Eugene, Oregon

Foreign Study, 1993
Obirin College, Tokyo, Japan
An intensive semester study of Japanese business, society, and language. Program included seminars with various Japanese companies.

Languages

Proficient in **Japanese** • Knowledge of **French**

Address

12345 Goshen Avenue #12 • San Francisco, California 90049 • (310) 555-1234

Scannable

7 Those Difficult Dates

Where should you place your dates? It all depends on how much importance you want to give them. If you have gaps in your employment history that you would rather explain in an interview, then the dates should be less obvious (pages 101, 103, 105, 109–111, and 115). You can even leave them off altogether and list totals instead (page 106), although your reader will automatically assume you have something to hide. You need to make the decision whether leaving the dates off will harm your chances of getting an interview more than putting the dates on your résumé.

Another reason to de-emphasize dates is your age. If you would rather not give your age away, then make the reader work to figure it out. Tuck dates against the text with parentheses (pages 101, 103, 105, 109, 111, 113, and 115) or bury them somewhere else in the résumé (page 110). You can selectively choose to leave dates off your education and show them only on your experience.

So, how far back should you go when listing your experience? The answer is simple. When your past experience stops being relevant to your job search, leave it off. The usual is 10 to 15 years in the past, unless there is something in your older experience that is critical to your qualifications. This will help to deflect interest from your age.

Accuracy and *honesty* are the most important considerations when it comes to dates. Don't lie! I had a client who chose to fudge on his dates and I didn't know about it. He was invited for an interview and then lost the job when previous employers were contacted and the dates didn't match. It wasn't worth it. Honesty is always the best policy.

There are many ways to make room for the dates. One is to establish a clear column of dates to the right of a résumé, which keeps the text lines short and makes the dates easy to find. You should not use this clear column of dates on the right if you are creating a scannable résumé since this style produces three newspaper-like columns.

Putting dates on the left gives them a great deal of importance. Since people read from left to right, information on the left of the page is read first and carries greater weight. Make sure you really want your dates to be that important before placing them in the left-hand column.

You may use months with years or years only. Some people feel more comfortable with a full accounting of their time and prefer the month/year method. However, making room for all those words becomes a problem if you choose to spell out the month, as in January 1989 to February 1993. Abbreviations or numbers for months make designing your résumé a little easier:

Jan. 1989 – Feb. 1993

or

Jan 1989 – Feb 1993

or

1/89 – 2/93

It is possible to stack the dates (as on pages 99 and 114) in order to make more room. For example:

Jan. 1989   January 1989
                    or
– Feb. 1993   to February 1993

Dot leaders . . . . can help draw the eye to the dates on paragraph-style résumés where it is difficult to create a clear column for the dates (pages 100 and 106–108). However, dot leaders should not be used in a scannable résumé.

There is no single, preferred method for the positioning of dates on a résumé. The key is to create a sense of balance by placing the dates in a position that is complimentary to the rest of your information, while keeping in mind how much importance you wish to give them and the scannability of your résumé.

METTE RIIS LERNER

Address
Møllegærdet 123
1234 Kolding, Denmark

Telephones
Tel: (75) 555-1234
Fax: (75) 555-1234

OBJECTIVE
A marketing management position with an internationally oriented firm that utilizes my marketing and finance skills

QUALIFICATIONS
- Degrees in Computer Management Science and International Business Management
- Demonstrated interpersonal skills, leadership qualities, and personal motivation
- Training and management experience
- Skilled administrator and communicator
- Broad multicultural and sociological knowledge

EDUCATION

MASTER OF BUSINESS ADMINISTRATION   June 1999
European University, Antwerp, Belgium
Selected courses: Multinational Business Management, International Finance and Trade, International Marketing, International Consumer Marketing, International Business Policy

CERTIFICATE OF ADVANCED STUDY   Jan. 1999
American Graduate School of International Management   – June 1999
Thunderbird Campus, Glendale, Arizona

BACHELOR OF SCIENCE *cum laude*   GPA 3.83/4.0   June 1996
COMPUTER MANAGEMENT SCIENCE
Armstrong University, Berkeley, California
Selected courses: Risk Management, International Money and Banking, Operations Management, Managerial Finance, Marketing

WORK EXPERIENCE

ASSISTANT RETAIL MANAGER   June 1997
Popp Dress, Kolding, Denmark   – Jan. 1998
- Achieved maximum sales potential through sales planning, merchandising, accurate inventory control procedures, and personnel management
- Supervised and trained department staff
- Exhibited high level of leadership and communication skills

COMPUTER CONSULTANT   Sep. 1996
Dun and Bradstreet Software Services, Inc., Los Angeles, California – May 1997
- Successfully completed Career Development Program (four-month intensive management training program in Atlanta, Georgia)
- Trained customers to fully utilize the software programs
- Worked under very tight time schedules
- Ensured customer satisfaction by maintaining constant communication and solving technical problems
- Researched software programs and replaced existing software with new releases

ASSISTANT TO BUSINESS MANAGER (Part-Time)   Mar. 1995
Armstrong University, Berkeley, California   – May 1996
- Wrote letters suggesting student financial status and corresponded with other departments
- Received and processed tuition/fees and made bank deposits

HONORS & ACTIVITIES
- The National Dean's List 1994, 1995
- The Dean's List every semester of undergraduate study
- Member of Sigma Kappa Phi Honor Society

INTERNATIONAL EXPERIENCES
- Graduate education in Belgium and the United States
- College education in the United States
- High school education in Denmark
- Traveled extensively throughout Europe and the United States

LANGUAGES
Fluent in **Danish** and **English** • Highly proficient in **Norwegian** and **Swedish**
Working knowledge of **German** • Knowledge of **French**

(Scannable)

JOAN LARKIN

1234 Doolittle Road • Monument, Colorado 80132 • (719) 555-1234 • criscito@aol.com

PROFILE
- Dedicated worker with strong customer service, meeting planning, and administrative experience.
- Optimistic team player with the ability to get along well with everyone.
- Quick learner who is open to change and new learning opportunities.
- Computer literate in Windows, MS Word, Excel, Outlook, WordPerfect, and Lotus 1-2-3.

EXPERIENCE

COLORADO INTERSTATE GAS, Colorado Springs, Colorado . . . . 1982 – present
Account Representative (Jan '95 – present)
- Negotiate terms and draft gas transport and storage agreements for small municipalities.
- Coordinate the approval of proposed agreements and ensure consideration of relevant comments before recommending approval and execution by management.
- Work closely with accounting, volume management/transmission, facility planning, engineering, certification, and operations departments to implement agreements.
- Responsible for extensive meeting planning, including site selection, facility contract negotiations, speaker recruitment, entertainment, food, audio-visual requirements, on-site management, and post-meeting evaluations.
- Saved $10,000 in charges relating to the annual sales customer meetings.
- Mediate between hotel staff and company employees during events and procure thank you gifts for speakers, saving more than $5,000 on a recent order.
- Coordinate the annual CIG International Golf Tournament and Sky Sox baseball outings.
- Provide marketing assistance to senior representatives and establish working relationships with existing and prospective customers.
- Prepare work-in-progress and special reports of transportation and storage activities.

Associate Account Representative (Mar '88 – Jan '95)
- Expedited the preparation and distribution of gas contracts.
- Prepared data for input into the computer, monitored monthly billings, and prepared reports and summary data.
- Arranged customer meetings and responded to customer requests and inquiries.

Senior Clerk (Feb '87 – Mar '88), **Clerk II** (July '82 – Feb '87), **Receptionist** (Apr '81 – July '82)
- Processed payment authorizations based on analysis of FERC regulations.
- Prepared reports, input data into the computer, and provided customer service.

SCHOOL DISTRICT 11, Colorado Springs, Colorado . . . . 1979 – 1982
Teacher's Aide
- Assisted kindergarten through sixth grade students individually and in small groups.
- Implemented lesson plans to present and reinforce learning concepts.
- Assisted in the preparation of adapted work materials for students with special needs.
- Supervised classes and assisted in the preparation of curriculum materials and lesson plans.

EDUCATION

REGIS UNIVERSITY, Colorado Springs, Colorado
Bachelor of Business Administration
- Completed all but 30 credits toward an undergraduate degree

PIKES PEAK COMMUNITY COLLEGE, Colorado Springs, Colorado
Associate of Science in Behavioral Sciences
- Dean's List, President's Honor Roll

CONTINUING EDUCATION
- Eight years of Meeting Professionals International
- Five years of seminars through the Colorado Oil and Gas Association
- CIG Classes: Dynamics of Customer Focus I and II, Excellence with People, Pipeline Rate Fundamentals, among others

GLEN A. MILLS

12345 Mill Creek Court • Colorado Springs, Colorado 80908 • (719) 555-1234

PROFILE

- Dedicated manager with a strong work ethic and the ability to build lasting client relationships.
- Experienced in operations management, sales, budget development, staffing, and cost control.
- Adept at communicating effectively with customers, vendors, and staff.
- Able to motivate employees to perform to their maximum potential.
- Exceptional organizational and planning skills; adaptable; enjoy new challenges.

EXPERIENCE

GENERAL MANAGER AND CO-OWNER
Mission Bell Inn, Manitou Springs, CO (1984 – present)

Key Accomplishments
- Successfully managed a family restaurant, increasing sales by 40 percent through quality food, exceptional service, and family value.
- Achieved a three-star rating from the Mobil Travel Guide.
- Won several "Best of the Springs" awards for the category.
- Maintained expenses below budget through accurate planning, waste reduction, purchasing, and cost-effective operating procedures.
- Planned and managed significant remodeling projects that enhanced the ambiance of the facility.

Management/Administration
- Accountable for budgeting, cost control, payroll, general accounting, and full profit and loss.
- Developed marketing campaigns to increase visibility of the restaurant; analyzed market demographics, defined the target market, and determined advertising placement.
- Wrote scripts and acted in television commercials; designed print advertisements.
- Planned menus, estimated food and beverage costs, and purchased inventory.
- Investigated and resolved food/beverage quality and service complaints, ensuring customer satisfaction and repeat business.
- Created new business through community involvement and active public relations programs.

Supervision/Training
- Recruited, hired, supervised, scheduled, and motivated a staff of up to 25 employees.
- Trained service staff to enhance customer service and increase profits through suggestive selling.
- Improved productivity and morale by initiating systems for accountability and by instituting effective training programs.

Community Leadership
- Past president (1993) of the Board of Directors, Manitou Springs Chamber of Commerce.
- Increased visibility of the city through effective leadership, improving visitor inquiries by 20 percent.
- Served as a member of the Economic Development Board charged with the responsibility of promoting the community throughout the United States.
- Member of the Manitou Springs Art Academy Board of Directors.
- Member of the Manitou Springs Historic Preservation Society.

EDUCATION

UNIVERSITY OF COLORADO, Colorado Springs
Bachelor of Science in Business Administration
- Completed three years toward this undergraduate degree

PIKES PEAK COMMUNITY COLLEGE, Colorado Springs
Associate of Science, Computer Programming

Scannable

101

LISA CAMFIELD

EXPERIENCE
1997 – present

ACTUATE SOFTWARE, San Francisco, California
Marketing Programs Manager
- Key player in taking Actuate, an Internet reporting company, from start-up to initial public offering.
- Manage all lead generation programs, including direct mail, events, web marketing, and telemarketing.
- Develop and implement monthly direct mail campaigns with an average response of 800 leads per campaign.
- Researched and developed Actuate's first online marketing strategy.
- Manage web advertising in publications, search engines, and product guides.
- Launched lead generation campaigns via e-mail and e-mail newsletters; created web forms to capture all responses.
- Created a customized web portal for Actuate prospects.

Team Manager, Business Development
- Generated qualified sales leads for field representatives through intensive inbound/outbound prospecting.
- Achieved 120 percent of quota, contributing to 20 percent of Actuate's annual revenue.
- Increased revenues by actively managing customer accounts.
- Developed partnership relationships with top application development companies.
- Trained new sales development team members on products, positioning, and phone skills.
- Created all phone scripts for sales development representatives.

1995 – 1997

ORACLE CORPORATION, Redwood Shores, California
Telesales Representative, Direct Marketing Division
- Responsible for sales and direct marketing of Oracle's products and services.
- Consistently surpassed license and support quotas.
- Averaged 200 contacts per week, resulting in the highest number of leads in a group of 50.
- Delivered product presentations and demonstrations.

Direct Response Representative, Direct Marketing Division
- Responsible for lead qualification and aggressive outbound telemarketing.
- Achieved 125 percent of quota for entire tenure with direct response.
- Positioned Oracle's product offerings and answered technical questions.
- Completed Oracle's comprehensive education program.

1994 – 1995

NEW TIMES, INC., Phoenix, Arizona
Account Executive – Sales and Marketing
- Generated new business through aggressive prospecting and telemarketing.
- Managed all aspects of customer accounts, including marketing plans, design and production of advertisements, and accounts payable.

EDUCATION
1992

MASTER OF INTERNATIONAL MANAGEMENT
American Graduate School of International Management, Thunderbird Campus, Glendale, Arizona

1990

BACHELOR OF ARTS (1990)
University of Arizona, Tucson, Arizona
- Major in English Literature, minor in Spanish Literature
- Honors program nominee for English literature, 1998; Humanities honors award, 1990
- Highly proficient in Spanish; proficient in French

1234 Larkin, Apt. 105 • San Francisco, California • (415) 555-1234 • E-mail: criscito@aol.com

Scannable

Catherine J. Brandt

1234 Connecticut Street, Apartment 12
San Francisco, California 94109
(415) 555-1234

BACKGROUND
- Dedicated trainer with a passion for working with people.
- Able to simplify complex subjects and to present them effectively.
- Competent problem solver who enjoys the challenge of creating efficiencies.
- Effective team player with strong communication and interpersonal skills.
- Knowledge of Windows 95, MS Word, Excel, PowerPoint, Lotus 1-2-3, and Internet browsers.

Training
- Fifteen years of teaching experience in both corporate and traditional higher education settings.
- Taught basic, intermediate, and advanced business, administrative, and management courses for Denver Technical College.
- Trained Total Healthcare site managers and staff in organizational practices and policies.
- Conducted regular meetings with physicians and staff to enhance communication.
- Conducted off-site informational meetings to recruit students directly from corporations.

Management
- Eleven years of experience in operations management and work flow supervision.
- Recruited, hired, supervised, and evaluated administrative and clinical staff.
- Developed pay-for-performance criteria and gained a working knowledge of FMLA/ADA processes.
- Experienced in developing departmental goals and establishing procedural guidelines.
- Broad knowledge of the management of accounting and payroll processes.

PROFESSIONAL EXPERIENCE

Practice Operations Manager, Total Healthcare, San Francisco, CA (Jan 1996 – Present)
- Managed the operations of eight separate medical clinics with 24 providers and 90 staff members specializing in family practice, internal medicine, and pediatrics.
- Recruited, hired, and evaluated staff and managers for the seven remote sites.
- Revamped physician schedules to increase gross revenue.
- Managed accounts receivable and billing; decreased accounts receivable days from 84 to 68.
- Developed and administered a $2 million budget; succeeded in bringing all offices within budget.

Medical Services Manager, Peak Medical Clinic, Colorado Springs, CO (Jan 1994 – Dec 1995)
- Recruited, hired, and scheduled support personnel for a 15-member family practice and internal medicine clinic.
- Served as a liaison between clinic physicians and executive director.
- Oriented and trained staff; evaluated and counseled employees regarding their performance.

University Representative Assistant, University of Phoenix, Colorado Springs, CO (Feb 1992 – Nov 1993)
- Served as customer service representative for the marketing department.
- Recruited and interviewed potential students; verified eligibility for programs.

Program Coordinator, Denver Technical College, Colorado Springs, CO (May 1988 – Jan 1992)
- Developed and implemented college associate degree programs in the healthcare field, including the medical assistant, administrative assistant, and transcription programs.
- Devised curricula, scheduled classes, set master calendars, hired instructors, arranged for facilities, and purchased books and class materials.
- Coordinated externship sites for students and followed up on evaluations.
- Contracted, trained, scheduled, and evaluated 15 faculty members.
- Counseled students on course schedules, curricula, and program requirements.
- Successfully obtained accreditation for new programs through the Accrediting Bureau of Health Education Schools within one year of program implementation.

EDUCATION

MASTER OF ARTS IN ORGANIZATIONAL MANAGEMENT (1994)
University of Phoenix, Colorado Springs, CO

BACHELOR OF SCIENCE IN BUSINESS EDUCATION (1979)
Winona State University, Winona, MN

Scannable

103

Robert P. Bentley

EXPERIENCE

INSTITUTE FOR INTERNATIONAL RESEARCH, Hartford, Connecticut   11/98 – Present
Free-Lance Conference Producer
- Developed three executive-level financial conferences for world's largest for-profit conference company
- Researched financial marketplace for industry trends and topics of concern
- Designed detailed forum agendas, including brochure copy and design
- Recruited 50 senior-level corporate executives
- Marketed individual conferences to the financial community through direct mail, advertising, and public relations

GERARD MONNEY INTERNATIONAL, Paris, France   1/98 – 10/98
Account Executive
- Analyzed distribution logistics and profit feasibility in the pharmaceutical industry
- Assisted in joint venture consultations
- Generated new-product publicity in local and trade press
- Defined corporate identity and designed corporate image promotional materials
- Initiated and oversaw all press conferences and trade shows

SHEARSON, LEHMAN, HUTTON, New York, New York   6/93 – 5/96
Account Executive Specialist
- Marketed and promoted new financial products in-house
- Supervised implementation of new computer system
- Conducted detailed seminars and training programs
- Served as corporate liaison to branch offices

GERARD MONNEY INTERNATIONAL, Paris, France   9/91 – 8/92
College Intern
- Researched U.S. and French pharmaceutical industry
- Interpreted drug descriptions and applications
- Performed various administrative tasks

EDUCATION

AMERICAN GRADUATE SCHOOL OF INTERNATIONAL MANAGEMENT   6/96 – 12/97
Thunderbird Campus, Glendale, Arizona
Master of International Management

Projects in International Marketing:
- Taco John's International/Taiwan
- Prima Diapers/Switzerland
- Tourism/Sri Lanka
- Gatorade/U.S.A.

BOSTON COLLEGE, Chestnuthill, Massachusetts   9/89 – 5/93
Bachelor of Arts
Major: Political Science/French

INSTITUTE DES ETUDES POLITIQUES, France   9/91 – 6/92
Junior Year Abroad Program

LANGUAGES

Highly proficient in **French**

ACTIVITIES

Travel throughout Europe, Africa, and the former Soviet Union
Treasurer/French Club, Toastmasters, Outdoor Adventure Club

ADDRESS

1234 Bentwood Drive, Hartford, Connecticut 06903   (203) 555-1234

GEORGE N. LATHAM

123 East Briarwood Drive • New York, New York 12110 • (518) 555-1234

QUALIFICATIONS
- *Extensive knowledge of international markets and product promotion*
- *Multinational commercial and trade consulting experience*
- *Developed experience in business planning and new business development*
- *Effective cross-cultural abilities in European and Asian business environments*

EDUCATION

AMERICAN GRADUATE SCHOOL OF INTERNATIONAL MANAGEMENT, *Glendale, Arizona*
Master of International Management *(January 1999)*

WESTERN NEW ENGLAND COLLEGE SCHOOL OF LAW, *Springfield, Massachusetts*
Juris Doctor *(May 1994)*

UNIVERSITY OF HONG KONG, *British Crown Colony of Hong Kong (June 1992 – August 1992)*
- *Legal study drawn from the resources of University of Hong Kong and Shanghai Institute of Foreign Trade focusing on the trade and commercial activities of the Pacific Rim*
- *Special emphasis on Chinese-Hong Kong Commercial Law, intellectual property rights, and the promulgation of joint venture law in the People's Republic of China*

UNION COLLEGE, *Schenectady, New York*
Bachelor of Arts, Political Science *(June 1989)*
- *Concentration in International Studies*
- *Senior thesis: The Cypriot Crisis and U.S. Strategic Interest in the Eastern Mediterranean*
- *Semester at* **College Year in Athens**, *Athens, Greece (December 1983 – March 1983)*

EXPERIENCE

CIBA-GEIGY CORPORATION, *Summit, New Jersey*
Product Management Intern *(June 1998 – Present)*
- *Participated in the drafting and presentation of marketing plan for ethical pharmaceutical product with sales of $100 million annually*
- *Assisted in the preparation of patient/physician marketing materials, including multimillion dollar national direct-to-consumer print campaign*
- *Prepared and presented to marketing management a comprehensive multi-year sales forecast relative to proposed second generation drug treatment*

KELLEHER AND FLINK, *Latham, New York*
Associate *(November 1995 – January 1997; October 1997 – May 1998)*
- *Commercial and corporate practice with emphasis in the areas of business planning, mortgage banking, commercial real estate, and bankruptcy*
- *Participation in all aspects of commercial litigation, including motion practice, pretrial conferences, and settlement negotiations*

ROEMER AND FEATHERSTONHAUGH, PC, *Albany, New York*
Associate *(September 1994 – November 1995)*
- *General litigation with emphasis in the areas of insurance defense, personal injury, matrimonial, medical malpractice, and commercial matters*
- *Responsible for prosecution and defense of claims*

WILKINSON AND GRIST, *British Crown Colony of Hong Kong*
Law Clerk *(June 1992 – September 1992)*
- *Assisted clients in intellectual property matters*
- *Researched Hong Kong legal considerations regarding foreign-based multinational corporations and the effects of labor, commerce, and trade issues*

SYSCO CORPORATION, *Albany, New York*
National Account Executive *(July 1989 – September 1991)*
- *Established and monitored national chain accounts that constituted 24 percent of branch sales*
- *Responsible for sales growth and procurement of additional volume accounts, with average annual rate of expansion over 105 percent*

LANGUAGES

Native in **English**, Proficient in **German**, Knowledge of **Greek**

HONORS & ACTIVITIES
- *American Jurisprudence Award for Academic Achievement in Antitrust Law*
- *New York and American Bar Associations*
- *American Graduate School of International Management Import/Export Club*

(Scannable)

109

Randy Sandstrum

1234 Nettlewood Place
Colorado Springs, CO 80918

Phone: (719) 555-1234
E-mail: criscito@aol.com

SUMMARY

- Highly motivated computer professional with more than ten years of combined management, supervisory, and technical experience, including:
  - Domestic/international project management
  - Technical support
  - Personnel staffing
  - Planning
  - Budgeting
  - Marketing
  - Asset management
  - Inventory management
  - Public speaking
- Recognized expert in systems administration, global help desk technology, and problem resolution.
- Skilled in developing business processes, internal/external operations, and customer relations.
- Exceptional written and verbal skills; adapt easily to multicultural environments.

COMPUTERS

Certifications: Microsoft Certified Professional (MCP), Microsoft Certified System Engineer (MCSE) June 1998
Networks: IBM 3270 and Shiva connectivity, desktop PC configuration, Ethernet and Token Ring topologies, X Window, Windows NT servers and workstations, Novell 3.x, NIC cards, Reflections, Exceed UNIX connectivity, Intergraph NFS, TCP/IP, IPX/SPX, NWlink
Operating Systems: MS-DOS, Windows 3.1/3.11/95, OS2 2.x, Warp, HP-UX UNIX
Software: Microsoft/Sybase/Watcom SQL Administration, MS Project, MS Word, Excel, PowerPoint, Access, Outlook, Lotus 1-2-3, Visio, Great Plains Accounting, MAPI and VIM mail packages, and various antivirus software (McAfee, IBM, etc.), Front Page 98, REMEDY and HEAT

EXPERIENCE

CONTRACTOR, Volt Technical/RHI Consulting, Colorado Springs, Colorado
1997–Present: Windows NT 4.0 systems administrator for the Hewlett-Packard AIT Division (Colorado Springs, Colorado) and consultant to Abacus Direct (Westminster, Colorado).
- Provided remote system administration for HP in South Queensferry, Scotland.
- Developed effective processes for meeting internal customer needs in Scotland.
- Integral member of the team responsible for developing the second largest NT network in the U.S.
- Developed a company-wide asset management program for Abacus Direct and provided technical support for Windows NT 4.0 server administration and PCs.
- Researched and developed internal service level agreements and procedures.

OFFICE TECHNOLOGY ADMINISTRATOR, City of Aurora, Aurora, Colorado
1996–1997: Directed the help desk and PC technical staff for the IT Department.
- Evaluated and implemented a new help desk call tracking system; purchased software.
- Supervised 25 technicians and contractors in a massive computer upgrade program.
- Developed processes and procedures for customers and the IT team.
- Realized a new vision of service for the IT Department.
- Improved customer mandates and negotiated service level agreements with internal management, which included all directors.

PRODUCT (PROJECT) MANAGER, Bendata/Astea International, Colorado Springs, Colorado
1995–1996: Responsible for the development of a new release of PowerHelp help desk software.
- Analyzed product potential and developed the project plan, resources, and release strategies.
- Worked closely with marketing manager to ensure the product met customer needs.
- Managed both foreign and domestic departments in research, development, quality assurance, and beta testing.
- Improved communication and processes needed for foreign development and sales teams.
- Negotiated software product enhancements and implementation for two major European companies.

EDUCATION

BACHELOR OF ARTS, Management and Human Relations (1995)

ASSOCIATE OF APPLIED SCIENCE, Microcomputer and LAN Specialist (1992)

ASSOCIATE OF APPLIED SCIENCE, Electronics (1992)
Certificate of Completion in Industrial Electronics

CONTINUING EDUCATION: Microsoft SQL 6.5 Administration, Windows NT 4.0 Core Technologies, Windows NT Administration, Windows NT Networking Essentials and Accounting I and II

Scannable

Cori Montalvo Beaubien

1234 San Pedro Avenue • Coral Gables, Florida 33156 • (305) 555-1234 • E-mail: criscito@aol.com

PROFILE
- Extensive international marketing experience at The Discovery Channel with trade and consumer initiatives.
- More than three years of advertising agency business management experience.
- Multilingual: Fluent in English and Spanish; working knowledge of Portuguese and French.

PROFESSIONAL EXPERIENCE

DISCOVERY NETWORKS LATIN AMERICA, Miami, Florida
Marketing Representative (1998 – present) and **Marketing Coordinator** (1998): Developed the annual marketing plan and budget proposal. Responsible for $3 million marketing budget. Managed the strategy development, creation, and execution of advertising, promotions, contests and sweepstakes, sales tools, presentations, events, collateral materials, direct mail advertising, and new media for The Discovery Channel, Discovery Kids, Animal Planet, and People + Arts brands.
- *Brand Management*: Developed Discovery Kids and People + Arts task force to collaborate on brand positioning and to tackle company-wide brand initiatives. Oversee strategic planning and research for sales-oriented marketing initiatives.
- *Advertising*: Oversee media strategy and creative processes for trade/consumer print, outdoor, and web advertising.
- *Promotions*: Concept, develop, and implement pan-regional and local promotions, contests, and sweepstakes. Work closely with legal and promotions agencies from concept through execution.
- *Production*: Supervise contest spots, vignettes, and interstitials from brief to storyboard, script, and air date.
- *Events*: Coordinate strategy and operations for the entertainment industry's largest Latin American trade event—The Upfront—which garnered a 20 percent increase in sales activity for 4Q 1998.
- *Direct Mail*: Extensive direct mail experience, varying from one-dimensional mailers to elaborate three-dimensional pieces with international and domestic distribution.
- *Multimedia*: Manage the development (content and design) of the Discovery Kids web site (LATAM). Supervise multimedia marketing efforts, including training the sales team using director presentations and initiating development of CD-ROM, web, and Internet activities.

TURKEL SCHWARTZ AND PARTNERS, Coconut Grove, Florida
Account Manager (1997 – 1998), **Multilingual Production Coordinator** (1996 – 1997): Managed advertising partnerships with Discovery Networks Latin America, LanChile Airlines, and Ralston Purina International. Collaborated on advertising initiatives from strategy development to execution. Presented all creative concepts to the client and conducted weekly status meetings in order to expedite projects.
- *Strategy and Research*: Developed strategic plans, cost analyses, advertising plans, competitive analyses, and new business pitches.
- *Production*: Supervised project time lines and collateral/print production; proofread and signed off on completed projects. Worked closely with production manager from sourcing, proofreading, pre-press, and press on all trilingual collateral jobs.
- *Traditional Media*: Managed media goals for clients and supervised media efforts through to completion.
- *New Media*: Initiated web marketing and advertising team.
- *Project Management*: Created and supervised production time lines and estimates for all Discovery Channel/Discovery Kids Latin America, Black and Decker Latin America, Ralston Purina International jobs. Worked closely with account team in the presentation of all collateral materials.
- *Translation*: Managed a team of translators, copywriters, and art directors in the creation and execution of all Spanish and Portuguese projects.

ACHIEVEMENTS
- Awards: 10+ Regional Addy Gold Awards from 1996 to 1999, 1998 Clio Award, 1998 Promax, Contender in the 1999 Cannes Advertising Festival, 1999 BDA Contender.
- Selected as Discovery Networks' most outstanding marketing performer in 1998.
- Ranked 8th in age group, female division of the 1998 Florida State Triathlon Championship, Gatorade Sprint Series.

EDUCATION

TULANE UNIVERSITY, New Orleans, Louisiana (May 1995)
Bachelor of Arts in English Literature, GPA 3.33
- Semester Abroad, Universidad Nebrisenssis, Madrid, Spain, Spring 1994 (European Relations and Business Affairs)

Scannable

111

Dawn M. Thomas

1234 Desierto Rico
El Paso, Texas 79912
(915) 555-1234

OBJECTIVE

A management position where education and experience, combined with positive interpersonal skills, initiative, and the capacity to motivate others, can be utilized to mutual benefit.

PROFILE

- Self-motivated, possess a high degree of professional integrity.
- Skilled in applying a logical, common sense approach to seeking practical solutions.
- Well-organized, inquisitive problem solver who enjoys challenges and thrives in a "people" environment.
- Communicate effectively when dealing with people of diverse interests and levels of authority—develop rapport easily and motivate others to maximum cooperation.

EXPERIENCE

1995 – 1999

SERVICEMASTER, Denver, Colorado
Manager, Kaiser Permanente . . . Managed 95 personnel in a clinical environment. Instilled a positive, service-minded attitude and a feeling of pride in a job well done by demonstrating a personal enthusiasm and team spirit. Maintained good public relations with facilities department and medical office administrators. Conducted bi-weekly inspections to ensure quality level is satisfactory or above. Accountable for a payroll budget of $1.2 million. Assumed responsibility for the department in the absence of the director.

Manager, Saint Anthony Central Hospital . . . Supervised 30 personnel in the maintenance of a 250-bed hospital. Maintained good public relations with patients, facility personnel, and medical staff. Trained employees in the proper use of chemicals. Inspected equipment to ensure clean conditions and good repair. Assumed responsibility for the department in the absence of the manager.

Human Resources Specialist . . . Recruited, screened, interviewed and hired for entry-level positions for 250-bed facility with a facility payroll of $400,000. Ensured that all standards are met by managers in handling all personnel actions. Performed pre-employment drug testing and criminal background checks. Conducted new hire orientation to include training of Occupational Safety and Health Administration requirements, infectious waste, hazardous communication, and personal protective equipment. Processed unemployment claims and handled workers' compensation cases.

1993 – 1995

GOODWILL INDUSTRIES, Colorado Springs, Colorado
Supervisor . . . Made changes in hiring, terminating, and employee evaluations of 35 personnel. Conducted monthly employee orientations. Maintained a $250,000 operating budget without exceeding it in any year. Coordinated with future and present property managers for placement of Attended Donation Centers. Reviewed records to establish trends in location effectiveness and merchandise type.

1986 – 1993

AMERICAN RED CROSS, Kitzingen, Germany
Bookkeeper . . . Managed $100,000 operating budget. Maintained accounts payable records, reviewed invoices and processed checks. Wrote and disbursed staff payroll. Implemented computerized accounting system and developed computerized inventory control/purchasing system for greater efficiency and cost effectiveness.

Counselor . . . Counseled service personnel and families requiring financial assistance and/or experiencing personal problems. Assisted in securing financial aid and making travel arrangements for emergency leaves. Outlined individual options and referred to other community resources.

EDUCATION

May 1995

BACHELOR OF SCIENCE DEGREE IN BUSINESS ADMINISTRATION
Regis University, Colorado Springs, Colorado

112

Scannable

CLEMENT R. FREEMAN

1234 Belden Drive • Los Angeles, California 90068 • Telephone: (213) 555-1234 • Fax: (213) 555-1234

QUALIFICATIONS
- Strongly motivated marketing professional with expertise in product development
- Excellent interpersonal and analytical skills
- Extensive customer service and consumer marketing experience
- Highly proficient in **Spanish**

EXPERIENCE

INDEPENDENT MARKETING AND MANAGEMENT CONSULTANT (August 1997 – Present)

Los Angeles Times, Los Angeles, California
- Developing and implementing a promotional program with Delta Airlines to place the *Los Angeles Times* on all international flights, giving the newspaper a more global presence
- Assisting in the search for a new distributor for the *Los Angeles Times* in Mexico
- Helping to acquire sales for the *Nuestro Tiempo* Spanish language newspaper
- Developed five-year marketing and sales plan for the *Nuestro Tiempo* Spanish newspaper

Globe Media Incorporated, Mexico City
- Account Manager for the *Los Angeles Times* in Mexico
- Secured advertising and assisted in the development of client brand awareness
- Recommended and successfully implemented structural changes in the office's staffing and operation
- Developed a computer database system for Globe's sales force in order to access pertinent client information

Freeman Cosmetics, Beverly Hills, California
- Formulated a proposal and bid for the $6.5 million Delta Airlines first class and business class amenity kit project
- Blended Delta's idea of an all-natural amenity kit with Freeman's current international marketing strategy

Assistance in Marketing, Long Beach, California
- Developed a Hispanic marketing research project for McDonald's Corporation
- Modified the English and Spanish questionnaires to reflect cultural variations between the Hispanic ethnic groups living in Southern California
- Assisted in the formation of the research test sample
- Recruited Hispanic questioners and monitored their performance

DELTA AIRLINES (1991 – 1997)

District Marketing Analyst
- Assisted in designing public relations campaign to assure Delta's eventual approval of their application for the Los Angeles–Hong Kong route
- Analyzed markets, evaluating regional demand trends and customer satisfaction
- Assisted in the development of flight services quality assurance program
- Managed international flight attendants as an International In-Flight Service Coordinator

COMPUTERS

MS Word, PowerPoint, Excel, @ Risk, Paradox, Lotus 1-2-3, FoxPro

EDUCATION

MASTER OF INTERNATIONAL MANAGEMENT (August 1996)
American Graduate School of International Management
Thunderbird Campus, Glendale, Arizona
- Emphasis in International Marketing and Sales
- Regional specialty in Latin America
- Analyzed Japanese airline industry for future growth patterns and outlook
- Winterim 1992 in Costa Rica and Nicaragua – Latin American Studies

BACHELOR OF ARTS (December 1994)
Antioch University, Yellow Springs, Ohio
- Major in Organizational Management
- Minor in Latin American Studies

 Scannable

JENNY L. HASKINS

Paraprofessional Accountant

1234 W. Rome Avenue, Phoenix, Arizona 85037

Phone: (602) 555-1234

EMPLOYMENT HISTORY

April 1999
through
Present

CONTROLLER
Omni Adams Hotel, Phoenix, Arizona
(Formerly Sheraton Phoenix Hotel)
Hired as Assistant Controller but ended as one of five controllers in three years. Managed and projected cash flow, working daily with banks, corporate office, and vendors. Supervised accounts receivable and payable. Performed usual accounting duties, including financial statements, audit schedules, budgets, and numerous special projects for owners. Utilized Lotus 1-2-3, WordPerfect, Datanamics, and Lodging Systems software.

September 1997
through
March 1999

ASSISTANT CONTROLLER/CONTROLLER
Happy Trails Resort, et al., Surprise, Arizona
(Subsidiaries of Western Savings and Loan Association)
Produced bank reconciliations, journal entries, sales and property tax returns, financial statements, reports, and budgets. Reconciled intercompany accounts, including on the books at the bank. Utilized Lotus 1-2-3 and did trouble shooting on Lodgistix hospitality software.

January 1997
through
September 1997

CONTROLLER
Outdoor Enterprises/RoadVantage Corporations
Surprise, Arizona and Carson City, Nevada
(Sister companies to Happy Trails, divisions of Thousand Trails, Inc.)
Performed cleanup and original bookkeeping, journal entry, and analysis work for multifaceted companies involved in travel package sales, insurance, road service packages, and Visa credit cards. Produced all financial statements, reports, and tax returns. Changed accounting system and setup on Lodgistix. Also used Lotus 1-2-3.

February 1994
through
January 1997

PARAPROFESSIONAL ACCOUNTANT
Deloitte Haskins and Sells, Phoenix, Arizona
Gained multi-industry experience through the Emerging Business Department. Provided range of client services from accounting cleanup and setup to financial statements, tax returns, reviews, and projected financial statements used in public offering. Produced tax returns for individuals, partnerships, and corporations, manually and on Fast-Tax software. Trained DHS personnel on Lotus 1-2-3 and used it extensively for client and administrative work. Used various software, mostly CYMA.

EDUCATION

August 1991
through
February 1994

ASSOCIATE OF ARTS
Glendale Community College, Glendale, Arizona
Major in Accounting

Scannable

MOIRA SHARP

1234 Alicia Point #201 • Colorado Springs, Colorado 80919 • Phone: (719) 555-1234

SUMMARY

- Proven sales and marketing executive with 18 years of sales management and corporate headquarters experience in all classes of trade, including specialty stores, department stores, discount centers, warehouse clubs, home centers, grocery stores, and distributors.
- Experienced in the management of sales teams and manufacturer's representatives.
- Successfully developed individuals to assume greater responsibility in a team-building environment.
- Consistent record of high achievement; exceptional administration and motivation skills.

EXPERIENCE

LEEGIN CREATIVE LEATHER/BRIGHTON, Colorado
Sales Manager, Rocky Mountain Region (March 1997 – present)
- Managed a 13-state territory with a sales volume of $11 million (Illinois and Iowa on the east, Idaho and Utah on the west).
- Increased effective core account base by 29 percent through category development.
- Achieved a growth rate of 25 percent in 1998 and 19 percent in 1997.
- Among the top 10 percent of sales managers nationwide; selected for the President's Club in 1998 for achieving a high level of sales excellence.
- Recruited, trained, and supervised eleven account executives and one area manager, mentoring two to achieve the Rising Star Award and three to the President's Club.
- Cultivated markets for handbags, watches, prestige fragrances, small leather goods, belts, fashion jewelry, sunglasses, and body and bath products with Specialty Ladies, Men's, Western, Casual, and Tourist/Resort stores.
- Developed educational program content for three biannual national sales meetings attended by 100 sales representatives.

CONAIR, INC., Arizona
Western Region Manager (May 1993 – November 1996)
- Responsible for the regional management of 13 western states, including 8 manufacturer's representative groups in the Personal Care Division.
- Developed core programs for wholesale clubs and department, drug, and grocery stores.
- Achieved 108 percent of quota over 1994 with total regional sales volume of $2.2 million.

SUNBEAM PRECISION MEASUREMENT/SUNBEAM-OSTER, INC., Arizona
Sales Manager, West (November 1991 – February 1993)
- Managed the western U.S. account base for the world's largest producer of appliances, grills, outdoor furniture, clocks, thermometers, and scales, including eight manufacturer's representative groups.
- Assumed national responsibility for The Disney Store, Disney Europe/Canada/Japan, The Price Company, Costco, Pace Warehouse Clubs, and J.C. Penney.
- Achieved regional sales volume of $15 million, 33 percent of the company's volume.
- Developed a warehouse club program that expanded sales in this trade class by 40 percent.
- Created private label and niche products for The Sharper Image, Costco, and Long's Drugs.
- Increased The Disney Store's 1991/92 sales volume by 506 percent.

EDUCATION

CARNEGIE-MELLON UNIVERSITY, Pittsburgh, Pennsylvania (1977 – 1978)

THE MANNES CONSERVATORY OF MUSIC, New York, New York (1978 – 1980)

CONTINUING EDUCATION
Completed a week-long Revlon management training program

DAWN D'AMORE POLIZZI

123 Partridge Lane • *Cherry Hill, New Jersey 08003* • *Phone: (609) 555-1234*

HIGHLIGHTS OF QUALIFICATIONS

- *Goal-oriented sales professional with more than ten years of experience in medical management and advertising sales; in-depth knowledge of medical terminology.*
- *Established reputation for increasing profitability through effective marketing.*
- *Enthusiastic and flexible with strong organization and communication skills.*
- *Self-motivated and energetic; comfortable working independently with little supervision.*
- *Skilled in negotiating and presenting material in a clear, concise, and understandable manner.*

RELEVANT EXPERIENCE

1993 – Present **MEDICAL OFFICE MANAGER, Runnemede Medical Center,** *Runnemede, New Jersey*
- *Marketed and managed the operations of a fast-paced doctor's office.*
- *Responsible for the overall profitability, operations, administration, and supervision of the medical center.*
- *Increased net profit in the first year by 50 percent and maintained steady annual growth of 15+ percent.*
- *Exceeded established goals in billing, patient enrollment, and collections.*
- *Successfully gained the participation of HMO insurance companies through an arduous application, on-site visit, and interview process.*
- *Implemented a new medical billing system for Medicare, Medicaid, HMO, and private insurance patients which reduced accounts receivable and improved the profitability of the center.*
- *Communicated with attorneys, patients, referral physicians, and insurance companies.*
- *Attended regular industry seminars, monthly pharmaceutical presentations, and national medical conventions.*

1992 – 1993 **SALES REPRESENTATIVE, AutoTrader Magazine,** *Aston, Pennsylvania*
- *Sold and serviced advertising accounts to car dealers, maintaining existing account base by providing exceptional customer service.*
- *Designed advertisement layouts and completed a two-day sales training course.*

1991 – 1992 **MANUFACTURER'S REPRESENTATIVE, 609 Wholesale,** *Williamstown, New Jersey*
- *Excelled at generating sales volume by coordinating outside promotions and through cold calling.*
- *Responsible for sales, account management, merchandising, and inventory control.*

OTHER EXPERIENCE

1998 – present **FASHION MODEL, Jo Anderson Modeling Agency,** *Cherry Hill, New Jersey*
- *Modeled high-fashion clothing in runway presentations to potential clients.*

1992 **ELEMENTARY EDUCATION TEACHER, Radix School,** *Williamstown, New Jersey*
- *Taught elementary and gifted/talented students, selling them on the concept of life-long learning.*
- *Developed lesson plans and teaching aids; planned activities and tutored special needs students.*
- *Managed the classroom, maintained records of student progress, and coordinated parent-teacher conferences.*
- *Participated in workshops, in-service programs, and other continuing professional development.*

EDUCATION

1991 **BACHELOR OF ARTS, Glassboro State College**
Major in Elementary Education with a Coordinate Minor in Psychology

1996 – 1997 **GRADUATE STUDIES, Rowan University**
Completed nine semester hours in Special Education Master's Program

Scannable

8 Geographic Location

With my international clients, the fact that they have worked, studied, lived, or traveled abroad strengthens their credentials for international jobs. Therefore, placing the geographic location of their work experience or schooling in a prominent location can be to their advantage.

Other times, it is only part of the overall design of the information. However, making it prominent does give it more importance, whether that was the intention or not.

When you really want the geographic locations of your past experience—or anything else on your résumé—to stand out, the easiest way to accomplish that is to make them flush right (pages 120–122) or to place them in the left-hand column of the résumé (page 118). Another alternative is to tab to a fixed place on the page for each location, as in the example on page 119.

All of the samples in this section will cause problems with a scanner, since they create multiple columns or place text in usual places, which confuses the OCR software. To avoid this, tuck the place names up against the text and use bold or italics to make them stand out instead.

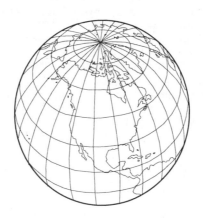

Rene Michelle Balboa

Address • Apartado 1234, Balboa, Panama • (507) 555-1234

WORK EXPERIENCE

July 1998 – Present
Balboa, Panama

DUANE & ASSOCIATES, INC.
Account Executive
- Accounts: Radisson Resorts (Bahamas), Aeromexpress Cargo (Aeromexico, Aeroperu, Mexicana), Metro Bank, Barbachano Tours
- Work closely with clients to fulfill marketing and advertising goals
- Coordinate production of print advertising, radio/TV spots, and collateral material
- Organize and oversee direct mailings

Sep. – Dec. 1997
Glendale, Arizona

HEWLETT-PACKARD – INTERAD
Marketing Research Director
- Conducted an in-depth market research study of the scanner market in China
- Developed international marketing strategy for product line

Summer 1997
New York, New York

FRITZ COMPANIES, INC.
Intern
- Assisted branch manager with sales support activities, including scheduling, follow-ups, proposal preparation, and obtaining competitive price quotes
- Culled and analyzed documentation for potential trade lane-specific sales leads

Jan. – May 1997
Glendale, Arizona

UNIVISION AND TELEMUNDO COMPANY
Consultant – Thunderbird Corporate Consulting Group
- Researched the Hispanic market in Albuquerque and Santa Fe
- Produced a report to assist in the selling of TV and radio advertising space

Summer 1994
Balboa, Panama

PANAMA CANAL COMMISSION – MARINE BUREAU
Student Assistant
- Supported tugboat operations by handling daily purchase requests and materials

Summer 1993
Geneva, Switzerland

UNITED NATIONS – ECONOMIC COMMISSION FOR EUROPE
Intern
- Researched, analyzed, and coded information concerning contracts between Eastern and Western European corporations

EDUCATION

December 1997
Glendale, Arizona

MASTER OF INTERNATIONAL MANAGEMENT
American Graduate School of International Management
Thunderbird Campus
Concentration: International Marketing

May 1996
Washington, DC

BACHELOR OF SCIENCE IN BUSINESS ADMINISTRATION
The American University
Major: International Business with a concentration in Marketing

May 1994
Leysin, Switzerland

ASSOCIATE OF ARTS
Institut Universitaire Americain de Suisse
Focus: International Business

Prior to 1993

All other education in Panama

LANGUAGES
COMPUTERS

Fluent in **English** and **Spanish** • Proficient in **French**
Paradox, WordPerfect, Lotus 1-2-3, BASIC

PERSONAL

Eligible to work in the United States and Latin America
Extensive travel experience to four continents

Pamela Ann Woodbury

WORK EXPERIENCE

M&M Mars   Hackettstown, NJ
Media Buying Analyst. Reviewed media purchasing procedures at Mars, Inc., including an examination of Agency of Record capabilities. Researched media buying alternatives and interviewed independent media service groups and corporate media centers. Created a spreadsheet system for efficient transfer of agency reports. Developed and recommended a spot market test and procedural changes for potential competitive advantages in media buying. (6/97 – Present)

Bloomingdale's   New York, NY
Executive Trainee and Assistant Department Manager. Assisted in merchandising a biannual merchandise volume of $19.3M in the Women's Coat Department and Leather Shop and managing a sales staff of 18 associates. "Superior" performance ratings led to assistant buyer responsibilities, including continued development of vendor relations and inventory reordering. (8/95 – 7/96)

International Commission for Jurists (ICJ)   Geneva, Switzerland
Lawyer's Aide. Attended and reported on hearings of the Human Rights Commission at the United Nations. Synthesized proposals for a "right to communication" and presented summary to UNESCO. Internship was conducted in French. (1/94 – 5/94)

Overseas Private Investment Corporation (OPIC)   Washington, D.C.
Marketing Intern. Researched and recruited U.S. companies to participate in investment missions to Third World countries. Prepared briefing books, researched talking points for countries, and updated all investment projects resulting from OPIC investment missions of 1987 through 1993. Position demanded rapid assimilation of complex information. (6/93 – 8/93)

Provident Bank   Cincinnati, OH
Operations Assistant, Installment Loan Department. Computed home equity and debt to income equations for mortgage loan applications. Position demanded rapid assimilation of complex information and writing detailed correspondence to private U.S. companies. (6/92 – 8/92)

EDUCATION

American Graduate School of International Management (Thunderbird Campus) Glendale, AZ
Master of International Management, GPA 3.8/4.0 (May 1998)

University of Michigan   Ann Arbor, MI
Bachelor of Arts in Political Science and French (May 1995)

LANGUAGES

Highly proficient in **French**, working knowledge of **German**, and knowledge of **Spanish**

COMPUTERS

Access, PowerPoint, PageMaker, Microsoft Word, WordPerfect, Excel, Quickbooks

ACTIVITIES

- *Front Line Forum*, Marketing Spokesperson
- *Das Tor*, AGSIM newspaper, Business Manager
- Ambassador Club, Campus Guide
- Recipient of Procter and Gamble Scholarship (NMSC)
- Kappa Kappa Gamma, Philanthropy Officer
- Ann Arbor Hunger Coalition

PERSONAL

Spent seven years in Belgium and six months in Switzerland. Traveled extensively throughout Europe, the former Soviet Union, and Central America. Active in sports, in particular, horseback riding, skiing, and tennis. Art enthusiast.

ADDRESS

1234 Sandstorm Place, Princeton, New Jersey, Phone: (405) 555-1234

Barbara J. Schreiber

PROFILE   Diversified, outgoing professional who combines an excellent academic background with vast international experience. Ambitious and creative, enjoys challenging projects. Detailed and skilled in setting priorities.

OBJECTIVE   To utilize marketing, managerial, communication, and analytical skills in an entry-level position with a multinational firm leading to a senior executive position with increased levels of responsibility

EDUCATION

AMERICAN GRADUATE SCHOOL OF INTERNATIONAL MANAGEMENT   Glendale, AZ
Thunderbird Campus   1998
Master of International Management – Marketing

ILLINOIS INSTITUTE OF TECHNOLOGY – CHICAGO KENT COLLEGE OF LAW   Chicago, IL
Juris Doctor – International Law and Business Law   1993

NORTHWESTERN UNIVERSITY   Evanston, IL
Bachelor of Arts – German Studies   1990

UNIVERSITÄT REGENSBURG   Germany
Completed courses toward German Studies degree   1989

GOETHE INSTITUT   Germany
Zertifikat Deutsch als Fremdsprache   1988

EXPERIENCE

CIRCUIT COURT OF COOK COUNTY   Chicago, IL
Office of the Chief Judge – Legal Research Division   1996
Staff Researcher

SUNRISE VILLAGE APARTMENTS   Glendale, AZ
Residential Leasing Representative   1995
- Conducted monthly market surveys of competing properties
- Marketed and leased apartment homes
- Increased and maintained occupancy levels at 97 percent

SHEA, ROGAL AND ASSOCIATES   Westchester, IL
Law Clerk   1992

CIRCUIT COURT OF COOK COUNTY   Chicago, IL
Law Clerk   1991

JAMES H. SCHREIBER, LTD.   Willow Springs, IL
Administrative Assistant   1990 – 1993
- Performed monthly billing and accounting
- Purchased, stocked, and sold merchandise for retail operations
- Reorganized and maintained the bookkeeping and filing systems
- Translated international invoices and correspondence

CRATE AND BARREL   Skokie, IL
Salesperson   1989

LANGUAGES   **German** – fluent • **French** – working knowledge

SKILLS   Windows, MS Word, Excel, Access, LEXIS/NEXIS, WESTLAW

12345 Woodbury Road • **Chicago, Illinois 60521 U.S.A.** • **Eve (708) 555-1234** • **Day (312) 555-1234**

PIA POSADA

EXPERIENCE	**INTERFACE ARNESSE INTERNATIONAL, INC.**	**Puebla, Mexico**	
	MANAGEMENT TRAINEE		Sept. 1999 – Present

- Conduct cross-cultural research on protocols and business customs for U.S. companies doing business with foreign countries
- Produced research for a tourism and trade seminar focused on Canada and Mexico
- Translation and revision of technical documents in Spanish and German
- Voice-over for International Visitors Program

WORLD TRANSLATION SERVICES   **Phoenix, Arizona**   1998 – 1999
TRANSLATOR AND INTERPRETER
- Translation of documents in Spanish, German, and French
- Simultaneous translator for Spanish/English hearings

HOTEL POSADA DE LA MISIÓN   **Taxco, Mexico**
HOTEL MANAGEMENT TRAINING PROGRAM   Winter 1998 – 1999
- Received management training in the following departments: Reservations, Front Desk, Restaurant/Bar, Kitchen, Housekeeping, and Accounting
- Conducted public relations activities and served as an interpreter

GRAFIBA S.A., Subsidiary of Reynolds Aluminum   **Barcelona, Spain**
EXECUTIVE ASSISTANT TO THE GENERAL MANAGER   1997
- Negotiated sales of manufacturing equipment to foreign customers
- Contacted potential customers and suppliers in seven different countries
- Translated documents and correspondence in Spanish, English, German, and French

ZDF GERMAN TV – SOCCER WORLD CUP   **Mexico City, Mexico**
TECHNICAL ASSISTANT TO THE PRODUCTION MANAGER   Summer 1994
- Organized interviews with well-known public figures
- Served as interpreter between German and Mexican TV crews
- Coordinated transportation of office crew and studio guests

EDUCATION   **MASTER OF INTERNATIONAL MANAGEMENT**   May 1999
American Graduate School of International Management
Thunderbird Campus   **Glendale, Arizona**
- Academic emphasis in Marketing and Management
- Relevant course work included International Marketing Management, Marketing Research, Finance and Trade, Business-to-Business Marketing, Direct Foreign Investment and Technology Transfer, and Tourism and Economic Development

BACHELOR OF SCIENCE IN POLITICAL SCIENCE   *cum laude*   1996
Oklahoma State University   **Stillwater, Oklahoma**
- Major in International Relations, Second Major in French, Minor in German

UNIVERSITÉ DE LA SORBONNE   **Paris, France**   Summer 1995
- Certificat de Langue Française

LANGUAGES   Fluent in Spanish, English, and German – Proficient in French

ACTIVITIES
- Member of Organizational Committee for two International Colloquiums on Latin American authors at Oklahoma State University
- Tae Kwon Do Instructor – Refereed and participated in tournaments; trained and supervised 15 students

OVERSEAS
EXPERIENCE
- Resided four years in Germany, fifteen years in Mexico, five years in the United States, and one year in Spain
- Traveled extensively through Mexico, the United States, and Europe

ADDRESS   Apartado Postal 123, Puebla, Pue. 72000 Mexico   (022) 555-1234

PRABUDDHA NATH BENGALI

EXPERIENCE
1998 – Present

PROJECT MANAGER
Infratest Health Research   Bombay, India
- Initiated client contact with pharmaceutical companies in Europe and the United States
- Designed qualitative and quantitative research studies to client specifications
- Coordinated international studies and conducted research briefings
- Analyzed data and made recommendations and conclusions
- Presented research findings to client
- Experienced in the areas of hypertension, cerebral vascular disease, osteoporosis, cancer, and diagnostic imaging equipment

1998 – 1998

MARKET RESEARCH ANALYST
Sandoz AG   Basel, Switzerland
- Performed qualitative and quantitative marketing research for mental health and cardiovascular products, both existing and in the research pipeline
- Participated in multinational repositioning exercise for important Sandoz product
- Interacted extensively with clinical research personnel

1997 – 1998

ASSISTANT MANAGER, NEW PRODUCTS DIVISION
Progressive Technologies, Ltd.   Gurgaon, India
- Set the groundwork for a foreign collaboration with Bausch and Lomb
- Facilitated licensing, transfer of technology agreements, company structure agreements, etc., with Indian government
- Researched markets in principal Indian cities to estimate market size
- Attended marketing seminars in the Middle East and Europe
- Consulted with financial experts regarding 5-year profit and loss estimates
- Visited B&L factory in Waterford, Ireland, to determine manufacturing process and inventory calculation methods
- Sourced indigenous equipment for the Indian factory

1996 – 1996

PRAKTICUM, MARKETING RESEARCH
Sandoz AG   Basel, Switzerland
- Conducted a multinational OTC study to identify high-growth areas and entry methods

EDUCATION
2000

MASTER OF INTERNATIONAL MANAGEMENT
American Graduate School of International Management   Glendale, Arizona

1997

SUBSIDIARY COURSES
Royal College of Medicine   London, England
- Cardiovascular Diseases and Treatments

1997

Sandoz AG   Weggis, Switzerland
- Quantitative and Qualitative Marketing Research

1995

BACHELOR OF ARTS IN INTERNATIONAL RELATIONS
Pomona College   Claremont, California

1991

HIGH SCHOOL DIPLOMA
Ecole d'Humanite   Hasliberg, Switzerland

LANGUAGES   English, German, Bengali, Hindi

INTERESTS   Extensive travel in Europe, U.S., Middle East, Kenya, and India
Acting, theater lighting design, skiing, swimming

ADDRESS   Rush 1, 12 Carmichael Road, Bombay 123, India   (022) 555-1234

9 Personal Information and References

There are very few times when personal information is appropriate on a résumé. Usually such facts only take up valuable white space, especially details such as age, sex, race, health, or marital status, and other information that potential employers are not allowed to ask anyway. There are exceptions to every rule in the résumé business, however! Here are some of them:

- International résumés in almost all cases require date of birth, place of birth, citizenship, marital status, sex, and a photograph.

- Students, or those who have recently graduated, often have a difficult time coming up with enough paid experience to demonstrate their qualifications. But, if they have held leadership positions in campus organizations or have supervised groups of people and organized activities on a volunteer basis, then an "Activities" section could strengthen those qualifications.

- A list of sporting interests would be helpful for a person looking for a sports marketing position.

- If you are looking for a job in sales where you would need to travel a great deal, or overseas where relocating an entire family becomes expensive, showing that you are unmarried and willing to travel could be helpful.

- Submitting a résumé to a U.S. company doing business in certain foreign countries could be another example. On such a résumé, an "Interests" section would show a prospective employer that your hobbies are compatible with the host country.

And the list goes on. It is important to use your judgment, since only you know best what qualifications are important in your field. For instance, on the third example in this section, you will notice that the author was a minister. In his line of work, it is very important to list a great deal of personal information that most employers would not need to know or even be allowed by law to request. In his case, the information he provided related directly to bonafide occupational qualifications for the job he was seeking.

❑ Photographs

Photographs on a résumé are required by foreign companies requesting a curriculum vita. However, in the United States, photographs are discouraged in all but

but a few industries. For instance, if you are trying for a job as an actor, model, newscaster, or in some other field where your appearance is, again, a bonafide occupational qualification, then a photograph is appropriate. Remember, there is an exception to every rule in the résumé business, so use your judgment.

❑ References

References are not usually presented on a résumé since most employers will not take the time to check references until after an interview. By then, they will have your completed application with a list of references. You also don't want to impose on your friends, associates, or former employers unnecessarily or too frequently. There is nothing wrong with taking a nicely printed list of personal references with you to an interview, however.

Here's one of those exceptions to the rule again. If an advertisement requests that a list of references be sent with the résumé and cover, then by all means supply the list. You don't want to be accused of not following directions!

Another thing: Avoid that needless line at the bottom of the résumé that says, "References available upon request". It takes up valuable white space that you need to define the sections of your résumé in order to draw the reader's eyes logically down the page.

Pretend you are an interviewer. You ask, "Will you provide references?" The interviewee replies, "Sorry, no, I can't do that." Will you even think twice about continuing to consider this candidate? I think not. It is assumed that you will provide references when requested.

AHMAD A. EL-GUIZA

Training Department
Egyptian Hospitals Program
P.O. Box 123, Cairo, Egypt

Tel. 04-1234567
Ext. 12345 or
56789, 54321

PERSONAL

Date of Birth	15 October 1963
Citizenship	Egyptian
Languages	Arabic, English, French
Health	Excellent
Marital Status	Married

EDUCATION

MSC/Diploma in the Practice of Education
Surrey University, Guildford, United Kingdom
May 1999

Bachelor of Arts English Language
Faculty of Languages, Ain Shams University, Cairo, Egypt
May 1983

EXPERIENCE

Language Instructor
Training Centre, NWAF Hospital
P.O. Box 100, Cairo, Egypt
July 1995 – Present

- Develop teaching materials for medical terminology and conduct classes for on-the-job trainees and civilian hospital staff.
- Conduct classes in beginning and intermediate English, and develop teaching materials for special-purpose English.
- Teach beginning and intermediate Arabic, and develop teaching materials.

Language Instructor
Training Centre, GAMA
King Abdul Military Hospital
P.O. Box 123, Riyahd, Saudi Arabia
May 1992 – July 1995

- Developed teaching materials for special-purpose Arabic classes.
- Taught classes in beginning and intermediate Arabic for non-Arabs.
- Conducted classes in Arabic for long-term inpatient children.

Language Instructor
Training Centre
Allied Medical Group
Joint Venture
P.O. Box 123, Riyahd, Saudi Arabia
June 1989 – April 1992

- Developed teaching materials for special-purpose English and Arabic classes.
- Taught classes in beginning and intermediate Arabic for non-Arabs and for long-term inpatient children.
- Conducted classes in English medical terminology for new Nurse's Aide Interpreters.
- Translated materials for in-service education, as needed.

Language Instructor
Staff Development
Whittier Corporation
P.O. Box 123, Riyahd, Saudi Arabia
April 1986 – May 1989

- Developed teaching materials for special-purpose Arabic and English classes.
- Taught classes in beginning and intermediate Arabic for non-Arabic speaking personnel.
- Conducted classes in Arabic literacy for Saudi civilian staff.
- Translated for various hospital development classes related to Arabic culture and traditions.

Classroom Teacher
El-Guiza Preparatory School
Cairo, Egypt
December 1983 – April 1986

- Taught English language classes to preparatory students.
- Maintained all records of student progress.

ADDITIONAL INFORMATION

- TOEFL, April 1998
- Graduate Record Examination, April 1993
- Typing Skills in English and Arabic

HENRY L. REILLY

U.S. Mailing Address • ABC Unit 12345, APO AE 09812-1234 • Phone (966) (4) 555-1234
Saudi Arabia Address • ABC DEFG P.O. Box 12, Tabuk, Saudi Arabia • Fax (966) (4) 555-1234

OBJECTIVE   Supervisor of Heavy Equipment Maintenance or related role in an international setting.

SUMMARY OF QUALIFICATIONS

- Achieved Master Craftsman status in the military/civilian heavy construction field.
- Over thirty years experience in mechanics, inspection, engineering, maintenance, and operation of dozers, graders, loaders/backhoes, forklifts, power generators, cranes, excavators, trucks, and cement mixers, including Caterpillar, Komatsu, John Deere, FMC Linkbelt, P&H, Galion, etc.
- Eleven years of active duty with the United States Armed Forces.
- U.S. Navy Construction Battalion (CB) experience for fourteen years, supervising and training CB units in all phases of the mechanics, maintenance, and operation of above-mentioned equipment.
- Over ten years of experience supervising and training Saudi Arabian Army construction engineers in all phases of mechanics, operation, and maintenance of construction and heavy equipment.
- Experienced in the supervision of multinational work forces, including Saudi Arabians, Americans, British, Filipinos, Koreans, and Jordanians.

EXPERIENCE

MAINTENANCE WORKSHOP SUPERVISOR / INSPECTOR (June 1993 to Present)
Saudi Maintenance Corporation (SIYANCO SOCP), Saudi Operation and Maintenance Co., Ltd. (SOMC), Tabuk, Saudi Arabia
Supervise and train Saudi military work force and civilian multinational mechanics assigned to the heavy equipment maintenance workshop on a Saudi military base.

Primary Responsibilities:
- Inspect, plan, direct, and supervise the operation and maintenance of all types of construction and heavy equipment and accessories.
- Organize and schedule heavy equipment repair shop operation to expedite completion of repairs.
- Analyze operational difficulties and provide corrective measures.
- Render technical assistance to subordinates.
- Conduct research, and requisition parts and supplies.
- Perform administrative functions, including payroll and timekeeping for subordinates, leave scheduling, and preparation of maintenance records and files.
- Directly supervise the work and performance of twelve mechanics and technicians.

Achievements:
- Greatly reduced turnaround time for repairs and overhaul of equipment under responsibility.
- Significantly decreased maintenance costs for repair parts and supplies to an acceptable level as a result of systematic planning, scheduling, and technical supervision of the maintenance and operation of heavy equipment.
- Enhanced the morale of subordinates through counseling and proper application of leadership.
- Promoted from Engineering Heavy Equipment Mechanic to Maintenance Workshop Supervisor in April 1999 because of exceptional technical skills and devotion to duty.

HEAVY EQUIPMENT MECHANIC (Civil Service WG-10/11) (March 1978 to May 1993)
Public Works Transportation, U.S. Naval Air Station, Kingsville, Texas
- Responsible for the maintenance, overhaul, and repair of all heavy and construction equipment, fire and crash trucks and equipment, and field and ground support equipment.
- Supervised and scheduled training of the Navy CB mechanics and operators on all heavy and construction equipment listed in the summary of qualifications section.

Scannable

EXPERIENCE
(continued)

HEAVY EQUIPMENT MECHANIC (June 1977 to February 1978)
Holders Equipment Rental Company, Corpus Christi, Texas
- Maintained and repaired all heavy and construction equipment.

ENGINEMAN FIRST CLASS PETTY OFFICER (E-6) (June 1966 to June 1977)
FIREMAN APPRENTICE FA2, U.S. Coast Guard
- Supervised mechanics and technicians aboard various ships (including five years of overseas tours) in maintaining engineering equipment, main propulsion engines and accessories, damage control, and the overhaul, repair, and operation of all heavy and construction equipment.
- Assignments also included various construction job sites and military base maintenance of heavy and construction equipment.

OTHER SKILLS
- Crane and machine shop equipment operator
- Welding
- Word processing and office equipment

EDUCATION
& TRAINING

Academic: Diploma, Waskom High School, Waskom, Texas, 1966
Industrial and Military: Various Military Institute Correspondence Courses from E-2 to E-7 on Engineman Petty Officer ratings and Warrant Officer Engineering from the U.S. Coast Guard Institute, Groton, Connecticut. On-the-job training (OJT) in heavy equipment operation and maintenance, as well as shipboard training in turbine engine mechanic fundamentals, U.S. Army Aeronautical Depot Maintenance Center, Corpus Christi, Texas.

AWARDS
- Department of the Navy Federal Service Length of Service Award for completion of 25 years of service, June 1992.
- Meritorious Service Certificate from DS/GS Supervisor, Saudi Maintenance Corporation (SIYANCO), August 1999.

PERSONAL DATA
- U.S. Citizen with valid passport
- Eligible for United Kingdom residency
- Excellent health, married
- Interests include racquetball, jogging, yoga, and bowling

Scannable

REV. RANDY J. WREN

1234 North 10th Lane • Phoenix, Arizona 85019 • (602) 555-1234

PERSONAL INFORMATION

Born: February 19, 1971, Davenport, Iowa
Height: 6' 2"
Licensed: General Council Assemblies of God
Married: March 14, 1991
Wife: Sandra, born April 4, 1972, Milwaukee, WI
Son: Andrew, born November 8, 1992
Daughter: Candace, born September 19, 1994

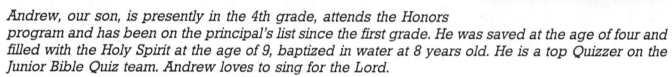

FAMILY

My wife: Sandy is my best friend and support in our home and ministry. She is warm, friendly, hospitable, and gifted. She has served as Children's Church Director, Bible Quiz Coach, and Assistant Missionette Teacher. Presently she is the Junior Bible Coach and works as a Dental Assistant. She is a spirit-filled believer.

Andrew, our son, is presently in the 4th grade, attends the Honors program and has been on the principal's list since the first grade. He was saved at the age of four and filled with the Holy Spirit at the age of 9, baptized in water at 8 years old. He is a top Quizzer on the Junior Bible Quiz team. Andrew loves to sing for the Lord.

Candace, our daughter, is presently in third grade and has been on the Honor Roll list all the way through 2nd grade. She was born again at age 7 and filled with the Holy Spirit and baptized in water. She loves to sing for the Lord. She is presently in Junior Bible Quiz and doing very well for her first year.

BACKGROUND

I was born in Iowa and raised in Phoenix, Arizona. My parents have always served the Lord. My grandfather was a Pioneering Pastor (55 years). I was saved and filled with the Holy Spirit at age 8 and called into the ministry.

MINISTRY VISIONS AND GOALS

To utilize my experience, education, and ideas • To see God build His church through the power of the Holy Spirit • To preach, teach, and lead people into a balanced Christian lifestyle – this includes worship to God, growth in Christ, caring for one another, and evangelism to our world • To challenge Christians to find and use their gifts and be motivated by the Holy Spirit.

MINISTRY EXPERIENCE

1999 – Present   Since last year we have been on the evangelism field. We have been holding revivals and concerts. I have been teaching and preaching on the use of the power of the Holy Spirit for today's Christians. We have seen many lives changed through Christ. Pastors have been uplifted and encouraged and filled with a new drive.

MINISTRY EXPERIENCE (continued)

1998 – 1999   ASSOCIATE/YOUTH PASTOR, South Mountain Assembly of God, Phoenix, Arizona
Area of Ministry:
Coordinated, planned, and directed all Youth Ministries
- Preached and taught weekly
- Planned curriculum and trained leaders
- Planned outings—youth retreats, family counseling camps
- Developed and directed fund raisers—Speed-the-Light

Coordinate, plan, and direct all Sunday school programs
- Taught Sunday school class
- Trained teachers, seminars, monthly meetings, visitation
- Taught new converts class, membership class

Pastoral care and administrative areas
- Assisted in preaching and pulpit ministries
- Performed counseling and visitation (family and one-on-one)
- Designed and produced special services—Western Round-up Sunday, Family Days

1995 – 1998   MINISTRY, North Freeway Assembly of God, Phoenix, Arizona
Coordinated the children's church for two years
- Recruited members
- Trained teams

Taught Sunday school for two-and-a-half years

Managed bus ministry
- Visitation
- Recruited leaders

EDUCATION

B.A. IN PASTORAL MINISTRY, American Indian Bible College, Phoenix, Arizona
Graduated 1998—Honor Roll, Dean's List, Valedictorian, Mission President

REFERENCES

James B. Doe
Arlington Hospital
123 North George Mason Drive
Arlington, Virginia 22205-3698
Phone: (703) 555-1234

Richard Mitchell
Cambridge Consulting Corporation
1234 N. Fairfax Drive, Suite 12
Arlington, Virginia 22203
Phone: (703) 555-1234

Stephen Gibbs, Ph.D.
Office of Institutional Research
Houston Community College
1234 Jackson Hill
Houston, Texas 77007
Phone: (713) 555-1234

Dennis Reilly
South Mountain Assembly of God
1234 Ashdown Forest Drive
Phoenix, Arizona 80991
Phone: (520) 555-1234

Heather Florio

Modeling and Fashion

▸ Helped plan and coordinate a fashion show for 200 people, Colorado Springs, Colorado	1997
▸ Modeled sportswear for the Brooks College Fashion Show, Long Beach, California	1997
▸ Swimsuit model for Back to the Beach swimwear store, Belmont Shores, California	1997
▸ Modeled business attire for the Angela Hill Television Show, New Orleans, Louisiana	1996
▸ Trained for three months with John Robert Powers Modeling School, Denver, Colorado	1994
▸ Assisted in organizing a Robinsons/May fashion show for a school fund raiser	1993

Acting and Singing

- ▸ One year of acting school at the Playwright's Workshop Theatre, Phoenix, Arizona
- ▸ Member of the St. Mary's High School choir and LTC trio (soprano)

Education

▸ Major in Fashion Merchandising, Brooks College, Long Beach, California	1997
▸ Liberal Arts Studies, Pikes Peak Community College, Colorado Springs, Colorado	1996

Customer Service, Clerical, Merchandising

- ▸ Skilled in assisting multinational clients and providing exceptional customer service.
- ▸ Made travel arrangements and assisted author on book tours.
- ▸ Accountable for accepting money from customers and opening/closing stores.
- ▸ Knowledge of WordPerfect, Windows, MS Word, Excel, Access, Hypercard, Paintbrush, etc.
- ▸ Contacted designers and wholesale representatives to arrange the purchase of inventory for upscale women's fashion boutiques; received, priced, and stocked inventory.
- ▸ Prepared visual merchandising displays using mannequins, alternatives, fabric drapes, suit/dress forms, lay down presentations, and fixtures.

Work History

▸ Administrative Assistant, ProType, Ltd., Colorado Springs, Colorado	1987 – present
▸ Sales Associate, Victoria's Secret, Colorado Springs, Colorado	1997 – 1998
▸ Sales Associate, Dillard's, Colorado Springs, Colorado	1997 – 1998
▸ Assistant Manager, Modiste, Colorado Springs, Colorado	1997
▸ Sales Clerk, Beyond the Beach, Belmont Shores, California	1997
▸ Cashier, Target, Colorado Springs, Colorado	1996
▸ Assistant to the Buyer, Posh at the Broadmoor, Colorado Springs, Colorado	1996

Challenge

▸ Participated in a Summit Adventure (Outward Bound), Yosemite, California	Summer 1995
▸ Spent three weeks testing my limits by climbing to the top of the tallest peak in California	
▸ Gained experience in rock climbing, Tyrolian traverse, and repelling	
▸ Spent a week in the Wind River Wilderness in Wyoming	

Interests

- ▸ Fashion, modeling, acting, singing, rollerblading
- ▸ Traveled throughout Europe (Germany, Holland, Austria, Luxembourg, France, Switzerland, and Italy); studied Italian; lived four years in Germany

1234 Ralph's Ridge
Colorado Springs
Colorado 80910
(719) 555-1234

10 Fonts and Bullets

Fonts (aka type style or type face) set the tone for the entire résumé. What is a font? It is that little bit of magic that enables humans to communicate in print. It is the alphabet set to music. It is art. Actually, a font is a set of curved, straight, or slanted shapes that your brain decodes into letters and then words, but that sounds too boring for a subject as fascinating as type style.

Every font has its own designer and its own personality. Each font projects a certain "feel." For instance, serif fonts (the kind with the little "feet" like the Utopia font used on this page) are considered more traditional. They are usually used as text fonts in books and magazines. Some samples include:

- Times Roman
- New Century Schoolbook
- Padua
- Bookman
- See pages 143–153 for more serif fonts

Sans (meaning "without" in French) serif fonts, on the other hand, have no "feet" and are considered more contemporary, as in:

- Helvetica (Arial)
- Avant Garde
- CG Omega
- Univers
- See pages 133–142 and 154–155 for more sans serif fonts

Although serif fonts are commonly used as text type for the main body of published works, you don't have to restrict yourself to these types of fonts for résumés. Either style produces equally impressive résumés.

Headline fonts and wild type faces have their place in design, but only in the headlines and only for very creative professions. Remember, you want your résumé to be easy to read. You will find many samples of headline fonts on pages 156–158.

In all my years of designing résumés, I have discovered that my clients don't have to understand the science behind fonts or the difference between serif and sans serif fonts, and neither do you. It is more important that you look at samples of good résumé fonts and then choose the one that makes your eyes "feel good." In other words, choose the one you like the best. Again, it comes down to personality.

If you are concerned about the scannability of your resume, remember that the fonts you choose play a major role. If you haven't read Chapter 3, now is the time to read it. Pages 20 through 22 address the scannability of fonts and bullets in particular.

❏ Bullets

Bullets are special characters used at the beginning of indented short sentences to call attention to individual items on a résumé. Short, bulleted sentences are easier to read than long paragraphs of text, and they highlight the information you want the reader to see quickly. Bullets also add some variety to a résumé and make it just a touch more creative.

In both MS Word and WordPerfect for Windows or Macintosh, clicking on "Insert" gives you access to a myriad of special characters that are not found on your keyboard. That is how the bullets in this section were created. Your printing capabilities might not allow you to have access to all of these dingbats/wingdings/symbols, but you can still be creative.

HELVETICA CONDENSED

1234, rue du Trabli ♦ 1236 Cartigny (Geneva) Switzerland ♦ Tel/Fax: 55.44.333.2222 ♦ E-mail: criscito@aol.com

PROFILE

♦ Global thinker with proven experience in developing successful marketing strategies and promotional materials in cross-cultural environments.
♦ Background in business development, strategic planning, sales, conference planning, and finance.
♦ Adept at motivating others, building trust, and positively impacting troubled client or employee relationships.
♦ Highly motivated, energetic, and results-oriented team player with excellent presentation and written communication skills.

EXPERIENCE

Recruitment and Human Resources
♦ Developed and directed the Thunderbird career management program in Europe.
♦ Provided the vision for ongoing development of innovative career services for students and alumni.
♦ Developed internships and job placement opportunities for graduate management students by calling on multinational corporations throughout Europe.
♦ Succeeded in increasing jobs and internships from ten to more than 100 per year.
♦ Created opportunities for students to visit major multinational corporations throughout Europe, which increased opportunities for students and enhanced the awareness of the university.
♦ Organized annual pan-European conferences to give human resource professionals the opportunity to discuss industry trends, compensation, and global workforce issues.
♦ Coached MBA students on job search strategies, resume and cover letter writing, interviewing techniques, and salary negotiation.

Marketing and Sales
♦ Created and implemented international marketing strategies for a U.S.-based clinical research organization that resulted in a five-fold increase in revenue and eventual sale of the company at a profit.
♦ Responsible for new business development and maintaining existing relationships with division heads of large pharmaceutical and biopharmaceutical clients.
♦ Developed marketing brochures, direct mail materials, and trade fair booth.
♦ Assisted the Motorola international marketing and sales manager in marketing radio and navigation equipment to international governments, multinational businesses, and individuals.
♦ Conducted original market research studies on the French advertising market, the market for factoring services, and the environment for Franco/American joint ventures (published in National Trade Data Bank).
♦ Developed, marketed, and sold trade communication programs to international housewares manufacturers, including Clairol, Panasonic, and Singer for *Housewares Executive*.

Finance
♦ Marketed and structured stock, bond, and hybrid security portfolios for more than 250 individual and small corporate accounts.
♦ Specialized in direct investment programs.
♦ Assisted in the overhaul of the accounting system for the Department of Commerce in Paris, France.

WORK HISTORY

The American Graduate School of International Management, Archamps, France   1997 – 1999
European Corporate Associate

HALIFAX CLINICAL RESEARCH INSTITUTE, Paris, France   1994 – 1996
Director of International Marketing

EMBASSY OF THE UNITED STATES OF AMERICA, Paris, France   1992 – 1994
Trade Event Recruiter/Exhibit Coordinator—U.S. Foreign and Commercial Service   1993 – 1994
Exhibit Attendant and Translator for Motorola, Paris Air Show, Le Bourget   1993
Marketing and Trade Promotion Intern—U.S. and Foreign Commercial Service   1992 – 1993

EDUCATION

MASTER OF INTERNATIONAL MANAGEMENT   1993
American Graduate School of International Management, Thunderbird Campus, Glendale, Arizona

BACHELOR OF ARTS, ART HISTORY (Minor in Economics)   1986
Barnard College, Columbia University

Scannable

133

ARIAL ITALIC

123 Adams Street
Denver, Colorado 80206
Phone: (303) 555-1234

PROFILE

- Results-oriented marketing professional with exceptional analytical and organizational skills.
- Entrepreneurial, energetic self-starter with broad experience in several different industries.
- Proven communication, leadership, management, and problem solving abilities.

EXPERIENCE

MANAGER, CONSUMER INSIGHTS (6/96 – 4/97)
Coors Brewing Company, Golden, Colorado

- Report and champion consumer data from Coors consumer hotline, including monthly executive summary to CEO and senior management team.
- Integral member of several cross-functional quality improvement teams, with responsibility for analysis and driving for results.
- Develop actionable tools to communicate relevant consumer hotline data across all levels of the organization and distribution channel.
- Recommend and facilitate system enhancement to accommodate more sophisticated reporting and analysis needs.

ACCOUNT EXECUTIVE, CLIENT SERVICES (2/95 – 5/96)
PROJECT DIRECTOR, CLIENT SERVICES (3/94 – 2/95)
ASSOCIATE PROJECT DIRECTOR, CLIENT SERVICES (3/93 – 3/94)
Information Resources, Inc., Chicago, Illinois

- Sold, delivered, and analyzed syndicated sales data and custom analyses to address business issues for Cereal Division, which represented approximately $3 million in revenue for IRI.
- Primary IRI contact for Kellogg's Ready to Eat Cereal Division—Consulted on pricing, trade promotion, distribution, category management, advertising, and regional and ethnic issues with all levels of brand management, market research, and sales organizations.
- Coordinated activities of individuals in several functional areas to ensure the execution and delivery of concurrent, large-scale custom analyses and weekly on-line delivery of syndicated data.
- Developed and delivered training programs on the use of IRI's proprietary database management software and expert systems, data, and methodologies for brand management, market research, and sales.

GENERAL MANAGER (9/87 – 9/89)
Lettuce Souprise You Restaurants Inc., Atlanta, Georgia

- General Manager with profit/loss responsibility for one unit grossing $1,300,000.
- Member of six-person start-up team responsible for launching and operating a chain of upscale soup and salad bar restaurants.
- Hired, trained, scheduled, and motivated staff of 55.

EDUCATION

MASTER OF INTERNATIONAL MANAGEMENT – MARKETING (5/92)
Thunderbird, American Graduate School of International Management, Glendale, Arizona

Significant Project: Consumer Marketing Consulting Project, DowBrands, Inc. (1/92 – 5/92)

- Generated and presented business plan to market plastic food storage bags and wraps in Mexico, including viability analysis, competitive analysis, product positioning, and promotion.
- Traveled to Mexico to conduct consumer and trade research.
- Selected to participate from a competitive field of advanced marketing students.

BACHELOR OF ARTS, University of Colorado, Boulder, Colorado (5/87)
Major: American Studies

SEMESTER ABROAD, Kent State University, Geneva, Switzerland (1/85 – 6/85)
International Studies Program

LANGUAGE

Working knowledge of **French**

COMPUTERS

Windows, Excel, Word, Access, PowerPoint, Harvard Graphics, Wilke Thornton CRS, Information Resources, Inc., Proprietary Database Management Software and Expert Systems

Scannable

134

ARIAL (HELVETICA)

SUMMARY
- ↦ Goal-oriented sales professional with successful experience in medical/surgical supply sales.
- ↦ Demonstrated ability to create client loyalty above and beyond the sales relationship.
- ↦ Strong background in building territories and using creative marketing approaches.
- ↦ Self-motivated and well-organized; comfortable working independently with little supervision.
- ↦ Personable with the ability to communicate well with people of diverse backgrounds and levels of authority.

EXPERIENCE

ACCOUNT MANAGER (1997 – present)
Bergen Brunswig Medical Corporation, Colorado Springs, Colorado
- ↦ Sold medical/surgical supplies, home health care products and equipment, personal health products, pharmaceuticals, and specialty products for the second largest pharmaceuticals distributor in the United States.
- ↦ Formulated, designed, and conducted sales presentations to primary care physicians, hospitals, managed care facilities, rehabilitation centers, and retailers.
- ↦ Planned and organized southern Colorado territory to increase market share.
- ↦ Grew the territory by 300 percent in less than two years, taking sales volume from $400,000 to $1.2 million per year.
- ↦ Used suggestive sales techniques to achieved sales of up to $180,000 per month.

DRIVING INSTRUCTOR (1990 – 1999)
Masterdrive, Inc., Colorado Springs, Colorado
- ↦ Taught accident avoidance and driving skills to beginning and experienced drivers.
- ↦ Implemented a driving rehabilitation program for head injury and stroke victims and those with phobic driving problems.
- ↦ Assisted senior drivers in finding solutions to age-related driving problems.
- ↦ Trained, coached, and evaluated new instructors.

MEDICAL SALES REPRESENTATIVE (1992 – 1997)
Colorado Springs Surgical and Supply Company, Colorado Springs, Colorado
- ↦ Sold medical supplies and maintained customer base through exceptional customer service.
- ↦ Increased territory sales from $200,000 to $750,000 per year with average monthly sales volumes of $45,000+.
- ↦ Added new accounts and expanded the Pueblo, Cañon City, and southern Colorado territories.

COURIER/SALES (1981 – 1992)
Federal Express, Colorado Springs, Colorado; Houston, Texas; and Memphis, Tennessee
- ↦ Managed the operations of the Hunstville, Texas, station for two years.
- ↦ Developed the account base from the ground up for this new location.
- ↦ Coordinated the pickup and delivery of packages from hundreds of accounts.
- ↦ Initiated contact with potential new accounts through phone and personal contact, generating significant increases in account base and volume.
- ↦ Upgraded volume from existing accounts and placed drop boxes.

EDUCATION

CONTINUING EDUCATION
- ↦ Graduate of the Dale Carnegie Sales Course.
- ↦ Completed courses and seminars in customer service, account retention, selling techniques, time management, and interpersonal skills.

BLAIR JUNIOR COLLEGE, Colorado Springs, Colorado (1989 – 1990)
- ↦ Completed course work in business and marketing.

MEMPHIS STATE UNIVERSITY, Memphis, Tennessee (1980 – 1982)
- ↦ Completed course work in business and marketing.

ADDRESS   1234 Mount Estes Drive, Colorado Springs, Colorado 80921   (719) 555-1234

Scannable

135

WEISSACH

PROFILE
- Experienced marketing/communications manager who enjoys challenges.
- Quick study with a strong work ethic and exceptional time management skills.
- A true leader who is calm under pressure and adept at problem solving.
- Committed team player with finely tuned interpersonal and communication skills.
- Proficient in IBM and Macintosh environments, Aldus Persuasion, PageMaker, MS Word, Excel, Access, CorelDraw, WordPerfect, and the Internet.

EDUCATION
BACHELOR OF SCIENCE, CORPORATE COMMUNICATIONS (June 1996)
Ithaca College, Roy H. Park School of Communications, Ithaca, New York

EXPERIENCE
LOAN OFFICER (1998 – present)
New Century Mortgage, Advanta Finance, Colorado Springs, Colorado
- Analyzed risk potential and made sound lending judgments on mortgage and home equity loans.
- Assisted customers in determining financial needs and recommended appropriate credit solutions.
- Interviewed loan applicants, set up and processed files, and prepared files for closing.
- Promoted and recommended products and services, answered customer inquiries, and advised customers of approval or denial.
- Built a strong base of referrals for nonconforming loans through effective outside marketing.

MANAGER ASSISTANT (1996 – 1998)
Enterprise Rent-a-Car, Chicago, Illinois and Colorado Springs, Colorado
- Assisted in the management of a car rental agency with a staff of six employees.
- Developed and coordinated a marketing plan for four distinct marketing districts; determined the target markets and surveyed potential customers.
- Developed training materials for the staff, significant improving response from new customers.
- Led the office in targeted sales to insurance customers.
- Responsible for balancing the daily cash receipts and collecting accounts receivable.
- Provided customer service to individual customers and insurance companies.

ACCOUNT MANAGER (1993 – 1996)
Public Relations Student Society of America, Ithaca College, Ithaca, New York
- Developed promotions for the events of local nonprofit organizations.
- Gained hands-on experience in the creation and production of newsletters and collateral materials.
- Designed and set up a profitable booth for the Apple Festival.
- Exceeded fund raising goals for the Cornell Mountain Bike Race.

PUBLIC RELATIONS MANAGER ASSISTANT (Summer 1995)
Regional Water Authority, New Haven, Connecticut
- Promoted summer classes for the Connecticut Water Center.
- Implemented a direct mail campaign; wrote press releases.
- Conducted telephone surveys with clients to determine customer satisfaction levels.
- Instrumental in the creation and layout of company brochures and newsletters.

ASSISTANT KITCHEN MANAGER (Summer 1994)
Steamers Bar and Grill, Guilford, Connecticut
- Maintained inventory, ordered food, and negotiated prices with vendors.
- Supervised five line workers as Head Line Cook.
- Investigated and resolved quality and service complaints, ensuring customer satisfaction.
- Maintained expenses below budget through accurate planning, purchasing, and waste reduction.

---

123 Pinon Drive • Colorado Springs, Colorado 80906 • (719) 555-1234

(Scannable)

Avant Garde Book

1234 Orchard Path Road * Colorado Springs, Colorado 80919 * (719) 555-1234

PROFILE

* Dedicated management professional with extensive hands-on experience in:
  - Office Management
  - Retail Management
  - Recreation Administration
  - New Business Development
  - Customer Relations
  - Sales/Marketing
  - Budget Administration
  - Forecasting
  - Staff Motivation
  - Purchasing
  - Inventory Control
  - Shipping/Receiving
* Skilled in combining quality and service to ensure exceptional customer satisfaction.
* Successful in product and service related environments where the ability to coordinate and control daily activities, manage projects, and interpret information has increased profitability.
* Knowledge of MS Word, Excel, Access, PowerPoint, Peachtree, and point-of-sale software.

EDUCATION

BACHELOR OF SCIENCE, RECREATION ADMINISTRATION (Fall 1999)
Eastern Illinois University, Charleston, Illinois

EXPERIENCE

MANAGEMENT/ADMINISTRATION

* Managed the daily operations of fast-paced retail stores, recreation programs, and service organizations.
* Developed and administered budgets; established long-term and short-term objectives.
* Hired, trained, scheduled, and motivated staff; evaluated performance and made recommendations for improvement or productivity.
* Identified and resolved existing and potential problems to achieve maximum return on investment and improve cash flow.

RETAIL

* Monitored flow of inventory, tracked deliveries, verified shipments, supervised warehouse, ensured proper handling of merchandise, and authorized payment of invoices.
* Investigated and selected vendors and worked closely with sources to facilitate timely delivery.
* Forecasted inventory requirements based on past performance, seasonal trends, and specials.
* Achieved an effective merchandise mix through knowledgeable selective buying.
* Created, placed, and evaluated advertising materials and merchandising displays to increase customer awareness and sales potential.
* Researched and resolved customer complaints and account discrepancies, ensuring customer satisfaction.

WORK HISTORY

Bookstore Coordinator, Colorado Technical University, Colorado Springs, CO   1999 – present
* Coordinated customer service and textbook ordering for 2,500 students.
* Established department operating processes and supervised two staff members.
* Developed customer service procedures, served as liaison between the customer and other departments, and ensured the delivery of exceptional customer service.
* Responsible for accounts receivable, cash handling, and month-end inventory of 200,000+ items.

Fulfillment Manager, Volleyball Information Products, Colorado Springs, CO   1997 – 1998
* Managed a publication and video partnership, including marketing, purchasing, order processing, customer service, inventory maintenance, shipping, bulk mailing, and payment processing.
* Performed the duties of the VIP Director from three days after hire date.
* Supervised, trained, scheduled, and evaluated the performance of customer service assistants.
* Sourced new products and followed through the development cycle to product production.
* Responsible for preparation of accounts payable/receivable and financial statements.
* Maintained database in Peachtree software and downloaded orders daily from the Internet.

Assistant Retail Manager/Buyer, West Point Gift Shop, West Point, NY   1989 – 1997
* Managed the retail operation with $2.2 million in annual retail sales and $1.2 million catalog sales.
* Hired, scheduled, and supervised a staff of 45 full-time, part-time, and seasonal sales associates.
* Sourced and purchased soft goods, books, gift items, videos, and novelty items.
* Planned and purchased an effective marketing mix and created merchandising displays.
* Developed inventory control procedures to support both retail and catalog operations.
* Served as interim manager for six months, increasing sales by 21 percent within 30 days and then trained a new manager who continued to increase sales.

Scannable

137

Univers

PROFILE
* Self-motivated professional with a diverse background in administration and contracting.
* Detail-oriented, quick learner who loves a challenge.
* Comfortable working independently and as an integrated team member.
* Strong written communication skills.
* Proficient in MS Word, Excel, Lotus, Quattro Pro, PowerPoint, Access, Windows.

EDUCATION

CONTINUING EDUCATION   1995
George Washington University
Introduction to Government Contracting

BACHELOR OF ARTS, LEGAL STUDIES GPA 3.69   1992 – 1994
College of Mount Saint Joseph, Cincinnati, Ohio

ASSOCIATE DEGREE IN BUSINESS GPA 3.41 *(cum laude)*   1989 – 1991
University of Cincinnati, Cincinnati, Ohio

MARKETING MAJOR GPA 3.5 (in major)   1987 – 1988
Xavier University, Cincinnati, Ohio

EMPLOYMENT

PRICING ANALYST, GTE (Contractor), Colorado Springs, Colorado   1996 – 1997
* Review statements of work to determine proposal requirements.
* Prepare equipment and services cost data for inclusion in bids.
* Interface with district business offices to gather and consolidate cost data.
* Update and track proposal process from submission to negotiation.
* Make formal presentations of proposals to corporate management for approval.

PROPOSAL COORDINATOR (Contractor), Science Applications International Corporation, Colorado Springs, Colorado   1996
* Assisted in the preparation of government requests for proposals.
* Prepared graphics and edited scripts used for presentations using PowerPoint.
* Modified existing proposals for best and final offer submission.
* Gathered data from all levels of corporate staff.

CONTRACT ADMINISTRATOR, Shelf Stable Foods, Cincinnati, Ohio   1995 – 1996
* Managed the administration of all current government contracts with values of up to $3 million.
* Responsible for generating major proposals, including planning, setting project timelines, and soliciting and coordinating input from others.
* Liaison for company with various government and defense contracting agencies.

LEGAL ADMINISTRATOR, General Revenue Corporation, Cincinnati, Ohio   1993 – 1994
* Managed the administration of all current state and federal licenses and bonds.
* Designed, developed, and implemented table to track state licensing requirements.
* Researched legal issues that had a direct impact on the company.
* Assistant to corporate attorney; conducted research using Lexus/Nexus, West-law, etc., for federal and state regulations affecting interstate collections.

COMMODITY ASSISTANT, Pierre Frozen Foods, Cincinnati, Ohio   1993
* Responsible for monitoring and tracking all commodity production and finished goods inventory.
* Prepared and submitted monthly accounting performance reports.

123-A Rimview Drive ✳ Colorado Springs, CO 80919 ✳ (719) 555-1234

Scannable

LUCINDA SANS

PROFILE
- Dedicated management professional with a strong international background.
- Experienced in administration, marketing, advertising, teaching, and travel.
- Effective team player with exceptional communication, interpersonal, and presentation skills.
- Well-organized problem solver with an innately inquisitive mind.
- Proven leader with the ability to motivate and manage professional staff members.

EXPERIENCE

MANAGEMENT/ADMINISTRATION
- Co-founded and managed the operations of a successful international advertising firm, generating $3–5 million in sales annually.
- Served as advertising manager responsible for supervising in-house and freelance staff.
- Developed and administered a $5 million annual budget with full P&L responsibility.
- Sourced and purchased computer network, office furnishings, and supplies.
- Negotiated with contractors to develop and install software applications.
- Continue to maintain an interest in the company, although not active in the daily management.

INTERNATIONAL
- Native born Italian who emigrated to the United States with an American wife.
- Fluent in English and Italian; proficient in French; working knowledge of Spanish.
- Traveled extensively throughout the United States, Canada, and Europe, including France, Germany, United Kingdom, Denmark, Norway, Belgium, The Netherlands, former Soviet Union, Yugoslavia, Greece, Switzerland, and Austria.
- Coordinated European tour groups for an operator specializing in educational programs to students and clients under the age of 26.
- Directed tours that included visits to significant cultural sites and foreign language courses.
- Increased bookings and sales of airline and train tickets by 10 percent each year.

MARKETING/ADVERTISING
- Owned and operated an advertising firm in Italy responsible for creating $10 million promotional campaigns for both prominent private corporations and state agencies.
- Brokered print services and coordinated the details of printing, video production, and conference presentations.
- Installed three Macintosh desktop publishing stations on a network, which increased in-house graphic and artistic capabilities and saved considerable time and cost over traditional layout, typesetting, and paste-up processes.
- Developed a low-budget promotional campaign for CTS Tours' Meeting Point at Termini Rail Stations in Rome, achieving first-quarter sales in the new office 10 percent ahead of projections.
- Experienced in the use of Quark X-Press, Aldus FreeHand, Adobe Photoshop, Adobe Illustrator, MS Word, MacWrite, PageMaker, and ClarisWorks.

HISTORY

PART-OWNER AND MANAGER, Antigone Multimedia srl, Rome, Italy	1988 – present
TOUR OPERATOR, CTS Tours, Rome, Italy	1985 – 1988
TEACHER, Private and Public High Schools, Rome, Italy	1979 – 1985

EDUCATION

MASTER OF ARTS, Modern Foreign Languages and Literature Universitá degli Studi di Roma "La Sapienza," Rome, Italy	1978
BACHELOR OF ARTS, Humanities and Philosophy Universitá degli Studi di Roma "La Sapienza," Rome, Italy	1977

123 East Willamette Avenue ∎ Colorado Springs, Colorado 80903 ∎ (719) 555-1234

Scannable

CG Omega (Optima)

1234 Ravenel Drive ‣ Colorado Springs, Colorado 80920 ‣ (719) 555-1234

PROFILE

- Quality oriented worker with a stable work history and exceptional attendance record.
- Background in failure analysis, quality control, production control, and training.
- Acknowledged expert in the fabrication of metal and optical piece parts; in-depth semiconductor and defense hardware manufacturing experience.
- Able to prioritize assignments, work independently, and cooperate as a team player.
- Skilled production control group leader with excellent interpersonal skills.

EXPERIENCE

ATMEL, Colorado Springs, Colorado (6/97 – present)
Failure Analysis Technician

- Made modifications, cut lines, and created jumpers and other circuit features on silicon wafers; modified packaged integrated circuits using focused ion beam (FIB).
- Sanded, polished, etched, gold coated, and analyzed samples with a scanning electron microscope (SEM).
- Worked from engineering drawings and change orders to ensure products matched specifications.
- Built test fixtures using manual soldering techniques.
- Developed a process for mounting and polishing samples that had been previously back ground, preventing broken samples and saving both time and money.

TEXAS INSTRUMENTS, INC., Dallas, Texas (9/82 – 4/97)
Key Accomplishments:

- Replaced a manual method of soldering joints with an automated flow soldering process.
- Suggested a design improvement that prevented an extensive amount of scrap of existing inventory.
- Recommended an alternative, comparable steel for constructing saw fixtures that permitted the production line to come back on line four days quicker.
- Submitted ten method-improvement reports in the first year with TI (quality control, manufacturing, and process improvement) that resulted in a $48,000 annual savings.
- Expedited parts through the optics fab shop when it was supposedly impossible.

Wafer Level Reliability/Failure Analysis Technician, Semiconductor Division

- Performed electrical tests of wafers and die using an HP-4156-A (semiconductor parameter analyzer) and HP-41501-A (SMU and pulse generator expander).
- Analyzed circuits using a scanning electronic microscope.

Certified Quality Control Inspector, Semiconductor Division

- Inspected wafers and die to ensure compliance with MIL-STD-105D.

Self-Directed Work Team Member, Missile Systems Division R&D

- Team member with cross-functional responsibilities for acceptance testing, assembly, scheduling, and production control of military hardware; DOD Secret Security Clearance.
- Presented daily status reports at morning production meetings.

EDUCATION

RICHLAND COMMUNITY COLLEGE, Dallas, Texas (1982)
Associate Degree in Applied Arts and Science, Manufacturing Engineering

TEXAS A&M ENGINEERING EXTENSION, Dallas, Texas (1995–1996)

- Semiconductor Physics and Chemistry I and II (40 hours), Semiconductor Processing Overview (12 hours), Microcontamination (8 hours), Mathematics for Semiconductor Technicians (16 hours)

CONTINUING EDUCATION

- MS Windows, Excel, ISO 9000, JIT, Statistical Quality Control, Six Sigma Concepts, Hazcom, Electrostatic Discharge, Statistical Process Control, and MIL-STD-2000 Certification

Scannable

Antique Olive

123 Sun Ridge Court • Woodland Park, CO 80863 • Fax: (719) 555-1234 • Phone: (719) 555-1234

PROFILE

- Experienced IT manager and programmer who thrives in a fast-paced, constantly changing, and challenging environment.
- Respected for the ability to build customer trust and close the sale.
- Loyal professional who is able to see the whole picture while managing the details.
- Adept at developing creative solutions and meeting challenges head on.
- Team player with exceptional communication skills; comfortable presenting to high-level executives.

COMPUTERS

Programming Languages: C, Visual Basic, SQL, SAS, EasyTrieve, Access, SyncSort, Excel macros, COBOL, PASCAL, JCL, REXX, TSO, EHLLAPI.

Operating Systems: MS-DOS, Windows NT/95, OS-2, MVS, UNIX.

Databases: Access, SAS, dBASE, Oracle, SQL Server, SyBase, ODBC, DAP.

Networking: TCP/IP, NetBEUI, Ethernet, Token Ring.

Hardware: Mainframes, minicomputers, microcomputers, Sun, HP, and IBM.

Application Software: MS Word, Excel, PowerPoint, Outlook, Exchange, MS Project, Crystal Reports, Extra, Monarch, SAS.

EXPERIENCE

Technical Consultant, MCI Call Center, Colorado Springs, Colorado (1997 – present)
- Evaluated and recommended solutions for internal help desk traffic in two call centers with a total of 200 employees.
- Wrote a business case for workforce management, including capital budgeting, requisitions, and cash flow analysis.
- Served as project manager for vendor implementation of IT systems.
- Evaluated vendor products and made purchase recommendations.
- Designed call reporting systems and wrote a program using Visual Basic and SAS to extract data from call center reports.

Marketing Product Manager, MCI, Colorado Springs, Colorado (1995 – 1997)
- Evaluated advanced technologies for MCI's multimedia division, including voice-recognition systems, voice processing platforms, high-speed consumer Internet access (ADSL), and bundling opportunities.
- Conducted market research and generated product ideas for small business markets and consumers.
- Worked closely with Telstra (Australia) and British Telecom (U.K.) in the development and implementation of an online video game product, including creation of a business plan and marketing strategy.
- Participated in trade shows and met with senior executives of multimedia companies to negotiate bundling opportunities.

Call Plan Manager, MCI, Dallas, Texas (1992 – 1995)
- Responsible for forecasting all of MCI's customer service calls (50 million calls per year).
- Analyzed call traffic data and developed reports for 3,000 agents and ten call centers.
- Integrated planning for all ten call centers to form an enterprise view of the operations.
- Determined budget and staffing impacts of call volumes on the call centers.
- Designed a real time database to route all MCI customer service call volume based upon the caller's usage patterns.
- Developed a new linear regression model for call planning using SAS and very complex statistical calculations.
- Created a mathematical model for a process that was previous manual and intuitive.

EDUCATION

Master of Arts, International Management (1994)
University of Texas, Dallas, Texas

Bachelor of Arts, Historical Studies (1990)
University of Texas, Dallas, Texas
Dual minors in computer science and marketing

Scannable

141

ARIAL NARROW

12345 W. Grisly Road ❑ Peoria, Arizona 85345 ❑ (602) 555-1234

OBJECTIVE A challenging customer service position in the financial services industry

QUALIFICATIONS
- ❑ Proficient on DLS and CPI systems for cashiering, customer service, letter writing, and payoffs
- ❑ New loan setup and documentation experience
- ❑ Excellent customer relations and problem solving skills; get along well with people
- ❑ Aptitude for numbers and skilled in math, organization, and reasoning
- ❑ Knowledge of Windows, MS Word, Excel, Access, and Lotus 1-2-3
- ❑ Type 50+ words per minute; 10-key by touch; microfiche experienced

EXPERIENCE

MERIDIAN MORTGAGE CORPORATION, Phoenix, Arizona (July 1999 to Present)
Payment Processor
- ❑ Prepared and posted all payments and payoffs to borrower accounts on both Data Link and CPI systems daily.
- ❑ Posted regular and modified payments, curtailments, reversals, special deposits, fees, and adjustments.
- ❑ Maintained daily suspense report, balanced batches, and prepared reports.
- ❑ Data entry for Investor Accounting Department.

Customer Service
- ❑ Answered phones and assisted customers by researching and completing histories, amortization schedules, credit verifications, payoff updates, letters of receipt, payment research, address changes, etc.
- ❑ Position required heavy emphasis on situations involving payments.

Receptionist and Other Duties
- ❑ First position was as Receptionist but quickly moved up to other areas.
- ❑ Letter Librarian duties included creation and maintenance of all office letters on both DLS and CPI systems.
- ❑ Prepared payroll and submitted biweekly; transferred payments to new servicers weekly.
- ❑ Operated and maintained various office machines.
- ❑ Maintained files for all monetary batch work and suspense reports.
- ❑ New loan setup and investor transfers.

SOUTHWEST SAVINGS & LOAN ASSOCIATION, Phoenix, Arizona (August 1997 to July 1999)
Vault Coordinator, Quality Control/Lending Operations Department
- ❑ Coordinated vault activities and supervised vault staff, including prioritization and delegation of daily work.
- ❑ Maintained vault records, documentation for other departments, monthly reports, and canceled files.
- ❑ Organized loan sales, RTC review projects, audits of loan files, and semiannual vault inventories.
- ❑ Managed retention procedures (preparation and shipping); created and utilized reports for files-out inventory.
- ❑ Ensured that department followed proper security guidelines.

Vault Clerk, Lending Operations/Loan Administration
- ❑ Retrieved, returned, maintained, logged, and microfiched files.

REPUBLIC AUTOMOTIVE PARTS, INC., Phoenix, Arizona (June 1994 to July 1996)
Front Office Secretary/Input Clerk
- ❑ Operated phone system (30 lines and intercom); typed letters and forms; sorted mail; maintained jobber files.
- ❑ Reconciled daily accounts for company store locations and input accounts payable.
- ❑ Maintained and input parts received in daily shipments; adjusted computer inventory.

File Clerk/Receiving Clerk
- ❑ Maintained accounts receivable files; purged invoice files; created and distributed monthly price sheets.
- ❑ Adjusted computer inventory; cross-referenced packing lists; ordered part shipments via computer; maintained receiving department files.

AMERICAN PAGING OF ARIZONA, Phoenix, Arizona (August 1995 to January 1996)
Administrative Assistant
- ❑ Handled customer complaints, solved problems, greeted clients, and answered phones.
- ❑ Prepared payroll, maintained employee files, scheduled meetings and appointments.
- ❑ Ordered supplies; typed invoices, charts, letters, memos; sorted and filed contracts.

CENTER CITY

1234 McBurney Boulevard, Colorado Springs, Colorado 80911

E-mail: criscito@aol.com

Phone: (719) 555-1234

PROFILE
- Creative management professional with more than 18 years of diverse experience.
- Self-starter with strong customer service, problem solving, and organizational abilities.
- Successful in taking risks and making management judgments while considering overall organizational objectives.
- Able to work effectively with people from diverse cultural backgrounds.
- Effective team player with strong interpersonal and communication skills.
- Proficient in MS Word, Excel, PowerPoint, Publisher, and Lotus 1-2-3.

EXPERIENCE

DEPUTY CLERK III   1990 – present
4th Judicial, El Paso County District Court, Colorado Springs, Colorado
- Set up and managed the Court's Self-Help Center to assist defendants who choose not to use an attorney.
- Coordinated clinics for divorce, custody, adoption, etc., staffed by volunteer attorneys.
- Wrote brochures, simplified language of existing materials, and created packets of forms and court procedures.
- Represented the 4th Judicial District on the State of Colorado Consumer Relations Board.
- Tracked expenses using spreadsheets and accounted for all funds.
- Developed policies and procedures for the El Paso County Combined Court Clerk's Office.
- Designed and set up a web site for the 4th Judicial District's home page.

INSTRUCTOR   1989 – 1990
YMCA Downtown Branch, Colorado Springs, Colorado
- Coordinated summer youth programs, including classes, instructors, advertising, and registration.
- Taught gymnastics and racquetball classes to teen-agers and young children.

SELF-EMPLOYED MUSICIAN   1979 – 1989
Classically Trained Guitarist, New Mexico, Texas, and Colorado
- Studied under Master Guitarists, Chet Atkins and Hector Garcia.
- Made several recordings, including one album of original music.

MANAGER   1977 – 1978
Santa Fe Motel, Santa Fe, New Mexico
- Managed all aspects of a 53-room motel in a vacation resort town.
- Hired, trained, and supervised a staff of three workers.
- Responsible for maintaining all financial records and administering the budget.

EDUCATION

MASTER OF BUSINESS ADMINISTRATION   October 1998
University of Phoenix, Colorado Springs, Colorado

GRADUATE STUDIES   1989 – 1990
Arapahoe College, Denver, Colorado

BACHELOR OF ARTS, ENGLISH LITERATURE   1977
University of New Mexico, Albuquerque, New Mexico
University of Oklahoma, Norman, Oklahoma

BOOK ANTIQUA

OBJECTIVE   An entry-level accounting position with the opportunity for growth.

PROFILE
- Self-motivated junior accountant with a recent undergraduate degree.
- Ambitious professional who enjoys the challenge of learning new things.
- Team player with strong communication and interpersonal skills.
- Dependable and meticulous; can see the big picture without getting lost in the details.
- Experienced in MS Word, Excel, PC Payroll, and proprietary accounting software.

EDUCATION

BACHELOR OF SCIENCE, ACCOUNTING   May 1999
Regis University, Colorado Springs, Colorado
Relevant Course Work: Advanced Accounting, Cost Accounting, Tax I/II, Governmental Accounting, Intermediate Accounting I/II/III, Principles of Accounting, Managerial Accounting.

EXPERIENCE

CENTURY SMALL BUSINESS SOLUTIONS/COMPREHENSIVE ACCOUNTING, Colorado Springs, Colorado   1998 – present
Staff Accountant
- Process 70 payroll accounts for 21 clients and prepare quarterly payroll reports, including federal, state, and unemployment reports.
- Calculate and prepare state, city, and county sales tax reports for 16 clients.
- Reconcile bank accounts to both the bank and client.
- Work closely with a certified public accountant to resolve complex problems.
- Input data and compile financial statements for 14 companies, including balance sheets, income statements, detailed general ledgers, trial balances, and cash flow statements.
- Calculate and process monthly federal tax deposits.
- Responsible for training a new payroll clerk.

ALAN D. RAPP, M.D., Colorado Springs, Colorado   1995 – 1998
Administrative Assistant
- Provided administrative assistance in a busy cardiologist's office.
- Scheduled appointments and communicated with contracting insurance offices.
- Posted procedures and payments to the computer system in a UNIX environment.
- Served as a liaison between the doctor and his patients, hospitals, pharmaceutical companies, and insurance companies.

CARDIAC ASSOCIATES, Colorado Springs, Colorado   1994 – 1995
Medical Receptionist
- Provided medical support for a cardiology practice.
- Answered multiple incoming lines and ensured that patients were satisfied.
- Scheduled routine and emergency appointments.

COMMUNITY SERVICE
- Active member of the Institute of Management Accountants (IMA)
- Assisted with a girls' softball league for the Parks and Recreation Program.

ADDRESS   1234 Summerset Drive, Apt. B ❖ Colorado Springs, Colorado 80920
Phone: (719) 555-1234 ❖ E-mail: criscito@aol.com

Gazette

PROFILE
- ❖ Dedicated study coordinator with a background in nursing and a strong work ethic.
- ❖ Reliable and hard working with the ability to make processes better and to add value.
- ❖ Team player with good communication and interpersonal skills.
- ❖ Versatile, quick learner who adapts easily to new situations.

CREDENTIALS
- ❖ Licensed Practical Nurse, State of Colorado
- ❖ Registered Pulmonary Function Technologist by the NBRC

EXPERIENCE

CLINICAL RESEARCH COORDINATOR (1997 – Present)
Asthma & Allergy Associates, PC, Colorado Springs, Colorado
- ❖ Coordinated studies for pharmaceutical companies.
- ❖ Interpreted protocols and researched patient database to find appropriate candidates.
- ❖ Gathered data on patients to meet inclusion/exclusion criteria.
- ❖ Recruited, screened, and enrolled patients in studies.
- ❖ Evaluated results and prepared work sheets and case reports for drug companies.
- ❖ Succeeded in over-enrolling studies through exceptional patient recruiting.

PULMONARY NURSE (1994 – 1996)
Big Thompson Medical Group, Aspen Medical Center, Loveland, Colorado
- ❖ Assisted pulmonologists in recertification of sleep studies.
- ❖ Completed certificates of medical necessity for insurance companies, Medicare, and managed care organizations.
- ❖ Coordinated clinical research and performed routine clinical nursing responsibilities, including phone triage, phlebotomy, limited scope x-rays, and patient education.

CLINICAL MANAGER/OWNER (1988 – 1994)
Major Medical Supply, Loveland, Colorado
- ❖ Built this medical supply company from the ground up to a base of 200 oxygen customers.
- ❖ Developed forms and education pieces; efficiently scheduled home visits for patients.
- ❖ Wrote policies and procedures and trained staff for JCAHO accreditation.
- ❖ Created a Better Breathers support group; coordinated mailings, arranged for speakers, and hosted meetings.
- ❖ Planned and supervised recreational trips for patients, ensuring that medical needs were met and developing good customer relations.

DIRECTOR OF CARDIOPULMONARY SERVICES/STAFF THERAPIST (1980 – 1988)
McKee Medical Center, Loveland, Colorado
- ❖ Managed 20 respiratory therapy staff in providing cardiac, EEG, and EMG services.
- ❖ Scheduled and trained staff, prepared budgets, and ensured quality of patient services.
- ❖ Coordinated several clinical research trials of drugs.
- ❖ Administered respiratory therapy treatments, pulmonary function tests, EEG tests, and attached Holter monitors.

EDUCATION

POUDRE SCHOOL OF PRACTICAL NURSING, Fort Collins, Colorado
- ❖ Completed one year of nursing studies

CONTINUING EDUCATION
- ❖ Respiratory Therapy Practical Training, St. Vincents Hospital, Leadville, Colorado
- ❖ Intensive Care Nursing Course, St. Vincents Hospital, Leadville, Colorado
- ❖ EEG Technician Training, North Colorado Medical Center, Greeley, Colorado
- ❖ Limited Scope Radiology Course, Aspen Medical Center, Loveland, Colorado

---

1234 Pine Ridge Road ❖ Woodland Park, Colorado 80863 ❖ (719) 555-1234

123 Luxury Lane
Colorado Springs, CO 80921

Phone: 719.555.1234
criscito@aol.com

PROFILE

➤ Goal-oriented technical sales professional with successful experience in:
  – Getting to the decision maker — Team building
  – Discerning customer needs and preferences — Leadership
  – Closing the sale — Upselling
➤ Respected for depth of product knowledge and enthusiasm for sales.
➤ Able to ask the right questions to get to the heart of customer needs.
➤ Effective team player with outstanding communication and interpersonal skills.
➤ Technically oriented; able to grasp new technologies quickly.

EXPERIENCE

SALES ENGINEER (1991 – present)
Omega Limited, Colorado Springs, Colorado
➤ Successfully sold electronic and computer components and subassemblies to large companies in a territory that covered Denver to Albuquerque.
➤ Achieved $2.1 million in sales, exceeding goals by $200,000.
➤ Acquired in-depth knowledge of computer subcomponents and their specifications.
➤ Position involved technically oriented sales to design engineers and the ability to prove that the represented product was better.

OUTSIDE SALES REPRESENTATIVE (1990 – 1991)
Minet Electronics, Colorado Springs, Colorado
➤ Colorado representative for a distributor of electronic components.

ASSISTANT MANAGER (1988 – 1990)
Avco Financial Services, Colorado Springs, Colorado
➤ Solicited new consumer and retail loan business.
➤ Received, processed, and closed loan applications, including personal and real estate loans.
➤ Evaluated the credit worthiness of clients and established credit limits.
➤ Collected delinquent accounts.

U.S. ARMY SERGEANT (1981 – 1988)
Communications Chief, Fort Carson, Colorado
➤ Planned and supervised telecommunication requirements for combat battalions.
➤ Supervised equipment installation, maintenance, and training.
➤ Motivated, supervised, and evaluated 38 personnel.
Senior Communication/Electronics NCO, Kaiserslautern, Germany
➤ Responsible for planning and coordination of tactical and administrative radio, telephone, and teletype operations in support of more than 22,000 personnel.
➤ Designed telephone systems to meet special user requirements.
➤ Planned and supervised war-time headquarters communications consisting of microwave, land line, and telecommunications systems.
➤ Coordinated communications support for major NATO exercise.
➤ Supervised 65 German national and U.S. military personnel.

COMPUTERS

➤ Proficient in Windows, MS Word, Access, PowerPoint, Internet Explorer, and WordPerfect.
➤ Selected by Microsoft to beta test Office 98 and Microsoft Network 2.5.

EDUCATION

BACHELOR OF BUSINESS ADMINISTRATION, U.S. Armed Forces Institute
➤ Completed three years of coursework toward an undergraduate degree

146

Scannable

CENTURY SCHOOLBOOK

1234 Whimsical Drive • Colorado Springs, Colorado 80917 • (719) 555-1234

PROFILE
- Experienced buyer with a strong work ethic and proven customer service skills.
- Dependable and flexible professional who is accustomed to working under tight deadlines.
- Detail-oriented and self-motivated; able to work independently with little supervision.
- Effective team player with strong communication and interpersonal skills.
- Proficient in Windows 95, Macintosh, MS Word, Excel, Lotus 1-2-3, and WordPerfect.

EXPERIENCE

SIGNAL PROCESSING TECHNOLOGIES, Colorado Springs, Colorado (1996 – present)
Buyer (1998 – present)
- Responsible for purchasing silicon wafers, computers, test and capital equipment, furniture, office supplies, maintenance contracts, uniforms, and services for this manufacturer of semiconductors.
- Effectively negotiated contracts to keep costs within budget.
- Reduced costs through improved sourcing, negotiations, and communications with suppliers.
- Improved efficiency of the purchasing department through consolidation of suppliers.
- Planned and coordinated annual parties for 200 employees, including facilities, food, entertainment, and gifts.

Customer Service Representative, Sales and Marketing Department (1996 – 1998)
- Provided customers with price quotes, delivery information, and collateral materials.
- Served as an escalation point for dissatisfied customers.
- Set up trade show booths for outside sales representatives.
- Tracked revenue and pending orders using sophisticated spreadsheets.
- Prepared commission reports for sales by location.

TEMPORARY AGENCY POSITIONS (1994 – 1995)
Administrative Assistant, Pacific Architects & Engineers, Fort Carson, CO (1 year)
- Assisted the safety manager in the daily operations of the office.
- Processed worker's compensation claims; scheduled and administered new employee training.
- Checked work sites for compliance with OSHA requirements and wrote accident reports.
- Maintained a detailed database of accidents and injuries.

Office Manager, Cripple Creek & Victor Gold Mine Co., Victor, Colorado (3 months)
- Managed the on-site office of the construction project manager and accountant.
- Reviewed and maintained construction contracts, specifications, and drawings.
- Responsible for subcontractor relations, filing, and telephone customer service.

WRICO CORPORATION, San Antonio, Texas (1992 – 1993)
Office Manager
- Managed the office of this busy distributor of hazardous chemicals.
- Processed accounts receivable and accounts payable; maintained customer accounts.
- Responsible for collections, order processing, and shipping and receiving.

U.S. ARMY RESERVES (1993 – 1994)
Operating Room Technician
- Completed an eight-month operating room technician school.

JUNGLE LABORATORIES, Cibolo, Texas (1988 – 1992)
Customer Service Representative
- Took orders for aquarium products from large-volume distributors and maintained close customer contact.
- Prepared extensive financial and sales reports.
- Resolved problems for clients and maintained exceptional customer satisfaction ratings.

EDUCATION

PIKES PEAK COMMUNITY COLLEGE, Colorado Springs, CO (1994)
- Liberal arts studies toward an Associate of Arts Degree

Scannable

147

BOOKMAN LIGHT

QUALIFICATIONS

Registered Dietitian with three years of varied nutritional experience.
Self-motivated professional with a strong background in counseling and planning.
Detail oriented, accurate, and well organized; able to learn quickly.
Team player with outstanding interpersonal, communication, and presentation skills.
Knowledge of MS Word, Excel, Windows, and Cbord computer software.

EXPERIENCE

Counseling and Health Promotion

+ Counseled patients with nutritional challenges, high cholesterol, diabetes, heart disease, renal failure, cancer, weight control, and gastrointestinal disorders.
+ Part of an interdisciplinary Health Care Team responsible for preparing patients for discharge and ensuring adequate nutritional care on return home.
+ Planned and coordinated community-wide programs for National Nutrition Month and National Diabetes Awareness Month.
+ Instructor of Slim for Life program through the American Heart Association of Colorado.
+ Presented "Food Pyramid and Healthy Eating" to students in the Pikes Peak Community College Nursing Program.

Clinical Nutrition

+ Managed the nutritional needs of patients in acute, subacute, and long-term care facilities.
+ Prepared in-depth assessments and care plans for patients requiring nutritional support, therapeutic diets, nutritional counseling, and dietary supplementation.
+ Constantly reviewed and revised the seven-day menu cycle in response to patient feedback.
+ Coordinated nutritional efforts between inpatient dialysis center and outpatient renal and diabetes care center.
+ Participated in patient rounds with physicians and interfaced with interns and nursing staff.

Administration and Training

+ Ensured patient satisfaction as part of the Continuous Quality Improvement Team.
+ Leader of the Nutritional Task Force, a nursing and dietary team for resolution of interdepartmental problems.
+ Developed clinical pathways for CVA, congestive heart failure, and bypass patients as a member of the Stroke Rehabilitation Team.
+ Member of an interdisciplinary team responsible for redesigning hospital processes to improve the efficiency and effectiveness of operations.
+ Assisted in redesigning the medical chart to reduce paperwork and simplify charting.
+ Planned and presented in-service programs for nursing and nutritional services staff.

WORK HISTORY

Clinical Dietitian, Penrose St. Francis Healthcare System, Colorado Springs, Colorado, 1995 – present
Clinical Dietitian, St. Thomas More Hospital, Cañon City, Colorado, 1994 – 1995

EDUCATION

Bachelor of Science in Nutritional Sciences, 1994
University of Oklahoma Health Sciences Center, Oklahoma City, Oklahoma

---

1234 South Boulder Road ✦ *Boulder, Colorado 80303* ✦ *(303) 555-1234*

Scannable

PALATINO

123 West Polk Street → Colorado Springs, Colorado 80907 → (719) 555-1234

PROFILE
- Dedicated child care provider with more than eleven years of experience.
- Fair and just with a commitment to setting a good example.
- Patient instructor who enjoys working with children.
- Effective team player with strong interpersonal and communication skills.

EXPERIENCE

SITE ASSISTANT
Children's World at Divine Redeemer, Colorado Springs, Colorado (1998 – present)
- Teach social, physical, and fundamental academic skills to children ages four to seven in the Educare Preschool Program.
- Coordinate activities in the after-school program for elementary school children.
- Supervise children during activities and counsel them when social, academic, or adjustment problems arise.
- Ensure a safe and clean environment; arrange interest areas, including a sports zone, challenge and nature programs, and Imagine That area.
- Develop and implement lesson plans and instruction aids/materials.
- Maintain attendance records, daily notes, and student accident reports.
- Assume responsibility for the site director in her absence.
- Communicate information to parents and accept payments.

FAMILY SUPPORT GROUP LEADER
U.S. Army, Fort Carson, Colorado (1998 – present), Graf/Hohenfels, Germany (1988 – 1990)
- Responsible for providing information, referral assistance, and social/emotional support for the families of active duty soldiers.
- Coordinated fund raising events, support group, activities, parties, and briefings.
- Recruited, trained, and managed volunteers; tracked and recorded volunteer hours.
- Supervised the meals on wheels program for families in need.
- Welcomed new families and made hospital visits.
- Developed telephone trees to facilitate communication of information.

KINDERGARTEN AIDE, **St. Michael School**, Annandale, Virginia (1997 – 1998)
- Assisted kindergarten teachers and filled in as a substitute teacher when needed.

NANNY, **The Loomis Family**, Arlington, Virginia (1996 – 1997)
- Assumed full responsibility for the care of two children, ages 4 and 5, in their home until the children were old enough to attend full-day kindergarten.

DAY CARE PROVIDER, **Self-employed**, Meridian, Idaho (1993 – 1995)
- Provided in-home care for preschoolers.
- Evaluated stages of development, designed curriculum, and ensured a loving and safe environment for children.

HOSTESS AND CHILD CARE PROVIDER
The Ethel Kennedy Family, Cape Cod, Massachusetts (Summer 1982)
- Lived in the summer home on the Kennedy estate.
- Hosted parties and tennis matches, ran errands, and did the shopping.
- Helped to care for the two youngest children when needed.

EDUCATION

UNDERGRADUATE STUDIES
Northern Virginia Community College, Alexandria, Virginia (1998)
Central Texas College, Killeen, Texas (1985)

Scannable

149

GARAMOND

1234 Stonedike Drive, Apt. B • Colorado Springs, Colorado 80907 • (719) 555-1234

PROFILE

- Experienced Advertising Manager with demonstrated success in:
  - Major accounts
  - Classified advertising
  - Retail accounts
  - Research
  - New product development
  - Sales and training
  - Budgeting
  - Coordination
  - Planning
- Practical problem solver with exceptional analytical and communication skills.
- Strong background in building territories and using creative marketing approaches.
- Demonstrated ability to create client loyalty above and beyond the sales relationship.

EXPERIENCE
Major Accounts

- Managed the major accounts sales team for *The Gazette,* a Freedom Corporation newspaper with a circulation of 121,000.
- Made sales presentations to senior management of major accounts in cities nationwide.
- Developed a new client base and expanded existing accounts to achieve $17 million in annual sales.

Research and New Product Development

- Directed the development of new products for *The Gazette,* including demographic and psychographic market research, feasibility studies, product design and packaging, budgeting, scheduling, implementation, sales, and P&L.
- Analyzed statistical and other market data and used the results to create sales presentations to advertisers; researched and analyzed competitive information.
- Developed the *Home in Colorado* magazine that won the 1999 Addy Award for best in-home publication with more than four colors.
- Created a sales and marketing product manual to delineate newspaper sections, ancillary products, and the demographics of the newspaper's core readership.
- Implemented the weekly *Peak Computing Magazine* from the ground up; responsible for product development and design, placement, distribution, setting advertising rates, sales, and creation of a companion Web site.
- Created an innovative research program for the *Times Advocate* (Team: Research) that provided the sales team with comprehensive and accurate demographic information to increase the effectiveness of client advertising.

Classified and Retail

- Directly supervised all commercial advertising sales functions for the *News-Chronicle* (a community newspaper with a circulation of 30,000), increasing revenues by 22 percent.
- Sold Pennysaver classified advertisements to commercial account advertisers.
- Increased gross sales by 131 percent, decreased new territory delinquencies by 40 percent, and achieved the top 10 percent of all sales executives.

Management/ Supervision

- Developed and managed sales budgets of up to $17 million; accountable for print bids, production costs, and full profit and loss.
- Hired, trained, supervised, and mentored up to seven sales representatives.
- Negotiated dollar volume contracts averaging $400,000, with highest being $1 million.
- Increased revenues for *Peak Computing* by 870 percent in 13 months and display advertisers by 400 percent, ultimately achieving $750,000 in annual sales.
- Managed the Porch Plus alternative delivery program for the *Times Advocate,* increasing revenues from $130,000 to $1.5 million.
- Collaborated with *The Orange County Register* to increase the market for Porch Plus.
- Served as co-chair of the San Diego North County Golf Expo, generating significant goodwill and $70,000 in new revenue.

EDUCATION

BACHELOR OF ARTS, Material and Logistics Management   1988
Michigan State University, East Lansing, Michigan

12 Delaware Road
Manitou Springs, CO 80829
Telephone: (719) 555-1234

SUMMARY OF QUALIFICATIONS

- Goal-oriented professional with a Bachelor of Arts degree in political science (with distinction).
- Skilled in political processes, community organization, research, and problem solving.
- Loyal team player with proven interpersonal, communication, and presentation skills.
- Energetic and self-motivated; able to handle multiple projects simultaneously and manage time efficiently.
- Proficient in WordPerfect, Windows 95, e-mail, Quickbooks, and Internet software.

RELEVANT EXPERIENCE

EXECUTIVE DIRECTOR   1998 – present
Cripple Creek Casino Association, Cripple Creek, Colorado
- Represent the gaming industry before local, regional, and state elected officials.
- Act as a spokesperson for the industry with news media.
- Responsible for nonprofit accounting, membership development, and the creation of group marketing opportunities.
- Work closely with the City Council, Planning Commission, Historic Preservation Association, State Gaming Commission, and Teller County Commissioners.
- Board Member of the Colorado Springs Convention and Visitor's Bureau charged with the responsibility of increasing tourism in the Pikes Peak region.
- Board Member of the Teller County Economic Development Council.
- Member of the Steering Committee for the Southeastern Teller County Planning Initiative.
- Member of the Steering Committee for the Cripple Creek Marketing Plan.

ELECTION COMMISSIONER
University of Colorado, Colorado Springs, Colorado   1996
- Increased voter turnout threefold to set a record for the university.
- Developed advertising campaigns and slogans.
- Organized "meet the candidate" events and solicited donations from local businesses and media.
- Served as co-chair of the Judicial Board, interpreting and executing the University constitution.
- Established guidelines and policies for the university Election Committee.
- Managed poll staffing, setup, and ballot counting; coordinated post-election banquet.

LEGISLATIVE INTERN
Assistant Minority Leader Diana DeGette, Denver, Colorado   1995
- Analyzed pending legislation, wrote speeches, and assisted in campaign activities.
- Coordinated and scheduled events; provided administrative assistance.
- Sat in on House floor and Judicial Committee sessions, took notes, and prepared reports.
- Maintained liaison with government agencies affected by proposed or pending legislation.
- Researched and assisted in preparation of legislation.
- Mediated between the Congresswoman, her constituents, the House of Representatives, and other government agencies.

PERSONNEL CONSULTANT   1990 – 1991
Adams & Associates, Anchorage, Alaska
- Recruited temporary employees and matched them with employer needs.
- Make cold calls to potential customers.
- Resolved problems between customers and temporary placements.

EDUCATION

BACHELOR OF ARTS, University of Colorado, Colorado Springs, Colorado   1996
- Major in Political Science
- Graduated with distinction while working full time to finance education

Serif Fonts

Sans Serif Fonts

Antique Olive . . . . The quick brown fox jumps over a lazy dog
Page 141 THE QUICK BROWN FOX JUMPS OVER A LAZY DOG

Aquiline Book . . . . The quick brown fox jumps over a lazy dog
Page 162 THE QUICK BROWN FOX JUMPS OVER A LAZY DOG

Arial Helvetica . . . . The quick brown fox jumps over a lazy dog
Pages 26, 27, 28, 29, 33, 44, THE QUICK BROWN FOX JUMPS OVER A LAZY DOG
57, 71, 83, 84, 88, 164, 165,
168, 169, 182, 193, 189, 212,
222, 223, 254–262, 266, 268

Arial Italic . . . . *The quick brown fox jumps over a lazy dog*
Pages 59, 61, 89, 109, 134, *THE QUICK BROWN FOX JUMPS OVER A LAZY DOG*
174, 175, 198, 269, 270

Arial Narrow (Helvetica Narrow) . . . . The quick brown fox jumps over a lazy dog
Pages 68, 125, 142, 228, 229 THE QUICK BROWN FOX JUMPS OVER A LAZY DOG

Arial Narrow Italic . . . . *The quick brown fox jumps over a lazy dog*
Pages 93, 185, 264 *THE QUICK BROWN FOX JUMPS OVER A LAZY DOG*

Avant Garde . . . . The quick brown fox jumps over a lazy dog
Pages 43, 105, 111, 137, 161, THE QUICK BROWN FOX JUMPS OVER A LAZY DOG
190, 196, 203, 252, 253

Avant Garde Italic . . . . *The quick brown fox jumps over a lazy dog*
Pages 72, 176 *THE QUICK BROWN FOX JUMPS OVER A LAZY DOG*

Century Gothic . . . . The quick brown fox jumps over a lazy dog
Page 180 THE QUICK BROWN FOX JUMPS OVER A LAZY DOG

CG Omega (Optima) . . . . The quick brown fox jumps over a lazy dog
Pages 50, 120, 140, 186 THE QUICK BROWN FOX JUMPS OVER A LAZY DOG

Chelmsford Book . . . . The quick brown fox jumps over a lazy dog
Page 82 THE QUICK BROWN FOX JUMPS OVER A LAZY DOG

Corporate Rounded . . . . The quick brown fox jumps over a lazy dog
Pages 40, 102, 238, 239 THE QUICK BROWN FOX JUMPS OVER A LAZY DOG

Corporate Rounded Oblique . . . . *The quick brown fox jumps over a lazy dog*
Page 116 *THE QUICK BROWN FOX JUMPS OVER A LAZY DOG*

Futuri Condensed . . . . The quick brown fox jumps over a lazy dog
Pages 56, 230–232 THE QUICK BROWN FOX JUMPS OVER A LAZY DOG

Headline Fonts
(for use only in creative industries and never as text fonts)

Agincort Italic . . . . *The quick brown fox jumps over a lazy dog*
No samples   *THE QUICK BROWN FOX JUMPS OVER A LAZY DOG*

AVALON QUEST . . . . THE QUICK BROWN FOX JUMPS OVER A LAZY DOG
No samples   THE QUICK BROWN FOX JUMPS OVER A LAZY DOG

Blox . . . . The quick brown fox jumps over a lazy dog
No samples   **THE QUICK BROWN FOX JUMPS OVER A LAZY DOG**

BodiniPoster . . . . **The quick brown fox jumps over a lazy dog**
No samples   **THE QUICK BROWN FOX JUMPS OVER A LAZY DOG**

Broadway . . . . **The quick brown fox jumps over a lazy dog**
Page 166   **THE QUICK BROWN FOX JUMPS OVER A LAZY DOG**

Brush Script . . . . *The quick brown fox jumps over a lazy dog*
Pages 118, 273   *THE QUICK BROWN FOX JUMPS OVER A LAZY DOG*

Buckingham . . . . The quick brown fox jumps over a lazy dog
Pages 56, 190   THE QUICK BROWN FOX JUMPS OVER A LAZY DOG

Bullwinkle . . . . The quick brown fox jumps over a lazy dog
No samples   THE QUICK BROWN FOX JUMPS OVER A LAZY DOG

Chili Pepper . . . . The quick brown fox jumps over a lazy dog
No samples   THE QUICK BROWN FOX JUMPS OVER A LAZY DOG

Clearface Contour . . . . The quick brown fox jumps over a lazy dog
No samples   THE QUICK BROWN FOX JUMPS OVER A LAZY DOG

Commercial Script . . . . *The quick brown fox jumps over a lazy dog*
Pages 43, 188, 267   *THE QUICK BROWN FOX JUMPS OVER A LAZY DOG*

CooperBlack (Copperfield) . . . . . . **The quick brown fox jumps over a lazy dog**
Pages 45, 298   **THE QUICK BROWN FOX JUMPS OVER A LAZY DOG**

Domenic . . . . **The quick brown fox jumps over a lazy dog**
Pages 65, 299   **THE QUICK BROWN FOX JUMPS OVER A LAZY DOG**

ExPonto . . . . *The quick brown fox jumps over a lazy dog*
Page 49   *THE QUICK BROWN FOX JUMPS OVER A LAZY DOG*

Frederick . . . . The quick brown fox jumps over a lazy dog
Pages 174, 203, 274 . . . . THE QUICK BROWN FOX JUMPS OVER A LAZY DOG

Freestyle Script . . . . The quick brown fox jumps over a lazy dog
Pages 236, 237, 271 . . . . THE QUICK BROWN FOX JUMPS OVER A LAZY DOG

Harem . . . . The quick brown fox jumps over a lazy dog
Pages 291, 295 . . . . THE QUICK BROWN FOX JUMPS OVER A LAZY DOG

Hobo . . . . The quick brown fox jumps over a lazy dog
No samples . . . . THE QUICK BROWN FOX JUMPS OVER A LAZY DOG

IVY LEAGUE SOLID . . . . THE QUICK BROWN FOX JUMPS OVER A LAZY DOG
PAGE 185 . . . . THE QUICK BROWN FOX JUMPS OVER A LAZY DOG

Jewel . . . . The quick brown fox jumps over a lazy dog
Pages 47, 51 . . . . THE QUICK BROWN FOX JUMPS OVER A LAZY DOG

Lalique . . . . The quick brown fox jumps over a lazy dog
No samples . . . . THE QUICK BROWN FOX JUMPS OVER A LAZY DOG

Linotext . . . . The quick brown fox jumps over a lazy dog
Page 303 . . . . THE QUICK BROWN FOX JUMPS OVER A LAZY DOG

Monotype Corsiva . . . . The quick brown fox jumps over a lazy dog
Page 289 . . . . THE QUICK BROWN FOX JUMPS OVER A LAZY DOG

Moravian . . . . The quick brown fox jumps over a lazy dog
Page 57 . . . . THE QUICK BROWN FOX JUMPS OVER A LAZY DOG

Murray Hill . . . . The quick brown fox jumps over a lazy dog
No samples . . . . THE QUICK BROWN FOX JUMPS OVER A LAZY DOG

Penwin . . . . The quick brown fox jumps over a lazy dog
No samples . . . . THE QUICK BROWN FOX JUMPS OVER A LAZY DOG

Poetica Chanceryl . . . . The quick brown fox jumps over a lazy dog
No samples . . . . THE QUICK BROWN FOX JUMPS OVER A LAZY DOG

Quetzalcoatl . . . . The quick brown fox jumps over a lazy dog
No samples . . . . THE QUICK BROWN FOX JUMPS OVER A LAZY DOG

Saddlebag . . . . The quick brown fox jumps over a lazy dog
Page 170 . . . . THE QUICK BROWN FOX JUMPS OVER A LAZY DOG

Sanvito Italic . . . . The quick brown fox jumps over a lazy dog
No samples   THE QUICK BROWN FOX JUMPS OVER A LAZY DOG

Schehererade . . . . The quick brown fox jumps over a lazy dog
Page 178   THE QUICK BROWN FOX JUMPS OVER A LAZY DOG

Shelley Volante . . . . The quick brown fox jumps over a lazy dog
Page 105   THE QUICK BROWN FOX JUMPS OVER A LAZY DOG

University Ornate . . . . The quick brown fox jumps over a lazy dog
Pages 46, 62   THE QUICK BROWN FOX JUMPS OVER A LAZY DOG

Viva Regular . . . . The quick brown fox jumps over a lazy dog
No samples   THE QUICK BROWN FOX JUMPS OVER A LAZY DOG

Write Bold . . . . The quick brown fox jumps over a lazy dog
Page 48   THE QUICK BROWN FOX JUMPS OVER A LAZY DOG

11 Graphic Lines

All of the résumés in this book were typeset using common word processing software (MS Word and WordPerfect for Windows). That means you can reproduce everything you see in these pages, including the graphic lines. These lines can be either horizontal, vertical, or full page borders.

Lines at the top of the résumé can be used to set the name and address section(s) apart from the text so the eye can be drawn to the most important information first.

Horizontal lines between sections allow the reader to focus on each section separately and draw the eye from section to section, especially when there is little room for extra white space (which can serve the same purpose). The creative use of horizontal or vertical lines adds pizzazz to the design of a résumé without appearing too overdone. Résumés created with such lines can be used in all but the most conservative of industries.

It is important, however, to avoid the use of too many lines with different thicknesses on the same page. The résumé can get "busy," which makes the reader work too hard. It is a good idea to use no more than two line widths per résumé. For instance:

This line is .02 inch thick.

And this one is .005 inch thick.

You might combine the two together.

The samples that follow will give you some ideas for ways to use lines in a résumé. There are lines on almost every résumé in this book, but the ones in this chapter and on pages 24, 25, 36, 37, 52, 65, 73, 88, 92, 93, 116, 134, 149, 172, 177, 178, 179, 186, 194, 199, 220, 224–226, 229, 236, 244–247, 249–251, 267, 268, and 272 might offer you even more unique ideas.

BEATRICE MONROE

PROFILE
* Caring teacher with more than 20 years of experience; Colorado Teaching Certificate (K-7)
* Strong background in elementary education, arts, math, language, and problem resolution
* Dedicated to creating stable learning environments and inspiring students to do their best
* Experienced in fund raising, grant writing, and program development

EDUCATION

POSTGRADUATE STUDIES (1985 – Present)
University of Colorado and Webster University, Colorado Springs, Colorado
* Eighty hours of postgraduate work in education
* Recipient of the first Space Foundation scholarship for Colorado Springs teachers (1986)

MASTER OF ARTS (1985)
Colorado College, Colorado Springs, Colorado
* Major in Elementary Education

BACHELOR OF ARTS (1969)
Southern University, Baton Rouge, Louisiana
* Major in elementary education, minor in history

EXPERIENCE

TEACHING
Queen Palmer Elementary School (5th Grade), Colorado Springs, Colorado (1995 – Present)
Emerson Junior High School (6th Grade), Colorado Springs, Colorado (1990 – 1995)
James Monroe Elementary School (6th Grade), Colorado Springs, Colorado (1985 – 1990)
Fremont Elementary School (1st and 6th Grades), Colorado Springs, Colorado (1976 – 1985)
Garfield Elementary School (4th and 5th Grades), Colorado Springs, Colorado (1971 – 1975)
* Taught academic, social, and motor skills to elementary and junior high students in team teaching, combination, and special classes
* Prepared objectives and outlines for courses of study and assisted in developing curriculum
* Counseled students when adjustment and academic problems arose and met with parents
* Prepared, administered, and corrected tests; kept attendance and grade records.

SPECIAL PROJECTS
* Assisted in coordinating the tutoring program at Queen Palmer Elementary (1995 – 1996)
* Taught outdoor education, wrote grants, and obtained funding for the High Trails program (1980 – 1996)
* Participated in District 11 Leadership in Science Training (1995 – 1996)
* Mentored students as part of the East Middle School Mentoring Program (1994 – 1995)
* As part of a team, developed the language and math curriculum for District 11 (1992 – 1993)
* Assisted with the Buddie System mentoring program between 6th and 2nd graders (1992 – 1993)
* Helped with the planning and development of the Special Needs Committee, Special Student Training (1991 – 1993)
* CSEA School Representative for James Monroe Elementary (1991 – 1992)
* Selected as the CSEA delegate to the Colorado State Delegate Assembly (1989 – 1990)
* First sponsor and coordinator for the Student Council at James Monroe Elementary (1990)
* Participated in the Peer Math Meet for 6th graders at Emerson Junior High (1990)
* Art coordinator and representative for James Monroe Elementary (1985 – 1990)
* Historian for James Monroe Elementary PTA Committee (1989)
* Holmes Junior High Accountability Committee representative (1980)
* Supervised a Colorado College student teacher (1978)
* Sponsor and dance instructor for 1st grade through 6th grade students (1972 – 1974)

AFFILIATIONS
National Education Association, Colorado Education Association, Colorado Springs Education Association (CSEA), Delta Sigma Theta, St. Mary's Catholic Church

Address * 123 Skyway Boulevard #222 * Colorado Springs, Colorado 80906 * (719) 555-1234

Henry Wight

1 Sandcastle Court
Pueblo, Colorado 81001
(719) 555-1234

PROFILE

- Professional manager with more than 20 years of materials management experience.
- Background in manufacturing, production control, master scheduling, material flow, capacity planning, inventory control, purchasing, and warehousing.
- Certified Practitioner of Inventory Management, American Production and Inventory Control Society.
- Able to see the big picture, motivate teams to excellence, and get results.
- Self-motivated and focused; comfortable working independently with little supervision.
- Effective team player with excellent interpersonal and communication skills.
- Knowledge of material requirement planning (MRP) software and spreadsheets.

EXPERIENCE

MFG. APPLICATION CONSULTANT, Born Information Services, Pueblo, Colorado (1998 – present)
Implement J.D. Edwards manufacturing software at client companies and provide after-purchase service. Advise clients on best practices and recommend effective solutions to manufacturing challenges. Customize the software to meet client needs and train users after installation.

MATERIAL CONTROL MANAGER, Atlas Pacific Engineering Company, Pueblo, Colorado (1987 – 1998)
Direct the production control, inventory control, and warehousing departments for a manufacturer of industrial/commercial food processing equipment. Oversee the staffing and scheduling of entire machine shops, welding, fabrication, and assembly areas. Directly hire, supervise, and evaluate three supervisors. Develop, implement, and manage operating budgets, allocating resources to achieve program goals. Purchase $11 million per year and oversee $80 million in production. Analyze customer requirements and ensure that their needs are met.

- Achieved and maintained 99 percent inventory accuracy on more than $8 million of materials while at the same time reducing inventories by 20 percent.
- Improved on-time shipments to 97 percent through the development and implementation of effective forecasting, production scheduling, and capacity planning.
- Successfully integrated three acquired companies into the system, improving their inventory accuracy and on-time shipments.
- Implemented J.D. Edwards material requirements planning software system.

PRODUCTION CONTROL MANAGER, NBI Corporation, Boulder, Colorado (1984 – 1987)
Managed the production of word processors in a company growing 50 percent per year. Scheduled production and workers. Managed the stockroom using MRP.

- Implemented just-in-time inventory philosophy, resulting in a 33 percent reduction in work in process.

MANAGER OF MASTER SCHEDULING, NBI Corporation, Boulder, Colorado (1981 – 1984)
Supervised production scheduling. Used marketing forecasts to develop short-term and long-term manufacturing strategy. Developed overall company business plan.

- Reduced finished goods inventories from $13.8 to $4 million in a company with an annual growth rate of up to 50 percent while meeting the goal of shipping products within three days of order receipt.

PLANNER, Sundstrand Aviation Company, Denver, Colorado (1978 – 1981)
Responsible for evaluating ship capacity relative to projected workloads.

- Assessed and advised plant and corporate management on the adequacy of computer-based MRP systems, leading to the re-implementation of the system.

EDUCATION

BACHELOR OF ARTS, PSYCHOLOGY, Stockton State College, Pomona, New Jersey

CONTINUING EDUCATION
- Financial Management Seminar, American Management Association
- Material Requirements Planning, Oliver Wight
- Management of Human Resources Seminar, Rocky Mountain Employers Council

PUBLICATIONS & AFFILIATIONS

- Author of "Sundstrand: A Case Study," chapter in *Computers in Manufacturing*, Auerbach, 1981.
- Member of the American Production Inventory Control Society (1976 – present); former officer of the Denver Chapter.
- Chairman of the Board (1994 – 1996), Pueblo Diversified Industries (a nonprofit organization that employs and develops the skills of handicapped people); member 1991 – 1996; coordinated a national search for a new chief executive officer.

Scannable

Genean Decker

123-C East Cheyenne Mountain Blvd. #333
Colorado Springs, Colorado 80906
Telephone: (719) 555-1234

PROFILE

- Creative professional with a diverse background in sales, finance, and administration.
- Self-starter with definitive problem solving and organizational abilities.
- Effective team player with strong interpersonal, communication, and presentation skills.
- Licensed in Colorado and California for Series 6 and 63, life, accident, and health insurance.
- Skilled in IBM and Macintosh computers, MS Word, Excel, PowerPoint, Claris Works, Windows, MS-DOS, and basic office equipment.

EXPERIENCE

FINANCIAL SALES

- Prospected and developed a client base for annuities, mutual finds, and life, disability, and long-term care insurance.
- Ranked nationally in the top third in sales with a major financial services company.
- Developed a strong knowledge of the principles of insurance, investing, and financial planning.

ADMINISTRATION

- Owned and managed a company that provided sign language interpreting services.
- Accountable for long-range planning, profit and loss, controlling costs, invoicing, bookkeeping, collecting accounts receivable, and monitoring financial performance.
- Supervised, motivated, and evaluated assistants; delegated work to team members.
- Coordinated an off-site seminar for 120 participants nationwide, including registration, record-keeping, fee collection, and arranging for guest and speaker lodging and transportation.
- Verified, printed, and distributed checks and submitted payment schedules to the state capital for reimbursement.
- Obtained quotes, assisted with formal bidding process, sourced vendors, and negotiated contracts for purchasing.

COMMUNICATION

- Developed and presented seminars to individual business owners.
- Worked with administrators, doctors, and other professionals to ensure clear communication between deaf and hearing parties.
- Maintained high levels of confidentiality for clients.
- Participated on the student evaluation team to assess skills and progress.
- Interviewed and screened personnel for perspective placement in positions.
- Acted as a liaison between parents and site director.

WORK HISTORY

Registered Representative, Prudential Preferred Financial Services, Colorado Springs, Colorado	1997 – present
Self-Employed, Sign Language Services, Colorado Springs, Colorado	1996 – 1997
Sign Language Interpreter II, Office of Education, Santa Clara, California	1995 – 1996
Head Teacher, Ames Child Care Center, Mountain View, California	1994 – 1995
Administrative Assistant, ChoiceCare Personnel, San Jose, California	1992 – 1993
Buyer Assistant, San Jose State University, Logistical Services, California	1988 – 1991

EDUCATION

BACHELOR OF ARTS, CHILD DEVELOPMENT   1994
San Jose State University, San Jose, California
- Minor in Deaf Education and Communications

Personal Resume of
ANTHONY S. McDONALD

1234 W. Cactus Avenue   Home: (602) 555-1234
Peoria, Arizona 85345   Fax: (602) 555-5678

- QUALIFICATIONS -

The entrepreneurial spirit, dynamic energy, and sagacity to help plan and lead a good business opportunity to its optimum profit, value, growth, synergism, and success. Extensive experience in financial planning, budgeting, negotiations, control, analysis, and reporting. An in-depth knowledge and extensive experience in general and cost accounting; computer operations, data processing and management information systems; billing, credit and collections; purchasing and inventory control. Creative skills in marketing, sales, new product development, pricing, and customer service. Excellent communication, organization, and problem solving skills and the leadership, discipline, enthusiasm, and ethics to effectively direct, develop, and motivate human resources.

- EXPERIENCE -

McDONALD GROUP, INC., Birmingham, Alabama
Corporate Construction Analyst/Manager, from November 1997 to March 1999, for sixteen cable television systems operated in Louisiana, Alabama, and Georgia. Major responsibilities/contributions:
- managed $20 million capital budget including negotiating, purchasing, and tracking of fixed assets and of materials and labor for the construction of cable extensions, upgrades, rebuilds, and fiber optic projects;
- development of automated systems to project costs, determine feasibilities, track capital expenditures, analyze variances, and control inventory.

AMERICAN TELEVISION AND COMMUNICATIONS CORPORATION, BIRMINGHAM DIVISION
(Subsidiary of TIME, INC.) Birmingham, Alabama
Financial Vice President, Board of Directors, from June 1993 to April 1997, for major metropolitan cable television systems and advertising business. Major responsibilities/contributions:
- strategic business planning with detailed capital and operating budgets, re-estimates and cash flow forecasts;
- effective management and accurate reporting of balance sheet position, P&L performance and source and use of funds, with supplemental reporting to SEC, FCC, franchising authorities, and other regulatory agencies;
- development and direction of general and cost accounting, billing, credit and collections, purchasing, inventory, computer and management information systems;
- development of strong internal control, audit, and accountability procedures;
- development and direction of human resources department policies and wage/benefit plans;
- analyses of demography, critical success factors, ROI, IRR, NPV, and cost variances;
- initiation and implementation of substantial revenue enhancement and cost containment programs;
- successful rate increase and re-franchising negotiations;
- due diligence and successful negotiations for acquisition of Bessemer Cable.

- EDUCATION -

BACHELOR OF SCIENCE DEGREE, ACCOUNTING
University of Akron, Ohio (June 1983)
Member Reserve Officers Training Corps (ROTC)

KRISTIN E. COX
1234 East Linda Vista
Flagstaff, Arizona 86004
(520) 555-1234

PROFILE
- Accomplished pianist and flutist with performance and teaching experience.
- Effective team leader with strong communication and interpersonal skills.
- Disciplined student who achieves goals through hard work and perseverance.

EXPERIENCE

Teaching
- Taught private piano and flute lessons at home, 30–60 minutes per student.
- Skilled in teaching to a child's ability while keeping the pace quick and interesting.
- Adept at using questioning tactics to validate understanding of students.
- Tutored elementary flute students as an assistant to band directors (1994–1996).
- Lectured and performed for local elementary schools (1997–1998).

Performance (Piano)
- Received an honorable mention at the Flagstaff Youth Orchestra Festival (1996).
- Performed with the Coconino High School Jazz Ensemble I (1996–1998).
- Recitals: James Anthony Honor Recital (1998), Northern Arizona University Summer Music Camp Honor Recitals, Junior and Senior Divisions (1993–1997), Karen Maison Studio of Piano Recitals (four times in 1997), Solo Suzuki Piano Books 3–5 Recitals (1991–1994).
- Performed three times a year for Northern Arizona University Preparatory School of Music Recitals (1986–1995).
- Piano ensembles: "A Grand Suzuki Concert" (1991), "Fall Spectacular" (1993).
- Played for services at Federated Church, Shepherd of the Hills Lutheran Church, and Trinity Heights Methodist Church as needed.
- Accompanied solo instruments during the Northern Arizona Solo and Ensemble Festivals at Northern Arizona University summer music camp, at recitals, and for school choirs and orchestras.

Performance (Flute)
- Received an honorable mention at the Flagstaff Youth Orchestra Concerto Festival (1997) and at the Flagstaff Youth Orchestra Concerto Festival (1995).
- Member of the Northwest Regional Orchestra Arizona (1996–1998), Arizona All-State Band (1996– 1998), Coconino High School Symphonic Band and Marching Band (1995–1998).
- Performed in the Northern Arizona University Summer Music Camp Honor Recitals, Junior and Senior Divisions (1995–1998).
- Participated in the Northwest Arizona Junior High School All-Star Music Festival (1995) and Flagstaff Youth Orchestra (1994–1995).

Volunteer
- Played a variety of popular music from many generations for a local nursing home.
- Member of the All Stars Leadership and Community Service Club (1995–1996).
- Youth Board Member for the Northern Arizona chapter of the American Red Cross (1997–1998).
- Served food at the Sunshine Rescue Mission and participated in National Honor Society community cleanup projects.

EDUCATION

Coconino High School, Flagstaff, Arizona (1995–1999)
- Selected for Who's Who Among High School Students (1996–1997).
- National Honor Society (1997–1998); Honor Roll (1995–1998).
- Attended the three-day Southwest Leadership Summit (1997).

Scannable

DAVID M. BOWEN
123 West Woodmen Road
Colorado Springs, Colorado 80919
(719) 555-1234

OBJECTIVE: A challenging, career-oriented position as a member of an electronics engineering technology team.

SUMMARY OF QUALIFICATIONS:
▸ Background encompasses experience in:
- Quality control/quality assurance
- Electronics/mechanics
- Precision-process maintenance
- Robotics transfer systems
- Fabrication
- Semiconductors
- Systems chemistry
- Pneumatic systems
- Vacuum systems
- Diffusion CMP
- Purchasing
- Computers

▸ Strong communication, leadership, management, and problem solving skills.
▸ Able to work with minimal supervision and as a cooperative team member.
▸ Detail-oriented, self-motivated work style; proven ability to master new skills quickly.

EXPERIENCE:
1996 – present

EQUIPMENT ENGINEERING TECHNICIAN
LSI Logic, Colorado Springs, Colorado
▸ Senior technician responsible for repairing electrical, robot, computer, communications, hardware, and I/O systems associated with the automated wet station, furnaces, Mirras chemical/mechanical processors, sorters, load pod transfers, Ontraks wafer cleaners, etc.
▸ Use SPC and COMETS to tracking problems that affect defect density, thereby improving yields.
▸ Design and implement system enhancements and install new equipment into the fabrication line.
▸ Interface with process and equipment engineers to evaluate system changes.
▸ Perform preventive maintenance on all automated wet stations and other equipment.

1994 – 1996

FIELD SERVICE ENGINEER AND SITE MANAGER
Submicron Systems, Inc., Colorado Springs, Colorado
▸ Senior technician responsible for repairing electrical, robot, computer, communications, hardware, and I/O systems associated with the automated wet station.
▸ Increased equipment availability from 78 to 94 percent in the first month by reducing down time.
▸ Responsible for the procurement, distribution, maintenance, and replacement of inventory.
▸ Prepared daily and weekly technical reports for senior management.
▸ Trained customer maintenance technicians in the operation and troubleshooting of equipment.
▸ Maintained 24-hour on-call status for technical assistance and emergency situations.

1990 – 1994

ELECTRONICS LINE MAINTENANCE TECHNICIAN
Digital Equipment Corporation, Colorado Springs, Colorado
▸ Tested, diagnosed, and repaired processors, options, peripherals, memories, and power supplies.
▸ Evaluated results of specialized testing on production change notices and wrote process flow procedures together with manufacturing engineers.
▸ Planned and implemented schedules, process manuals, schematics, and diagrams.
▸ Assured post-production quality for newly developed systems, VAX/VMS, and related subsystems.
▸ Conducted monthly, quarterly, and yearly preventive maintenance.
▸ Carried out failure analysis procedures in dispositioning high-capacity disk drives.
▸ Tracked failures and otherwise monitored yields to determine trends.
▸ Facilitated meetings, trained personnel, and disseminated information to team members.

EDUCATION & TRAINING:
1994

BACHELOR OF SCIENCE IN ELECTRICAL ENGINEERING TECHNOLOGY
BACHELOR OF SCIENCE IN TELECOMMUNICATION ELECTRONICS TECHNOLOGY
Colorado Technical College, Colorado Springs, Colorado
▸ Additional emphasis in mathematics
▸ Maintained a 3.5 grade point average while working full time
▸ Special Project: Designed and built a working prototype of a DC variable power supply

CERTIFICATIONS, Digital Equipment Corporation, Colorado Springs, Colorado
▸ ISO 9000 Process Technician, Six Sigma Production, Team Concepts, Total Quality Management, Safety, Cleanroom Protocol, Technical Updating, and Process/Manufacturing

Scannable

Aaron Corell

QUALIFICATIONS
- Result-oriented and imaginative interactive designer.
- Well-developed organizational, project management, trouble shooting, and problem solving abilities.
- Effective team player with strong presentation and communication skills.
- Experienced in Windows 95/NT, MS-DOS, and Macintosh environments.
- Proficient in HTML, JavaScript, 3D Express, CGI, Photoshop; knowledge of Java, PERL, Lingo, Director, and Corel.

EXPERIENCE

INTERACTIVE DESIGNER, Interactive Papyrus Corp., Dallas, Texas (1996 – Present)
- Developed Web sites for companies such as Hewlett-Packard, Educational Marketing Network, and Information Management Research (www.imrgold.com, www.lodestone.com, www.wildart.com, www.ipapyrus.com, and www.hp.com/go/scanjet)—interactive CD portfolio available with sample projects.
- Met with clients to assess their needs and time lines.
- Project manager responsible for setting work flow schedules for designers and ensuring that deadlines were met.
- Managed databases using SQL and ODBC, maintained the server, and performed usability interface testing for Web sites.
- Developed projects using Director software (Center for Creative Leadership).

CREATIVE ENTREPRENEUR, Colorado Springs, Colorado (1995 – 1996)
- Created World Wide Web presences for businesses using copy editing, HTML programming, and graphic manipulation skills.
- Developed Internet capabilities as a consultant for Interactive Papyrus.
- Tested pre-release software for Optika Imaging Corporation.
- Generated wireframe 3D objects and provided software support for 3D technologies.
- Created a snowboarding Web site and a complete business plan for a San Francisco development group, generating interest in the sport with creative ideas.

SNOWBOARD INSTRUCTOR, Squaw Valley, Olympic Valley, California (1994 – 1995)
- Taught fun, safe, and respectful snowboarding.
- Demonstrated extreme levels of the sport and promoted equipment.

SKI INSTRUCTOR, Rasthaus am Chiemsee, Bavaria, Germany (1993 – 1994)
- Observed and critiqued individual technique, improving performance at all experience and age levels.

SALES ASSOCIATE, Serta Mattress Factory, Arvada, Colorado (1992 – 1993)
- Managed the daily operations of the store, assisted customers in selection of merchandise, and coordinated promotional events.
- Responsible for bookkeeping, recordkeeping, inventory control, product ordering, merchandising, and coordination of operating procedures with management.

EVENTS DIRECTOR, Associated Students, Denver, Colorado (1991 – 1992)
- Optimized the events budget and created an account that would not "roll over," providing a continuous year-to-year budget.
- Managed the office and supervised a staff of ten in event coordination and promotion.

SUPERVISOR, Roadway Express, Inc., Aurora, Colorado (1990 – 1992)
- Supervised outbound dock production for an international freight hauling company, overseeing crews of up to 15 Teamsters.
- Implemented a daily electronic inventory tracking system and maintained records of overages, shortages, and damage.

EDUCATION

BACHELOR OF SCIENCE, BUSINESS ADMINISTRATION (1992)
University of Colorado, Denver, Colorado
- Major in Marketing

ADDRESS

12 Luxury Lane, Dallas, Texas 80921, (719) 555-1234, E-mail: criscito@aol.com

Scannable

Christopher Taunton

SUMMARY

A **Professional Engineer** and **Project Manager** with eleven years experience in Consulting, Project Engineering, and Contract Administration. Major strengths include:

♦ Program Management   ♦ Problem Solving   ♦ Innovation

PROFESSIONAL EXPERIENCE

06/98 – 12/99   **PACIFIC CONSULTANTS INTERNATIONAL**   Tokyo, **Japan**

Consultant to one of the largest private Japanese consultant firms. Assigned to infrastructure and development programs in Southeast Asia funded by Japanese agencies and the World Bank.
♦ Assisted with feasibility studies, project evaluations, and proposals

Contracts Advisor for the Jakarta-Merak Tollway project   Jakarta, **Indonesia**
♦ Formulated and amended contract specifications, documents, and drawings
♦ Enhanced communications between our design team and site managers

01/98 – 05/98   **INTERNATIONAL EDUCATION SERVICES**   Tokyo, **Japan**

English Language Instructor to Japanese corporations, banks, and finance houses. Taught technical English to Japanese engineers and managers.

09/97 – 12/97   **C.H. ENGINEERING SERVICES**   Taunton, **U.K.**

Independent Consultant to the construction industry. Established my own business in order to finance my move to Tokyo.

10/93 – 09/97   **PICK, EVERARD, KEAY & GIMSON**; Consulting Engineers   Taunton, **U.K.**

Project Manager of a multidisciplinary team engaged in environmental engineering. Responsible for project appraisal, costing, design, contract specification, tender evaluation, and contract administration. Public and private sector, $0.2 million to $2.5 million value.
♦ Produced civil, electrical, and mechanical contract documents
♦ Designed and supervised a major water pipeline diversion, value $1 million
♦ Coordinated structural, hydraulic, and biological designs of wastewater plants
♦ Established contract periods and specified key contract requirements
♦ Rescheduled design and services work to achieve project deadlines
♦ Monitored contractor performance on site, produced financial evaluations, and reported progress to the client

01/91 – 09/93   **TAYLOR WOODROW**; Project Managers   Heysham Nuclear Power Plant, **U.K.**

Acting Section Engineer on one of the largest construction projects in Europe. Responsible for site supervision, operations planning and resourcing, and the design, manufacture, and implementation of site engineering systems.
♦ Supervised subcontractors and trained six graduate engineers on site
♦ Ordered materials, outlined bonus proposals, drafted progress reports
♦ Formulated strategic work programs from critical path analysis
♦ Documented information used to pursue financial claims for contract delays
♦ Devised tests, models, and method statements to verify construction techniques and quality assurance
♦ Supervised night shift operations and improved liaison between day and night shifts to achieve program completion

ADDRESS   123 Broadway Chadderton, Oldham 0699JH Lancashire, England   (061) 555-1234

Scannable

167

MARK S. GANTT

1234 Pennsylvania Avenue, N.W., #333
Washington, D.C. 20006
E-Mail: criscito@aol.com

Home: (202) 555-1234
Pager: (800) 555-5678
Fax: (202) 555-1234

PROFILE

- Seven years of experience in the legal aspects of international business transactions, with skills including:
  - Joint Venture Management
  - International Legal Research
  - Work Experience Abroad
  - International Litigation
  - Trade Regulations
  - Language Skills (German, Japanese)
  - Software and Technology Licensing
  - International Tax Plan Implementation
  - Contract Drafting and Review
  - Internet Ventures

EXPERIENCE

Co-Founder and Director (Operations/Legal)

**DigiView/Ed-X, LLC
Washington, D.C.**

1997 – present

- Developed and implemented an innovative distance learning Web site to provide continuing education and certificate programs through audio, video, text, and graphics.
- Assisted in the development of the information architecture for the site.
- Contributed to site design and managed the technical experts.
- Provided legal advice in licensing, IP matters, and entity creation.
- Managed the project and created Gantt charts for meeting project milestones.

Director, International Operations and Planning

**Medaphis Corporation
BSG/Imonics Division
Cary, North Carolina**

1996 – 1996

- Supported corporate international operations on a cross-functional (legal, financial, managerial) basis involving all organizational levels of the software development division of a Fortune 500 company.
- Managed the legal formation of the company's European subsidiary, including creation of corporate entities and assistance with the international tax plan, transfer pricing study, and international financial structure.
- Assisted with the legal formation and management of a corporate joint venture between the Imonics division and Bertelsmann AG for the provision of systems integration and software engineering in Germany.
- Supported the legal needs of a DM 100 million project with the German telecommunications authority, Deutsche Telekom, including the provision of core software license, drafting of labor and other agreements, complying with German residency and work permit regulations for U.S. technical team, and assisting local project team with day-to-day management issues.
- Completed the negotiations and drafting of an offshore software development joint venture located in Secunderabad, India.

Office of Executive Liaison

**U.S. International Trade Commission
Washington, D.C.**

1994 – 1996

- Assisted in the preparation of Schedule XX and other materials for the Uruguay Round of the General Agreement on Tariffs and Trade (GATT) which were incorporated into the United States' final offer at Marrakech in 1995.
- Researched and drafted opinions on GATT issues and its effect on the creation of the World Trade Organization using original source materials.
- Drafted the Annex implementing the 1995 Special 301 IPR retaliatory action against China.
- Briefed Commission members on issues related to the implementation of the North American Free Trade Agreement (NAFTA) and the impact of NAFTA on the Maquiladora program in Mexico.
- Assisted the Office of the United States Trade Representative with the implementation of trade agreements, including negotiation materials for Chile's accession to NAFTA and World Customs Organizations revisions to the Harmonized Tariff Schedule.

Attorney/Legal Consultant

**Redeker, Schön, Dahs & Sellner
Bonn, Germany**

1991 – 1994

- Advised U.S. and Japanese clients with queries on German and international law and assisted with the development of a foreign client base.
- Participated in international tax planning for German multinational companies.
- Assisted in the creation of a consortium agreement for research and development of infrastructure between the various telecommunication authorities of the European Union.
- Researched investment opportunities in state-owned manufacturing enterprises in eastern Germany for American clients.

EXPERIENCE (continued)

Attorney/Legal Intern

Pluta & Knorr
Ulm, Germany

Fall 1990

- Advised clients in the United States and Europe on international business transactions—joint-ventures, software licensing, and technology transfer agreements, among others.
- Counseled German companies on American law as it related to the pharmaceutical, software, and computer industries.
- Prepared a joint-venture agreement between a German company and the Ministry of Health of the former USSR for a pharmaceutical research laboratory in Moscow.
- Researched and prepared briefs on topics of international law including transactions, litigation, East-West trade, and computer law.

Associate Attorney

Williams, Blizzard
& McCarthy
Houston, Texas

1989 – 1990

- Litigated domestic legal issues in an av-rated law firm with an extensive commercial, medical malpractice, and personal injury practice.
- Negotiated and prepared real estate contracts between developers and residential builders.
- Assisted with the transnational litigation in Federal district court of a breach of contract between a U.S. manufacturer and a European subsidiary located in the United States.

EDUCATION

McGeorge School of Law
Sacramento, California

Master of Law (LL.M.), 1991
- Transnational Business Practice (top 10 percent)

Southern Methodist University School of Law
Dallas, Texas

Juris Doctor, 1988
- Trial Finalist, SMU School of Law Trial Advocacy Competition, 1988

American Graduate School of International Management (Thunderbird)
Glendale, Arizona

Master of International Management, 1986
- Emphasis on International Finance and Japanese language
- Full scholarship from the Japanese Ministry of International Trade and Industry (MITI) to the Boeki Kenshu Centa, Fujinomiya, Japan, 1986

Texas A&M University
College Station, Texas

Bachelor of Business Administration, 1984
- Major: Finance
- Distinguished student, Texas A&M University, 1981, 1982, 1983

FOREIGN STUDIES

Universität Salzburg
Salzburg, Austria

Postgraduate legal studies (LL.M.) in Germanic and European Union laws, international business transactions, and transnational arbitration, 1990

Inns of Court School of Law, London, U.K.

Studied the legal issues of Eurobond placement, international syndicated term loans, and other financial topics, 1988

Boeki Kenshu Centa (IIST)
Fujinomiya, Japan

Graduate-level business courses in the Japanese economy, language, and international finance, 1986

BAR MEMBERSHIPS

- Member, State Bar of Texas
- Admitted to practice before the U.S. Court of International Trade
- Admitted to practice before the Supreme Court of the United States

LANGUAGES

- Highly proficient in German.
- Proficient in Japanese (Monbusho Level 4).

ACTIVITIES

Central and East European Law Initiative (CEELI)
American Bar Association
Washington, D.C.
1996 – present

- As a volunteer project attorney, edited analyses of draft laws proposed for former communist nations in Central and Eastern Europe with the assistance of experts in the fields of law and politics.
- Prepared thematic concept papers on election law, labor law, and other legal subjects for use by the legislatures of Russia, Belarus, Latvia, Lithuania, Ukraine, and Kazakhstan.

Lisa Taylor

PROFILE

- Self-motivated sales professional with more than twelve years of proven experience.
- Top performer with a strong background in building new territories and using creative marketing approaches.
- Respected for the ability to get to the decision maker and close the sale.
- Demonstrated ability to create client loyalty beyond the sales relationship.
- Entrepreneurial thinker who works well independently or as part of a team.

EXPERIENCE

SALES REPRESENTATIVE (1992 – present)
Unisource, Denver, Colorado

- Sold paper products, chemicals, and cleaning supplies to large corporate and government clients, including hospitals, hotels, casinos, City of Denver, and Coors.
- Formulated a strategic plan for the territory and grew the account base by 350 percent through effective cold calling and account development.
- Created and conducted sales presentations to upper-level management, assessed their needs, and developed unique customer applications.
- Successfully regained former customers through effective marketing and follow-up.
- Designed and executed training programs for key clients.
- Achieved the President's Club through exceptional sales performance; ranked the number one salesperson in the Denver metropolitan territory.

SALES REPRESENTATIVE (1988 – 1990)
Moore Business Forms, Denver, Colorado

- Sold customized business forms to companies in the Denver territory.
- Increased sales to existing customers and developed the territory by 178 percent.
- Designed special forms to fit proprietary computer systems.
- Created a forms management program for the Poudre Valley Hospital.

SALES REPRESENTATIVE (1985 – 1988)
Pitney Bowes, Denver, Colorado

- Developed markets for Pitney Bowes copiers throughout 20 zip codes in the Denver metropolitan area.
- Consistently exceeded production quotas by as much as 250 percent, producing nearly half a million dollars a year in sales.
- Honored as one of the top five Pitney Bowes salespeople in the state of Colorado.
- Completed a comprehensive Pitney Bowes professional sales training program.

EDUCATION

BACHELOR OF ARTS IN BUSINESS MARKETING
Colorado State University, Fort Collins, Colorado

CONTINUING EDUCATION

- Ongoing sales and motivation training, Dale Carnegie course
- Hazardous materials, OSHA, material safety data, and SARA regulatory training

---

1234 Grand Cypress Lane • Lone Tree, Colorado 80124
Phone: (303) 555-1234 • Mobile: (303) 555-5678 • E-mail: criscito@aol.com

Scannable

12 Graphic Design Elements

The following résumés aren't extremely elaborate in their use of graphic design elements. They are still basically conservative résumés with just a little something added to make them stand out.

Keep in mind that the graphic should be directly related to your industry. You wouldn't put a world globe on a waitress's résumé or drafting tools on a paramedic's. In some more conservative professions (banking, accounting, upper management, etc.) graphics on a résumé are not recommended, even if they are small and conservative.

The résumés on pages 172–178 use graphics that reflect an international focus (as does page 93), whereas the graphics on pages 177, 180–183, and 185 reflect the person's industry.

By becoming a little more inventive, you can incorporate scanned letters or figures that reflect your personality more than the industry (see pages 184 and 186 in this section and pages 271 and 274 elsewhere).

The use of the graphics in this chapter is fine on a scannable résumé. The scanning software will ignore your graphics as long as they don't touch any of the words on the page. However, using a graphic image as the first initial of your name (like the résumés on pages 143, 184, 186, 203, 212, and 267) will cause your name to be spelled wrong in the electronic database after scanning. Avoid such graphic images that are part of your name in a scannable résumé.

Those in more creative industries—the arts, entertainment, advertising, graphic design—have a license to be even more creative. You could definitely get away with the résumés in this chapter, but you can be as creative as the résumés in Chapter 17.

Jessica Lee Titus

EXPERIENCE

President, Associated Students Legislative Council   November 1998
American Graduate School of International Management   May 1999

- Managed and supervised 25 officers
- Supervised application of a $70,000 budget
- Made presentation to Board of Directors
- Liaison to Board of Trustees
- Member of the Academic Council
- Conducted meetings on a weekly basis

Vice President, Associated Students Legislative Council   August 1998
American Graduate School of International Management   November 1998

- Supervised publication of campus directory
- Regulated club activities
- Allocated over $10,000 of student funds
- Organized all campus elections
- Coordinated school-sponsored activities
- Organized charity ball for Red Cross

Customer Service Counselor   July 1997
BancFlorida, Sarasota, Florida   January 1998

- Opened and closed accounts
- Responsible for training of new tellers
- Received and resolved customer complaints
- Controlled access to safety deposit boxes
- Balanced bank records of negotiables
- Participated in numerous training programs

Bank Teller   May 1995
BancFlorida, Sarasota, Florida   August 1995

- Operated cash drawer of $10,000
- Maintained positive customer relations
- Verified commercial deposits
- Balanced branch records

Bank Teller   May 1994
Dauphin Deposit Bank and Trust Company, Harrisburg, Pennsylvania   August 1994

- Participated in a 6-week training program
- Developed customer service skills
- Replaced vacationing employees
- Operated and balanced cash drawer

EDUCATION

Master of International Management   May 1999
American Graduate School of International Management, Glendale, Arizona
Concentration: International Marketing and French

Bachelor of Arts   May 1997
Eckerd College, St. Petersburg, Florida
Major: French ▪ Minor: Management
Completed comprehensive exams in major with a 4.0/4.0

LANGUAGES

Proficient in **French** and **Danish**
Knowledge of Lotus 1-2-3, WordPerfect, BASIC, dBASE III, and MS Word

OVERSEAS EXPERIENCE

Youth for Understanding Exchange Student, Borup Skole, Borup, Denmark   1991 – 1992
Eckerd College Independent Study, Paris, France   January 1997

ACTIVITIES

Vice President of Women's Rugby Club, Co-Coordinator for Career Services
Fashion Show, Development and Volunteer Committees, French Club

ADDRESS

12345 Casey Key Road, Nokomis, Florida 34275   (813) 555-1234

172

DeBrinka C. Lamar

PROFILE
- Dedicated travel professional with a background in customer service.
- Self-motivated and well organized; able to thrive in a fast-paced environment that involves managing multiple tasks simultaneously.
- Even-tempered team player with exceptional communication and interpersonal skills.
- Extensive travel experience in Mexico, Puerto Rico, Hawaii, and the continental U.S.
- Experienced in System 1, Lotus 1-2-3, WordPerfect, and Quicken software.

EXPERIENCE

GERRI'S TRAVEL, Lamar, Colorado   1996
Travel Agent
- Planned itineraries and arranged accommodations and other travel services for both individual and group customers.
- Consulted with customers to determine destinations, modes of transportation, travel dates, financial considerations, and accommodations required.
- Provided travel information regarding points of interests, special events, local customs, and travel regulations.
- Booked and ticketed airline, cruise, and rail reservations.
- Computed cost of travel packages and collected payments.

INSTANT REPLAY, INC., Pueblo West, Colorado   1993 – 1995
Vice President
- Placed and maintained video poker machines in fraternal organizations.
- Responsible for business planning, bookkeeping, payroll, tax returns, accounts payable, and accounts receivable.

PACIFICO AVEDA, Denver, Colorado   1992 – 1993
Account Executive
- Promoted Aveda cosmetics and hair care products to top salons.
- Responsible for team building and training of salon owners and stylists.

THE CROSSING HEALING ARTS CENTER, Colorado Springs, Colorado   1988 – 1992
Office Manager
- Managed the Colorado Springs and Limon offices of several holistic healing professionals, including a nutritionist, chiropractor, psychotherapists, and massage therapists.
- Instrumental in improving profitability of the health care professionals.
- Responsible for payroll, accounts payable, and accounts receivable.
- Arranged appointments, answered telephones, and greeted patients.
- Interviewed, hired, scheduled, trained, and supervised a staff of six.

MARRIOTT, Colorado Springs, Colorado   1991
PBX Operator (part-time)
- Operated PBX switchboard to relay incoming, outgoing, and interoffice calls.
- Assisted guests by supplying information and recording messages.

EDUCATION

NORTH AMERICAN SCHOOL OF TRAVEL, Scranton, Pennsylvania   1995 – 1997
Master Travel Course (August 1997)
Course work included: Today's Travel Industry, Introduction to Airlines and Ticketing, Airline Reservations and Ticketing, Steamship Travel and Cruises, How to Use the North American OAG, Rail and Motorcoach Travel, Hotels, Resorts and Tours, Customer Service

UNIVERSITY OF SOUTHERN COLORADO, Pueblo, Colorado   1983 – 1985
Major in mass communications, minor in computers

BLAIR JUNIOR COLLEGE, Colorado Springs, Colorado   1982 – 1983
Advanced Secretarial Science

ADDRESS   1234 Mountain Top Lane, Colorado Springs, Colorado 80919   (719) 555-1234

Fernando F. Barbosa

1234 Collins Avenue, Miami Beach, Florida 33140

(305) 555-1234

QUALIFICATIONS
- *Master's degree in International Management with a focus in Marketing*
- *Extensive experience in Latin American cable TV markets*
- *Experience in consumer brand management, sports marketing, and capital markets*
- *Multilingual—Fluent in* **Portuguese, Spanish,** *and* **English**
- *Strong analytical ability*

EXPERIENCE

DISCOVERY NETWORKS, *Miami, Florida (1995 – present)*
Advertising Sales Regional Director for Latin America
- *Became Regional Director in 1997, adding the responsibility for advertising sales operations in the entire Latin America region for the Discovery Channel, People and Arts Network, Animal Planet, Discovery Kids, and Travel Channel.*
- *Created the Latin America sales strategy for three new networks, including Discovery Kids, Animal Planet, and People and Arts Network.*
- *Assisted in the successful creation of a strategic alliance between Discovery Networks and the BBC; facilitated the acquisition of the Travel Channel.*

Advertising Sales Senior Manager for Latin America
- *Developed and maintained international business in the entire Latin America region.*
- *Successfully increased the number of clients from 2 to more than 30 in the 1995–96 season, representing revenues of $3.7 million for Discovery Networks.*
- *Exceeded individual and departmental sales goals by 5 percent in 1996.*
- *Managed the advertising sales operation in Brazil and Argentina.*
- *Supervised sales planners, assistants, and a 25-person international sales team.*
- *Ensured the proper scheduling and billing of media proposals.*
- *Compiled research and ratings to create presentations for new business development.*
- *Prepared industry analysis, managed departmental budgets, and tracked the inventory sellout levels.*

GOLDMAN, SACHS AND CO., *New York, New York (1994 – 1995)*
Associate, Latin American Equity Group
- *Managed instruction, settlement, and reconciliation of Latin American equities on behalf of GS&Co. and its clients.*
- *Interacted with traders, sales reps, clients, and managers in all areas of equities trading, including prime brokerage, arbitrage and derivatives trading.*
- *Developed procedures and system enhancements for reducing failed transactions.*
- *Planned and developed information flow to assist risk arbitrage desk.*
- *Liaison between the Latin American Equity Group and custodian banks.*
- *Contributed strategic, financial, risk management, and operational solutions to the opening of a regional office in Mexico.*
- *Led the investigation and resolution of failing transactions.*
- *Monitored agency and proprietary accounts.*

PHILIP MORRIS INTERNATIONAL, KRAFT GENERAL FOODS, *Mexico City, D.F. (1993)*
Assistant Brand Manager
- *Researched the possibility of brand cannibalization among Kraft powdered soft drinks.*
- *Orchestrated the development and improvement of the Kraft brand image in Mexico through a million dollar ad campaign entitled "Stars in the Kraft Kitchen."*
- *Developed a profit per square meter analysis on the three largest supermarket chains in Mexico City for KGF major brands.*
- *Forecasted sales quotas for all regional divisions.*
- *Developed a brand development index and created a sales history presentation for KGF powdered soft drinks (Kool-Aid, Tang, Frisco).*

174

Scannable

EDUCATION

MASTER OF INTERNATIONAL MANAGEMENT *(May 1994)*   *GPA 3.80/4.0*
American Graduate School of International Management   *with honors*
Thunderbird Campus, Glendale, Arizona
- *Conducted extensive marketing research and created advertising program
  for Pepsico's introduction of Mirinda soft drinks in the Phoenix area*
- **International Consumer Marketing Seminar**
- **Marketing for U.S. Hispanics Seminar**

EFFECTIVE ADVERTISING SEMINAR *(July 1993)*
J. Walter Thompson, *Mexico City, D.F.*

BACHELOR OF BUSINESS ADMINISTRATION *(July 1992)*   *GPA 3.81/4.0*
Southern Arkansas University, *Magnolia, Arkansas*   *magna cum laude*
- *Major: Business Administration (Outstanding Business Student Award)*
- *Minor: French*

**ACTIVITIES &
ACHIEVEMENTS**
- *Academic All-American—Tennis (1991 – 1992)*
- *Member of the SAU Tennis Team (1988 – 1992)*
- *Captain of the soccer team at SAU for four straight years (1989 – 1992)*
- *Competitive triathlete*
- *Active member of the Aircraft Owners and Pilots Association (AOPA)*
- *Active member of Angel's wings, a charity organization*

LICENSES

PRIVATE PILOT LICENSE, INSTRUMENT RATING *(August 1997)*
Husta Aviation, *Miami, Florida*
- *Golden Wings Award for best pilot in the 1997 class*
- *Member of ADF Airways flying team*

EVERETT C. ATHERTON JR. ——————————————

education

Thunderbird, American Graduate School of International Management
  Master of International Management   *May 1998*
    Emphasis on Mandarin Chinese, Asian Studies, International Marketing and Trade

Stanford University
    Intensive Modern Chinese language program   *Summer 1997*

Menlo College, *Atherton, California*
  Bachelor of Arts   *1996*
    Major: Philosophy • Minor: Business Administration
    Honors: Dean's List (five semesters) • Most Outstanding Humanities Major, 1992

international study programs

Southeast Asia Today   *Winter 1996*
    Selected to represent Menlo College in a student delegation to Hong Kong, Malaysia, Thailand, Singapore, and China. Formally conferred with leaders in both public and private sectors. Analyzed foreign and economic policies to assess the relative significance of uncertainty in the region and evaluate both market and resource opportunities of multinational endeavors in the East.

Semester in Paris   *Spring 1992*
    Resided in Paris as a full-time student, studying French language, the humanities, and contemporary politics. Took advantage of the intellectually stimulating environment through extracurricular pursuits and immersion in Parisian culture.

work experience

Malke-Sage Galleries – *Installation Manager*   *1992 – 1995*
    Head of corporate sales installation department for a prominent San Francisco bay area firm specializing in fine art and limited edition work. Approximately $1.8 million in annual sales with five locations on the peninsula. Successfully devised and implemented program to handle record level of corporate sales. Personally responsible for coordination of $60,000 in installations and general client satisfaction.

et sequens

Languages: *Proficient in Mandarin Chinese and French*
Computer Skills: *MS Word, WordPerfect, Lotus 1-2-3, Excel, dBASE IV, and BASIC*
Eastern Thought: *Authored thesis investigating the relationship between Lao Tzu's Tao Te Ching and the Western philosophical problem of freewill versus determinism*
Martial Arts: *Five years of Tae Kwon Do study; rewarded both in rank and competition*
Travel: *Extensive international travel, particularly in Europe and Asia*

Present Address • P.O. Box 1234 • Glendale, Arizona 85306 • (602) 555-1234
Permanent Address • 123 Albino Way • Woodside, California 94062 • (415) 555-1234

Scannable

CARLA J. ARLUN

PROFILE

- **DESIGN** – Experienced interior designer with a strong work ethic.
- **ORGANIZATION** – Detail-oriented design professional who is self-motivated and capable of handling multiple tasks simultaneously, meeting deadlines, and working efficiently.
- **TEAM WORK** – Known for working well with others, contributing to a team environment, and maintaining a positive attitude.
- **COMMUNICATION** – Outstanding interpersonal, written, and oral communication skills; able to present well to both groups and individuals.
- **CREATIVITY** – Creative and innovative problem solver; can quickly translate customer requirements into pleasing design schemes.
- **TECHNICAL** – Computer literate on IBM and Macintosh; competent in manual drafting and CAD.

EDUCATION

BACHELOR OF SCIENCE, INTERIORS MERCHANDISING   1994
University of Wyoming, Laramie, Wyoming
- Self-financed 100 percent of education while maintaining a 3.7/4.0 grade point average

Courses
- Principles of design, drawing, drafting, space planning, color theory, textiles, art history, architectural history, housing, historical furnishings, marketing, communications, retailing, merchandising, accounting, and architectural engineering

Honors
- Who's Who of American Students, Honor Graduate, President's Honor Roll, Dean's List, National Collegiate Engineering Award, Golden Key Honor Society, Phi Beta Phi Honor Society, Phi Upsilon Omicron Honor Society

EXPERIENCE
Design
- Design consultant for four large home builders; selected interior and exterior finishes.
- Consulted with residential clients on design projects involving space planning, color selection, painting, wall coverings, floor coverings, and accents.
- Assisted customers in selecting home furnishings and developing creative, functional floor plans.
- Learned furniture construction and sizes, characteristics of wood types and upholstery, and furniture sales techniques while selling Country Classics furniture.
- Created appealing merchandise displays.

Sales/Marketing
- Applied effective sales techniques to sell furniture, floor coverings, ceramic tile, accents, and art.
- Sold annuity investment plans through home presentations.
- Solicited and maintained accounts for a busy manufacturer; developed creative promotional strategies.

Management
- Managed an 1,100-acre farm business and supervised farming operations.
- Controlled inventory and handled shipping and receiving for a manufacturing firm.
- Active in the management of several family-owned business, including a manufacturing company, bingo supply distributor, bingo hall, and food service company.

Financial
- Settled creditor claims and oversaw estate funds and assets, including organizing five years of finances for back taxes and effectively arbitrating creditor/heir disputes.
- Experienced with computerized inventory and customer records management programs.
- Maintained/balanced computerized and manual journals (parts and service sales, cash receipts, disbursements, accounts receivable, etc.) and prepared financial statements.

WORK HISTORY

Interior Designer, Arlun Floor Coverings and Design Center, Colorado Springs, CO 1995 – 1997
Bookkeeper/Assistant to Manager, Kotby Motors, Laramie, WY   1994 – 1995
Sales Associate, Earth, Wind, and Fire Gallery, Laramie, WY   1994
Administratrix, James A. Roland Estate, Laramie, WY   1990 – 1994
Marketing Representative, Marketing Corporation of America, Laramie, WY   1993
Manager/Sales Representative, Coincepts and Prairie Food Services, Laramie, WY 1988 – 1991

ADDRESS   1234 Split Rock Drive, Colorado Springs, Colorado 80919   (719) 555-1234

Stacy S. Sheiver

1234 East Kiowa
Colorado Springs, CO 80909

Phone: (719) 555-1234
E-mail: criscito@aol.com

PROFILE

- Creative sports administrator with varied experience in both domestic and international arenas.
- Effective team player with strong interpersonal and communication skills.
- Cross-culturally sensitive professional who has traveled throughout Egypt, Australia, Italy, France, Switzerland, and Greece.
- Knowledge of Spanish and skills in American Sign Language.
- Proficient in WordPerfect, MS Publisher, MS Word, PowerPoint, Lotus Notes, Survey Pro, and the Internet.

EDUCATION

MASTER OF SCIENCE IN EDUCATION, Northern Illinois University, DeKalb, Illinois   1994
- Emphasis in Sports Management; self-financed 100 percent of college expenses.

BACHELOR OF ARTS IN COMMUNICATIONS, Northern Illinois University, DeKalb, Illinois   1992
- Emphasis in Media Production; received Outstanding Major Award.

CONTINUING EDUCATION
- Completed in-depth training on rehabilitation and substance abuse at the Betty Ford Center, Professional in Residence Program, Palm Springs, California.

INTERNATIONAL EXPERIENCE

- One of three Americans selected to attend the **International Olympic Academy** (IOA), Olympia, Greece; selected to serve as delegation leader.
- **Olympic Games**, Atlanta, Georgia, drug testing team member.
- **Paralympic Games**, Atlanta, Georgia, drug testing team member.
- International observer at the Australian Sport Drug Agency, Australia's IOC Accredited Drug Testing Laboratory, Australian Institute of Sport in Canberra, and the Canadian Centre for Ethics in Sports.
- Brought together 40 top drug-control administrators, IOC laboratory directors, and IOC Executive Committee Member Anita DeFrantz to discuss research topics in drug control as the Program Organizer of the International Research Conference in San Diego, California (1/97).
- Worked as an international business intern in Egypt for the winter of 1991–1992; examined the operations and marketing strategies of the Suez Canal Authority; studied private and public businesses throughout the country.
- Participated in an international exchange to Perth, Australia, to assist with drug testing at the Swimming World Championships.

PROFESSIONAL EXPERIENCE

UNITED STATES OLYMPIC COMMITTEE (USOC), Colorado Springs, Colorado   1994 to present
Drug Education Administrator
- Administered the USOC Drug Education Program and managed a $250,000 budget.
- Coordinated yearly dissemination of more than 25,000 pieces of educational resources to National Governing Bodies, athletes, and others.
- Interviewed, hired, supervised, and evaluated education program staff members.
- Provided input and reviewed international agreements.
- Created educational campaigns, including the coordination of poster designs, video productions, photo shoots, post-production processes, and resource development.
- Successfully managed the conceptualization, content, production, and distribution of USOC drug education materials.
- Developed and implemented education material inventory and tracking system.

UNITED STATES OLYMPIC COMMITTEE (continued)
- Coordinated all aspects of international meetings, crew chief training seminars, committee meetings, etc., including site selection, hotel contracts, meeting agendas, transportation, correspondence, logistics, faculty appointments, entertainment, and evaluation.
- Worked with SGMA, MusiCares, and the U.S. Department of Education, among others, in developing alternative avenues for drug education.
- Made a presentation to high-level representatives from bid cities for future Pan American and Olympic games.
- Authored articles for *Olympic Coach* and write-ups for the World University Games, Pan American Games, USOC Fact Book, and the USOC Annual Report.
- Assisted legal staff with writing the protocol for the new No Advance Notice drug testing program.
- Served as crew chief for drug testing operations at different sporting events throughout the United States.
- Appointed by the Human Resources Director to the USOC Employee Advisory Committee.
- Member of the USOC Family Days Committee.

MEDIA SERVICES, DeKalb, Illinois   1992 to 1993
Media Production Assistant
- Wrote scripts and edited/produced videos.
- Hired and trained student assistants.
- Taught gripping, lighting, cameras, and microphone mixers for studio and remote productions.

NORTHERN ILLINOIS UNIVERSITY, ATHLETIC DEPARTMENT, DeKalb, Illinois   1990 to 1991
Promotions and Marketing Assistant

HEAD TENNIS INSTRUCTOR, Mt. Prospect, Illinois   1989 to 1991

COMMUNITY SERVICE

- United States Association for Blind Athletes (USABA)
- Coordinated the opening reception and opening ceremonies for the IPC Cycling World Championships
- Member of NIU Sport Management Curriculum Advisory Board
- Volunteer at the Ironman Triathlon in Kona, Hawaii
- Relay for Life Team Captain and Jonquil Ball Fund Raising Committee, American Cancer Society
- Wheelchair tennis instructor and volunteer
- Volunteer, Athletes Against Drugs
- Fund Raiser, Hike to the Peak, Pikes Peak Pain Center
- Scorekeeper for Nuveen Men's Senior Professional Tennis Tour
- Member, IHSA All-State Tennis and Badminton Teams
- Blind Ski Guide
- President, Sigma Sigma Sigma social sorority
- Interests: tennis, table tennis, golf, running, skiing, travel, and people

KENNETH M. JACKSON
1234 Bridgewater Drive
Colorado Springs, CO 80916
(719) 555-1234

OBJECTIVE   A position as a Photo Process Engineer

EXPERIENCE   **ATMEL**, Colorado Springs, Colorado (1995 – present)
Process Technician (1997 – present)
• Collaborate with engineers to determine materials, parts, dimensions, and tolerances necessary for operating wafer fabrication equipment.
• Authorized to make decisions on production hold lots, stopped processes, and down equipment.
• Initiate and implement corrective action to resolve process and equipment problems.
• Trouble shoot out-of-control SPC issues and perform routine equipment checks.
• Write and modify operating specifications, reports, and documentation of experiment results.
• Train and certify operators; participate on preventative action and work area teams.
Photo Specialist (1996 – 1997)
Wafer Production Operator (1995 – 1996)
• In-depth experience with the ASM 2500/5000 Stepper and develop inspect.
• Manufacture 6-inch memory chip wafers and perform minor trouble shooting on the line.
• Experienced in the use of the Daninippon 60A Coater, UV Bake, OTI Vacuum Bake, and DNS Developer.
• Operate Comet computer system for wafer tracking, including MASS11 word processing and e-mail.
• Trained peers in operations and protocols as a buddy trainer.
• Perfect attendance; able to work with minimal supervision.

TERRANOMICS LANDSCAPE MANAGEMENT, INC., Colorado Springs, Colorado (1992 – 1995)
Foreman, Mowing Crew
• Supervised all aspects of mowing operations, including scheduling and training of workers.
• Ordered and maintained inventory of supplies.
• Performed preventive maintenance on all equipment.
• Maintained a safe work environment.

UNITED STATES ARMY, Fort Carson, Colorado (1987 – 1992)
ARMY NATIONAL GUARD, Fort Carson, Colorado (1992 – present)
Team Leader
• Implemented orders and directives.
• Supervised training and activities of subordinates.
• Evaluated performance and provided written and oral counseling.
• Ensured proper collection and reporting of intelligence data.
• Trained National Guard forces for Saudi Arabia.
• Commended for outstanding leadership skills.

EDUCATION   **UNIVERSITY OF COLORADO**, Colorado Springs, Colorado (1996 – present)
• Working toward a Bachelor of Science in Electrical Engineering.
• Completed 113 credit hours.

PIKES PEAK COMMUNITY COLLEGE, Colorado Springs, Colorado (1993 – 1996)
• Completed 59 credit hours toward a degree in electrical engineering.
• Computer programming classes in VAX, Fortran, and Computer Science I and II (C++).

UNITED STATES ARMY, Fort Carson, Colorado (1992)
Primary Leadership Development Course (PLDC)
• Selected for the Commandant's List for superior performance.
• Scored 192 out of 200 on the E-5 promotions board.

HONORS   Army Service Ribbon, National Defense Service Medal, Three Army Achievement Medals, Army Good Conduct Medal, Army Commendation Medal, Expert Infantry Badge

Scannable

DONNY W. STEELE

1234 N. 37th Avenue #123 • Glendale, Arizona 85301 • (602) 555-1234

QUALIFICATIONS
- 10 years as a Medical Technician
- Experienced in Medical, Surgical, Family Practice, Dermatology, Allergy, and Emergency Room Medicine
- CPR Certified and EMT-Basic Licensed

EXPERIENCE

MEDICAL SERVICE SPECIALIST, U.S. Air Force   1991 – Present
- Assisted professional medical personnel in planning, providing, and evaluating patient care, including inpatient, outpatient, emergency services, and disaster preparedness
- Served as ambulance driver and emergency medical technician
- Performed aeromedical evacuation duties

PATIENT CARE
- Triage, vital signs, venipuncture for IVs, controlling hemorrhage, resuscitation, emergency management of burns and shock
- Dressing changes, casting, splinting
- Assisted in minor surgery (suturing, anesthetics)
- Administered oxygen and respiratory treatments
- Eye and ear irrigation, Foley catheterization, enemas
- Trained to assist physicians with chest tube insertion, paracentesis/thoracentesis, lumbar puncture, external and internal cardiac pacemakers, cricotracheotomy, central line or subclavian IV line insertion

TESTING
- Drew blood, performed urine strains, computerized PT counts
- Performed tympanograms, pulmonary function studies, and throat cultures
- Immunizations and testing for social diseases
- Allergy testing and injections
- Accomplished well-baby checks (vitals, weight, head circumference, length)

EQUIPMENT
- EKG, code cart, defibrillator, vitals monitoring, intubation and airway equipment
- Cleaned instruments, sterile setup, infection control
- Prepared minor surgery packs and Pap packs

MANAGEMENT
- Scheduled appointments and received patients at reception desk
- Supervised more than six workers at any given time
- Obtained, stored, and disposed of supplies and linens
- Maintained medical records, observing and reporting observations in patient progress notes and team conferences

EDUCATION

ASSOCIATE DEGREE IN ALLIED HEALTH SCIENCES   in process
Community College of the Air Force   38 credits
Rio Salado Community College, Phoenix, Arizona
Southwest Virginia Community College, Richlands, Virginia
Ferrum College, Virginia

TRAINING

Medical Service Specialist, Sheppard AFB, Texas (240 hours)   1992
Pharmacology Course, Luke AFB, Arizona (20 hours)   1992
I.V. Therapy Course, Luke AFB, Arizona (20 hours)   1993
Noncommissioned Officers Preparatory Course (191 hours)   1995
Noncommissioned Officers Leadership School (in residence)   2000

 Scannable

181

Joe Dunham

12345 N. 91st Avenue
Peoria, Arizona 85345
(602) 555-1234

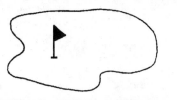

SUMMARY OF
QUALIFICATIONS

Diverse and accomplished individual offering an established track record in all aspects of a PGA golf professional. Expertise includes all facets of management, wholesale/retail, golf lessons, club design and repair, cart maintenance, tournament operation, and public relations. Excellent liaison and troubleshooting skills.

EMPLOYMENT
OVERVIEW

ESTRELLA GOLF CLUB
Goodyear, Arizona

Assistant Golf Pro   12/98 – Present
High-visibility position involving operations of assisting golf director, shipping, receiving inventory control, merchandising, golf club repair, tournament operations, starter, tee times/reservation, cashier responsibilities/deposits.

WHISPERING PALMS COUNTRY CLUB
Rancho Sante Fe, California

Golf Instructor   4/98 – 6/98
Position requiring strong leadership to individuals seeking beginning, intermediate, and advanced training, also golf club repair.

DIXON LAKE PARK
Escondido, California

Ranger Aide   6/97 – 6/98
Maintained direct involvement in enforcing park policies, general maintenance, reservations, and collecting monies.

DUNHAM HILLS GOLF CLUB
Milford, Michigan

Greenskeeper   3/96 – 10/96
Duties included inspection of equipment, repairs, turf grass grooming, and maintenance.

EDUCATION

PGA BUSINESS SCHOOL II   10/98
Phoenix, Arizona

PGA BUSINESS SCHOOL I   11/95
Phoenix, Arizona

SAN DIEGO GOLF ACADEMY   2/93 – 11/94
Rancho Sante Fe, California

SPECIALIZED
ACCOMPLISHMENTS

PLAYERS ABILITY TEST (PAT)   5/96
Arrowhead Ranch Golf Course

182

D. L. McDonald
Painter

EXPERIENCE

PAINTING
- Journeyman with 15 years of experience
- Experienced in all phases of painting from preparation of surfaces to spray/brush/roll
- Drywall repairs, texturing, taping, popcorn finish
- Furniture and wood finishing/refinishing
- Repainting of all types
- Industrial and commercial jobs
- New construction, custom and tract homes
- Government contract work
- Insurance painting—water and smoke damage repair
- Experienced with all types of interior and exterior paint—latex, oil, varnish, lacquer, stains, synthetics, primers, epoxy, Elastimeric coatings, etc.

EQUIPMENT
- Scaffolding, man lifts, scissor lifts, ladders
- Airless sprayers with extension wands and all other associated equipment
- Air compressors
- Texturizing guns
- Electrostatic machines
- All hand tools and sanders used for painting and wood finishing

MANAGEMENT
- Foreman—directed seven workers for government contracts; four workers for 70-home subdivision tract project
- Experienced in all aspects of company ownership, including job bidding and planning, personnel management, marketing, public relations, budgeting, and bookkeeping

WORK HISTORY

1999	Master Group Project Management
1990 – 1999	Self-Employed, D. L. McDonald Painting, Visalia, CA, and Phoenix, AZ

- McDonald Construction, General Contractors
- Fistelaro Construction, General Contractors
- Ghaster Painting, Inc.
- John Doe, Realtor
- Jane Doe, Realtor
- Grand Painting

1989 – 1990	Atkins Construction, Visalia, CA
1988 – 1989	Shy, Inc., Builder, Visalia, CA
1987 – 1988	Parker Painting Contractors, Visalia, CA
1985 – 1986	Roache Painting Contractors, Visalia, CA
1983 – 1984	Price Painting Contractors, Visalia, CA
1982	Visalia Unified School District, Visalia, CA
1981	Furniture Stripping Shop, Van Nuys, CA

1234 Port Lane • Indianapolis, Indiana 46517 • (219) 555-1234

Katherine Steven

1234 Apogee View
Colorado Springs, CO 80906
Phone: (719) 555-1234
Cellular: (719) 555-5678

OBJECTIVE: A position with a progressive company where expertise in sales and marketing can improve the company's bottom line.

PROFILE

- Driven sales and marketing professional with 14 years of successful experience.
- Demonstrated ability to create client loyalty above and beyond the sales relationship.
- Self-motivated and focused; comfortable working independently with little supervision.
- Team player with exceptional communication and interpersonal skills.
- Track record of consistently generating significant revenues.

EXPERIENCE

SALES/MARKETING

- Marketed and generated student enrollments for undergraduate and technical education programs.
- Successfully gained new clients through effective marketing, special events, professional sales presentations, and follow-up.
- Coordinated marketing and advertising for television, radio, and newspaper ads.
- Personally interviewed, telephoned, and used direct mail to recruit prospective students.
- Generated leads through cold calls to Job Training Program Assistance, Veteran Affairs, Vocational Rehabilitation, and companies offering tuition reimbursement.
- Created special events at local military installations to market to military members and their dependents.
- Provided career counseling to students regarding future job placements in their respective fields of study.
- Generated leads by cold calling and referral for an advertising company.
- Sold advertisement spots in magazines, brochures, and newspapers.

ACCOMPLISHMENTS

- Promoted to Director of Admissions in 1997 based on production, show rate, and leadership abilities.
- Top producer for the last 7 years, earning up to $3 million each year from recruitment of 170 students.
- Consistently exceed sales quotas by 10 percent per year.

MANAGEMENT/ADMINISTRATION

- Hired, trained, supervised, and evaluated four admission representatives.
- Created work schedules and provided continuous sales training for all representatives.
- Ensured timely completion of financial aid plans, student advisor information, enrollment agreements, registrations, examinations, and orientations.
- Generated weekly, monthly, and annual statistical reports to evaluate enrollment versus leads for the Admissions Department.

WORK HISTORY

Director of Admissions/Admissions Representative   1991 – 1999
Denver Technical College, Colorado Springs, Colorado

Advertising Sales Representative   1990 – 1991
Ad Mail, Colorado Springs, Colorado

Admissions Representative   1988 – 1990
Denver Technical College, Colorado Springs, Colorado

Admissions Representative   1984 – 1988
Adelphi Business College, Colorado Springs, Colorado

EDUCATION

Denver Technical College, Colorado Springs, Colorado   1991 – 1999
- Completed course work in business, management, and computers

Continuing Education
- Carl G. Stevens and Dick Gardner's Sales Techniques
- Excelling as a First-Time Supervisor, Career Track Seminar

LORI MANSON

1234 South Overview Drive, San Ramon, California 94583, Phone (510) 555-1234

OBJECTIVE   *A challenging teaching position utilizing creativity and a true desire to educate*

EXPERIENCE   *TEACHER/CENTER SUPERVISOR*   *Oct. 1998 – Dec. 1999*
Turtle Mountain Head Start, *Belcourt, North Dakota*
- *Manage six center employees and evaluate job performance through biannual reviews.*
- *Complete comprehensive monthly reports to reflect inventory control, accounts payable/receivable, and adherence to federal health and safety regulations.*
- *Design learning environment to meet educational development objectives.*
- *Educate handicapped and nonhandicapped students in both individual and group sessions according to their needs.*
- *Document assessment findings and review with central staff and parents.*
- *Assist coordinator for handicapped children with preparation of individual education plans (IEPs) in accordance with PL94-142.*
- *Participate in Comprehensive Developmental Team (CDT) staffing meetings to review IEPs.*
- *Screen, assess, and record observations and evaluations of child development, including referrals for cognitive, language, vision, health, and social development.*
- *Responsible for classroom schedule, subject matter, selection of materials and media, development of learning activities, and documentation of plans.*

DAY CARE FACILITATOR   *May – Oct. 1998*
Tykes Daycare, *Belcourt, North Dakota*
- *Provided day care services to children ages infant to eight years.*
- *Processed customer invoices and calculated payment schedules.*

CROP INSURANCE CLERK   *Jan. 1994 – June 1995*
Agricultural Stabilization and Conservation Service, *Rolla, North Dakota*
- *Assessed and processed client insurance claims.*
- *Distributed crop insurance payments to ASCS members.*
- *Monitored damage claims and revised records to reflect adjustments.*

EDUCATION   *BACHELOR OF SCIENCE*   *GPA in major 3.47*   *May 1999*
University of North Dakota, *Grand Forks*
Major: Elementary Education with emphasis in Science/Bilingual Education

ASSOCIATE OF SCIENCE, cum laude   *GPA 4.0*   *May 1996*
Turtle Mountain Community College, *Belcourt, North Dakota*
Major: Early Childhood

HONORS
- *Bureau of Indian Affairs Scholarship*   *1995 – 1999*
- *North Dakota Indian Affairs Commission Scholarship*   *1996 – 1999*
- *Who's Who in Junior and Community Colleges*   *1995 – 1996*
- *President's List and Dean's List (UND and TMCC)*   *1994 – 1999*

ACTIVITIES
- *American Indian Higher Education Consortium (AIHEC) Member*   *1994 – 1996*
- *North Dakota Association for the Education of Young Children (NDAEYC)*   *1996 – 1999*
- *University of North Dakota Indian Association*   *1996 – 1999*
- *Head Start Council Member*   *1996 – 1999*

LANGUAGES   *Knowledge of **Michif** • Communication skills in **Spanish***

SHAY STEEL

1234 Quicksilver Drive
Colorado Springs, Colorado 80922
Telephone: (719) 555-1234

STRENGTHS

- Dedicated teacher with the desire to instill in children the passion to be life-long learners.
- Able to set and maintain high expectations with the belief that children will rise to them and be reliable, respectful, responsible, and ready to learn.
- Outgoing and patient instructor who enjoys working with children.
- Effective team player with strong interpersonal, communication, and presentation skills.
- Knowledge of Hyperstudio, Storyweavers, WordPerfect, MS Word, Windows, MS Publisher, and the Internet.

BACKGROUND

Teaching
- Taught academic, social, and motor skills to elementary students.
- Experienced in team teaching (5-member team), combination, and multi-age classes (kindergarten through fifth grades).
- Prepared objectives and outlines for courses and assisted in developing curriculum.
- Designed learning environments to meet development objectives and state standards.
- Adapted lesson plans for students with special needs, including those with learning disabilities and ADHD.
- Developed a cooperative learning foundation using partners and the buddy system.
- Integrated reading, science, social studies, writing, and math into skills-based and structured learning environments.
- Developed a skills-based reading unit using a wide variety of materials.
- Created and taught lessons about Germany and Australia in order to help children think with open minds and understand other cultures as well as their own.
- Tutored individual students in reading and math.
- Prepared, administered, and corrected tests; kept attendance and grade records.

Communications
- Counseled students when adjustment and academic problems arose.
- Facilitated student-led conferences with parents.
- Recruited parents to assist with field trips.
- Recorded observations of child development.

EDUCATION

BACHELOR OF ARTS   May 1999
University of Colorado, Colorado Springs
- Major: Psychology
- Minor: English
- Completed an additional 11-month Teacher Education Program (TEP)
- Colorado Elementary Education Certificate

TEACHING EXPERIENCE

Student Teacher, Jackson Elementary, Colorado Springs, Colorado	1999
Teaching Associate, Jackson Elementary, Colorado Springs, Colorado	1998
Teaching Associate, Steele Elementary, Colorado Springs, Colorado	1998
Teaching Associate, Penrose Elementary, Colorado Springs, Colorado	1998
Teaching Observations, 30 classrooms, Colorado Springs, Colorado	1998
Junior Achievement, Jordahl Elementary, Colorado Springs, Colorado	1997
Tutor, Harrison and Longfellow Elementary, Colorado Springs, Colorado	1996 – 1997

13 | Paragraph Style

Good advertisements are designed in such a way that the reader's eye is immediately drawn to important pieces of information using type and graphic elements, including bold, italics, and headline fonts, and so forth. Then the design must guide the reader's eye down the page from one piece of information to the next with the use of white space or graphic designs between short paragraphs.

In this science of typography, very long lines of text (longer than six or seven inches, depending on the font) and large blocks of text (more than seven typeset lines) are considered to be tiring to the reader's eye. If you look closely at textbooks, magazines, and newspapers, you will notice that the information is usually typeset in columns to reduce line lengths, and journalists intentionally write in short paragraphs because they are more reader friendly.

How does this science translate into the design of a résumé? As a general rule, you should keep your lines of text no longer than seven inches—five to six inches is even better—and your paragraphs shorter than seven lines of text each. Many people find it difficult to cram the description of a job and its accomplishments into a single paragraph while following this rule. Therefore, you will often see bulleted sentences used instead of paragraphs on résumés.

If you prefer the paragraph style, there are some tricks of the trade that can help you make your résumé more readable:

1. Divide your experience into related information and use several shorter paragraphs under each job description (pages 188, 192, and 194).

2. List the job summary in paragraph form and then use bullets to highlight your achievements (page 188).

3. Use left headings instead of centered headings (pages 188 and 192) or put dates in a left column (page 191) to make the line lengths shorter. This won't work, however, when the shorter line length forces your information into very long paragraphs. It is better to have longer line lengths and shorter paragraphs.

Full justification—where all the lines end at the same place on the right margin—makes paragraph-style résumés look more formal. Ragged right margins generally give a more informal appearance (see pages 185 and 186). Full justification creates a neater appearance any time the lines of text run all of the way to the right margin, even in bulleted résumés. However, you can choose either style and not go wrong. Again, it is just a matter of your personal preference.

Sandra L. Wesson

1234 South Hoyt Court
Littleton, Colorado 80123
Phone: (303) 555-1234
E-mail: criscito@aol.com

PROFILE

Dedicated sales representative with more than 18 years of experience with retail headquarter, convenience store, and natural food accounts, including:

- Retail sales/marketing
- Merchandising
- Territory management
- Strategic planning
- Trade shows
- Display set-up
- Plan-o-grams
- Store resets
- Management/administration
- Budgeting
- Employee recruiting
- Training/development

Self-motivated and determined sales professional with a proven record of effectively managing large territories and increasing profitability. Skilled in getting to the decision maker and communicating with all levels of management. Knowledge of Windows 95, MS Word, Excel, PowerPoint, e-mail, and the Internet.

EXPERIENCE

DIRECTOR OF CHANNEL MARKETING (1995 – present)
Marketing Specialists, Aurora, Colorado
Manage the channel marketing efforts for this international broker of grocery products, health and beauty aids, and general merchandise. Represent 30 manufacturers to more than 1,200 convenience stores, 100 natural food stores, and 80 headquarter accounts in a seven-state territory. Recruit, interview, hire, train, and supervise a retail sales supervisor and six merchandisers.

Personally represent more than 2,000 items to convenience stores and natural food markets, including Earth Science, Arrowhead, Nabisco, Texaco/Havoline, and Blistex. Aggressively call on headquarters of McLane, Coremark, Rainbow Natural Foods, and Wild Oats at least once a month. Create strategic plans for merchandisers, including territory assignment, routing, sales binders, survey sheets, and reporting. Develop and manage the marketing budget and determine placement of advertisements, promotions, and donations.

- Took store sales from zero to more than $400,000 in monthly sales within one year.
- Gained a 50 percent increase in distribution from General Mills in the territory.

SERVICE MANAGER (1989 – 1995)
Sell-Thru Services, Austin, Texas
Successfully managed 3,000 accounts and as many as 30 sales representatives in a territory that covered Colorado, Albuquerque, and West Texas. Developed a thriving territory in Colorado's previously untapped ski areas. Responsible for the headquarters of M&M Mars, Tropicana, Hunt Wesson, and Sky Box. Other major accounts included Kraft General Foods, Best Foods, General Mills, Kimberly Clark, and Procter and Gamble.

Implemented plan-o-grams and store resets; performed category analyses and determined market share through competitive analysis of IRI and Nielsen data. Set up trade shows and displays (end caps, lobby, and in-line); instrumental in designing and setting up a 3,000-case display.

- Selected to trouble shoot territories in seven major markets (Colorado, Albuquerque, West Texas, San Francisco, Kansas City, New Orleans, and Houston).
- Interviewed, hired, and trained new territory managers and sales representatives and improved profitability.

MERCHANDISER (1981 – 1989)
M&M/Mars, Inc., Hackettstown, New Jersey
Managed a territory with 100 retail accounts. Responsible for all merchandising functions, including product freshness, display building, resets, and plan-o-grams.

EDUCATION

ARAPAHOE COMMUNITY COLLEGE, Littleton, Colorado
- Courses in finance, marketing, and computer applications.

CONTINUING EDUCATION
- Classes and seminars in business management, computer software, and IRI data analysis.

ADAM L. GREEN

12343 North Ashby Lane
Livingston, New Jersey 07039
Telephone: (973) 555-1234

SUMMARY OF QUALIFICATIONS

Dynamic sales professional with a background in marketing and merchandising. Experienced in national representation, manufacturing, and retail sales. Proven ability to maintain profitable client relationships. Effective team player with strong interpersonal, communication, and presentation skills. Self-motivated; comfortable working independently with little supervision. Knowledge of Windows, MS Word, Excel, Access, PowerPoint, and Lotus 1-2-3.

RELEVANT EXPERIENCE

MOORE RESPONSE MARKETING, New York, New York (1997 – Current)
Senior Account Coordinator
Manage all facets of direct mail production for Citibank account exceeding $10 million in revenue. Act as a liaison between client and several internal printing facilities in Green Bay, Wisconsin. Involved with hiring, training, and supervising of Account Coordinators. Strategically estimate and price mailings to client, monitor job costs and prepare invoicing for monthly mailings. Participate in new creative development ideas for over 50 million mailing pieces in 1998. Create and implement numerous internal management processes and manufacturing reference tools, including an extensive proofing process.

MELARD MANUFACTURING CORPORATION, Passaic, New Jersey (1990 – 1997)
National Sales and Service Representative (1996 – 1997)
Developed nationwide marketing plans for bath accessories and plumbing products. Helped create a sales presentation for Home Depot that landed their entire bath accessory aisle. Contributed to the doubling of sales to $100 million during the last fiscal year. Served as a liaison between customers and importers to better meet customer needs. Met regionally with customers to refine local preferences. Team leader for customer installations of product displays and aisle resets.

Service Representative (Summers, 1990 – 1995)
Formulated national and local marketing strategies for the National Sales and Marketing Coordinator. Traveled extensively throughout the United States, representing the sales department and promoting the latest marketing strategies. Interfaced with and developed rapport with major customers, including Home Depot, Wal-Mart, Lowes, K-Mart, and Hechinger/Home Quarters.

SUMMER OLYMPIC GAMES, Atlanta, Georgia (1996)
Kiosk Manager
Supervised ten employees in the sale of official Olympic apparel at the 1996 Summer Olympics. Host for the German guests of Lufthansa Airlines.

ART PLUS, Springfield, New Jersey (1993 – 1994)
Sales Assistant
Assisted the president of the company with the daily management operations. Scheduled art demonstrations and traveled the East Coast conducting sales presentations. Delivered and installed valuable paintings, portraits, and sculptures at numerous corporate headquarters, including Johnson and Johnson, Merck, DuPont, and ADP.

EDUCATION

BACHELOR OF SCIENCE DEGREE IN MARKETING (1996)
University of Maryland, College Park, Maryland
School of Business and Management • Minor in Economics

Larry O'Keefe

12345 60th Drive • Sun City, Arizona 85351 • (602) 555-1234

QUALIFICATIONS

- Production Control
- Inventory Control
- Production Planning
- MRP Implementation

- Real Estate Sales
- Property Evaluation
- Market Forecasting
- Budget Control

EXPERIENCE

1997 – 2000   REAL ESTATE AGENT, O'Keefe Realty

As a licensed agent, sold residential real estate in the Sun City/Sun City West area. Successfully sold both single-family homes and condominiums/apartments. Also was proficient in developing comparative analysis reports and sales forecasting plans for both home buyers and sellers, using advanced computer software programs.

1996 – 1997   OPERATIONS MANAGER, AAA Transport Company

Responsible for all freight loading and unloading into and out of the terminal, both long haul and local delivery. Also served as terminal dispatcher. Worked with both local and national representatives to acquire contracts for inbound and outbound rail and truck freight.

1994 – 1996   PRODUCTION PLANNER, ITT Cannon

Responsible for the production and shipment of major cables and harnesses for customers such as McDonnell and Hughes. This included the initial staging, production tracking, parts storage control, and final assembly. The above requirements were initiated through the use of an MRP system, which required continual input of data and control of production parameters. Product line represented shipments valued at approximately $8 million per year.

1992 – 1994   PRODUCTION CONTROL SUPERVISOR, Advanced Semiconductor Materials America

Supervised and trained subassembly planners and expeditors, which included timely and accurate staging, reviewing MRP guidelines and monitoring scheduled receipts and allocations. Previous responsibilities as a Senior Planner for the low pressure/diffusion wafer processing systems involved the implementation of two MRP II systems, proper control of allocations, and timely staging at the top assembly level. Improved delivery performance to better than 95 percent on major systems.

1990 – 1992   INVESTIGATOR/ANALYST, Subcontractor to Law Firm

Investigated and analyzed law firm property and assets held in various trusts and estates. Position involved contact with local and state government agencies, real estate brokers, and financial institutions. Prepared reports to provide information for estate heirs and for the preparation of tax returns. Arranged financing for various investment and construction projects. Served as registered process server for legal documents.

1988 – 1990   MANAGER, RAW MATERIALS AND BULK SCHEDULING, Revlon, Inc.

Ordered and controlled all materials needed for the production of bulk used in all Phoenix-produced products. Also determined the quantity and dates for the production of all bulk to correspond with product requirements. Supervised three executives and five clerical personnel. Prior position was Supply/Demand Manager, which included analysis of marketing forecasts, calculation of production frequency, and auditing of inventory positions.

EDUCATION

Master of Business Administration • Indiana University, South Bend, Indiana • 1988
Bachelor of Arts, Economics • Hanover College, Hanover, Indiana • 1973

Scannable

STEVEN J. WILLIAMS

1234 W. Anderson Drive • Phoenix, Arizona 85023 • (602) 555-1234

PROFESSIONAL OBJECTIVES

Immediate Objective: To obtain a sales representative position within the consumer product market.
Long-Range Objective: To assume increased responsibilities and serve in various levels of management.

EXPERIENCE RELATING TO SALES/MANAGEMENT

1998 – Present

FACTORY SALES/SERVICE REPRESENTATIVE
SHERWIN WILLIAMS COMPANY, Cleveland, Ohio
After completing college, was hired to service an area that includes the entire state of Arizona and the city of Las Vegas, Nevada. Primary customers include the three largest retail outlets in the area, i.e., Sears, Wal-Mart, Kmart, and other selected smaller retailers. Achieved total territory sales of over $704,000 and received Gold Shoe Award, among other achievement recognition rewards. Primarily responsible for factory orders, but also assist in merchandising, inventory control, and promotional activities. Conduct product knowledge sessions on an ongoing basis, including one-on-one and group sessions with customer personnel. Resolve end-user complaints. Responsible for company car, territory budget management, expense reporting, and other corporate paperwork.

1991 – 1997

SALES
SEARS, ROEBUCK AND COMPANY, Phoenix, Arizona (Metrocenter)
Commission sales within the hardware and lawn and garden departments. Primary responsibilities include assisting customers in their purchasing process, overcoming their objections, closing the sale, and providing follow-up assistance. Assist management with inventory control and product display maintenance. Served on the Courtesy Committee in 1987. Three-time winner of the store's monthly Courtesy Award. Winner of the 1986 Courtesy Award of the Year. Recipient of the Vice President's Symbol of Service Award in 1985.

1988 – 1991

ASSISTANT STORE MANAGER
FOREMOST LIQUORS, Downers Grove, Illinois
Shared responsibility for the operation of a franchised retail store. Primary responsibilities included inventory control of wine and delicatessen goods. Assisted in billing, payroll, receiving, hiring, and training. Was direct supervisor of 10 employees.

1985 – 1988

ASSISTANT STORE MANAGER
FRANK'S NURSERY SALES, INC., Franklin Park, Illinois
Originally hired as a stock boy but later became manager trainee, co-assistant manager, and then assistant manager. Shared the responsibility for the entire operation of a retail chain store. As a working manager, primary responsibilities included bookkeeping, payroll, and inventory planning and control. Was also responsible for staffing, scheduling, and training new employees. In addition to management activities, secondary responsibilities included receiving, stocking, store maintenance, and constructing store displays. Directly supervised 25 employees.

EDUCATION RELATING TO SALES/MANAGEMENT

Dec. 1997

B.S. DEGREE, Arizona State University, Tempe, Arizona
Major in Marketing. Courses most related: Principles of Selling, Principles of Retailing, Consumer Behavior, Sales Management, Marketing Communications, Strategic Marketing, Human Behavior in Organization, Marketing Research, Business Policies.

1995

A.A. DEGREE, Glendale Community College, Glendale, Arizona
Major in Business Administration. Courses most related: Accounting, Business Communication, Data Processing.

Scannable

191

Lou Farleigh

1233 West Kimberly Way
Glendale, Arizona 85308
(602) 555-1234

SUMMARY OF QUALIFICATIONS

Retail Manager with over 20 years experience in supermarket and department store operations with a major regional chain. Proficient in business planning and budgeting; employee training and motivation; enforcement of company standards and practices; and customer relations and services. Able to effectively delegate and monitor multiple employees and tasks concurrently.

ACCOMPLISHMENTS

- Consistently achieved bonuses for my store's operational profitability by careful attention to payroll budgets, gross profitability, inventory controls, and merchandise turnover.

- Recognized as a strong staff motivator able to develop a team attitude while enforcing company policies and procedures.

- Began with Smitty's as a courtesy clerk and progressed rapidly through the ranks to the position of supermarket manager.

PROFESSIONAL QUALIFICATIONS

SMITTY'S OF ARIZONA, Phoenix, Arizona   *1991 – Present*

Store Manager (6 years)

Store manager for six years prior to a company-wide reorganization and again at present, with responsibilities for both supermarket and department store operations with a total staff of 300–350 and gross revenues of over $35 million. Consistently met company standards of profitability and productivity while staying within budget guidelines and concurrently developing a loyal and dedicated employee team.

Supermarket Manager (7 years)

Manage all aspects of retail grocery operations at a busy store for this large regional grocery and department store chain. Direct the activities of 250 employees through delegation and supervision of eight subordinate managers. Departments include meat, bakery, produce, grocery, dairy, restaurant/snack bars, delicatessen, and floral department.

Key responsibilities include planning and executing budgets and business profit projections; developing and implementing employee motivation and training programs; delegating and ensuring company standards and practices; and instituting and maintaining ongoing customer relations and service activities. Also responsible for quality control and maintenance of the store and its facilities.

Key strengths include the ability to develop and control a profitable inventory mix and institute effective merchandising to serve those needs. This includes extensively training employees in customer service and public relations.

Prior positions held at Smitty's included: Assistant Supermarket Manager, Grocery Manager, Front End Manager, Night Manager, Department Manager, Receiving Manager, and Journeyman Clerk.

ROCHESTER HOUSING AUTHORITY, Rochester, New York   *1987 – 1991*

Housing Manager

Managed a staff of 30 people involved in renting and managing apartments and single-family housing in several locations. Collected rents. Handled evictions. Oversaw maintenance and repairs.

TWO GUYS DISCOUNT STORES, Harrison, New Jersey   *1982 – 1986*

Department Manager

Responsible for front-end operations with approximately 100 employees and the accounting department.

EDUCATION

FARLEIGH DICKINSON UNIVERSITY, Madison, New Jersey
Major: Education/Mathematics

(Scannable)

Joseph A. Emberwood

12345 Circle Drive   Sun City, Arizona 85351   (602) 555-1234

PROFESSIONAL EXPERIENCE

PROGRAM REVIEW MANAGER
Neighborhood Reinvestment Corporation
Atlanta, Georgia (3/90 to 5/99)

Completely responsible for managing capacity-building activities among 75 community development organizations in 18 states. Supervised remote professional staff and organizational development consultants. Conducted or managed the conduct of intensive "organizational audits" under difficult conditions or in complex situations requiring the utmost sensitivity. Met stringent annual quota of "audits" conducted. Received many compliments on the caliber of staff hired.

PROGRAM MANAGER, CENTRAL INTAKE
Chicago Energy Savers Fund
Chicago, Illinois (12/88 to 3/90)

Directed operations for a city-wide program offering energy-related loan and construction assistance to homeowners. Ensured that production quotas were met and quality of work was maintained in a fast-paced environment. Supervised technical and clerical staff. Underwrote hundreds of good-quality loans originated by my office and fifteen others. Directed loan closing and escrow management operations, routinely solving staff, customer, and contractor problems every step of the way. Became known as the "damage control" specialist, called upon to deal with the most difficult personalities. My own employees made our office the **top producer** of all.

FIELD SERVICES OFFICER
Neighborhood Reinvestment Corporation
Chicago, Illinois (7/85 to 12/88)

Completely responsible for on-site management assistance to voluntary community development agencies in ten cities, three states. Independently conducted successful training in fund-raising, strategic planning, fiscal management, and personnel administration. Routinely intervened in crises ranging from critical cash shortfalls to impending litigation of construction jobs in trouble.

NEIGHBORHOOD DIRECTOR
Little Village Division
Neighborhood Housing Services of Chicago, Inc.
Chicago, Illinois (12/80 to 7/85)

Completely responsible for developing, then operating successful housing rehab program. Recruited, trained, and provided administrative support to Board of Directors and other volunteers. Prepared and managed annual budget and work plan. Recruited, selected, trained, and evaluated four-person staff. Provided credit analysis, financial counseling, and loan packaging services for primarily Spanish-speaking clients.

EDUCATION

Bachelor of Science in Economics, Illinois State University, 1980

Spanish Language Training, Berlitz School of Languages, 1985
(attained fluency with 2,000-word vocabulary in four weeks)

Sandra L. Valfleur

1234 West Greenway Road #123 • San Francisco, California 85306 • (602) 555-1234

Professional Experience

Communications Director   **Vern Jones Oil and Gas Corporation (VJOG)**
September 1999 – Present   San Francisco, California
Lobbied for the oil and gas industry through the state legislature. Worked with state and county agencies to obtain permits. Ensured positive relations with investors through written communication and general meetings.

President   **Jones Four Corporation (JFC)**
February 1992 – December 1998   Healdsburg, California
Jones Four Corporation produced wine, marketed under the brand name Valfleur Winery. Developed the corporation's identity package, i.e., brand name, logo, brochures, trademark, bottles, and cartons. Determined wine styles, volumes, and varietals purchased from the vineyards. Researched potential markets. Developed and implemented marketing plan.

In 1987, Valfleur Winery produced 17,000 cases, 11,000 cases of Chardonnay from our Jimtown Ranch vineyard, 3,000 cases each of Sauvignon Blanc and Cabernet Sauvignon purchased from other vintners. The wines were marketed in approximately twenty (20) states. The company was sold in 1988.

Administrative Assistant   **Vern Jones and Associates**
July 1990 – February 1992   Sacramento, California
Established the accounting system, meeting all requirements of state and federal filing. Created and implemented a system for management of investments. Conducted research and feasibility studies on possible new ventures. From these studies emerged two companies: Jones Four Corporation in 1982 and Vern Jones Oil and Gas Corporation in 1985.

Education

Master of International Management   May 1999
American Graduate School of International Management   Glendale, Arizona
Thunderbird Campus

Bachelor of Business Administration   January 1998
National University   Sacramento, California

Language, Skills, and Affiliation

- Proficient in French (U.S. State Department Level 3)
- Extensive training in all aspects of the wine industry
- Elected Affiliate of American Society of Enologists
- Board of Director for Yolo County Child Sexual Abuse Treatment Center
- Member of San Francisco Ballet Auxiliary Association
- Outdoors enthusiast including skiing, running, mountain biking, hiking, and golf
- President of the International Wine Tasting Club – Thunderbird

International Exposure

- Summer study abroad in France 1998
- 1988 – 1990 lived in the Bahamas and France while employed with Club Med
- Extensive international travel

194

Scannable

GREGG M. DIETHRICH

EDUCATION

Master of International Management   Glendale, Arizona **1997 – 1999**

AMERICAN GRADUATE SCHOOL OF INTERNATIONAL MANAGEMENT. Specializing in Financial Management, Marketing, and International Trade. Developed a Lotus 1-2-3 based accounting system for a small business and used computer-based modeling to determine optimal asset acquisition and investment strategies. Conducted international market research for consumer and industrial products and subsequently created appropriate marketing strategies and advertising campaigns.

Bachelor of Science in Commerce-Finance   Santa Clara, California **1996 – 1997**

SANTA CLARA UNIVERSITY. Emphasis in Financial Decision Analysis and Investments with a minor in Asian Studies. Used computerized formulations of NPV, IRR, WACC, and risk and return analysis to determine alternative investment strategies and to support financial management decisions such as asset acquisition and lease/purchase evaluations.

Overseas Study Program   Tokyo, Japan **1988 – 1989**

SOPHIA UNIVERSITY. Enrolled in Business and Asian Culture seminars. Exposed to international business environment through semiweekly visits to multinational companies. Worked directly with president of Inoue Art Products, assisting in development/implementation of public relations campaigns for international clients.

WORK EXPERIENCE

Project Director   Poland **1999**

INTERNATIONAL DEVELOPMENT EXCHANGE. Co-authored program designed to introduce and support free-market economic operations in former centrally planned economies. Responsible for implementing pilot project in Poland. Duties included: Managing program development, supervising Western business consultants, assisting Polish managers and government personnel in their professional activities, developing a strong working relationship with business and education groups and government committees in order to ensure significant indigenous support and continued successful economic development.

Financial Manager   Phoenix, Arizona **1995 – 1997**

THE DIETHRICH GROUP. Designed computerized reporting formats and evaluated business data, including: forecasts, operating cost/benefit analysis, cash flow estimates, budget requirements, financial statement projections, return analysis, and long-range planning.

General Manager/Partner   Saudi Arabia **1994 – 1995**

SEA AND SUN SPORTS. Conceived, designed, and successfully implemented/managed business plan serving sports and leisure market. Responsible for complete operations of three retail and training facilities for activities, including boating, fishing, martial arts, scuba diving, skiing, squash, surfing, tennis, and travel. Activities included international recruitment, purchasing, and charter services.

Managing Director   Saudi Arabia **1991 – 1994**

LAKOS INTERNATIONAL. Responsible for entire joint venture operations, encompassing agricultural, industrial, and consumer products. Duties included: monitoring of manufacturing; overseeing shipping, customs clearance, and inventory control; supervising hiring/training and management of sales, installation, and service personnel; development of distribution channels/dealer network; reconciliation and compilation of relevant accounting and financial reports/statements; and distribution of profits. Also responsible for introduction of revolutionary well inspection and repair service.

TECHNICAL SKILLS

Foreign Languages: Proficient in Japanese. Knowledge of Arabic and Spanish.

ADDRESSES

Permanent • 12345 East Campus Drive • Mesa, Arizona 85282 • (602) 555-1234
Current • 12345 N. 59th Avenue, #123 • Glendale, Arizona 85306 • (602) 555-1234

Scannable

195

RONALD V. DANIELS

1234 Stanley Avenue • Key Largo, Florida 34640 • (813) 555-1234

AREAS OF KNOWLEDGE AND EXPERIENCE

SALES AND MARKETING:
Sales Training and Motivation
New Home Marketing
Market Research
Product Development
Feasibility Studies

ADVERTISING:
Design/Layout
Copy Writing
Radio/TV Commercials
Film Production

REAL ESTATE:
Licensed Real Estate Broker
Property Acquisition
Land Development
Property Management

GENERAL CONSTRUCTION:
Residential
Commercial
General Contracting
Condo Conversions

FINANCE:
Licensed Mortgage Broker
Loan Packaging
FHA/VA Financing
Project Funding

EXPERIENCE

OWNER / MANAGER   Mar. 1995 – Present
Debron Group, Inc. (Builder Developer), Daytona Beach, Florida
Full responsibility for managing all aspects of our three companies: *Debron Realty* specializes in marketing new homes for area builders. We built a reputation as an aggressive and innovative sales group with over 1,500 new home sales to our credit. *Debron Development* purchases raw land and develops it into fully improved building lots for resale or our own use. *Debron Homes*, one of the top three volume builders of custom designed single-family homes in the Daytona Beach area.

SALES MANAGER   Apr. 1994 – Mar. 1995
ITT/CDC—Sheraton Corporation (Land Developer), Palm Coast, Florida
Headed up a new home sales division. Planned advertising and marketing programs for this 80,000 acre city on Florida's northeast coast. During our first year we sold $5,000,000 in new homes in a previously untapped market. Reason for change: Left to pursue an opportunity in Daytona Beach's growing housing market.

DIVISION MANAGER   Nov. 1992 – Apr. 1994
Beacon Homes (Builder Developer), Hudson, Florida
Managed "Beacon Woods," a 7,000-acre planned unit development. Was responsible for all sales activity for five model centers. Hired, trained, and motivated sales staff. Planned marketing programs to increase traffic and developed out-of-state broker contacts. Produced a company record of *500* new home sales in 1983. This represented a 300 percent increase over 1992, despite high interest rates.

PROJECT MANAGER   Feb. 1988 – Nov. 1992
Deltona Corporation, Ocala, Florida
Managed all aspects of this 15,000-acre planned community called "Marion Oaks." Responsible for land sales, housing sales, golf course operations, advertising, marketing, sales training, and office operations. Reason for change: Economic cutbacks within the corporation.

EDUCATION

BACHELOR OF ARTS IN BUSINESS ADMINISTRATION
John Carroll University, Cleveland, Ohio • Major in Management

SPECIAL STUDY
American Management Association Seminars • Dale Carnegie Sales Seminars
University of South Florida, Marketing and Psychology

PROFESSIONAL MEMBERSHIPS

National Association of Homebuilders, Daytona Beach, Florida
Daytona Beach Homebuilders Association, Chairman, Sales/Marketing Council
Sales/Marketing Executives, Tampa, Florida

Scannable

14 Functional versus Chronological

There are three basic types of résumés—reverse chronological, functional, and a combination of the two.

A reverse-chronological résumé arranges your experience and education in chronological order with the most recent dates first. One of the most frequent questions I am asked as a résumé writer is, "Do I have to list all of my jobs? It makes me look so old!" My answer is always, "No, you don't have to list every single position you have ever held. The trick is to pick and choose the ones that are relevant to your objective." You can also eliminate low-level positions and positions that duplicate later experience. *Relevant* is the keyword here!

More than half of the résumés in this book are reverse-chronological, but that doesn't mean a different type of résumé might not fit your needs better. This chapter will show you what is possible with a functional résumé in case that style better fits your needs.

A functional résumé organizes your work experience by the functions you performed regardless of date. The functional résumé highlights your skills and potential instead of your work history. It allows you to play down gaps in your experience and is especially good for those people entering the job market for the first time. If you are reentering the job market, for example, after raising children, this type of résumé also allows you to list volunteer experience and community or school activities.

List your functional paragraphs in their order of importance, with the items listed first that will help you get the particular job you are targeting. Refer to step 10 in the twelve-step résumé writing process outlined in Chapter 2 of this book for ideas on how to rearrange your résumé sentences to better capture your reader's attention.

You should know that there are very rare times when I would recommend a purely functional résumé, however. In the 1980s, true functional résumés developed a bad reputation because applicants were not listing where they gained their experience. It made recruiters suspicious that the applicant was trying to hide something. A combination functional/chronological résumé will avoid this problem. Always list a brief synopsis of your actual work experience at the bottom of your functional résumé with your title, employer, and the dates worked.

Outside of this chapter, you will find other functional résumés on pages 35, 42, 43, 50, 58, 64, 65, 71, 75, 77, 82, 88, 133, 148, 150, 164, 183, 184, 234, 238, 244, 246, and 271. On pages 208, 209, 214, and 215 you will find true chronological résumés that have added functional subdivisions under each job.

Betty Warren

12345 Capella Drive • Monument, Colorado 80132 • Phone and Fax: (719) 555-1234

HIGHLIGHTS OF QUALIFICATIONS

Thirteen years of professional management experience
Background in event management, marketing, training, and coaching
Strong communication and presentation skills; self-motivated, dependable, and people oriented
Knowledge of Windows 95 and Excel computer software

PROFESSIONAL EXPERIENCE

Management/Administration

- Hosted the Virginia Slims of Denver tournament (Kraft General Foods World Tour).
- Co-chair of the Player Services Committee for The Challenge (Nuveen Men's Senior Tour, Jimmy Connors, John McEnroe, Bjorn Borg, Yannick Noah), The Broadmoor, Colorado Springs, 1997.
- Experienced in all aspects of event management and tournament directing, including logistics, transportation, security, safety, coordination of activities, recruitment of volunteers, publicity, and scheduling of celebrity appearances.
- As a college coach, recruited and counseled athletes, selected staff, developed budgets, raised funds, planned trips, made travel arrangements, scheduled activities, and publicized events.
- Revitalized underperforming club programs and achieved significant profitability.
- Recruited, hired, and supervised professional teaching staff, front desk, food/beverage, and maintenance personnel.
- Developed budgets and managed general pro shop operations and tennis/racquetball/fitness facilities.
- Responsible for vendor selection, ordering and purchasing of inventory and supplies.
- Developed office policies and procedures in order to ensure efficiency of operations.

Marketing/Promotion

- Coordinated media appearances and press conferences for celebrities, including transportation and security.
- Experienced in marketing, advertising, and promoting special events and tennis clubs.
- Integral part of a team responsible for developing event promotional materials, ticket sales, and newspaper advertising.
- Designed and advertised programs and created promotional brochures; assisted in publication of newsletters.
- Sponsored by Head Sports, Fila, Reebok, and the Aspen Leaf Corporation to promote their products.

Tennis

- Played in the U.S. Women's Pro Circuit; held #1 state ranking in the Colorado Tennis Association and #1 sectional ranking in the Intermountain Tennis Association; served on the Regional Ranking Committee for Division III colleges.
- Taught tennis to juniors, adults, and seniors; coached college men's and women's tennis teams.
- Certified with the United States Professional Tennis Association.

Sports Medicine/Rehabilitation

- Interviewed patients, conducted assessments, and measured body fat in Phase I of the rehabilitation program.
- Monitored stress testing (blood pressure and EKG) and other pre- and post-tests; designed exercise prescriptions for patients and supervised their twelve-week programs (Phase II).
- Educated patients in nutrition, medications, and stress management and designed follow-up programs (Phase III).
- Assisted in city-wide program to test fitness levels of Denver firemen.

EMPLOYMENT HISTORY

1985 – 1998	**Manager/Director of Tennis, Events Manager, Head Tennis Pro, and Coach**, Colorado Springs and Denver, Colorado: Colorado College, Cheyenne Mountain Country Club, Broadmoor Tennis, Woodmoor Country Club, Heatherridge Racquet Club, Gates Tennis Center, and University of Colorado
1984 – 1984	**Ski School Supervisor, Jr. Racing Coach**, Ski Broadmoor, Colorado Springs, Colorado
1981 – 1983	**Exercise Physiologist in Cardiac Rehabilitation**, Humana Hospital Aurora, Denver, Colorado
1980 – 1981	**Internship in Cardiac Rehabilitation**, Humana Hospital Aurora, Denver, Colorado

EDUCATION

MASTER OF ARTS, University of Denver, Denver, Colorado (1981)
Major: Sport Science • Emphasis in Exercise Physiology and Cardiac Rehabilitation

BACHELOR OF ARTS, Western State College, Gunnison, Colorado (1977)
Major: Physical Education • Athletic Scholarships for Women's Varsity Tennis and Volleyball

Scannable

MARK ELLIS WILLIAMS

123 East Willamette • Colorado Springs, Colorado 80903 • (719) 555-1234

TEACHING PHILOSOPHY

A teacher's goal is to connect students to the cultural, social, political, and economic events of history so that, through comparison and contrast, they can become excited about their current and future experiences. Films, literature, drama, art, newspapers, diaries, and field experiences can stimulate active learning experiences that engage students in a personal connection with the common and extraordinary dilemmas of each historical period. Students should be stretched past the memorization of facts to learn how historical peoples were engaged in very relevant human struggles. The classroom should be where students learn to investigate, formulate, criticize, and articulate the diverse views of the human experience.

HIGHLIGHTS OF QUALIFICATIONS

Experience in public and private secondary and higher education
Strong communication and presentation skills
Able to relate to a wide range of educational aspirations
Responsible, flexible, self-motivated, team-oriented problem solver

EXPERIENCE

TEACHING
- Graduate of the University of Colorado Teacher Education Program; graduate degree in history
- Taught social studies, civics, history, English, and literature courses to high school and middle school students
- Designed learning environment to meet educational development requirements, adapting teaching style to accommodate both individual and group needs
- Developed curriculum materials to meet state standards and lesson objectives, incorporating experiential learning wherever possible (mock trials, field trips, etc.)
- Counseled students with adjustment and academic problems and met with parents
- Member, National Council for History Education and Phi Alpha Theta national history honor society

ADMINISTRATION
- Administered a 50-person staff as Youth Camp Director
- Developed curriculum and activity plans for as many as 200 youth
- Stabilized the program over twelve years to achieve maximum occupancy rates
- Interviewed, hired, trained, supervised, and evaluated restaurant staff
- Responsible for marketing and management consulting

EDUCATION

1996	**Master of Arts in History**	University of Colorado, Colorado Springs, Colorado James Madison Fellow
1991	**Teacher Education Program**	University of Colorado, Colorado Springs, Colorado
1990	**Bachelor of Arts in History**	University of Colorado, Colorado Springs, Colorado Magna Cum Laude, Highest Honors in History
1999	**Social Studies Internet and Leadership Training Program**	University of Northern Colorado, Greeley, Colorado

EMPLOYMENT HISTORY

1997 – present	**Teacher**	Palmer High School, Colorado Springs, Colorado
1991 – 1996	**Substitute Teacher**	Colorado Springs School Districts 11 and 20
1993 – 1994	**Teacher**	Woodland Park Middle School, Woodland Park, Colorado
1982 – 1991	**Youth Camp Director**	Sierra Bible Camp, Palo Alto, California
1983 – 1987	**Restaurant Manager**	Baskin-Robbins, Palo Alto, California Old Chicago, Colorado Springs, Colorado
1979 – 1982	**Admissions Counselor**	Columbia Christian College, Portland, Oregon

Scannable

199

LEE DAVID MADISON

QUALIFICATIONS
- Seasoned leader with 25 years of senior-level management experience coupled with significant marketing and high-tech computer/communications expertise in the Silicon Valley.
- Able to effectively motivate executive management and operating personnel to achieve maximum results.
- Skilled in applying logical but creative approaches to problem resolution.
- Effective in successfully completing projects under tight budgets and time limitations.
- Possess a high degree of professionalism and dedication to exceptional quality.

ACHIEVEMENTS
- Helped GTE Sprint grow from a $100 million start-up company to a $2 billion enterprise by developing, installing, and maintaining new consumer-oriented technologies.
- Built Computer Intellectics from a -$100,000 company to a $30+ million organization with 85 technical professionals and managers, saving $274,000+ a year for more than 11 years.
- Pushed state-of-the-art technology envelope to feasible limits to build one of the first commercial ISDN global networks.
- Provided design guidance and supervised the installation of Bank of America's European network for international money transfers.
- Significantly increased functional capabilities of Ungermann-Bass' Support Technology Department without increasing the budget or adding personnel.
- Introduced incentive and recognition programs to promote productivity and reduce turnover.
- Historically delivered projects on time and under budget while utilizing only available staff and resources.

Management
- Provided technical administration, leadership, and long-range business planning.
- Developed and managed budgets of up to $21.6 million.
- Responsible for strategic planning, profit and loss, financial activities, and resource allocation/utilization.
- Extensive experience in marketing, tactical response to meet competitive threats, pre- and post-sales support, customer relations, and successful proposal preparation and presentation.
- Evaluated vendors and ensured conformance with specifications.
- Experienced in technical marketing support, competitive analysis and response, and market research.
- Supervised integrated teams of up to 126 technical professionals and managers, in addition to contractors and support staff.
- Developed data utilization and optimization techniques for management.

Technical
- Extensive experience in voice/data communications system design and development, communications implementation and planning, and integration of large-scale computer systems.
- Background in technology assessment and feasibility, communications analysis, database design, client-server architectures, systems integration and installation, and systems generation.

EDUCATION

MASTER OF BUSINESS ADMINISTRATION   1978
California Western University, Santa Ana, California

BACHELOR OF SCIENCE, ELECTRONIC ENGINEERING   1976
California Western University, Santa Ana, California

CONTINUING EDUCATION
Numerous technical courses at IBM Institutes, postgraduate courses, and seminars in technology subjects

WORK HISTORY

President/CEO, Lee Schur Engineering, Inc., San Mateo, California	1990 – Present
Director, Program Management, Storage Technology Corporation, Louisville, Colorado	1990
Director, Support Technology, Ungermann-Bass, Inc., Santa Clara, California	1989 – 1990
Project Director, Software Engineering, Hewlett-Packard, Cupertino, California	1988 – 1989
Consulting Systems Engineer, Bank of America, San Francisco, California	1985 – 1988
Director of Technical Planning, GTE Sprint Communications, Inc., Burlingame, California	1983 – 1985
President/CEO, Technology Marketing International, Burlingame, California	1982 – 1983

ADDRESS

1234 Capstan Way, Colorado Springs, Colorado 80906   (719) 555-1234

Scannable

EXPERIENCE

LEE SCHUR ENGINEERING, INC., San Mateo, California (1990 – Present)
Developed and established a successful computer/communications consulting company dedicated to resolving leading-edge technology challenges for large corporate clients. Provided senior-level technical assistance in data and voice communications, computer interconnectivity, client-server architectures, and the integration of dissimilar network and computer systems.

Round the Bend Software Development (12 months) – IS Consultant, Chairman of the Board
• Structured and staffed the senior levels of this startup company.
• Led the software development team effort to resolve the legacy program problems created by the Year 2000 programming bug.

Mediatel (2 months) – Consultant
• Re-engineered network design and RAS definition for international network expansion.
• Developed rollout and implementation plans and schedules for the proposed network.
• Reviewed all documentation and prepared for ISO 9000 acceptance.

Aspect Telecom (3 months) – Consultant Network Engineer
• Senior member of the technical team responsible for the installation, testing, and support of an ISDN switch capable of handling full multispan ISDN PRI functionality, including voice, data, fax, and full-motion video.

Airtouch/EDS Consortium (2 months) – Project Manager
• Managed the new product installation, testing, and rollout planning for the Airtouch/Tandem SIXS system for cellular telephony, including wireless voice, data, and fax transmission.

Raynet Division of Ericsson (6 months) – Senior Engineer/Architect
• Developed and defined functional product specifications for the Broadband Raynet Video System (RVS) to provide fiber-to-the-curb and video-on-demand, full-function ISDN capability.

British Telecom/North America (3 months) – Senior Technical Consultant
• Integrated British Telecom's EDI electronic mail Internet (EDINet) with IBM, H-P, Tandem, DEC, and other platforms using X.400 and X.435 file transfer and message handling systems.
• Wrote and supported the technical portion of the proposal that resulted in $100 million contract award from Ford Motor Company.

Levi Strauss & Co. (3 months) – Project Manager/Network Consultant
• Defined the requisite technologies and topologies; conducted cost studies and wrote business case analyses supporting the cost-benefit ratios, performance studies, resource utilization, technology justification, and cost reduction and system re-engineering rationales for presentation to upper management for Levi's Global Communications Network, including data center site selection and justification.

Universal Communications (UNICOM) (6 months) – Program Manager
• Provided consultation services on a number of voice/data support and development activities, including customer support and training oversight, marketing support, and evaluation studies, among others.

STORAGE TECHNOLOGY CORPORATION, Louisville, Colorado (1990)
Director, Program Management
• Managed the machine interconnectivity program between STK's products and all other major vendors and mass-storage users; provided technical leadership and direction and guided the development efforts.
• Responsible for long- and short-term product line direction.
• Ensured the feasibility and viability of the newly developed interconnectivity products, ensuring that they met customer requirements, program objectives, and corporate strategic goals and objective.
• Managed cross-functional project teams and interdepartmental activities to achieve consensus.
• Defined strategic direction and business objectives; assured financial and technical conformance.

UNGERMANN-BASS, INC. (Division of Tandem Computers), Santa Clara, California (1989 – 1990)
Director, Support Technology
• Senior executive within the customer support organization with responsibility for new product hardware and software launch activities and customer support.
• Restructured and reorganized a department of 24 technical professionals to produce a 60 percent to 70 percent increase in response capability without adding to existing resources.
• Led a series of software development and communications interconnectability projects involving major clients throughout the world.
• Managed pre-release problem escalation, beta testing, and new product testing.

201

Gail B. Arif

OBJECTIVE A career position in a progressive and creative environment with increased administrative responsibilities

EXPERIENCE **Office and Clerical** . . . Experienced as an office manager, site supervisor, secretary, bookkeeper, and account clerk. Developed special interest college classes, researching subject matter, finding lecturers, scheduling classes, and assisting students with registration. Managed a city business license program. Organized and followed through with nonprofit fund raisers, including planning, assembling, pricing, advertising, and enlisting workers.

Skills . . . include public communication, accuracy, neatness, attention to detail, organization of work, time management, and ability to work on own with limited supervision. Have acquired skills in typing, word processing, filing, 10-key calculator, standard office machines, IBM System 36 computer, IBM personal computer, IBM and BPI software.

Public Relations and Communications . . . Positions held in the past have required extensive contact with the public, including good oral and written communications skills. Designed and distributed flyers, news releases, and worked on developing public relations between a college and its surrounding communities. Taught groups of 10 to 40 children or adults. Worked on large regional conferences involving up to 350 participants from conception to completion. Communicated information to employees regarding insurance benefits, payroll deductions, salaries, and leave balances. Researched, distributed, and explained revenue and expenditures to management to be used in budget projections.

Sales . . . Experienced in florist shop sales, fabric sales and cost estimation, furniture and appliance showroom sales, church and school fund raisers, garage sales, wholesale showroom sales of accessories, and sales to decorators. Served customers in a manner that would generate and/or continue their goodwill, satisfaction, and return business. Presented good showroom image by setting up and maintaining effective and attractive merchandise displays.

Bookkeeping and Inventory Management . . . Prepared payroll for a large staff. Responsible for accounts payable, accounts receivable, general ledger, record keeping, scheduling, computer setup and data entry, records management, bank deposits, purchasing, filing freight claims, research and retrieval of information, calendar and fiscal year-end reports, W-2s and 1099 preparation, quarterly and year-end tax reports, insurance benefits, payroll deductions, correspondence, and ordering, inventory, and distribution of office supplies. Responsible for estimating and expediting orders for supplies/merchandise, phone/wire orders, scheduling and delivery.

Creative . . . Adept in interior design, color coordination, textile design and selection, floral design and arrangement, handicrafts, layout of flyers and posters for sales and fund raisers, showroom displays of furniture and accessories, visual aids for teaching, designing and sewing clothing, assisting in wardrobe and accessory selection.

EMPLOYMENT HISTORY

Site Supervisor, Rio Salado Community College, Surprise, Arizona	1/94 – 6/99
Chiropractic Assistant, Weathersby Chiropractic, Glendale, Arizona	1/93 – 5/93
Secretary/Bookkeeper, Maverick Masonry, Inc., Phoenix, Arizona	3/92 – 10/93
Account Clerk, City of Novato, Novato, California	4/80 – 10/92

EDUCATION **Bachelor of Science in Home Economics**, University of New Hampshire

ADDRESS 1234 W. Athens Street · Peoria, Arizona 85382 · (602) 555-1234

Scannable

JOHN D. VINSON

1234 Oro Blanco Drive
Colorado Springs, CO 80917
Telephone: (719) 555-1234

SUMMARY

Fifteen years of experience in maintenance and repair of electronics and communications equipment. Background in quality control and quality assurance programs. Skilled in leading by example and inspiring others to better performance. Committed to honesty and the highest caliber character. Secret security clearance.

PROFESSIONAL HIGHLIGHTS

Technical Experience
- Repaired traffic control equipment, including motion detectors, current monitors, traffic control computers, power supplies, and integrated circuit boards.
- Experienced in the use of oscilloscopes, multimeters, signal generators, and computers (Windows, MS Word).
- Chemically treated integrated circuit dies before and after photo processes to etch circuit patterns using high-tech robotic equipment and electron microscopes.
- Set up, operated, repaired, tested, and maintained high-frequency communications equipment for eleven years.
- Responsible for Vinson communication systems, satellite burst communications equipment, FM/AM/UHF and digital radio receivers/transmitters, telephone switchboards, field telephones, satellite phone uplinks, fax machines, power generators, and other electronic and communications equipment.
- Assembled and diagnosed components of various systems with calibrated test equipment, including oscilloscopes, multimeters, and signal generators.
- Maintained bench stock of repair parts, supplies, and technical publications.
- Honored for increasing efficiency ratings from 60 percent to 95 percent.

Quality Control
- Managed a quality assurance program.
- Maintained quality and reliability standards to ensure optimum performance.
- As Communications Inspector, inspected communications equipment being turned in for replacement.

Management and Supervision
- Managed an electronic repair shop with accountability for vehicles and communications equipment valued in excess of $10 million.
- Directed the production control of high-frequency equipment to ensure steady work flow.
- Supervised up to forty maintenance technicians and/or operators.
- Provided professional guidance to staff and initiated/scheduled training of employees.
- Designed and presented hands-on training programs.

EMPLOYMENT HISTORY

1996 – present	**Electronic Technician**, Safetran Traffic Systems, Colorado Springs, Colorado
1996	**Cleanroom Operator**, Atmel, Colorado Springs, Colorado
1993 – 1995	**Satellite Repair Supervisor**, U.S. Army, 50th Signal Battalion, Fort Bragg, North Carolina
1992 – 1993	**Communications Electronics Shop Foreman**, U.S. Army, 307th Signal Battalion, Korea
1989 – 1992	**Communications Supervisor**, U.S. Army, 10th Special Forces Group, Fort Devens, Massachusetts
1984 – 1989	**Communications Inspector**, U.S. Army, 317th Maintenance Company, Germany

EDUCATION

Central Texas College
25 credit hours in Electronics and Electricity
14 credit hours in Basic Law Enforcement • Management Coursework

United States Army
Burst Communications Systems Maintenance • Primary Technical Course • Field Radio Repairer Course
Noncommissioned Officer Academy, Primary Leadership Course

Scannable

CORY CHARLESTON

1234 Orchard Path Road • Colorado Springs, Colorado 80919 • (719) 555-1234

PROFILE
- Dedicated management professional with extensive hands-on experience in:
  - Office Management
  - Retail Management
  - Recreation Administration
  - New Business Development
  - Customer Relations
  - Sales/Marketing
  - Budget Administration
  - Forecasting
  - Staff Motivation
  - Purchasing
  - Inventory Control
  - Shipping/Receiving
- Skilled in combining quality and service to ensure exceptional customer satisfaction.
- Successful in product and service related environments where the ability to coordinate and control daily activities, manage projects, and interpret information has increased profitability.
- Knowledge of MS Word, Excel, Access, PowerPoint, Peachtree, and point-of-sale software.

EDUCATION

BACHELOR OF SCIENCE, RECREATION ADMINISTRATION (Fall 1999)
Eastern Illinois University, Charleston, Illinois

SUMMARY

MANAGEMENT/ADMINISTRATION
- Managed the daily operations of fast-paced retail stores, recreation programs, and service organizations.
- Developed and administered budgets; established long-term and short-term objectives.
- Hired, trained, scheduled, and motivated staff; evaluated performance and made recommendations for improvement of productivity.
- Identified and resolved existing and potential problems to achieve maximum return on investment and improve cash flow.

RETAIL
- Monitored flow of incoming and outgoing inventory, verified shipments, supervised warehouse, ensured proper handling of merchandise, and authorized payment of invoices.
- Investigated and selected vendors and worked closely with sources to facilitate timely delivery.
- Forecasted inventory requirements based on past performance, seasonal trends, and special needs.
- Achieved an effective merchandise mix through knowledgeable selective buying.
- Created, placed, and evaluated advertising materials and merchandising displays to increase customer awareness and sales potential.
- Researched and resolved customer complaints and account discrepancies, ensuring customer satisfaction.

EXPERIENCE

Bookstore Coordinator, Colorado Technical University, Colorado Springs, CO   1999 – present
- Coordinated customer service and textbook ordering for 2,500 students.
- Established department operating processes and supervised two staff members.
- Developed customer service procedures, served as liaison between the customer and other departments, and ensured the delivery of exceptional customer service.
- Responsible for accounts receivable, cash transactions, and monthly inventory of 200,000+ items.

Fulfillment Manager, Volleyball Information Products, Colorado Springs, CO   1997 – 1998
- Managed a publication and video partnership, including marketing, purchasing, order processing, customer service, inventory maintenance, shipping, and payment processing.
- Performed the duties of the VIP Director from three days after hire date.
- Supervised, trained, scheduled, and evaluated the performance of customer service assistants.
- Sourced new products and followed through the development cycle to product production.
- Responsible for preparation of accounts payable, income statement, and balance sheet.
- Maintained database in Peachtree software and downloaded orders daily from the Internet.

Scannable

EXPERIENCE
(continued)

Assistant Retail Manager/Buyer, West Point Gift Shop, West Point, NY   1989 – 1997
- Managed the retail operation with $2.2 million in annual retail sales and $1.2 million catalog sales.
- Hired, scheduled, and supervised a staff of 45 full-time, part-time, and seasonal sales associates.
- Sourced and purchased soft goods, books, gift items, videos, and novelty items.
- Planned and purchased an effective marketing mix and created merchandising displays.
- Developed inventory control procedures to support both retail and catalog operations.
- Served as interim manager for six months, increasing sales by 21 percent within 30 days and then trained a new manager who continued to increase sales.

Assistant Retail Manager, G.H. Bass Shoe Outlet/Van Heusen, Central Valley, NY 1988 – 1989
- Turned around the operations of a faltering retail outlet store, achieving the largest sales volume of Bass outlets in the United States.
- Responsible for merchandising, staff development, financial analysis/management, payroll, floor plans, inventory controls, and customer relations.
- Determined merchandise needs and sales potential; organized six-month inventory layout and accountability for merchandise.

Assistant Director, Day Care Center, U.S. Military Academy, West Point, NY   1986 – 1988
- Responsible for program management, marketing, and planning of recreational and supplemental learning activities to foster physical, cognitive, and emotional development in infants, preschoolers, and school-age children.
- Sponsored and marketed monthly child advocacy and parental awareness meetings.
- Collaborated with parent associations, school districts, service agencies, and various community organizations.

Director, Child Development Center, Stewart Air Base, Newburgh, New York   1985 – 1986
- Directed the operations of a large child development center, including strategic planning, budgeting, marketing, program development, coordination of special events, and supervision of 38 personnel.
- Designed and implemented developmental programs for full day, hourly, preschool, and latchkey children from 6 weeks to 12 years old.
- Ensured that programs were in compliance with military and local government regulations.

Program Director, Naperville YMCA, Naperville, IL   1980 – 1985
- Director of YMCA youth, aquatic, and senior programs.
- Formulated curriculums and trained staff and volunteers.
- Managed 23 employees, including teachers, office staff, and volunteers.
- Organized fund-raising events to raise money for scholarships.
- Prepared budgets based on historical and projected data.
- Served as resource person for the development of all programs.

Scannable

Rose Lincoln

1234 Stonehaven Drive
Colorado Springs, Colorado 80906
(719) 555-1234

HIGHLIGHTS OF QUALIFICATIONS

Dedicated, hard-working management professional with a strong work ethic.
Highly motivated self-starter who needs little supervision and can manage multiple priorities with ease.
Effective team builder with exceptional communication and presentation skills.
Quick learner who adapts easily to new situations and enjoys solving challenging problems.
Computer skills: Windows, MS Word, Excel, Macintosh, and proprietary software.

AREAS OF EXPERTISE

Sales/Marketing	Supervision	Price Structuring
Customer Relations	Training	Negotiations
Management	Evaluation	Sales Tracking

PROFESSIONAL EXPERIENCE

Management/Administration

- Managed operational performance of sales team to ensure performance standards were met.
- Provided leadership, direction, coaching, and training of 10 sales consultants.
- Conducted performance reviews, identified problems, counseled employees, and took proactive measures to correct problems.
- Conducted regular strategy sessions with staff to increase productivity.
- Determined staffing levels; interviewed and hired new employees.
- Developed and administered objectives, operating policies and procedures, budgets, and strategic action plans for achieving goals.
- Interfaced with underwriting and other internal departments to set price structures, negotiate rates, and develop new products and proposals.
- Developed and researched comprehensive reports from various data sources for management.
- Designed and implemented statewide format to ensure accurate case set-up for contract renewal and revisions.
- Assisted with development of statewide service standards that ensured efficient maintenance and effective education of existing clients.
- Created and maintained tracking mechanisms for effective prospecting and sales forecasting.

Customer Relations/Sales

- Responsible for the Southern Colorado sales team, which brought in 40 percent of 1,200 gross new sales for the entire state.
- Assess client needs, made sales presentations, prepared proposals, negotiated rates, compared providers and benefits, and negotiated/closed the sale.
- Met or exceeded sales quota of 400 enrollments per month, generating $200,000+ per year in new revenue.
- Accountable for meeting or exceeding membership growth for 13,000 existing clients.
- Successfully negotiated annual contract renewals and consistently increased intrinsic growth for 85 existing clients.
- Developed and revised marketing/sales proposals utilized by national sales and service personnel.
- Developed positive relationships with clients and brokers and enhanced their knowledge of managed health care philosophies and system procedures.

EMPLOYMENT HISTORY

Sales Manager, PacifiCare (formerly FHP), Colorado Springs, Colorado	1996 – Present
Sales Consultant, FHP (formerly TakeCare/Lincoln National), Colorado Springs, Colorado	1995 – 1996
Customer Service Manager, Spectranetics, Colorado Springs, Colorado	1992 – 1994
Account Manager, Service Representative, Enrollment Plan Administrator	
Lincoln National Corporation (formerly Peak Health Plan), Colorado Springs, Colorado	1979 – 1992

Scannable

KATHLEEN HERALD

123 MANITOU PLACE
MANITOU SPRINGS, COLORADO 80829
TELEPHONE: (719) 555-1234

PROFILE

★ Energetic and persuasive sales professional with a talent for closing the sale.
★ Creative and persistent; skilled in listening with empathy and assessing client needs.
★ Effective team player with strong interpersonal and communication skills.
★ Self-motivated; comfortable taking the initiative and working independently.
★ Knowledge of Macintosh, MS Word, Excel, Pagemaker, and Lotus 1-2-3.

EXPERIENCE

SALES/MARKETING
★ Originated new individual and corporate accounts, generating $25,000 in new business each year.
★ Maintained good working relationships with established clients.
★ Assisted customers in assessing needs and designing new signage products.
★ Learned all aspects of sign fabrication and promotion, including design, production, sales, and marketing.
★ Persuaded customers to purchase upscale cosmetics in a highly competitive market.
★ Generated new, younger client base and introduced fresh products to existing clients.
★ Consistent top sales performer; developed repeat clientele through effective sales techniques.
★ Collaborated with colleagues to win multiple regional sales competitions.
★ Convinced the *Scottsbluff Star-Herald* of the need for a biweekly column on college issues; wrote and published fifty articles for this daily newspaper with a circulation of 25,000.
★ Served as academic advisor for the yearbook; supervised production and marketing; personally responsible for achieving $1,200 in ad sales; exceeded book sales quotas by more than $1,000.

ADMINISTRATION AND TEACHING
★ Interviewed, made hiring recommendations, supervised, and evaluated teachers.
★ Researched and presented comprehensive benefits plan proposal.
★ Assisted administration in building and supporting a school-wide student behavior plan.
★ Led a team of three teachers in the design and implementation of weekly lesson plans.
★ Developed a year-long curriculum to meet defined goals and objectives.
★ Taught English and reading to seventh and eighth grade students, generating buy-in for new concepts and enthusiasm for lifelong learning.
★ Assisted students in building mental, physical, and social skills.
★ Established ongoing contacts with parents; counseled students with adjustment and academic problems.

WORK HISTORY

Sales and Account Representative, Northglen Signs, Northglen, Colorado, 1996 – present
Teacher, Watson Junior High School, Widefield, Colorado, 1996 – 1998
Lead Teacher, Williamsburg Child Development Center, Lincoln, Nebraska, 1995 – 1996
Sales Consultant, Clinique Cosmetics, Scottsbluff, Nebraska, 1993 – 1994

EDUCATION

BACHELOR OF SCIENCE, University of Nebraska, Lincoln, 1994
★ Major in Secondary Education, English, and French
★ Cumulative GPA 3.8/4.0; Dean's List all semesters
★ Nominated to the USA All-Academic Team
★ Scholarships: ACT, Elks Club, Grone Memorial, UNLTC
★ Member of the Teachers College Outstanding Teacher Selection Committee

Scannable

207

JAMES L. VAN OVERDALE

1234 Nicklaus Court • Decatur, Illinois 62526-9316 • Phone: (217) 555-1234 • E-mail: criscito@aol.com

PROFILE

- Experienced senior executive with proven success in starting, leading, and rebuilding corporations to profitability.
- Expertise in strategic planning, infrastructure development, operations management, regulatory compliance, sales, and marketing.
- Track record of improving net income through team-centered management, leadership, staff development, and effective communication skills.
- A true leader who is not afraid to tackle difficult tasks and build an organization from the ground up.
- Hard-working, detail-oriented professional with a common-sense approach to problem solving.

EXPERIENCE

PRESIDENT, FirsTech, Inc., Decatur, Illinois (1997 – 1999)
Recruited to resuscitate this bill payment processor after the devastating loss of two of the company's largest accounts. Responsible for development of the corporate vision, strategic and financial planning, operations efficiency, management reporting system, and quality control processes. Directed 80 full-time staff members, 40 temporaries, and 5 directors and officers.

Management

- Built an innovative management team, increased accountability, instilled a greater sense of urgency, and improved morale.
- Developed job descriptions, performance evaluation system, and compensation program designed to attract, retain, and reward high-caliber staff.
- Led the management team in the development and implementation of internal controls, project management, and client service structures that drove revenue growth by 26 percent and improved client satisfaction as indicated by survey results.
- Reduced operating expenses by 23 percent and increased client base by 60 percent in the first year, generating $6 million in annual gross revenues from more than 42 million transactions.

Sales and Marketing

- Implemented a financial management system to evaluate profitability by product, which refocused sales efforts on more profitable product lines.
- Recruited a new sales force and established a formal fee schedule for services, resulting in a pretax net increase of 184 percent in one business unit and an overall revenue increase of 26 percent.
- Personally negotiated with the most profitable client to retain and expand service offerings, which resulted in a new three-year contract with a projected revenue increase of 82 percent.
- Leveraged professionalism and integrity to attract and retain such clients as CellularOne, Sprint PCS, The March of Dimes, and Chrysler Financial Corporation.

Technology

- Formed a strategic business alliance with CheckFree Corporation, the nation's largest electronic bill payment processor.
- Retained a consulting firm to conduct a Year 2000 audit that identified all mission-critical systems; took corrective action to test and upgrade all PCs, point-of-sale terminals, mainframes, and local area network.
- Developed and implemented an action plan to correct deficiencies in information technology documentation, contingency planning, and system security identified by an audit commissioned during first year in office.

PRESIDENT, Corporate Network Brokerage Services, Inc., Overland Park, Kansas (1989 – 1996)
Assumed full profit and loss responsibility for this institutional investment management firm, including sales, operations, administration, and regulatory compliance. Bought and sold securities, and provided reliable and ethical investment services to credit unions nationwide. Served more credit unions than any other broker/dealer or investment advisor in the United States (according to a trade publication survey). Opened a profitable branch office.

Infrastructure Development

- Led this start-up company to $2.5 million in revenues in six years with more than 400 accounts nationwide.
- Directed the development of new services that grew to more than $6.5 billion in managed assets in four years.

Scannable

EXPERIENCE
(continued)

Corporate Network Brokerage Services, Inc. (continued)
- Achieved a 210 percent increase in net income while reducing expenses by 14.5 percent.
- Maintained an unblemished examination record from such regulatory agencies as the Securities and Exchange Commission and the National Association of Securities Dealers during a period of rapid expansion.
- Designed and implemented a new incentive compensation program that contributed to a volume increase of 7.7 percent.
- Conducted dozens of presentations to audiences as large as 300 people, receiving praise for the ability to clearly communicate complex information and professionally attract new clients.

VICE PRESIDENT, CUNA Brokerage Services, Inc., Overland Park, Kansas (1986 – 1989)
Managed the operations of the only branch of a national investment firm for financial institutions (the predecessor organization to Corporate Network Brokerage Services). Registered principal responsible for supervising a staff of six in the purchase and sale of securities. Active contributor to corporate strategic planning, budgeting, and business development.
- Achieved high levels of customer service and revenues of $500,000.
- Successfully transitioned clients from CUNA Brokerage Services to the new company.

EDUCATION

MASTER OF BUSINESS ADMINISTRATION, University of Kansas, Lawrence, Kansas (1992)
BACHELOR OF SCIENCE, University of Missouri, Columbia, Missouri (1977)

COMMUNITY SERVICE

- Board of Directors, Community American Credit Union (1997)
- Supervisory Committee, Yellow Financial Credit Union (1996 – 1997)
- Development Committee, Kansas City Christian Schools (1996 – 1997)
- Steering Committee, Capital Development Campaign, Johnson County YMCA (1996 – 1997)
- Vice President, Parent/Teacher Fellowship, KC Christian (1996 – 1997)
- Director of Children's Program, Bible Study Fellowship, Prairie Village, Kansas (1996 – 1997)
- Advisory Cabinet, Moundford Free Methodist Church, Decatur, Illinois (1999)
- Adult Class Leader, Moundford Free Methodist Church, Decatur, Illinois (1999)
- Youth Soccer Coach and Assistant Baseball Coach

Scannable

CHRISTOPHER A. HIGHFIELD

Current Address:
123 South Forest #444
Ann Arbor, Michigan 48104
Phone: (734) 555-1234

E-mail: criscito@aol.com

Permanent Address:
1234 Cypress Pointe Court
Ann Arbor, Michigan 48108
Phone: (734) 555-5678

PROFILE

- Dedicated basketball coach and team manager with four years of university-level experience.
- Hard working and well organized; able to work independently with little supervision.
- Proven leader who works well under pressure and develops resourceful solutions to problems.
- Effective team player with strong communication and interpersonal skills.

EDUCATION

BACHELOR OF ARTS, The University of Michigan, Ann Arbor, May 2000
- Major in Sports Management and Communications
- Concentration in Coaching
- Minor in English

EXPERIENCE

Coaching
- Trained youth athletes in basketball camps and worked closely with professional athletes to develop basic skills.
- Oversaw the development of up to 120 campers (elementary to high school age).
- Analyzed player performance and instructed them in game strategies and techniques to prepare for competition.
- Observed players to determine the need for individual or team improvement.
- Created and judged individual skills competition awards for youth sports camps.

Team Management
- Collected and processed data for triathlon/duathlon Team USA events as an intern with the national governing body for the sport of triathlon.
- Managed uniform inventory, including timely ordering and delivery for events.
- Hired, trained, and supervised 12 student managers for the University of Michigan men's varsity basketball team.
- Responsible for player relations, including one-on-one tutoring in academic subjects, physical training, and personal appearances.
- Controlled gratis tickets for the players valued at $600 per game.
- Videotaped, edited, and organized varsity practice and game films.

Promotion/Marketing/Sales
- Promoted Nike sports on the University of Michigan campus.
- Distributed Nike gear at various university athletic functions.
- Marketed USAT and Team USA at the grassroots level.
- Hosted potential University of Michigan basketball recruits, providing entertainment and campus tours to convince the players to sign with the team.
- Promoted the Michael Jordan Basketball Camp through handouts, flyers, and mall kiosks.
- Supervised summer promotions for Moe's Sport Shop and sold collegiate merchandise.
- Modeled sportswear and monitored outdoor sales during special events.

WORK HISTORY

Head Student Manager, UofM Men's Varsity Basketball, Ann Arbor, MI, 1995 – present
Team USA Administrative Projects Intern, USA Triathlon, Colorado Springs, CO, Summer 1999
Youth Team Coach, Michael Jordan Basketball Camp, Chicago, IL, Summers 1997 – 1999
Youth Team Coach, UofM Basketball Camp, Ann Arbor, MI, Summers 1995 – 1998
Youth Team Coach, Univ. of Virginia Girl's Basketball Camp, Charlottesville, VA, Summer 1998
Youth Team Coach, Ball State Univ. Basketball Camp, Muncie, IN, Summer 1996, 1998
Student Manager, UofM Men's Varsity Basketball, Ann Arbor, MI, 1995 – 1997
Youth Team Coach, Penn State University Basketball Camp, State College, PA, Summer 1997
Nike Campus Representative Assistant, Univ. of Michigan, Ann Arbor, MI, 1995 – 1997
Youth Team Coach, University of Illinois Basketball Camp, Champaign, IL, Summer 1996

(**Scannable**)

JEFF SOBOLIK

1234 Fletcher Drive • Colorado Springs, Colorado 80916 • (719) 555-1234

HIGHLIGHTS OF QUALIFICATIONS

More than eight years of successful experience in sales, marketing, business management,
new business development, communications, delegating, outsourcing, and customer relations
Able to apply a logical, common sense approach to problem solving
Effective team player with strong communication and interpersonal skills

EXPERIENCE

SALES, MARKETING, CUSTOMER RELATIONS

- **Marketing Manager** for Josh and John's Homemade Ice Cream:
  - Developed marketing campaigns to sell ice cream through major grocery stores and chains.
  - Earned a reputation for outstanding account management and control.
  - Orchestrated resources to yield optimal growth and customer satisfaction; provided a full range of product volume discount programs.
  - Planned strategies to target and develop new accounts while maintaining existing accounts; successfully opened up several major profitable new accounts.
  - Introduced products to customers previously unaware of product capabilities through demos and trade shows.
  - Overcame distance barriers by offering persuasive advantages over competition, tasting being the first.
  - Made cold calls, created buying programs that best fit customer needs and future demands.
  - Prepared weekly, monthly, and/or quarterly sales reports and inventory reports.
  - Supervised 10 employees, coordinating deliveries, pick-ups, and inventory management.
  - Directed and trained staff in time management skills.
- **Small Business Consultant** for MCI Communications:
  - Switched customers from one long distance carrier to MCI by backing up agreements and thoroughly following up to ensure customer satisfaction.
  - Consistently exceeded all sales expectations; among top sales representatives for number of switched sales per month.
- **Territory Manager** for Finzer Imaging Systems:
  - Successfully sold copiers and fax machines, including digital black and white and color machines.
  - Consistently maintained 160% to 340% of quota in a competitive arena.
- **Account Executive** for VoiceStream Wireless
  - Sold cellular telephones and services to businesses and consumers; provided after-sale customer service for the territory.
  - Achieved 129% of quota in the first month on the job and continued to meet or exceed quota every month.

BUSINESS MANAGEMENT, OPERATIONS, PUBLIC RELATIONS

- **Business manager** in charge of operations for Project Freefall:
  - Initiated this successful skydiving event at Edwards AFB in California.
  - Received national media exposure, raising more than $300,000 by obtaining corporate/individual sponsorships.
  - Negotiated broadcasting rights to ESPN's Expedition Earth program, October 1992.
  - Promoted event through excellent public relations, fundraising actions, and sponsorships.
  - Received notoriety and the challenge of accepting additional assignments in the future.
- **Business manager** in charge of operations for Operation Motherload:
  - Successfully initiated, organized, promoted, coordinated, and marketed this world record skydiving event.
  - Scheduled more than 50 participants and delegated responsibilities for on-time completion of event.
  - Aggressively designed and developed innovative marketing strategies through various press conferences and releases.
  - Build business relationships and maintained public relations.

WORK HISTORY

1999 – Present	Account Executive	VoiceStream Wireless	Colorado Springs, CO
1996 – 1998	Territory Manager/Sales	Finzer Imaging Systems	Colorado Springs, CO
1996	Co-Owner/Sales	The Yellow Sheet	Colorado Springs, CO
1994 – 1996	Small Business Consultant/Sales	MCI Communications	Colorado Springs, CO
1993 – 1994	Marketing Director	Josh and John's Homemade Ice Cream	Colorado Springs, CO
1988 – 1993	Business Manager/Operations	Operation Motherload	Colorado Springs, CO
1990 – 1992	Media Technician	Cheyenne Mountain Conference Resort	Colorado Springs, CO

(Scannable)

211

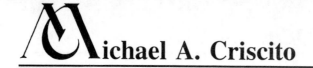

Michael A. Criscito

1234 Amstel Dr., Colorado Springs, CO 80907
Phone (719) 555-1234 • Fax (719) 555-1234

SUMMARY OF EXPERIENCE

SUPERVISION
- Seven years of experience managing accounts payable, receivables, inventory, shipping, and customer service for an international business support service
- Established maintenance control and work flow procedures for Air Force shops
- Supervised and motivated subordinates to exceptional performance
- Coordinated 16 personnel, 4 vehicles, and thousands of food packs for Meals on Wheels
- Served for two years as Branch Technical Order and Training Monitor
- Augmented quality assurance teams in mobility and logistics planning

VEHICLE PROGRAM ADMINISTRATION
- Managed the largest vehicle program at Bitburg Air Base, West Germany, for three years with flawless inspections
- Coordinated vehicle maintenance and rotation; investigated accidents and abuse/misuse
- Commended for dramatically improving the squadron's vehicle management program
- Maintained $117,000 worth of radios at an exceptional operations rate

TRAINING MANAGEMENT
- Served four years as Unit Training Manager—made dramatic improvements in career development courses (CDC), upgrade training programs, class scheduling, and forecasting of training needs
- Overhauled the CDC course exam pretesting program, increasing completion rates by 400 percent with higher average test scores and no failures
- Developed pretesting appointment and tracking system and created flow charts

AIRCRAFT AND FLIGHTLINE
- Flightline Expeditor—assured that all aircraft on the flying schedule were configured as specified; supervised maintenance crew and four load crews
- Two years of experience in component repair, troubleshooting electronic systems
- Performed integrated combat turnarounds
- Weapons Load Crew Chief—launched and recovered aircraft, and loaded ordinance
- Inspected, maintained, installed, modified, and repaired bomb, rocket, and missile release, launch, suspension, and monitoring systems; gun and gun mount systems; and related munitions handling, loading, and test equipment for a total of 12 years
- Supervised and performed in-shop maintenance and functional checks on pylons, bomb racks, launchers, bomb release dispensers, guns, and other components
- Trained personnel in troubleshooting complex electronic components and use of associated test equipment, cockpit/explosive/flightline safety, radiation hazards, and other subjects

WORK HISTORY

Vice President, Operations, ProType, Ltd., Colorado Springs 1992 – Present
Aircraft Armament Systems Technician, U.S. Air Force 1972 – 1992

EDUCATION

ASSOCIATE DEGREE IN ARMAMENT SYSTEMS TECHNOLOGY partially completed
Community College of the Air Force 42 credits

RELEVANT TRAINING

Flightline Weapons Maintenance Management (34 hours)	1988
Section Supervisor OJT Course (12 and 24 hours)	1987
OJT Trainer Orientation (24 hours)	1980
Noncommissioned Officer Leadership School (Management) (191 hours)	1978
Maintenance Management and Data Collection System (30 hours)	1975

PERSONAL DATA Private pilot's license • Current CPR certification • Top Secret Security Clearance

Scannable

15 Executive Résumés

Webster defines an executive as "a person whose function is to administer or manage affairs of a corporation, division, department, group of companies, etc." This can be the president, director, chief executive officer, chief financial officer, chief information officer, controller, executive director, vice president, general manager, treasurer, principal, owner, and the list goes on.

Generally, a person in such a position has strategically worked his/her way to the top echelons of management over a period of at least ten years. Executives tend to have many relevant past positions, credentials, achievements, published articles, speaking engagements, community service activities, and other important qualifications.

In order to reflect this experience, an executive résumé is almost always more than one page. In fact, an executive résumé can be as long as it needs to be in order to convince the reader that the candidate has what it takes to manage an organization effectively.

Just because an executive résumé is long, however, doesn't mean it should be wordy. The same good writing described in Chapter 2 is even more important in an executive résumé. Because the number of applicants for an executive position is generally not as large as for lower-level positions, every word of an executive's résumé will be read many times before a decision is made. Make sure every word you write serves a purpose!

As a general rule, executive résumés should be conservative in style. Senior-level management is considered a very sober position with considerable responsibility, so there is no room for frivolity or creativity. That doesn't mean, however, that the design of an executive résumé must be boring. The effective use of type style, white space, and discrete graphic lines can make your résumé stand out in the crowd.

Lance G. Ingersoll

123-C East Cheyenne Mountain Blvd. #333 • Colorado Springs, Colorado 80906
Phone: (719) 555-5678 • Cellular: (719) 555-1234 • E-mail: criscito@aol.com

PROFILE
- Global thinker with strong marketing, business development, and technology experience.
- Proven ability to gain the confidence of customers, employees, and senior management.
- True leader who inspires confidence in employees by empowering them to do their jobs and respecting them for their accomplishments.
- Creative problem solver with the ability to develop visionary solutions to complex business and technical challenges.
- Experienced in MS Word, Excel, Access, PowerPoint, Netscape, Internet, networks, etc.

EXPERIENCE

VICE PRESIDENT, DIRECTOR OF MANUFACTURING   1991 – 1999
K&R Products, Inc., Colorado Springs, Colorado
Developed new business and directed the operations of an international manufacturer of custom medical, commercial, and industrial hardware using high-end engineering resins. Hired, supervised, and motivated 2 plant managers and 65 staff members, including operators, technicians, and customer service representatives, representing a growth of 540 percent over 1991 staffing levels. Purchased and installed two complete wide area network systems.

Achievements
- Responsible for growing this privately held corporation from a $2 million family-owned business to a $10 million, world class manufacturing and service organization.
- Achieved 19 percent pretax profits in 1998 and 22 percent expected pretax profits in 1999.
- Expanded operations by opening two new manufacturing plants.
- Negotiated agreements for the start-up of an international manufacturing plant in Guadalajara, Mexico.

Business Development
Traveled extensively to customer locations throughout the United States and Mexico to develop new markets and build business with key customers.
- Acquired an exclusive contract for all of Ingersoll Rand's plastic injection molding business, increasing annual sales by $3 million.
- Built strategic alliances with suppliers and customers and created win-win partnerships by assessing needs, discovering niches in the market, and developing innovative products.
- Used strong engineering experience to develop unconventional techniques, processes, and products that created new profit centers for the company and provided turnkey products to customers, including printing, welding, and assembly.

Multi-plant Growth
Managed the site selection, capital equipment purchases, tenant improvements, staffing, production design, ramp-up, and customer acquisition for two new plants.
- Designed a 30,000 square foot plant using SPC-controlled Toshiba injection molding equipment, high cavitation molds, full hot runner systems, robotic automation, and load-cell conveyance systems for an extremely high-volume production environment.
- Created a state-of-the-art, automated production line in Colorado Springs that ran 24 hours a day and produced 250 million parts per year, serving as a model for the industry.

Production
Responsible for capacity planning and implementation of just-in-time production processes. Qualified sub-tier suppliers and sourced second operation components. Developed thin film PVD/plastic hybrid products for industrial uses.
- Competed with 500 tier-one suppliers to win the 1998 Ingersoll Rand (AHG) supplier quality award for achieving 0.00 defects per million on all delivered products.
- Achieved ISO 9000 and 9001 compliance by qualifying suppliers, developing quality standards, and implementing new administrative, accountability, and production procedures.
- Integrated cell manufacturing with demand flow technology to reduce in-process units and streamline the manufacturing process, increasing production by 200 percent.
- Managed the outsourcing of more than $1 million in production tooling.

Scannable

EXPERIENCE
(continued)

PRESIDENT, GENERAL MANAGER   1988 – 1991
California Precision Optical, Santa Cruz, California
Managed the operations of this importer of sunglasses and optical lenses from Italy, Austria, France, and Japan. Developed markets with retail stores (Macy's, Sunglass Hut, etc.) and optometric practices. Traveled internationally to source suppliers for new products. Hired and supervised a staff of 15 and purchased new computer systems for all three locations.
• Expanded the optometric portion of the business from one location to three.
• Built a new facility from site selection through grand opening.
• Developed coating specifications for all lens product manufacturing.

VICE PRESIDENT, DIRECTOR OF OPERATIONS   1982 – 1988
Bucci, Inc., Scotts Valley, California
Created market name recognition for an importer of high-end sports and fashion sunglasses and accessories. Traveled extensively throughout the United States, Japan, and Europe to negotiate contracts with suppliers and conduct trade shows. Developed new thin film lens designs in collaboration with international suppliers. Established material specifications and quality standards for all injection molded products. Negotiated contracts with U.S. and international tooling suppliers to custom manufacture injection molded products.
• Grew the company from three employees with a quarter million dollars in sales to a major force in the optical industry with $4.5 million in annual revenue and 50 employees.
• Started in product development and rapidly advanced to production manager, national sales manager, and then director of operations.

ENGINEERING TECHNICIAN   1979 – 1982
Santa Barbara Research Center, Santa Barbara, California
Worked closely with twelve engineers in the film coating group of this division of Hughes Aircraft Corporation. Manufactured film coatings for the detector arrays used in satellites and missile guidance systems using e-gun, sputter, ion etch, and thermal system technologies.
• Developed a coating technology for Capton electronic cables that allowed Hughes to use the cabling in a new satellite application.
• Learned the science of film deposition through intensive on-the-job-training.

EDUCATION

UNIVERSITY OF CALIFORNIA, Santa Barbara
One year of math and science studies. Self-educated during successful, uninterrupted career.

CONTINUING EDUCATION
Graduate of the 13-week Dale Carnegie Executive Management Program, Dale Carnegie Sales Program, GE Polymer Science Training, Ingersoll Rand Demand Flow Technology Course, and Toshiba America Process and Maintenance Training

Scannable

HUEY P. ALLEN, JR.

1234 Stargrass Drive • Colorado Springs, Colorado 80918 • (719) 555-1234 • E-mail: criscito@aol.com

PROFILE

- Goal-directed project manager with the ability to lead by example and motivate others to excel.
- Proven "smoke jumper" with a strong background in business development, requirements analysis, proposal development, business process re-engineering, problem resolution, and customer satisfaction.
- Respected for the ability to solve problems and get things done when others give up.
- Twenty-three years of experience in command and control information and telecommunications systems development and analysis, test and evaluation (T&E), modeling simulations, and verification, validation, and accreditation (VV&A).
- Effective team player with exceptional communication, interpersonal, and presentation skills.
- Skilled in preparing and presenting briefings to high-level executives on systems, test requirements, operational concepts, and mission support equipment.
- Detail-oriented and analytical; able to manage the details while seeing the whole picture.
- Completing a Project Management Professional (PMP) certification (October 1999).

EXPERIENCE

THE BOEING COMPANY, Joint National Test Facility (JNTF), Schriever AFB, Colorado (1998 – present)
Acting T&E Site Manager, Deputy Director of Operations
Lead an integrated product team of engineers in the testing, validation, and integration of communications and computer systems for critical missile defense initiatives at the world's number one modeling and simulation facility. Provide leadership, direction, and supervision to military and contractor data communications experts. Set project scope, direction, and time lines to meet customer expectations; create comprehensive project schedules, contingency plans, cost estimates, and performance criteria. Accountable for a $100 million budget and assignment of project resources. Create budget databases, generate monthly project status reports, and participate in the financial management review board. Supply technical expertise in system evaluation methodology, test requirements analysis and development, data analysis, and preparation of technical reports. Monitor and control work in progress for technical adequacy and budget compliance. Develop strategic plans to address competitive advantages, action plans, operational necessity for upgrades, and total estimated life cycle costs of integrating future technology. Position requires frequent contact with government customers and presentations to high-level Pentagon executives.

- Received consistently high scores on all award fee evaluations for excellence in project management; delivered all contract items within budget and on schedule.
- Successful in planning and budgeting scalable information systems that accommodated a variety of internal and external customers.
- Championed an aggressive team-building approach to work flow management that contained costs while greatly enhancing product quality and efficiency.
- Used information technology to enable business process improvements that reduced travel and staffing by 10 percent.

THE BOEING COMPANY, Joint National Test Facility (JNTF), Schriever AFB, Colorado (1994 – 1998)
Task Order Manager
Managed the development of both the Joint Theater Missile Defense Planner and Global Command and Control System Segment projects. Defined research and development program requirements. Coordinated with senior government and commercial organizations to ensure continuity and accomplishment of program objectives within cost, schedule, and risk guidelines. Led a multi-disciplinary team of engineers and administrative personnel.

- Defined and initiated two entirely new projects that were the first to implement Department of Defense VV&A guidelines.
- Consistently achieved high scores during the semi-annual award fee evaluation period.
- Achieved cost savings of 15 percent on each program for two years.
- Succeeded in developing new business that resulted in a 100 percent increase in staffing and budget for three consecutive years.
- Served as organizational representative to the Department of Defense VV&A Technical Working Group.
- Wrote and presented two professional papers at the 1997/98 Summer Simulation Conferences.
- Selected to serve on a T&E/VV&A panel and presented a white paper at the Military Operations Research Society's 1998 conference.
- Created standards for estimating the true personnel cost of proposed software changes, providing a management tool for assigning limited resources to critical missions.
- Developed metrics to measure, identify, and reduce cost drivers of software development.

216

Scannable

**EXPERIENCE
(continued)**

McDONNELL DOUGLAS AEROSPACE, DoD Advanced Programs, Huntsville, Alabama (1992 – 1994)
Test and Evaluation/Systems Analyst
Responsible for systems engineering and integration to support the development of the Space Defense Initiative (SDI) Global Protection Against Limited Strike (GPALS) program. Planned demonstration/ validation tests and developed requirements for system elements. Served as the designated point of contact to resolve major integration issues across multiple organizations (Army, Navy, Air Force). Allocated system requirements to the elements through their respective engineering contractors. Resolved critical technical parameters, exit criteria, and operating issues from an overall system perspective. Developed the concept of operations for contingency planning to support the battle management and command, control and communications segment of GPALS and command authority devolution.

- Selected as a final candidate for the MDA Silver Eagle Award, a recognition given to only 50 of Boeing's 175,000 employees worldwide for outstanding performance.
- Selected as the system engineering representative to the government-chaired GPALS Configuration Control Board; provided technical guidance to the chairman on system engineering, integration, and test matters.
- Clearly defined system requirements, resulting in a 20 percent increase in staffing and budget to support program development.

McDONNELL DOUGLAS ESC, Command and Control System, Memphis, Tennessee (1991 – 1992)
Site Manager for Memphis Operations, Cost Account Manager
Managed the operations of the Global Operations Command Center contract for Federal Express. Ensured that all tasks assigned to the site were accomplished within budget and schedule constraints, while maintaining strict adherence to quality standards. Coordinated all third-party vendor subcontracts, including direct supervision of more than 12 training classes. Established and directed the Command and Control Lab, a development test and evaluation laboratory supporting the strategic, systems, database, and software engineering efforts. Established and implemented the operations and administrative procedures for the site. Served as the program manager's on-site customer liaison.

- Achieved operational readiness status one month before deadline.
- Developed and implemented cost containment plans that reduced operating costs by 10 percent.

**PROFESSIONAL
DEVELOPMENT**

PROJECT MANAGEMENT PROFESSIONAL (PMP) (October 1999)
Project Management Institute
- Completing a rigorous training program for the project management profession's most globally recognized and respected certification credential.

EDUCATION

COLORADO TECHNICAL UNIVERSITY, Colorado Springs, Colorado (1997 – present)
- Completing a Bachelor of Science in Management Information Systems/Systems Engineering.

LOUISIANA TECHNICAL UNIVERSITY, Ruston, Louisiana (1980 – 1983)
- Computer Science major.

**COMMUNITY
SERVICE**

El Paso County Commissioners, Colorado Springs, Colorado
- Appointed as chairman of a county-commissioned study panel to identify long-term development plans for 125 square miles of El Paso County.

SECURITY

Possess a current Top Secret SSBI security clearance, performing additional duties as Facility Security Officer and COMSEC Custodian.

Scannable

217

JANICE M. WEILAND

Post Office Box 12345
Colorado Springs, CO 80949
(719) 555-1234

SUMMARY

Substantial banking experience as a manager with responsibility for credit support and commercial lending. Managed loan review audits, developed loan policies and procedures, trained junior lenders and analysts, directed loan officers in accomplishing portfolio objectives, and instilled the importance of sound credit skills and lending practices.

PROFESSIONAL EXPERIENCE

COLORADO NATIONAL BANK (First Bank System), Colorado Springs, Colorado   1996 to Present
Vice President/Manager of Private Banking, Southern Colorado
Manage client relationships of high-profile professionals and executives and their related businesses or practices, providing an array of credit and depository products. Responsible for developing and executing a strategy to build market share while maintaining credit quality and profitability.

THE WEILAND GROUP, INC., Colorado Springs, Colorado   1990 to 1996
President
Established a bank consulting firm providing risk management services to financial institutions. Conducted ongoing loan review audits, including analysis of credit strengths and weaknesses, reporting of documentation exceptions, and preparation of watch list summaries. Consulted in determining allocations to the loan loss reserve, including presentations to senior management and the Board of Directors. Developed loan policies and procedures consistent with regulatory requirements while maintaining and strengthening the institution's credit culture.

COMMERCE BANK, N.A., Cherry Hill, New Jersey   1989 to 1990
Vice President/Credit Manager
Managed a department of ten credit analysts and support staff. Responsible for the underwriting of commercial loans. Established a credit training program for commercial lenders, selected participants, and provided an environment conducive to the development of sound credit skills. Managed delinquent loans while maintaining acceptable ratios.

CORESTATES, Philadelphia, Pennsylvania   1983 to 1989
Vice President/Credit Review (1987 to 1989)
Managed credit audits of commercial lending divisions, including the assignment of ratings, compilation of credit risk data, and analysis of portfolio characteristics. Analyzed and recommended loans to Credit Committee for approval. Served on the Transactional Products Exposure Committee responsible for identifying and controlling credit risk inherent in non-credit products and services.

Vice President/Credit Product Management (1986 to 1987)
Managed credit offerings as products, conducted competitive market research, and implemented more efficient operating procedures. Doubled the bankers' acceptance portfolio while reducing out-of-pocket expenses by $350 million. Served on the Loan Information System Committee responsible for ongoing MIS enhancements.

Vice President/Commercial Lending (1983 to 1986)
Managed a $200 million portfolio consisting of corporate accounts located in the Middle Atlantic region. Created and implemented a business plan that resulted in a 42 percent increase in loan outstandings. Generated new customer relationships, improved credit quality, and achieved target portfolio yield.

Scannable

IRVING TRUST COMPANY, Chicago, Illinois   1982 to 1983
Assistant Vice President/Commercial Lending
Developed and executed a marketing strategy for the sale of credit and non-credit services to small middle-market companies. Identified and qualified key prospects and prepared new business plans as measurement tools. Originated new business relationships while augmenting and improving existing ones.

FIRST CHICAGO CORPORATION, Chicago, Illinois   1976 to 1982
Assistant Vice President/Commercial Lending (1978 to 1982)
Marketed credit and non-credit services to large corporate and regional customers and prospects. Designed creative financing approaches, negotiated loan agreements, restructured debt, and offered unique cash management systems. Managed and monitored junior lending personnel.

First Scholar Training Program (1977 to 1978)
Assigned to the Capital Markets Division, Treasury Department, and Commercial Lending Division. Exposed to municipal underwriting, trading and sales, the monitoring of short-term liabilities, coordination of funding subsidiaries, preparation of comparative financial reports for management review, and presentation of economic and competitive data to lending units.

Analyst/Control Division (1976 to 1977)
Generated reports and analyzed financial results of Capital Markets and International Divisions. Participated in corporate planning process.

EDUCATION

NORTHWESTERN UNIVERSITY/KELLOGG SCHOOL OF BUSINESS (1979)
Master of Management with an emphasis on financial and marketing management

SUFFOLK UNIVERSITY (1975)
BSBA, *magna cum laude,* major in marketing

AFFILIATIONS

State of Colorado Economic Development Commission (1994-95)
El Paso County Planning Commission (1995)
State of Colorado Women's Economic Development Council (1995)
Robert Morris Associates, Southern Colorado Group, Board of Directors (1994-97), Chair (1996-97)
Robert Morris Associates, South Jersey Group, Board of Directors (1990-92), Secretary (1992)
National Association of Women Business Owners, Pikes Peak Chapter, Founding President (1995)
National Association of Women Business Owners, Mile High Chapter, Board of Directors (1994-95)
Northwestern University, Women's Professional Network (1993-97)
Northwestern University, Alumni Club of Philadelphia, President (1989-92)
University of Colorado Foundation, Women's Endowment Fund, Steering Committee (1995-97)
University of Colorado, College of Business, Business Advisory Council (1996-97)
Girl Scouts, Wagon Wheel Council, Board of Directors (1996-97)
Southern Colorado Women's Chamber of Commerce
Founding President (1993-94), Board of Directors (1996-97)
JOBS Committee, Colorado Springs, Colorado (1993-94)
Small Business Advisory Council, Colorado Springs, Colorado (1993-94)
Center for the Prevention of Domestic Violence, Board of Directors (1997)

Scannable

HENRY W. GABLE

1234 Sunlight Way • Penrose, Colorado 80132 • (719) 555-1234

SUMMARY OF QUALIFICATIONS

Professional health care administrator with 25 years of experience in diverse management settings, including multi-hospital, specialty hospital, general hospital with multiple freestanding clinics, university hospital with large outpatient practice (1,600 visits per day), and general hospital with 150-physician management service organization (MSO). Experience in the implementation of Medipac (HBO), Shared Medical System (SMS), and Meditech computer systems. Comprehensive background in the management of:

- Multi-million-dollar budgets
- Cost containment and savings innovations
- Utilization review
- Admissions and registration
- Billing
- Accounts receivable
- Credit and collections
- Medical records and coding
- Charge entry and charge description master
- Cashier posting and reconciliation
- Internal audit

- Defensive insurance audits
- Managed care reimbursement
- Medicare compliance controls
- Ambulance/helicopter billing
- Transplant/organ procurement
- Customer service
- Information desk
- Volunteer escort service
- Language interpretation service
- Electronic mail room operations
- Switchboard operations

EDUCATION

BACHELOR OF SCIENCE IN BUSINESS ADMINISTRATION
Robert Morris University, Pittsburgh, Pennsylvania
Graduated with Honors • Dean's List • Phi Theta Pi International Honor Fraternity

EXPERIENCE

DIRECTOR OF PATIENT FINANCIAL SERVICES . . . . 1998 – present
Boulder Community Hospital, Boulder, Colorado
Managed the financial services of two hospitals (329 beds), three medical centers, and a 65-physician MSO. Contacted by the Colorado Hospital Association and asked to lobby the General Assembly of the State of Colorado to enact House Bill 99-1250 into law. Succeeded in getting the bill passed, ensuring prompt payment of health insurance claims to hospitals and physicians from contracted managed care carriers.

CENTRAL BUSINESS OFFICE DIRECTOR/CONSULTANT . . . . 1997 – 1998
Precedent Health Center, Precedent Health Management (MSO), Denver, Colorado
Hired as a consultant to develop and implement all registration and business office processes and procedures for a new hospital and 150-physician MSO within a one-year time frame.

DIRECTOR OF BUSINESS SERVICES . . . . 1995 – 1997
University Hospital, Denver, Colorado
Managed 210 FTEs and an annual budget of $12 million for this 500-bed teaching hospital with a large outpatient practice (1,600 visits per day). Reduced accounts receivable from 87 to 39 days. Recovered $1.2 million in incorrectly paid managed care reimbursement. Increased the bottom line $8 million by converting Colorado indigent care patients into Medicaid patients with significantly higher reimbursements.

DIRECTOR OF PATIENT ACCOUNT SERVICES . . . . 1988 – 1995
Penrose-Saint Francis Healthcare System, Colorado Springs, Colorado
Centralized the business office and admissions functions of three hospitals with a total of 620 beds, four large clinics, and a 75-physicians MSO. Managed 120 FTEs with an annual budget of $6.5 million. Successfully reduced accounts receivable from 99 to 50 days. Instrumental in establishing Novare Collection Services, an independent collection agency formed for the Sisters of Charity.

DIRECTOR OF PATIENT FINANCIAL SERVICES . . . . 1984 – 1988
Rose Medical Center, Denver, Colorado
Managed 120 FTEs and an annual budget of $5.5 million for a 410-bed hospital and nine clinics. Reduced accounts receivable from 110 days to 58 days. Oversaw installation of the Shared Medical System (SMS) computer system.

DIRECTOR OF PATIENT FINANCIAL SERVICES . . . . 1972 – 1984
Magee Women's Hospital, Pittsburgh, Pennsylvania
Directed the financial services operations of this obstetrical and gynecological hospital with 384 beds and 187 bassinets (part of the University of Pittsburgh Health Center). Managed 85 FTEs with an annual budget of $3 million. Reduced accounts receivable from 85 to 44 days.

AFFILIATIONS

Advanced Member of the Healthcare Financial Management Association
President (1982 – 1984) of the Patient Accounting Managers Association
National Member of the American Guild of Patient Account Management
Chairman of the Colorado Provider Committee
Member of the Institute of Internal Auditors

RANDALL R. SANGER

1234 Rancheros Lane ▸ Colorado Springs, Colorado 80922 ▸ (719) 555-1234

PROFILE

▸ Demonstrated success in materials management positions for more than 12 years, including:

- Cost control/cash flow   - Purchasing/receiving   - Medical/Surgical
- Administration   - Inventory systems   - Pharmacy
- Operations   - Distribution   - IV infusion therapy
- Contract negotiations   - Managed care   - Home health care

▸ Self-motivated leader with strong interpersonal, communication, and motivation skills.
▸ Able to organize and prioritize multiple projects with divergent needs; love challenges.
▸ Knowledge of Excel, PowerPoint, MS Word, Windows, Matkon, Enterprise Systems, and Legacy.
▸ Certified Senior Material Management, American Hospital Association.
▸ Certified Registered Central Service Technician, Purdue University, Indianapolis, Indiana.

EXPERIENCE

CORAM HEALTHCARE, Denver, Colorado
National Director, Materials Management (1996 – 1998)

▸ Responsible for the general operations of the Material Management Department for a national home health/IV infusion company, including the coordination, implementation, installation, and training for a major national infusion pump conversion saving more than $4 million.
▸ Maintained and set up national contracts for $110 million in pharmacy and $20 million in med/surg, personally saving Coram $12 million through effective negotiations.
▸ Provided instruction and guidance for 112 branches nationwide, ensuring 98 percent compliance with the purchasing program.
▸ Worked with senior management in the field to ensure appropriate articulation in all branches.
▸ Presently converting all med/surg inventories to consignment and changing the cash flow pattern to provide extended vendor payment of only the product used and allowing for reimbursement closer to the time of product payment to improve cash flow.
▸ Set up a preferred provider relationship with Coram's resource network.
▸ Coordinated contracts for a mail order prescription service; chair of the formulary/standards committee.

CENTURA HEALTH, Colorado Springs, Colorado
Director, Materials Management (1994 – 1996)

▸ Accountable for the overall management of the materials management division, including purchasing contracts, central services, processing, and the hiring and supervision of 44 full-time employees.
▸ Managed the distribution of supplies to more than 51 separate sites totaling 1,000 acute care beds and 1,000+ long-term care beds.
▸ Maintained at least a 90 percent national contract compliance rate at all locations.
▸ Implemented a patient procedure based supply delivery system for reduction of inventory and waste.
▸ Coordinated a successful department re-engineering to reduce overhead, including writing new job descriptions, changing department hours, downsizing employees, expanding services, and co-managing an operating room instrumentation program.
▸ Implemented a managed care supply program to further drive down health care costs.
▸ Served as a member of the implementation team to align all Sisters of Charity institutions into a regionally managed organization with initial savings of $15 million over five years.

PENROSE ST. FRANCIS HEALTHCARE SYSTEM, Colorado Springs, Colorado (1988 – 1994)
Manager, Supply, Processing and Distribution (1994)

▸ Regional Manager of the SPD material management departments with responsibility for patient supply revenue exceeding $30 million per year, budgeting, and compliance.
▸ Supervised the acquisition of supplies, services, and equipment.
▸ Responsible for supply processing and distribution, including surgical processing, sterilization, instrumentation control, and transportation.
▸ Maintained a point-of-use stockless inventory program, saving $2.5 million per year.
▸ Developed the concept for a centralized processing plant to service the two regions.
▸ Achieved a 90 percent contract compliance rating with the system's group purchasing organization.

Processing Manager (1992 – 1993)

▸ Managed three off-site central service departments and an off-site warehouse.
▸ Processed all sterile products, monitored the quality assurance departments, and ensured adherence to JCAHO, CPA, and OSHA rules, guidelines, and recommendations.
▸ Maintained a consistently favorable profit margin.
▸ Trained and supervised more than 45 staff members, ensuring ongoing education.
▸ Planned and implemented a stockless inventory control system resulting in a multi-million dollar partnership with a national distributor.

(Scannable)

EXPERIENCE
(continued)

PENROSE ST. FRANCIS HEALTHCARE SYSTEM, Colorado Springs, Colorado (continued)
Surgical Stores Manager (1991 – 1992)
▶ Supervised the surgical stores, two buyers, and one purchasing assistant involved in the acquisition of all med/surg needs, including supplies and capital equipment for surgery, heart cath lab, emergency, cardiology, birth center, ICU, CCU, and central services department.
▶ Planned and implemented a central distribution department.
▶ Constructed an automated system that increased picking efficiency by more than 400 percent.

Surgical Stores Coordinator (1990 – 1991)
▶ Developed and implemented the surgical stores inventory control system.
▶ Controlled and reduced both official and unofficial inventories by more than $1 million.

Medical/Surgical Buyer (1990)
▶ Reorganized work flow, instilled leadership and accountability among the staff, and improved the working environment.
▶ One of the first acute care facilities in the United States to discontinue the use of ETO sterilizing gas and move to alternative sterilization of surgical products.
▶ Purchased supplies and capital equipment for the surgery, heart cath lab, respiratory, emergency, and trauma departments.

Health Care Buyer (1988 – 1990)
▶ Built a new department to reduce surgical inventory; designed and built a low unit of measure storeroom.
▶ Reduced surgical inventory by more than $.5 million and improved service efficiency by 400 percent.
▶ Purchased supplies and capital equipment for the nursing, administration, information services, radiology, rehabilitation, and cardiology departments.

SISTERS OF CHARITY HEALTHCARE SYSTEM, Colorado Springs, Colorado
Manager, Reprographic Facility
▶ Built a reprographics center from the ground up to service seven acute and five long-term care facilities.
▶ Implemented the architectural design and equipped the facility to fulfill the goals set by the region.
▶ Generated an average of $2 million per year in revenue, with an annual budget of more than $500,000.
▶ Managed the daily operations and supervised a staff of 14.
▶ Interfaced with large hospital systems to develop specific goals and a marketing plan to attract patients.

EDUCATION

REGIS UNIVERSITY, Colorado Springs, Colorado
▶ 58 credits toward a Bachelor of Business Administration

PIKES PEAK COMMUNITY COLLEGE, Colorado Springs, Colorado
▶ Associate of Industrial Arts Degree

AFFILIATIONS

▶ Member of the American Hospital Association (AHA)
▶ President of the local chapter of the American Society of Healthcare Materials Managers (ASHMM)
▶ Member of the Advisory Board for School District 11, Regis University, University of Phoenix, and Pikes Peak Community College

LOUISE ELSEVIER

ADDRESS

123 Woodland Avenue, Summit, New Jersey 07901
Phone: 908-555-1234

E-mail: criscito@aol.com
Fax: 908-555-5678

PROFILE

- Results-oriented executive with experience in new product development and marketing.
- Expertise in start-ups, new business development, electronic and Internet products, consumer packaged goods and services, business-to-business markets, and international markets.
- Background in consumer products, publishing, travel, credit card, and financial industries.
- Skilled in all aspects of the marketing process from international need identification research to product testing and roll-out.
- Well-developed communication, negotiation, personnel, and project management abilities.
- Highly motivated, energetic, positive team player with a "roll-up the sleeves" attitude.

EXPERIENCE

REED TRAVEL GROUP, Secaucus, New Jersey (1995 to 1998)
Vice President, Global Travel Agency Channel
Directed the marketing efforts of a key division of Reed Elsevier, a $6 billion publishing company and the largest provider of travel content in the world (*Travel Weekly, Hotel and Travel Index, Official Airline Guide, Official Hotel Guide,* etc.). Responsible for global marketing, strategic planning, product development, needs assessment, direct response advertising, and development of strategic alliances with travel agencies and intermediaries. Fully accountable for profit and loss and business development efforts at key accounts worldwide.
- Consistently generated margins of more than 30 percent.
- Produced $42 million in revenue annually in print and electronic products and services.
- These subscription sales generated indirect revenues of $150 million annually in advertising sales.
- Successfully converted print media into electronic formats customized to each client's needs.
- Supervised staff on three continents and traveled extensively.

Vice President, Marketing and Communications, Business Development and Technology Solutions
Global responsibility for product development, competitive and market evaluation, strategic planning, and project management for electronic-based travel services. Defined evolving market opportunities for electronic products.
- Identified and assisted in the $20 million acquisition of a technology start-up company to complement electronic and Internet product development processes.
- Managed a $5 million development budget, consistently completing projects under budget.
- Provided situation analysis, customer needs identification, concept optimization, product testing, and business case development.
- Developed the company's first electronic competitive intelligence database.
- Directed the development of new Intranet products, including the Electronic Travel Store and Travel Weekly Crossroads.
- Created product definition, look and feel, component selection, and back-end reporting.

SAFECARD SERVICES, INC., (acquired by Cendant) Jacksonville, Florida (1994 to 1995)
Director, New Product Development
Directed the development of new products for five strategic business units for this provider of third-party credit card products.
- Created new product development processes for rapid, successful market entry through the direct mail channel; initiated and established Internet sales channel.
- Developed a business plan and managed new product development for the emerging travel strategic business unit.
- Managed primary qualitative and quantitative consumer market research, which resulted in the development of new product consumer benefit strategies for travel-related products and services.
- Conducted primary customer research to evaluate enterprise-wide customer relationships.
- Negotiated contractual relationships with credit card companies.
- Headed the marketing team that assessed companies targeted for merger or acquisition; led the purchase of National Leisure Group, a company that sells consumer travel packages.

Scannable

EXPERIENCE
(continued)

AMSOUTH BANK, Jacksonville, Florida (1993 to 1994)
Marketing Director
Managed all aspects of the bank's marketing, including new product development and execution, market research, competitive/market analysis, database management, advertising, public relations, and direct marketing.
- Designed and executed an employee and customer incentive plan that expanded direct deposit accounts to the highest level in the bank's history.
- Initiated market segmentation study that identified targets by brand usage, product perceptions, and needs, resulting in significant decreases in targeted marketing/advertising expenditures.

BUSINESSHIP INTERNATIONAL, Coral Gables, Florida (1991 to 1992)
Vice President, Marketing
Coordinated the marketing and sales of "The Business Kit," an entrepreneurial skills training program for children. Developed eleven new international consumer products from concept to "works-like, looks-like" presentation models within a 90-day period.
- Created a database and executed a direct mail campaign that increased the user base by 15 percent.
- Developed an interactive "Business Kit" with CompuServe and marketed the product to users via direct mail campaigns to the CompuServe network.

HASBRO, INC., Pawtucket, Rhode Island (1989 to 1990)
Senior Product Manager, Boys Toy Group
Successfully led staff and a multifunctional team in the development of integrated marketing and merchandising programs, new product strategies, multimillion dollar advertising campaigns, new packaging designs, and pricing policies for several key brands, including GI Joe and Transformers.
- Increased profits by 15 percent on existing brands by decreasing material costs.
- Negotiated licensing agreements worth $5 million in incremental income.

COLONIAL RESTAURANT EQUIPMENT, INC., New Bedford, Massachusetts (1986 to 1989)
Co-Owner
Directed every aspect of marketing, finance, and general operations.

WARNER LAMBERT, INC., Morris Plains, New Jersey (1982 to 1985)
Product Manager, Lubriderm Lotion and New Products
Assistant Product Manager, Effergrip and New Products
Retail Sales Representative, Consumer Health Care Products
Assistant Product Manager, Schick Razors and Blades

GENERAL MILLS, INC., Minneapolis, Minnesota (1981 to 1982)
Marketing Assistant, Bacos and Bugles

EDUCATION

MASTER OF BUSINESS ADMINISTRATION (1981)
Baruch College, City University of New York
- Concentration in Marketing and Advertising

BACHELOR OF SCIENCE IN BUSINESS ADMINISTRATION (1979)
Boston University
- Major in Marketing, Minor in Finance

PATRICIA A. DOMINICAN

OBJECTIVE

A key management position in an international environment with responsibilities for strategic planning, new business development, and international marketing management.

QUALIFICATIONS

- Thirteen years of sales, marketing, and general management experience
- Advanced Degree in International Management
- Proven management skills in new product development and expansion
- Skilled in negotiations, people management, and interpersonal skills
- Excellent communication, analytical, and leadership abilities

PROFESSIONAL EXPERIENCE

CONSULTANT . . . . 1996 – Present
Trosclair Marketing, San Rafael, California
Consultant to small/medium firms. Strategic business planning; sales/marketing planning; service and product packaging; new business development; television production planning and implementation.

REGIONAL SALES MANAGER, WESTERN UNITED STATES . . . . . . 1994 – 1996
Showtime Networks, Inc., San Francisco, California
Within first 9 months negotiated $19+ million in new revenue. Within first 12 months increased distribution by 10.2 percent. Key strategist for 11 Area Managers in financial and sales negotiations; key strategist for introduction of new pay-per-view service. Training and development of management team.

NATIONAL SALES MANAGER . . . . 1993 – 1994
Varicom, Inc., San Francisco, California
National Sales Manager, promoted from Western Regional Manager, San Francisco, California. Managed national distributor sales; managed sales to Western Region television stations, both network and independent.

CONSULTANT 1993
Trosclair Cable Marketing, San Rafael, California
Consultant to cable television management, specializing in marketing management, public/community affairs, and employee training. Analyzed a proposed California legislative bill, and designed and directed the campaign to the bill's defeat.

REGIONAL MANAGER, NORTHWEST . . . . 1989 – 1992
Home Box Office, San Francisco, California
Regional Manager, Northwest, promoted from Regional Coordinator: Sales to and marketing planning for 150+ cable television managements. Directed cooperative product promotion campaign for 20+ metropolitan cable firms. Analyzed and planned multi-product positioning. Managed field representatives. Conducted numerous client training programs.

DIRECTOR/EXECUTIVE PRODUCER OF TELEVISION STATION . . . 1986 – 1989
Marin 11, Viacom Cablevision, Inc., San Rafael, California
Designed and directed start-up, and managed award-winning television profit center for a community television station. Created and programmed 300+ television programs. Established community/media support and participation. Hired, trained, and managed employees; developed and managed three college intern programs. Nine national awards for excellence attained within first three years of operation.

226

(Scannable)

PROFESSIONAL EXPERIENCE

DIRECTOR OF DOMINICAN DAY CAMP . . . . 1984 – 1986
Dominican College of San Rafael, California
Creator and strategist for the foundations and operations of a recreational day camp. Directed the camp, which attracted capacity attendance the first year. Wrote procedures/operations/programming manuals. Hired/trained staff. Developed sales/marketing campaign and materials. Awarded the coveted *American Camping Association* accreditation in record time.

SAVINGS AND LOAN INSTITUTIONS / BANKING . . . . 1980 – 1986

EDUCATION

MASTER OF INTERNATIONAL MANAGEMENT . . . . May 1999
American Graduate School of International Management
Thunderbird Campus, Glendale, Arizona
Emphasis: International Marketing Management; Asia
Special Projects:
• Developed feasibility study for entry of new product into the Japanese market
• International Consumer Marketing Seminar
• Market research survey for development of new service between Japan and U.S.A.
• Study of telecommunications in the Pacific Rim

BACHELOR OF ARTS, SPEECH COMMUNICATION, *cum laude* 1986
Dominican College of San Rafael, San Rafael, California

LANGUAGES

Knowledge of Japanese

AWARDS

Ace Award for Cable Television Excellence 1985
Ace Award for Cable Television Excellence 1986
Who's Who in Cable Television 1986–87
1975 Outstanding Senior Student Nominee, Dominican College

PROFESSIONAL ACTIVITIES

Women In Cable, San Francisco Chapter – President, Vice President, PR Chair 1987–93
Bay Area Cable Club – Program Chair 1995
American Women in Radio and Television – Executive Board 1987–93

COMMUNITY ACTIVITIES

Mother Lode Musical Theatre, Inc. – Executive Board
San Rafael Chamber of Commerce – Executive Board
Marin Ballet – Executive Board
Cultural Affairs Service League – Charter President

INTERESTS

Travel in United States, Mexico, Canada, Asia

ADDRESS

Current Address:
1234 W. Greenway Road, #123
Glendale, Arizona 85306
(602) 555-1234

Permanent Address:
1234 Lincoln, #123
San Rafael, California 94901
(415) 555-1234

Scannable

Michael L. Linnenburger, CBI, CBE

1234 Los Padres Trail
Fort Worth, Texas 76137

Office: (972) 555-1234
Home: (817) 555-5678

Objective   A position as a computer network systems engineer for a company concerned about the integration and design of their operational network.

Experience

Williams Telecommunications Group (WilTel), Dallas, Texas . . . . 1996 to Present
SENIOR NETWORK SYSTEMS ENGINEER
- Provide support in resolving network problems either directly on site or via telephone.
- Engineer, design, and conduct tradeoff studies on network projects for various clients.
- Upgrade and configure network equipment (servers, hubs, switches, and routers) for use on operational networks.
- Assemble and distribute systems to operational users.

Meridian Oil, Incorporated, Fort Worth, Texas . . . . 1994 to 1996
SENIOR STAFF INFORMATION SYSTEMS AND TECHNOLOGY ANALYST
- Set up and managed the Internet connection using SMTP, DNS, and a firewall.
- Supported outlying offices with either direct on-site or phone support for resolving network problems.
- Set up and maintained a company-wide virus scanning software on both servers and clients.
- Developed and conducted training and update classes for VINES administrators company-wide.

United States Air Force . . . . 1973 to 1994
Twenty-one years of progressively more responsible service and training positions which included contact with manufacturers, service contractors, and major computer suppliers. Extensive specialized training at both Department of the Air Force and manufacturers' schools.

CHIEF, HARDWARE SERVICES DIVISION, ACADEMIC COMPUTING SERVICES
Department of the Air Force, Dean of Faculty, USAF Academy, Colorado (1993 to 1994)
- Supervised an office of 10 technicians, with a wide range of responsibilities including the installation of a 65-server Banyan VINES network with 6000+ clients.
- Prepared and conducted training for group and building VINES administrators for the USAF Academy.
- Worked with the dual broadband system for distribution of VAX cluster output and connections.
- Engineered design and trade-off studies; assembled and distributed systems to operational users.
- Supported base-level contracting with technical information needed to complete purchase requests.
- Improved process methods, reducing expenditures and minimizing total man-hours for all projects.

PROGRAM MANAGER FOR COMPUTER INFORMATION SYSTEMS
Training System Program Office, Wright-Patterson AFB, Ohio (1990 to 1993)
- Managed and provided engineering support for a 12-server Banyan VINES network with 400+ clients.
- Completed an upgrade of the network from 10base2 client wiring to 10baseT wiring, which included WAN connections to an off-site work location during the upgrade with no loss of work time.
- Designed and deployed an extension of the network to a division of the organization located in Utah, using Internet for connectivity.
- Engineered design and trade-off studies; supported base-level contracting with technical information.
- Assisted in leading a team of 13 functional experts in defining, acquiring, and fielding a family of maintenance training devices.

FIELD ENGINEER, DEFENSE METEOROLOGICAL SATELLITE PROGRAM (DMSP) GROUND SYSTEM
1000 Satellite Operations Group, Offutt AFB, Nebraska (1983 to 1986)
- Evaluated proposals for any changes to the Satellite Ground Control Facility.
- Lead Engineer on embedded microcomputer applications for controlling the DMSP Ground System links and equipment.
- Test Engineer for installation of new electronic systems.
- Controlled equipment failures and coordinated with DMSP SPO, three contractors, and two detachments when failure trend analysis indicated needed action.

228

Experience (continued)

MASTER INSTRUCTOR AND SCIENTIFIC MEASUREMENTS TECHNICIAN (1978 to 1980)
- Instructor for three key areas of the Scientific Measurements Technician School: Introduction to Programming and Computers, Seismic Analysis, and Seismic Field Station Operation.
- Updated portions of the course for new requirements and technologies, resulting in manpower and resources savings and more effective learning.

Education

College Degrees
- Master of Science, Systems Management, Air Force Institute of Technology
- Bachelor of Science, Electrical Engineering, Texas A&M University
- Applied Associate of Science, Instructor of Technology, CCAF
- Applied Associate of Science, Electronics Engineering Technology, CCAF
- Applied Associate of Science, Ground Radar Systems Technology, CCAF
- Applied Associate, General Studies, Mississippi Gulf Coast Junior College

Certifications and Honors
- Certified Banyan Instructor, 1994 (Basic/Advanced VINES Administration and 6.0 Update Courses)
- Certified Banyan Engineer, 1993 (Recertified 1994, 1995, 1996)
- Certified Banyan Specialist, 1993 (Recertified 1994, 1995, 1996)
- Inducted into Sigma Iota Epsilon, 1987

Banyan Courses
- Train-the-Trainer Update for VINES Administration (VINES 6.0), Banyan, 1996
- VINES 6.00 Engineering Update, ABUI Training Institute, 1995
- Train-the-Trainer for VINES Administration (VINES 5.5), Banyan, 1994
- Advanced VINES Administration and Planning (VINES 5.5), Banyan, 1994
- Basic VINES Administration (VINES 5.5), Banyan, 1994
- VINES 5.5 Engineering Update (VINES 5.5), Banyan, 1993
- Technical Tools II (VINES 5.0), Banyan, 1993
- Technical Tools I (VINES 5.0), Banyan, 1992
- VINES Gateways, Banyan, 1992

Other Courses
- NetBuilder II Configuration and Bridging, 3Com, 1997
- NetBuilder II IP Routing, 3Com, 1997
- Product Overview (Genesys CTI), Genesys, 1997
- Installation and System Administration (Genesys CTI), Genesys, 1997
- FastCall/FastView Installation and Operation, Nortel, 1997
- LANRover Installation and Operation, Shiva, 1996
- Systems Engineering Course, Systems Management and Development Corp, DSMC, 1992
- Computer Resources Acquisition Course, AFMC SAS, 1992
- Advanced Systems Acquisition Management Course, AFSC SAS, 1989

Activities

Enterprise Networking Association (ENA) .... 1990 to Present
Formerly known as Association of Banyan Users International (ABUI)
Immediate Past President/Secretary (1997 to Present). President, Board of Directors, with responsibility for overseeing corporate operations as CEO (1995 to 1997). Secretary, Board of Directors, with responsibility for overseeing minutes and corporate records (1994 to 1995). Chairman for Asynchronous Technical Wizards Interface Group (TWIG) with the responsibilities of overseeing session content at the semiannual conferences, conducting session, and coordinating the tracking of member requirements with a Banyan representative as related to asynchronous and WAN issues (1990 to 1994).

Scannable

CHARLES MCFEE

1234 Bergen Hill Drive • Evergreen, Colorado 80439 • (303) 555-1234 • E-mail: criscito@aol.com

PROFILE

- Experienced mechanical/design engineer and project manager with expertise in:
  - ▸ HVAC and Piping
  - ▸ Industrial Ventilation
  - ▸ Environmental Control
  - ▸ Nuclear Particulate Containment
  - ▸ Power Generation
  - ▸ Vibration Analysis
  - ▸ Safety Engineering
  - ▸ Facilities Engineering
  - ▸ Heavy Equipment Installation
  - ▸ Ship Building
  - ▸ Energy Use Analysis
  - ▸ Oil and Gas
  - ▸ Feasibility Studies
  - ▸ Managerial Analysis
  - ▸ Process Assessment
  - ▸ Procedural Development
  - ▸ Quality Assurance
  - ▸ Technical Editing/Training
- Self-motivated professional who is able to see the whole picture while managing the details.
- Adept at applying logical but creative approaches to problem resolution.
- Effective leader with strong communication, presentation, and team building skills.
- Proficient in Windows, MS Word, Excel, PowerPoint, MS Project, Lotus 1-2-3, and the Internet.

CERTIFICATIONS

- Registered Professional Mechanical Engineer (PE)
- Certified Safety Professional Credential (CSP)
- Certified Plant Engineer (CPE)
- Certified Vibration Analyst

BACKGROUND

Management

- Managed large, multi-million dollar engineering projects both domestically and overseas.
- Formed and supervised multi-disciplinary design teams; hired and supervised four design engineers.
- Successfully directed the operations of the mechanical engineering design departments of mid-sized engineering firms.
- Conducted client needs assessments, developed and managed budgets, created timelines, and served as client liaison for projects valued in excess of $50 million.
- Performed feasibility studies, equipment operability evaluations, economic analyses, cost-benefit analyses, project engineering, energy use analysis, and process development.
- Served as both team member and subject matter expert in numerous program and management assessments for Kaiser Hill Oversight Engineering.
- Prepared statements of work and nonconformance/safety resolution reports; ensured safety compliance.
- Lead developer and editor for process procedures and sight engineering requirements manual.

Engineering

- Expertise in the engineering design, analysis, and installation of mechanical/steam equipment, state-of-the-art electronic control hardware, industrial and nuclear HVAC, exhaust hood systems, and plant utilities in industrial, health care, laboratory, institutional, manufacturing, and commercial facilities.
- Projects often required skills in special air flow design, heating, cooling, humidification, dehumidification, safety system analysis, industrial ventilation, noise control, radiation protection, personnel protective clothing, chemical hazard protection, qualitative/quantitative hazard analysis, quality control and reliability, design parameters, maintainability, materials handling, inspection and control procedures, facilities planning and layout, environmental analysis and design, waste management, air quality management, and the creation of equipment and construction specifications.
- Diverse experience in the design and installation of HVAC and mechanical systems (piping, steam, chilled water, hot water, fire protection, exotic special gases, breathing air, etc.).
- Designed filtration systems, including HEPA filter fan plenums, portable/stationary air handling systems, charcoal absorbers, caustic/acid air scrubbers, and thermal DOP testing of HEPA filter systems.
- Identified hazards and devised appropriate safety measures to reduce exposure to contaminants and noise.
- Member of the ASHRAE technical committee responsible for devising the standards for clean rooms/spaces; very familiar with the requirements for clean room design from Class 100,000 to Class 1.
- Extensive knowledge of OSHA regulations, EPA standards, building/mechanical codes, fire protection codes, ventilation regulations, and equipment seismic qualifications.
- Experienced with nitrogen, ethylene oxide, oxygen, argon, helium, compressed control air ($-40°$ dewpoint), vacuum distribution, steam distribution, high-quality personnel breathing air, humidifiers, natural gas, propane, fuel oil, diesel, sanitary waste, process waste (fluorinated caustic, sodium hydroxide, potassium hydroxide, acids/caustics), and low relative humidity designs using Kathabar and desiccant drier systems.

EDUCATION

MASTER OF BUSINESS ADMINISTRATION IN MANAGEMENT, Webster University, St. Louis, Missouri
BACHELOR OF SCIENCE IN MECHANICAL ENGINEERING, University of Alabama, Tuscaloosa, Alabama

Scannable

EXPERIENCE

SENIOR PRINCIPAL MECHANICAL ENGINEER   1991 – present
KAISER/HILL COMPANY, LLC, Golden, Colorado (Operating Plant Facility)
Subject matter expert on nuclear, industrial, and commercial HVAC and piping engineering systems and standards, including multiple-stage .3 micron HEPA filtration systems. Emphasis on the design of low humidity, glovebox, and hooded laboratories and automatic control systems. Responsible for analysis and design of HVAC controls, mechanical design of pumping and piping systems, plant-wide vibration/balancing analysis, IAQ sampling, ventilation requirements, environmental systems, safety, and regulatory compliance. Part of the engineering team responsible for the decontamination, decommissioning, and demolition of a 40-year-old, three million square foot nuclear weapons production facility. Served as team lead for engineering review and technical editing of site design process and requirements documents. Analyzed economic feasibility and ensured quality control.
Notable Projects:
- Renovation of low temperature/low humidity process in a nuclear facility.
- New isolation airlock for nuclear plenum entry.
- Development of plant engineering design process manual.
- Revision and reorganization of plant engineering standards.
- Investigation of potential and actual nuclear accident scenarios.

DIRECTOR OF MECHANICAL ENGINEERING   1990 – 1991
DUNN CONSULTING ENGINEERS, Dallas, Texas (International Engineering Design Firm)
Established project criteria and objectives and prepared engineering design plans and CSI specifications for commercial, health care, and industrial facility turnkey projects. Marketed services directly to clients. Efficiently managed multi-disciplinary engineering teams. Designed control systems, central chiller/boiler plants, and pumping/piping systems. Analyzed and designed acoustics.
Notable Projects:
- Park Hyatt at Pelican Hills, Irvine, California (new 450-room luxury resort hotel).
- Methodist Hospital (Redbird), Dallas, Texas (prenatal, emergency room, surgery, patient rooms, and boiler/ chiller plant, combination of new construction and renovation).

MANAGER OF MECHANICAL ENGINEERING   1989 – 1990
CAMPOS ENGINEERING, INC., Dallas, Texas (Engineering Design Firm)
Directed engineers, design technicians, and CAD drafting personnel in the design and construction of HVAC and environmental control systems, operating suites, isolation areas, and a laminar flow operation suite for exposed bone surgery. Analyzed noise and designed vibration abatement to protect human hearing and improve safety.
Notable Projects:
- Parkland Hospital, Dallas, Texas (new laboratories and surgical facility).
- Presbyterian Hospital, Dallas, Texas (new hypobaric chamber/exam center).
- American Heart Association, Dallas, Texas (new 175,000 square foot national headquarters office).
- Cen'Tel Communication Systems, Dallas, Texas (new office/computer center).

PROJECTS ENGINEER   1985 – 1989
HENNINGSON, DURHAM, AND RICHARDSON, INC., Dallas, Texas (International A&E Design Firm)
Made marketing presentations to clients for mechanical HVAC systems, central chiller/boiler plant layouts, pumping/piping system design, and electronic environmental controls. Identified inventive solutions to unique problems. Coordinated internal and external project teams and prepared plans and CSI specifications.
Notable Projects:
- King Abdulazis University Health Sciences Center, Jeddah, Saudi Arabia (new, 100,000 square feet).
- Folsom Prison, Represa, California (new 3,200-bed prison facility).
- Frito Lay, Dallas, Texas (renovation of semi-works and hard bit line facilities/steam boiler plant).
- Dallas County Courthouse, Dallas, Texas (new 750,000 square foot courts/office/jail facility).
- Del Norte State Prison, Del Norte, California (new 2,000-bed maximum security facility).
- Gwinnett County Justice Center, Lawrenceville, Georgia (new 580,000 square foot courts/office/jail/parking/computer room facility).
- Quincy Veterans Hospital, Quincy, Massachusetts (energy systems evaluation)
- Lew Sterret Justice Center, Dallas, Texas (energy systems evaluation and boiler/chiller renovation).
- Santa Ana Hospital, Santa Ana, California (new prenatal, surgery, and psychology wings).
- Argonne National Laboratories, Chicago, Illinois (renovation of chemistry building laboratory).

Scannable

EXPERIENCE
(continued)

DESIGN ENGINEER   1983 – 1985
ARJO ENGINEERS, INC., Dallas, Texas (Engineering Design Firm)
Prepared HVAC computer load calculations and layouts for air distribution and electro-mechanical systems. Created equipment specifications, drawings, and mechanical pumping/piping systems designs. Served as liaison to outside project architects, vendors, and building owners.

PROJECT COORDINATOR   1978 – 1983
J. RAY MCDERMOTT INTERNATIONAL, INC., New Orleans, Louisiana (International Oil Field Operations)
Coordinated worldwide projects for sophisticated electronic, electrical, hydraulic, and other mechanical and electrical equipment systems. Accountable for budgeting, design, equipment procurement, supervision of installation, and final evaluation of turnkey projects on the company's ocean-going fleet of ships. Traveled worldwide and lived overseas.

FIELD ENGINEER   1976 – 1978
GENERAL ELECTRIC, MECHANICAL/NUCLEAR DIVISION, New Orleans, Louisiana (Field Service Engineering)
Lead technical advisor for electro-mechanical installation of steam turbine electric generators, switch-gear controls, main propulsion steam turbines, double reduction gear trains, and related integrated circuit control systems for large crude oil, LPG tankers and navy combat ships. Extensive background in steam and gas turbine technology. Inspected and analyzed vibrations of high-speed steam turbines, gear trains, and other rotating equipment.

AFFILIATIONS

- American Society of Heating, Refrigeration, and Air-Conditioning Engineers (ASHRAE), active voting member of the Technical Committee's Nuclear Subcommittee, Industrial Ventilation Committee, Laboratory Systems Committee, and Industrial Air Conditioning Committee
- Member of the American Society of Safety Engineers (ASSE)
- Member of the Association of Facilities Engineering (AFE)
- Association of Energy Engineers (AEE)

INTERESTS

Licensed Aircraft Pilot • Licensed Scuba Diver • Non-smoker • Cross-country Skier • Martial Arts

Scannable

16 | Curriculum Vitae

Remember when I said that there is an exception to every rule in the résumé business? Well, here's another one. In most cases, résumés should be concise and limited to one or two pages at the most. You will carefully select your information to provide a synopsis. In the professions, however, a much longer résumé is expected and the longer the résumé, the better your chances of getting an interview. Those industries generally include medicine, law, education, science, and media (television, film, etc.). If you are applying for a job in a foreign country, long résumés with more detail and a considerable amount of personal information are the norm (see Chapter 9).

Such a professional résumé is called a *curriculum vita* (CV) from the Latin meaning "course of one's life" (literally like running a race—and you just *thought* your life was a rat race!). For those of us who have trouble knowing how to spell the word, *vita* is singular and *vitae* is plural.

A successful CV will include not only education and experience but also publications (books, magazines, journals, and other media), certifications, licenses, grants, professional affiliations, awards, honors, presentations, and/or courses taught. Anything relevant to your industry is appropriate to use on a CV, and the résumé can be as long as it needs to be to present the "course of your life."

A CV—or any résumé with multiple pages for that matter—must contain a header with your name and page number on each successive page. Should the pages become separated, the reader should be able to easily put your subsequent pages in their proper order and with *your* résumé!

GARY A. MILLER

123 El Paso Boulevard • Manitou Springs, Colorado 80829 • (719) 555-1234

PROFILE
- Experienced administrator with a background in education.
- Doctoral degree in educational administration from the University of Colorado.
- Current Type D Certificate as Superintendent of Schools.
- Able to serve as a participant, facilitator, or leader of both large and small groups.
- Proven communication, organizational, management, and problem solving skills.

EXPERIENCE
Administration
- Efficiently administer the use of all district facilities, property, and funds with a minimum of waste.
- Maintain a current knowledge of all state and federal laws, rules, and regulations affecting the operations of the school district.
- Developed an asbestos management plan and coordinated projects to remove asbestos throughout the district; completed 16 hours of asbestos awareness training.
- Chair of 20 visiting resource teams for the North Central Accreditation Association, including two teams that visited the Lewis-Palmer School District.
- Scheduled the summer use of fields and buildings for the district.
- Coordinated the multi-year plan for district-wide replacement of copiers.

Supervision
- Supervise all employees of the school district; directly supervise the Administrative Assistant for Business and the Directors of Transportation, Food Service, and Buildings/Grounds.
- Inspire, lead, guide, and direct every member of the administrative, instructional, and support services teams in setting and achieving the highest standards of educational excellence.
- Represented the district in the selection of all employee fringe benefit plans, and wrote the board policy directing the management of the plans.

Financial
- Responsible for the overall financial planning of the district, including forecasting of revenue and expenditures, preparation of the annual budget, and presentation of the budget to the board of education and the public.
- In concert with the administrative team, developed a multi-year capital expenditure plan funded by the capital reserve fund allocation.
- Directly responsible for the investment of bond issue proceeds during the periods when the funds were not needed.
- Worked with the district's investment banking firm to refund outstanding debt in order to access lower interest rates, thereby saving taxpayers thousands of dollars in bond interest payments.
- Provide management oversight of the business/bookkeeping/accounting department.
- Developed, maintained, and updated the chart of accounts used to account for all district revenue and expenditures.
- Eliminated an annual deficit in the food service fund.

Bond Issues
- Manage the investment of district funds and the administration of the bond redemption fund.
- Met with Moody's in New York in 1986 to present information that resulted in an improvement in the district's bond rating.
- Facilitated the work of two different bond issue committees, achieving voter approval of bond issues in 1975 and 1986 that allowed for the construction of a new middle school and extensive additions/renovations to all four district schools.
- Acted as the "owner's representative" during the construction resulting from the bond issues, authorizing contractor payments and completing the projects under budget and on time.
- Made recommendations to the board of education for bond companies and auditing firms.

Communication
- Serve as liaison between the school board, school district, and the community.
- Established and maintain a public relations program to keep the community well informed of the activities and needs of the school district.
- Report directly to the board of education the monthly and quarterly financial status of the district.
- Adjunct Professor for Denver University; taught school finance in their Weekend Administrative Preparation Program in the Pikes Peak region.

Scannable

WORK HISTORY	**Superintendent of Schools**, Manitou Springs School District 14, Colorado	1974 – Present
	Director of Curriculum, Manitou Springs School District 14, Colorado	1972 – 1974
	Principal, Manitou Springs Elementary School, Colorado	1970 – 1972
	Counselor/Teacher, Manitou Springs High School, Colorado	1966 – 1970

EDUCATION

DOCTOR OF EDUCATION, Educational Administration   1982
University of Colorado, Boulder, Colorado

MASTER OF ARTS, Guidance and Counseling   1969
University of Colorado, Boulder, Colorado

BACHELOR OF ARTS, Psychology and Distributed Social Studies   1966
University of Colorado, Boulder, Colorado

AFFILIATIONS

- North Central Accreditation Association, State Committee Member
- American Association of School Administrators
- Colorado Association of School Executives
- Pikes Peak Area Superintendent's Association, Past Chair
- Pikes Peak Board of Cooperative Educational Services, Executive Council, Past Chair of the Superintendent's Advisory Council
- Pikes Peak Leadership Academy, Founding Governing Board Member, Treasurer
- Manitou Springs Arts Academy, Charter Member of the Board of Directors
- Manitou Springs Chamber of Commerce, Pride Council
- Manitou Springs Public Library, Board of Directors, Past President
- Plains and Peaks Library Systems, Governing Board, Past Chair
- Phi Delta Kappa, Past President, Past Vice President/Programs, 1985–1987

PRESENTATIONS WORKSHOPS

- "Effective Administration," Guest Lecturer, University of Denver Weekend Administration Program, Colorado Springs
- "Effective Teaching," Guest Lecturer, University of Colorado, Colorado Springs
- "Time Management," Pikes Peak BOCES Winter Workshop, Colorado Springs
- "Teacher Evaluation," Pikes Peak BOCES Winter Workshop, Colorado Springs
- "Teacher Performance Appraisal," Southeast BOCES Superintendents' Workshop
- "Target-Based Teacher Appraisal," Lewis-Palmer School District Staff In-service
- "Writing and Implementing Performance Targets," Wiley School District Staff In-service
- "Merit Pay," Phi Delta Kappa Workshop, University of Northern Colorado, Greeley
- "Merit Pay," University of Colorado, Spring Conference
- "Counselor Appraisal," Adams State College

Scannable

Laura M. Santos

1234 Van Pelt Avenue #4 • Hollywood, California 93105 • (805) 555-1234

QUALIFICATIONS

Creative film professional with experience in writing, field production, offline editing, research, camera, and sound
Detail oriented and well organized; comfortable taking the initiative and working independently
Adept at juggling multiple priorities and working under pressure to meet time-sensitive deadlines
Effective team player with strong interpersonal and communication skills
Thrive in positions that require traveling worldwide
Produced documentaries in South Africa, Mozambique, Botswana, Maldives, Hawaii, and the Continental United States
Undergraduate degree from Georgetown University in English and Fine Arts

FILM EXPERIENCE

Outer Bounds	**Discovery International** **National Geographic International** Distributed through HIT	**Writer, Researcher, Offline Editor (Editor of One Episode):** 39-part, half-hour adventure magazine showcasing the world's foremost documentary cameramen; featured extreme sports, expeditions, human adventure, and nature segments
Sharks of the Wild Coast *Shark Attack Files II* *In Search of the Giants* *Sharks of the Atlantic*	**The Discovery Channel** *Shark Week 1997* *Shark Week 1998*	**Writer, Editor, Field Producer, Production Manager, Researcher, Sound Recordist, Assistant to the Cameraman**
Snow Monkeys	**The Discovery Channel** *Nature World of Mitsuaki Iwago* NHK Broadcasting (Japan) Distributed by Media Int'l Corporation	**Writer, Researcher:** hour-long documentary shown at Wildscreen 1996 International Documentary Filmmakers' Festival
Penguins of South Georgia Island	**The Discovery Channel** *Nature World of Mitsuaki Iwago* NHK Broadcasting (Japan)	**Writer, Researcher:** hour-long documentary shown at Wildscreen 1996 International Documentary Filmmakers' Festival
Wolves of Poland *Crocodiles of the Ganges* *Capuchin Monkeys of the Amazon*	**The Discovery Channel** *Nature's Secret World* NHK Broadcasting (Japan) Distributed by Media Int'l Corporation	**Writer, Researcher, Offline Editor:** 13 half-hour long documentaries in production
Legends of Killer Sharks	**The Discovery Channel** *Shark Week 1996*	**Assistant to the Director**
Code Red	**The Discovery Channel**	**Production Coordinator:** one-hour submarine show

WORK HISTORY

Writer, Field Producer, Editor, Bergen & Associates, Inc., 1996 – present
Director of Development, Halfway House of Santa Barbara, 1994 – 1996
Writer, Olde Times, 1994 – 1996
Public Relations Coordinator and Educator, Cancer Foundation, 1993 – 1995
English Teacher, USAID, Prague, Czech Republic, 1992 – 1993

MANAGEMENT AND OTHER EXPERIENCE

- Coordinated field budgets, historically succeeding in bringing films in under budget.
- Scheduled locations, interviews, cast, and team members.
- As director of development for a residential facility for disabled children, wrote grants, raised funds, and served as community liaison.
- Generated record-setting funds for the facility's summer camp and directed the activities of the camp.
- Developed and coordinated a gala tennis affair and other community fund-raising events.
- Created all literature for the organization and designed a monthly newsletter.
- Served as public relations coordinator for a foundation, created and implemented fund raising events, developed grant proposals, supervised telemarketing staff, maintained financial records, collected and evaluated donor profiles, taught in-house seminars, developed a speakers bureau, edited literature, and designed logo.
- Developed preschool curriculum for young children in the Czech Republic, taught English, and lectured to Czech teachers on implementing the curriculum.
- Directed the Appalachian Craft Fair at Georgetown University to generate revenue for impoverished artists.
- Coordinated and led 15 students in the Spring Break in Appalachia program; assessed community needs and began construction of a water shed and community common house; assisted teachers in the local elementary school.
- Researched and wrote a feature length screenplay showcased at Sundance Institute 1995.
- Author of *Whale's Song*, a children's story.

EDUCATION

BACHELOR OF ARTS IN ENGLISH AND FINE ARTS
Georgetown University, Washington, D.C., 1991
Recipient of Lannon Fellowship for Writing, 1990
Nominated as Georgetown's delegate for the Poetry Festival at University of Maryland, 1991
Delegate to the Middlebury's Bread Loaf Writing Conference, 1991
New Press literary and graphics editor; coordinated the literary section for the *Journal on Issues of Gender*
Dean's List, six semesters

TOBI STEINBERG

1234 Camelot Court • Colorado Springs, Colorado 80904 • (719) 555-1234

PROFILE

- Experienced mental health professional with a diverse background in inpatient and medical psychiatric assessment and therapy, including:
  - Social work
  - Individual therapy
  - Group therapy
  - Teaching
  - Evaluation
  - Disposition
  - Crisis intervention
  - Domestic violence
  - Thought field therapy
  - Stress management
  - Suicide prevention
  - Victim assistance
- Licensed Professional Counselor, Certified Licensed Massage Therapist.
- Creative team player with exceptional communication and presentation skills.
- Able to "think outside the box" and use new psychotherapy techniques.
- Knowledge of MS Word and Excel on IBM and Macintosh systems.
- Working knowledge of Spanish.

EDUCATION

MASTER OF ARTS, COUNSELING/PSYCHOTHERAPY, 1982
Western State College, Gunnison, Colorado
- Emphasis on Stress Management Techniques; Graduate Research Assistant, Teaching Assistant

BACHELOR OF ARTS, SOCIOLOGY/EDUCATION, 1974
Potsdam State University, Potsdam, New York
- Minor in Theatre Arts; Member of Potsdam Players, Photography Club, Student Government

CONTINUING EDUCATION
- Child Custody Evaluation, Thought Field Therapy, Suicide Prevention, CPI (nonviolent crisis intervention), Hospice Volunteer

EXPERIENCE

PSYCHOTHERAPY
- Provided crisis intervention, evaluation, and disposition planning in both inpatient and medical psychiatric settings; evaluated patients using involuntary hospitalization criteria.
- Furnished therapy in stress management, marriage counseling, addictions, family dysfunction, and health.
- Facilitated group therapy sessions and provided individual and family counseling.
- Interfaced with community agencies, hospitals, government agencies, and the juvenile court system in planning patient care.

TRAINING/INSTRUCTION
- Taught Psych 101, 102, Intro to Human Services, and Social Services Perspectives at the undergraduate level for Pikes Peak Community College.
- Graduate level instructor for Regis University in Psychology, Human Growth and Development, and other human services courses.
- Received consistently high student evaluations for teaching approach and effectiveness.
- Fine-tuned curriculum, making the subjects understandable to non-psychology majors.
- Led professional in-service classes and supervised volunteer training programs.
- Developed a successful family education program and curriculum for Head Start.
- Taught parenting and substance abuse classes, community education seminars, and educational seminars to area families and community professionals.

ADMINISTRATION
- Integral member of the team responsible for developing and supervising the entire mental health program for the Community Partnership for Child Development in Colorado Springs.
- Supervised a staff of four family service workers.
- Assisted in all levels of planning and development of Colorado's first safehouse program.
- Revamped crisis information statistics, call sheets, and other forms to improve productivity.
- Created a more efficient filing system for patient information.
- Author of numerous articles for local newspapers relating to contemporary mental health issues.
- Wrote a weekly column for *The Chronicle-Pilot*, Crested Butte, Colorado.

238

Scannable

WORK HISTORY

Crisis Intervention Specialist, Psychiatric Evaluator   1994 – present
Cedar Springs Hospital, Colorado Springs, Colorado

Instructor/Mentor, Graduate Counseling Program   1995 – 1997
Regis University, Denver, Colorado

Adjunct Instructor, Psychology and Social Work   1992 – 1995
Pikes Peak Community College, Colorado Springs, Colorado

Family and Adolescent Therapist   1992 – 1994
Brockhurst Ranch, Penrose-St. Francis Hospital, Colorado Springs, Colorado

Family Services/Mental Health Coordinator   1991 – 1992
Community Partnership for Child Development (Head Start), Colorado Springs, Colorado

Senior Mental Health Therapist, Crisis Evaluator   1989 – 1992
Pikes Peak Mental Health Center, Colorado Springs, Colorado

Therapist   1983 – 1988
Midwestern Colorado Mental Health Center, Gunnison, Colorado

Self-Employed (self-financed graduate and undergraduate education by   1974 – 1988
owning and operating various successful catering businesses)

Education Specialist   1979 – 1981
Boulder County Safehouse, Boulder, Colorado

Education Specialist   1974 – 1978
Planned Parenthood of Northern New York, Saranac Lake, New York

COMMUNITY SERVICE

Vice President, Board of Directors   1983 – 1989
Crested Butte Mountain Theater, Crested Butte, Colorado
• Grant writer, producer, actor, director, public relations

Committee Member   1985 – 1989
Fat Tire Bike Festival, Crested Butte, Colorado

Assistant Director   1974 – 1979
Saranac Lake Community Theater
• Producer, director, actor, community educator, public relations

AFFILIATIONS

• Southern Colorado CISD Team (Crisis Intervention Stress Debriefing)
• Southern Colorado LPC Association, member of Legislative Committee
• American Counseling Association
• International Association of Marriage and Family Counselors

Regina M. Carpenter

1234 Blodgett Drive
Colorado Springs, CO 80919

E-mail: criscito@aol.com

Phone (719) 555-1234
Fax (719) 555-1234

PROFILE
- Dynamic school administrator with diverse experience in:
  - Management/supervision
  - Organizational development
  - Total quality management
  - Strategic planning
  - Budgeting
  - Staff development
  - School law
  - Scheduling
  - Special education
  - Counseling
  - Assessment
  - Standards of learning
- Proven communication, organizational, management, and problem solving skills.
- Dedicated professional with a personal commitment to educational excellence.

CREDENTIALS
- Educational Administration Endorsement (K–12), State of Virginia
- Principal Endorsement (K–6), State of Virginia
- Supervisor of Special Education and Related Services, Speech Disorders, Hearing (K–12), State of Virginia
- Clinical License in Speech Pathology and Audiology, State of Virginia
- Administrator License, Director of Special Education, State of Colorado
- Principal, Speech Language Pathologist, State of Colorado
- Audiologist, State of Colorado
- Certificate of Clinical Competence (CCC), American Speech, Language, and Hearing Association

EXPERIENCE

ACADEMY DISTRICT TWENTY, Colorado Springs, Colorado   1998 – present
Director of Special Education, Resource, and Support Services
- Developed and administered special education services and programs for a small suburban school district with 20,000 students.
- Fostered social, emotional, physical, and intellectual development by providing students with a broad, challenging, and academically rigorous curriculum tailored to their special needs.
- Provided leadership in the identification of best practices, staff development, and ongoing program evaluation.
- Hired, supervised, and evaluated 70 staff members, including resource teachers, speech language pathologists, occupational therapists, physical therapists, nurses, aides, and office support staff.
- Designed resource programs for mild to moderately handicapped students.
- Developed a database of students and resources that provided an accurate count of students, which increased federal and state funding.
- Wrote successful sliver grants that generated more than $50,000 from the Colorado Department of Education.

NORFOLK PUBLIC SCHOOLS, Norfolk, Virginia   1975 – 1998
Senior Coordinator, Special Education Instructional Services (1992 – 1998)
- Administrative coordinator for all instructional services to disabled students within the Norfolk Public Schools, a mid-sized urban school district with 40,000 students.
- Directly supervised nine program administrators, a transition and employment specialist, and an adaptive physical education specialist.
- Responsible for the management of more than 500 teachers, therapists, and assistants.
- Developed effective programs of recognition for student and staff achievements.
- Created a climate conducive to professional growth and self-actualization.
- Developed annual master schedule, projected staff and resource needs, prepared the annual budget, allocated resources for sustainability, and administered funds to minimize waste.
- Served as liaison to secondary and elementary department chairpersons, SECEP, and correctional youth reinstatement coordinator.
- Developed curriculum and created an effective learning climate for social, emotional, physical, and academic achievement for mild to severely disabled students.
- Implemented a transition workshop program for students entering the workplace, including job shadows, career exploration experiences, on-the-job training, and job placement.
- Created an adaptive physical education and vocational programs for mentally disabled students.
- Supervised student schedules, attendance, grades, and cumulative records.
- Instrumental in contracting the participation of Norfolk Public Schools in norming the Word Test in cooperation with Lingusystems.

240

EXPERIENCE
(continued)

- Key player in causing the Norfolk Public Schools to be designated as one of four school systems nationally to receive and implement the CASE system, a comprehensive record and data collection system for special education.

Principal, Summer School (1991 – 1998)
- Administered the Special Education Extended Annual School Year and Secondary Summer School programs.
- Planned and implemented summer education for more than 200 students.

Principal, Norfolk Detention School (1992 – 1998)
- Directed the development of an education program for students in detention education.
- Supervised seven teachers and seven counselors.

Coordinator of Speech and Sensory Programs (1986 – 1992)
- Administered programs for the communicatively disordered, vision/hearing/orthopedically impaired and supervised 173 professionals.

Program Leader (1977 – 1986)
- Led programs for the multi-handicapped/developmentally delayed, speech and language services, communication disorders.
- Provided instructional support to 120 special education teachers and assistants.

Speech and Language Pathologist (1975 – 1977)
- Itinerant teacher serving regular education and multi-handicapped students.

EDUCATION

POSTGRADUATE STUDIES, *Virginia Polytechnic Institute, Old Dominion University, George Washington University, Adams State College, and Norfolk State University*
- Completed 53 hours in supervision and administration of education, special education, and related services.
- Fellow, Danforth Leadership Institute for Administrators (Summer 1989)

MASTER OF ARTS, *Cleveland State University,* Cleveland, Ohio
- Major in Speech Pathology and Audiology.
- Concentration in the areas of special education, speech language, hearing disorders, and service delivery to all disabling conditions.

BACHELOR OF ARTS, *Queens College, City University of New York,* Queens, New York
- Major in Communications Arts and Sciences.
- Received the New York State Regent Scholarship.
- Concentration in communication, education, psychology, speech, language, and hearing problems for the disabled.

AFFILIATIONS
- National Association of Elementary School Principals
- Council of Exceptional Children
- Council of Administrators of Special Education

Regional
- Member, Committee on Student Teaching Competencies, Hampton University Communications Department
- Member, Committee on Student Teaching and Externships, Old Dominion University

Virginia
- State of Virginia Delegate to Educational Consistency for Virginia's Incarcerated Youth
- State of Virginia Delegate on Transition Services
- State of Virginia Delegate to the Committee on Mental Retardation, American Speech, Language, and Hearing Association
- State of Virginia Delegate to the Task Force Committee of Therapies in School, Virginia State Department of Education
- Contributor Editor to the Task Force on Speech/Language Severity Rating Scales, Task Force on Speech and Hearing Guidelines, Task Force on Preschool Handicapped, and Task Force on Developmental Language Instruction, Virginia State Department of Education

Colorado
- Member of the State Medicaid Consortium

VALERIE R. CASE, RN, BSN

12345 West River Birch Drive #111 • Brookfield, Wisconsin 53045 • (414) 555-1234

PROFILE

Goal-directed, results-oriented professional with a strong medical background and education. Skilled communicator, persuasive and adaptable. Self-motivated with high energy, initiative, and focus. Keen insight into the needs and views of others—able to listen and identify issues or problem areas and form innovative solutions. Professional, personable, and articulate in presentation. Areas of strength include:

- Comprehensive Medical/Nursing Knowledge
- Communication/Negotiation/Facilitation
- Problem Solving/Decision Making
- Program Management/Assessment

- Client/Community Relations
- Flexible/Assertive/Adaptable
- Presentations/Training
- Documentation/Writing

EXPERIENCE

ACCOUNT MANAGER (8/97 – present)
Bio-Rad Laboratories, U.S. Diagnostics Sales Division, Hercules, California
Successfully sell lab instruments and other QC products to more than 150 laboratories, teaching hospitals, medical centers, and physician offices in the Wisconsin territory. Account manager for the Mayo Clinic, Rochester, Minnesota.
- Plan and manage a $1.4 million territory to increase market share for Bio-Rad products.
- Set appointments and deliver key message through sampling, merchandising, and visual aids.
- Develop new and effective marketing strategies; maintain excellent customer relations.

PUBLIC HEALTH NURSE (6/96 – 8/97)
El Paso County Department of Health and Environment, Colorado Springs, Colorado
Provide nursing services to individuals, family, and community groups in the home, clinic, and community center. Initiate and conduct home visits within the community. Identify physical, social, and emotional needs of clients.
- Evaluate and manage a monthly caseload of 25-30 clients.
- Assess client needs, design and implement comprehensive care plans.
- Educate and counsel patients about health, wellness, and parenting, as well as other areas as needed.
- Research, develop, and maintain community resources; initiate referrals for clients and families.
- Conduct immunization and well-child clinics.

ADULT DAY HEALTH CARE NURSE (3/95 – 5/96)
Interfaith Services, Inc., Sun City, Arizona
Provided direct and indirect supervision of program health aides and volunteer nurses. Scheduled volunteer nurses to assure proper nursing coverage. Provided skilled nursing care and administered medications.
- Developed strong community relations through networking and liaison representation with resource agencies.
- Designed and conducted orientation classes.
- Trained volunteer nurses and aides.
- Assisted Director and Program Manager with development and implementation of policies.
- Served as Center Supervisor in the absence of the Director.

242

EXPERIENCE (continued)

REGISTERED NURSE (1/95 – 3/95)
Nurses PRN, Phoenix, Arizona (a national temporary nursing service/home health agency)
Provided staff relief as needed for home health agencies and nursing homes. Monitored vital signs, ensured safety and support, and coordinated medication administration with physicians.
- Assessed and coordinated nursing care needs.
- Instructed patients on catheter care.
- Educated clients in the areas of nutrition and diet.

REGISTERED NURSE (8/94 – 11/94)
Good Samaritan Regional Medical Center, Phoenix, Arizona
Provided direct patient care on a 45-bed medical/oncology/hematology unit within a 600-bed teaching hospital.
- Served as Team Leader; directed technician staff.
- Supervised and administered patient medication and dosing; interpreted doctors' instructions.
- Monitored and treated complications due to chemotherapy and brachytherapy, including pain management, hypercalcemia, and infectious processes.

EDUCATION

BACHELOR OF SCIENCE DEGREE IN NURSING (1994)
Valdosta State University, Valdosta, Georgia
Selected Achievements: Dean's List, Who's Who Among Students in American Universities and Colleges, "Excellence in Nursing Award," Sigma Theta Tau Nursing Honor Society

BACHELOR OF ARTS IN POLITICAL SCIENCE (1986)
University of Washington, Seattle, Washington

CONTINUING EDUCATION: 35 contact hours, including AIDS Impact HIV/AIDS Series, CVC Care and Maintenance, Chest Tube Learning Module, Peripheral IV Therapy, Trach Care and Suctioning, Epidemiology and Prevention of Vaccine-Preventable Diseases by the Centers for Disease Control and Prevention, Child Physical Assessment, Tuberculosis

LICENSES

California State Nursing License (#533662)
Arizona State Nursing License (#086346)
Colorado State Nursing License (#111048)

Scannable

DAVID H. PEARLMAN

ADDRESS

Home: 1234 Parkview Boulevard, Colorado Springs, Colorado 80906

Office: 1234 East Kiowa, Colorado Springs, Colorado 80903

Phone: (719) 555-1234

Fax: (719) 555-1234

PROFILE

- Licensed attorney in private practice since 1969 (Colorado and New Mexico).
- Board Certified Civil Trial Specialist, National Board of Trial Advocacy, with extensive litigation experience (initially certified 1980, recertified 1985, 1990, and 1995).
- Recognized specialist in workers' compensation law by the New Mexico Legal Specialization Board.
- Admitted to practice before the U.S. Court of Appeals, 10th Circuit; U.S. District Court for the District of New Mexico; U.S. District Court for the Western District of Texas; District Courts of the State of Colorado; and all courts in the State of New Mexico.
- Successful Federal Administrative Law Judge applicant (awaiting placement).
- Extensive experience in the preparation and trial of injury claims resulting from both workers' compensation and off-the-job injuries.
- Exceptional knowledge of administrative procedures, rules of evidence, and trial practices.
- Able to communicate clearly and concisely with people of diverse backgrounds and levels of authority.

EXPERIENCE

- Member of a three-attorney panel appointed by the New Mexico Court of Appeals to issue advisory decisions in pending civil appeals.
- Wrote the advisory decision in the appeal of *Miller v. NM Dept. of Transportation,* the essence of which was adopted by the New Mexico Supreme Court.
- Selected twice in fifteen months as an arbitrator for the New Mexico trial-level court to arbitrate cases with damage claims less than $15,000, using procedures similar to those governing American Arbitration Association proceedings.
- Currently prepare from three to five jury trials per year.

Personal Injury

- Lead counsel or sole counsel for the injured plaintiff/worker in at least 30 jury trials with a minimum trial length of three days, plus another 50 non-jury trials of at least two days.
- Since 1983, have prepared and prosecuted to conclusion, either by trial or settlement, over 650 workers' compensation cases involving both physical and economic injuries.
- Interviewed witnesses, propounded and responded to interrogatories, requested productions and admissions, took and defended depositions, briefed interlocutory motions, filed requested findings and conclusions in non-jury cases, and prepared and argued requested instructions in jury trials.
- Developed considerable experience in determining when the record should be closed or supplemented.

Expert Witnesses

- Defined case issues and facts, then determined what type of expert witnesses would be needed.
- Located highly competent and persuasive experts in the required field.
- Consulted with and prepared the experts based on the definition of the issues and facts.
- Examined and cross-examined all types of fact witnesses and expert witnesses from nearly all areas of medicine and many scientific fields.

Management

- Managed a private law practice for more than twenty years, including all aspects of administration, accountability for profit and loss, controlling costs, and achieving revenue objectives.
- Recruited, supervised, motivated, and evaluated employees, including clerical staff and paralegals.
- Met deadlines for pretrial procedures, trials, and appellate briefings by effectively utilizing attorney associates and support staff.
- Designed a complete set of recurring forms to manage a typical workers' compensation claim from initial client interview through requested findings and conclusions.
- Competent in IBM, Windows, and WordPerfect computer software.

EDUCATION

JURIS DOCTOR
University of New Mexico School of Law, Albuquerque, New Mexico

1969

GRADUATE SCHOOL
University of New Mexico, Albuquerque, New Mexico
- 18 hours of Modern European History

1966 – 1967

BACHELOR OF ARTS
University of Minnesota, Minneapolis, Minnesota

1965

Scannable

SIGNIFICANT CASES

- *Nick Andler v. City of Gallup and NM Self-Insurer's Fund,* NM Dept. of Labor, Workers' Compensation Administration No. WCA 92-03246.
- *Greene v. Proto/Stanley-Proto,* San Juan County, N.M. District Court No. CV-88-540-3, 1993 (jury verdict, products liability case, eight-day trial, $282,000 plus costs)
- *Vickaryous v. City of Albuquerque,* Bernalillo County, N.M. District Court No. CV-91-02098, 1992 (alleged police negligence in failing to take keys from DWI driver resulting in paraparalysis)
- *Chevron Resources ex rel. Blatnik v. New Mexico Superintendent of Ins.,* 838 P.2d 988, 114 N.M. 371 (Ct. App. 1992)
- *Johnson v. Sears, Roebuck and Co.,* 832 P.2d 797, 113 N.M. 736 (Ct. App. 1992)
- *Richardson v. Farmers Ins. Co.,* 811 P.2d 571, 112 N.M. 73 (S. Ct. 1991)
- *Roybal v. Mutual of Omaha,* USDC, DCNM No. CIV 88-01195 SC, 1991 ($300,000 settlement on appeal breach of insurance contract claims for nonpayment of benefits health/major medical policy)
- *Cano v. Smith's Food King,* 781 P.2d 322, 109 N.M. 50 (Ct. App. 1989)
- *Strong v. Sysco Corp./Nobel Sysco,* 776 P.2d 1258, 108 N.M. 639 (Ct. App. 1989)
- *Rodriguez v. X-Pert Well Serv., Inc.,* 759 P.2d 1010, 107 N.M. 428 (Ct. App. 1988)
- *Jimmy Davis, et al. v. Aztec Drilling, et al.,* San Juan County, N.M. District Court, 1988 (seven-day jury trial, natural gas field explosion, bifurcated liability and damages trials; settled for $500,000 for Jimmy Davis following jury verdict on liability)
- *Thompson v. Ruidoso-Sunland, Inc.,* 734 P.2d 267, 105 N.M. 487 (Ct. App. 1987)
- *Robert Shattuck v. Lovelace Medical Center,* Bernalillo County, N.M. District Court No. CIV 85-03953, (medical/hospital malpractice case settled after two days of trial for $800,000, Nov. 1987)
- *John Sauters v. Jack B. Kelley: American Western Securities, Inc., et al.,* USDC, DCNM No. CV 84-0826 HB, 1986 (bench decision for $180,000 minority shareholders dilution action against broker-dealer and principal broker)
- *Bledsoe v. Garcia,* 742 F.2d 1237 (10th Cir. 1984)
- *Garrison v. Safeway Stores,* 692 P.2d 1328, 102 N.M. 179 (Ct. App. 1984)
- *Moreno v. Marrs Mud Co.,* 695 P.2d 1322, 102 N.M. 373 (Ct. App. 1984) (exception to "firemen's rule" absolute assumption of risk defense to tort claim by policeman/fireman recognized)
- *Kathy Penley v. Buena Suerta Ranch, Inc., et al.,* USDC, DCNM No. CIV 82-0878, JB, 1984 ($60,000 jury verdict in breach of bailment contract by horse owner v. horse ranch and trainer)
- *Patterson v. City of Albuquerque,* 661 P.2d 1331, 99 N.M. 632 (Ct. App. 1983)
- *Montgomery v. Professional Mut. Ins. Co.,* 611 F.2d 818 (10th Cir. 1980)
- *Gonzales v. Stover,* 575 F.2d 827 (10th Cir. 1978)
- *Martin v. Duffie,* 463 F.2d 464 (10th Cir. 1972)

AFFILIATIONS

- American Bar Association
- Colorado Bar Association
- New Mexico Bar Association
- Association of Trial Lawyers of America
- New Mexico Trial Lawyers Association (Board of Directors, 1987 – 1988)
- Colorado Trial Lawyers Association
- Albuquerque Lawyers Society
- Who's Who Among Professionals

PRESENTATIONS

- "Workers' Compensation: Calculation of Disability Benefits Under the New Grid Systems," New Mexico Trial Lawyers Association, 1994.
- "Direct Examination of a Cardiologist in Heart Attack Cases" and "Establishing Disability with the Dictionary of Occupational Titles," New Mexico Trial Lawyers Association, 1993.

WORK HISTORY

PRINCIPAL, David H. Pearlman Trial Lawyer, LLC, Colorado Springs, Colorado	1997 – present
STAFF ATTORNEY, McDivitt Law Firm, Colorado Springs, Colorado	1995 – 1997
PRESIDENT, David H. Pearlman, P.A., Albuquerque, New Mexico	1980 – 1995
PARTNER, Pearlman and Diamond, Albuquerque, New Mexico	1979 – 1980
PRESIDENT, David H. Pearlman, P.A., Albuquerque, New Mexico	1976 – 1979
PARTNER, Pearlman and Shoobridge, Albuquerque, New Mexico	1975 – 1976
PARTNER, Aldridge, Baron, Pearlman and Campbell, Albuquerque, New Mexico	1973 – 1975
PARTNER, Aldridge and Pearlman, Albuquerque, New Mexico	1971 – 1973
PRESIDENT, David H. Pearlman, P.A., Albuquerque, New Mexico	1969 – 1971

Scannable

Jeanette LeBlanc, Ph.D.

1234 Elkton Drive, Suite 333 • Colorado Springs, Colorado 80907
Phone: (719) 555-1234 • Home: (719) 555-5678 • E-mail: criscito@aol.com

Professional Profile

- Experienced professional trainer with more than ten years of diverse background as a trainer, consultant, and manager.
- Proven ability to teach and train adult learners in group settings.
- Skilled in facilitating individual, group, and organizational learning and change.
- Faculty member at several universities nationwide.
- Board Certified Counselor by the National Board of Certified Counselors.
- Team player with exceptional interpersonal and communication skills.

Education

Ph.D., Administration/Management, Walden University, 1994
- Specialization in Psychology of Human Behavior and Organizational Development

Master of Science, Community Counseling, Georgia State University, 1991

Bachelor of Science, Liberal Arts/Psychology, University of the State of New York, 1989

Professional Experience

Training and Education

- Delivered training programs and keynote presentations, including the following topics:

▸ Leadership Development	▸ Team Building	▸ Supervision Skills
▸ Stress Management	▸ Ropes Course	▸ Conflict Resolution
▸ Change Management	▸ Creativity	▸ Women's Issues
▸ Management Development	▸ Interpersonal Skills	▸ Diversity
▸ Effective Communication	▸ Career Development	▸ Character and Ethics

- Received outstanding evaluations from a wide range of clients such as DuPont, U.S. Army, Americorps, PDI, and the U.S. Air Force.
- Planned and implemented a certification series for trainers on: needs assessment, adult learning and training techniques, computer-based training and training evaluation.
- Taught college courses in over 20 psychology and management subject areas.
- Doubled student enrollment by emphasizing experiential learning, interactive lectures and exercises, guest speakers, field trips, and internship programs.

Leadership and Management

- Founded and operated a successful training and development company focusing on adventure-based learning and corporate retreats.
- Consultant to the United States Air Force Academy on issues of character, diversity, and human relations.
- Academy representative to the Defense Advisory Committee on Women in The Services (DACOWITS), which advises the Secretary of Defense.
- Officer in charge of the Corbin Council, USAFA, for gender relations at the Nation's Service Academies.
- Supervised a staff of human services professionals responsible for assessing client needs and developing and administering comprehensive treatment plans.
- Significantly increased agency referral rates by improving interagency communications and public relations with more than 150 state organizations.
- Played a key role in human resource management, employee professional development, and conflict resolution.

Counseling

- Conducted research with inventors to study creativity for psychological and organizational applications.
- Advised clients on career planning through group instruction and individual sessions.
- Developed curriculum and counseled clients in life/career choices.
- Provided mental health counseling to groups, families, and individuals of all ages in diverse clinical settings to facilitate resolution of treatment goals.
- Developed and facilitated seminars and psychoeducational groups for clients.
- Chaired a committee to create policies and procedures for an innovative clinical technique.

Scannable

Work History

President, Corporate Adventures and Retreats, Colorado Springs, CO	1998 – present
Independent Consultant, Trainer, Speaker	1994 – present
Ropes Course Facilitator, Alpine Tower, USAFA, CO	1998 – present
Faculty Member, University of Phoenix, Colorado Springs, CO	1998 – present
Faculty Member, Central Michigan University, Mt. Pleasant, MI	1998 – present
Chief of HR Program Evaluation; Consultant and Trainer, USAFA, CO	1997 – 1998
College Instructor/Intern Supervisor, Upper Iowa University, LA	1994 – 1997
Group Psychotherapist, Vernon Community Action Council, LA	1994 – 1996
Social Services Coordinator/Supervisor, Twin Cedars, GA	1991 – 1993
Adolescent Counselor, Bradley Center Hospital, GA	1990 – 1991
Psychological Assistant, Twin Cedars, GA	1989 – 1990
Library Technician, Civil Service, McGraw Library, Munich, Germany	1988 – 1989
Crisis Counselor, Army Community Service, Munich, Germany	1988 – 1989
Military Policewoman, U.S. Army, Munich, Germany	1986 – 1988

Professional Affiliations and Honors

- American Society for Training and Development, Pikes Peak Chapter.
- Past Vice President of Professional Development, Pikes Peak Chapter of ASTD.
- National Speakers Association and Colorado Speakers Association.
- American Seminar Leaders Association.
- Toastmasters International, CTM Award, served as Education VP and Membership VP.
- National Association of Female Executives.
- National Board of Certified Counselors.
- Selected for inclusion in *Who's Who in American Education, Who's Who in the World, Who's Who of American Women,* and *Who's Who in the South and Southwest* by the Marquis Board for Outstanding Achievement.
- Received numerous community service awards in Germany, Louisiana, Georgia, and Iowa.

Publications

Published Works
- "Addressing Gender Relations at the Nation's Service Academies," *Checkpoints* magazine, 1998.
- *The Human Dynamics of Invention,* University Microfilms International, Ann Arbor, Michigan, 1995.
- "An Examination of Theoretical Perspectives of Societal Development, Futurism, and Corporate Transformations," *International Journal of Futurics,* scheduled for publication in 1998.
- *Upper Iowa University Internship Manual,* Fort Polk Center, Spring 1994.
- "Train for a Career in Human Services," *The Guardian,* June 1995.
- Manuscript for *Peak Performance* book in progress.

Scholarly Papers at the Doctoral Level
- *Principles of Societal Development and the Future: An Examination of Theoretical Perspectives of Societal Development, Futurism, and Corporate Transformations,* 1992.
- *Human Development: A Three-part Module that Examines Theoretical Perspectives of Human Development, Career Development, and Military Career Transitions,* 1993.
- *Organizational and Social Systems: A Critical Analysis of Systems Theory for Corporations through Utilization of Management Information Systems and Global Computerization,* 1994.
- *Research Design, Analysis and Theory: Scholarly Inquiry of the Quantitative/Qualitative Paradigms with Utilization of Case Study Design as Proposed Methodology,* 1994.
- *Advanced Case Study in Applied Change: An Examination of Major External Degree Programs in a Variety of Disciplines.*

Scannable

College Courses Taught

- *MSA 620—Effective Administration and Organizational Behavior:* The course provides a framework for understanding the behavior of employees within dynamic organizations to include human behavior principles, job design, and human performance.

- *GEN 323—Professional Ethics and Social Responsibility:* This course focuses on integrating the knowledge, beliefs, and values provided by insights from business, management, and the social sciences as they relate to ethical decision making.

- *BA 390—Complex Organizations:* An exploration of the structural and functional characteristics of formal organizations, such as corporations, government agencies, schools, etc. Special attention is given to such topics as theories of management from Taylor to Theory Z; the relations between the internal structure of organizations and the different forms of social stratification throughout American society (class, racial, ethnic, and gender stratification systems); and the new forms of management strategy in the global economy.

- *BA 371—Training and Development:* This course involves the evaluation and study of trends in human resource training, education, and development activities within organizational settings.

- *PSY 499—Special Project:* Individualized independent investigation with supervision. Consent of the instructor is required.

- *PSY 454—Issues and Ethics in the Helping Professions:* An analysis of issues and ethical problems involved in the helping professions and programs.

- *PSY 440—Industrial Psychology:* A study of the relationship between the individual worker and the work environment. Emphasis is on the exploration and application of the most influential theories. Topics include organizational dynamics, work motivation, job satisfaction, personnel selection and training, and work group influences.

- *PSY 403—Internship:* Supervised field experience in a selected setting. Consent of faculty and written report are required.

- *PSY 384—Social Welfare Programs and Policies:* An analysis of social policies in the United States, with emphasis on the dimension of choice and alternative policies, along with assessment of contemporary social welfare issues, programs, and legislation.

- *PSY 376—Gerontology and Aging:* This course is designed to provide a comprehensive multidisciplinary introduction to the subject of human aging, with particular emphasis on its social and sociopsychological aspects.

- *PSY 360—Abnormal Psychology:* A survey of the major classifications of psychopathology, including conceptual approaches to the understanding of psychopathology, etiology, and treatment.

- *PSY 335—Biology and Behavior:* An exploration of the relation of biological function and human behavior; the role of genetic, hormonal, and neurological factors in intelligence, sex differences, biological rhythms, and emotional disorders. Disturbances produced by agents such as drugs and disease are studied.

- *PSY 283—Human Behavior in the Social Environment:* An analysis of individual, group, and cultural influences on human behavior. The emphasis is on contrasting levels of analysis and application to a variety of environmental settings.

- *PSY 276—Methods in Human Services:* This course explores the assumptions, strategies, and techniques used in the delivery of human services, as well as problem identification and skill development.

- *PSY 260—Sex Roles:* An analysis of the changing cultural notions and social realities regarding male/female roles and relationships. Topics may include: cross-cultural research concerning gender differences; the role of various socializing agents in shaping sexual identities; and the effects of gender differences on political and economic processes.

- *PSY 232—Group Dynamics:* An analysis of group behavior in small and large groups of various types. The focus is on social interaction in the formation and operation of groups, and on the social systems approach to understanding group behavior.

- *PSY 221—Introduction to Human Services:* A survey of the professions, programs, and agencies involved in the delivery of human services.

- *PSY 210—Social Psychology:* This course presents the social aspects of human behavior, including person perception, social cognition, attitude formation and change, attribution, prosocial behavior, and interpersonal attraction.

- *SOC 333—Criminology:* An analysis of various forms of crime, as well as various elements of the criminal justice system. The emphasis is on theories of crime and juvenile delinquency. Topics will include: street crime, organized crime, white-collar crime, and the role of substance abuse in criminality and delinquency.

- *SOC 240—Cultural and Racial Minorities:* This course provides sociological perspectives for analysis of racial and ethnic minority groups, along with an examination of the development of American ethnic groups and the current position of ethnic and racial groups in the structure of modern America.

CAROL S. KLEINMAN, Ph.D., R.N.

PROFILE

- Experienced university professor and academic administrator.
- Able to bring real-world nursing and health care administration experience to the classroom.
- Effective team player with strong communication and interpersonal skills.
- Known for dynamic presentation style and the ability to reach any student.

TEACHING EXPERIENCE

PROFESSOR AND DIRECTOR OF HEALTH SERVICES ADMINISTRATION (1997 – 1999)
PROFESSOR OF GRADUATE NURSING
Clarkson College, Omaha, Nebraska

- Taught selected courses in health services administration, all courses in the nursing administration major, and core courses in graduate nursing curricula.
- Consistently received among the highest student reviews of all the faculty in the college.

ADJUNCT PROFESSOR (1993 – 1997)
School of Nursing, Barry University, Miami, Florida

- Taught core courses in the graduate nursing curriculum.

ASSISTANT PROFESSOR AND COURSE COORDINATOR (1978 – 1986)
School of Nursing, City College of New York

- Coordinated teaching team in upper junior level integrated nursing course.
- Taught all psychiatric content throughout the undergraduate nursing curriculum, including clinical teaching in psychiatric inpatient settings.
- Member of the Course and Standing Committee; Chair of the Evaluation Committee; Member of the Community Mental Health Liaison Committee.

COURSES TAUGHT

GRADUATE NURSING COURSES:

- Nursing Theories and Concept Development
- Theories and Concepts of Advanced Nursing Practice
- Social Context of Health Care
- Theories and Concepts of Nursing Administration
- Psychosocial Assessment and Intervention in Primary Care
- Thesis Development

GRADUATE HEALTH SERVICES ADMINISTRATION COURSES:

- Operations Management
- Organizational Theory and Behavior
- Human Resources Management
- Reimbursement and Managed Care
- Thesis Development

EDUCATION

CERTIFICATES
Imago Relationship Therapy, Institute for Imago Relationship Therapy (1991)
Clinical Fellowship in Hypnotherapy, Kleinman Prince Center for Hypnosis (1979)

Ph.D., BEHAVIORAL SCIENCE, Specialization in Psychotherapy (1983)
Florida Institute of Technology, School of Professional Psychology

- Dissertation: "Attitudes Toward Mental Illness by Student Nurses from Various Ethnic Groups"
- Honors: Graduate Assistantship (2 years)

MASTER OF SCIENCE, Psychiatric-Mental Health Nursing (1975)
Adelphi University, School of Nursing

- Thesis: "A Conceptual Model of Female Homosexuality from the Perspective of Analytical Psychology"
- Honors: NIMH Traineeship for Graduate Study, Sigma Theta Tau

BACHELOR OF SCIENCE IN NURSING, Major in Psychiatric Nursing (1973)
State University of New York at Stony Brook

- Honors: Graduated cum laude

Scannable

EDUCATION **(continued)**	**ASSOCIATE OF APPLIED SCIENCE IN NURSING** (1971) **Kingsborough Community College, City University of New York**

- Honors: Salutatorian (third in a class of 1,000), Phi Theta Kappa, Dean's List, President's Award, Department of Nursing Award

ADMINISTRATIVE
EXPERIENCE

DIRECTOR, HEALTH SERVICES ADMINISTRATION (1997 – 1999)
Nebraska Health Services, Omaha, Nebraska

- Directed the graduate program in Health Services Administration; responsible for operations management, budgeting, curriculum design, faculty supervision, and student recruitment initiatives.
- Developed and implemented a complete redesign of the curriculum based on market analysis.
- Involved in developing innovative new Internet-based distance learning programs.
- Created a program that allowed students to obtain dual graduate degrees.
- Developed incentives and interfaces between the undergraduate and graduate programs of the college to prevent loss of graduate students to competitive schools.
- Member of the Heartland Healthcare Executive Group; revitalized this regional chapter of the American College of Healthcare Executives, developed relationships with health care leaders in the community, and served as faculty advisor.
- Member of the Business Advisory Council and Academic Life Committee.

DIRECTOR, BEHAVIORAL HEALTH SERVICES (1993 – 1996)
Broward General Medical Center, Ft. Lauderdale, Florida

- Responsible for the administrative and clinical management of the behavioral health department of the fourth largest integrated health care delivery system in the nation.
- Directed the 98-bed inpatient service, crisis stabilization unit, psychiatric emergency services, specialty treatment unit, and mental health initiatives within primary health centers.
- Developed a consultation and liaison service to trauma and other hospital departments.
- Managed an expense budget of more than $7 million and a staff of 135 FTEs.
- Developed a re-engineering plan that modernized the care delivery model and restaffed the department, saving $400,000 a year in salary and benefit expenses.
- Absorbed all of the county mental health services valued at $4 million.
- Wrote a certificate of need for 30 additional beds that received state approval.
- Rewrote the department's policy and procedure manual; implemented a new quality assurance program.
- Member of the Board of Directors of the Mental Health Association of Broward County; chair of the Fund Raising Committee (increased funding from $4,000 to $30,000 a year).
- Member of the Judicial Task Force that developed procedures for identifying and treating offenders with mental health care needs within the county.

EXECUTIVE DIRECTOR (1992 – 1993)
American Day Treatment Centers of Miami, Florida

- Directed all administrative and clinical operations of a freestanding, for-profit center that provided adult, adolescent, and geriatric partial hospitalization programs.
- Developed this new program from the ground up, including definition and marketing of products, programs, and services.
- Responsible for managing the construction project, purchasing capital equipment, and staffing.
- Administered a $2 million budget, achieving profitability within twelve months.

DIRECTOR, OUTPATIENT SERVICES (1986 – 1992)
Green Oaks Psychiatric Hospital, Dallas, Texas

- Created and directed the outpatient department of a 106-bed psychiatric hospital, including adult, adolescent, and chemical dependency partial hospitalization programs.
- Developed and implemented programs and services, making them profitable in less than a year.
- Grew the program to 25 staff members in a dedicated 10,000 sq. ft. office space with a $2 million budget and 50 patients per day.
- Responsible for strategic planning, marketing, referral development, and regulatory compliance.

Scannable

AFFILIATIONS

American Organization of Nurse Executives
American Nurses Association
American Psychiatric Nurses Association
Association of University Professors of Health Administration

SELECTED PUBLICATIONS & PRESENTATIONS

- Kleinman, C. (In press). "Nurse executives." *Journal of Health Administration Education.*
- Kleinman, C. (April 4, 1999). "Graduate education for the twenty-first century nurse." Poster presentation for the Fourth State of the Art of Nursing Conference, University of Nebraska Medical Center.
- Kleinman, C. (November 11, 1998). "Reflections of an aging nurse." Keynote address, Omicron Epsilon, Sigma Theta Tau.
- Kleinman, C. (January 16, 1997). "Psychological aspects of menopause." Grand Rounds, Department of Psychiatry, Broward General Medical Center.
- Kleinman, C. (March 17–18, 1994; August 16–17, 1994; February 18–19, 1993; August 24–25, 1993; March 4–5, 1992, August 10–11, 1992). "Enhancing and expanding established partial hospitalization programs." American Association for Ambulatory Behavioral Healthcare Seminar.
- Kleinman, C. (April 26, 1991). "Setting up partial hospital programs for accreditation and other key aspects of program success." Texas Association of Partial Hospitalization Annual Meeting.
- Kleinman, C., and Halperin, D. (April 10, 1990). "Cults: Fact or fiction?" Southwestern Conference on Cult Issues, Dallas, Texas.
- Kleinman, C., and Halperin, D. (April 9, 1990). "Cult awareness." Early Morning on WKQZ-TV, Dallas, Texas.
- Kleinman, C. (April 13, 1989). "Partial hospitalization: The wave of the future." Third Annual Psychiatric Nursing Symposium, University of Texas at Arlington.
- Kleinman, C. (1982). State Board Review Examination: Grant-funded development of 240 test items for New York State nursing examination, City College of New York.
- Kleinman, C., and Collins, C. (1980). "Discharge planning game: An alternative teaching strategy." City College of New York.

ADDRESS

1234 Pierce Plaza #3, Omaha, Nebraska 68124, Phone: (402) 555-1234, E-mail: criscito@aol.com

Scannable

VIVIAN MALCOLM, B.Ed., M.Ed., Ed.D.

12345 Ridgeway Drive • Sun City, Arizona 85351 • (602) 555-1234

SYNOPSIS:

Twenty-eight (28) years in adult, college, primary, elementary, and high school in the gamut of: lecturer, core professor, classroom teacher, student counselor, educational researcher, and public speaker.

Demonstrated ability encompassing a broad spectrum of skills involving training sessions with student teachers and psychology interns, conferences, workshops, social, civic, religious, and public relations activities.

Years of successful experience in establishing and maintaining rapport with students, teachers, administrators, and community leaders. Speaker and lecturer with experience in the direction of educational, cultural, church programs, community, business, and public relations activities throughout the United States, the Caribbean Islands, France, and England.

ACADEMIC TRAINING:

1980	*Doctor of Education, Administration and Supervision* – University of Illinois, Champaign
1976	*Master of Education, Counseling and Guidance* – Chicago State University, Chicago
1974	*Bachelor of Education, Kindergarten and Primary* – Chicago Teachers College

ADDITIONAL GRADUATE STUDY:

1990–91	Illinois Institute of Technology
1988	Roosevelt University, Chicago, Illinois
1987–88	University of Illinois, Circle Campus, Chicago, Illinois

PROFESSIONAL EXPERIENCE:

2000	*Instructor* – Essentials of Psychology, Gateway Community College, Phoenix, Arizona
1996–99	*Psychologist* – Dysart Unified School District #89, El Mirage, Arizona
1996	*Instructor* – Applied Education Psychology, Spring Semester, Northern Arizona University, Coolidge
1996	*Instructor* – Introduction to Psychology, Spring Semester, Central Arizona College, Eloy and Coolidge, Arizona
1995–96	*Contractual Psychological Testing* – Pinal County Special Education Program, Casa Grande, Arizona
1995	*Contractual Psychological Testing* – Proviso Area for Exceptional Children, Maywood, Illinois
1994	*Contractual Psychological Testing* – Chicago Board of Education
1994	*Student Teacher Supervisor* – Winter Trimester, Northeastern University, Chicago
1977–92	*School Psychologist* – Chicago Board of Education

1977–92 *School Psychologist* – Chicago Board of Education
Description: The scientific study and evaluation of the behavior of children and their educational problems, with the purpose of facilitating learning and total human adjustment. Duties and responsibilities included:

- Performance of psychological diagnosis and evaluations.
- Writing educational prescriptions.
- Recommending instructional goals and approaches.
- In cooperation with multi-disciplinary team, serving as resource person to teachers, administrators, students, and parents.
- Providing support and guidance in mainstreaming program.
- Providing short-term individual counseling and guidance to the child.
- Interpreting psychological findings and counseling parents regarding pertinent recommendations and possible courses of action.

- Consulting with and interpreting psychological findings and recommendations to individual teachers, teacher discussion groups, school counselors and administrators regarding individual differences, discipline, remedial programs, and psychological aspects of working with exceptional children.
- Participating in selection of suitable curricula for special programs such as perceptually and emotionally handicapped children (as well as gifted), et al.
- Serving as liaison with community organizations, hospitals, and institutions on referral services and necessary follow-up.
- Supervising psychologist interns when programs are operant.
- Conducting in-service for schools and institutions.
- Conducting stress workshops for Desegregation Institute under Title IV (Chicago Board of Education and Northeastern University).
- Participant: Operation Higher Achievement, Grant School and District Nine (motivational program for better achievement).

ADDITIONAL PROFESSIONAL EXPERIENCE:

1986–88	*Core Professor* – Field Experience Program, National College of Education, Evanston, IL
1976–77	*Interned as School Psychologist* – Chicago Board of Education
1971–76	*Kindergarten Primary Teacher* – Gresham Elementary School
1965–71	*Kindergarten Primary Teacher* – Beale Elementary School

SUPPLEMENTAL EXPERIENCE:

Consultant – Malcolm X College
Travel Agent – Trains, Boats and Planes Travel Agency

WORKSHOPS CONDUCTED:

- Strategies for Successful Teaching in a Culturally and Ethnically Diverse Classroom – Dysart School District, El Mirage, Arizona, October, 1996
- Discipline, Your Child and School Success – Pinal County Special Programs, Eloy, Arizona, January, 1996
- Can I Live Longer by Managing Stress? – Illinois Park and Recreation State Convention, Hyatt O'Hare, Chicago, November 1993
- Stress and Burnout – Northeastern University, Desegregation Institute, '86 to '89

PUBLICATION:

Dissertation: *An Evaluation of Gains Made by Chicago Public and Catholic School Students Who Were Serviced by the Summer Diagnostic Clinic in Area B*, 1980

AFFILIATIONS AND MEMBERSHIPS:

- Member, National Sorority of Gamma Phi Delta
- International School Psychology Association
- National Association of School Psychologists
- Chicago Association of School Psychologists
- National Sorority of Phi Delta Kappa, Mu Chapter
- Phi Delta Kappa, Fraternity – Education Honors Society
- Kappa Delta Pi – Education Honors Society
- Member, Board of Directors – Englewood Community Health Organization
- Member, Illinois Council for Exceptional Children
- Member, Advisory Board – Primary Health Care Services

JODY L. PELUSI, RN, RT, FNP, AOCN, PhD

1234 West Cortez • Glendale, Arizona 85304 • Phone: (602) 555-1234 • SSN: 555-55-5555

EDUCATION

INSTITUTION	YEARS	DEGREE
University of Arizona College of Nursing Tucson, Arizona	1992 – 1999	Ph.D. Major: Nursing Minor: Public Administration/Policy
Arizona State University College of Nursing Tempe, Arizona	1990 – 1991 1987 – 1990 1983 – 1987	FNP MS (Community Health) BSN
Scottsdale Community College Scottsdale, Arizona	1990	General Electives
Phoenix Community College Phoenix, Arizona	1984 – 1985	General Electives
Glendale Community College Glendale, Arizona	1979 – 1983	General Electives
Northern Arizona University College of Radiologic Technology College of Nursing Flagstaff, Arizona	1972 – 1976 1972 – 1975	Associate Degree Associate Degree in Nursing

LICENSES AND CERTIFICATIONS

FNP – Arizona #351 (prescribing privileges)
RN – Arizona #RN-032327
RT – Arizona #CRT-2727 (Radiology and Radiation Therapy)
AOCN – Advanced Oncology Certified Nurse (National) 1996
OCN – Oncology Certified Nurse (National) 1986, 1990
CPDP – Cancer Prevention/Detection Certification
BLS (Basic Life Support) Instructor – #3054990001874
Cancer Chemotherapy Provider – Oncology Nursing Society, 1999 – 2001

TRAINING

- *Partners Against Pain*, Purdue Frederick, 1999
- *Lung Cancer and Gemzar Training*, Eli Lilly, 1999
- *Breast Awareness Training*, ACS, 1999
- *Xeloda Speakers Training*, Roche, 1999
- *Ambassador 2000 Training Program*, Nutrition Support Expert, Pain and Fatigue, ongoing
- *Genetic Train the Trainer Program*, ASCO, Chicago, Illinois, 1997
- *Look Good Feel Better Media Training Program*, American Cancer Society, San Diego, California, 1997
- *Breast Cancer Spokesperson Training,* American Cancer Society, Atlanta, Georgia, 1996
- *Governor's Wives Training Program on Women's Health Issues,* American Cancer Society, Palm Springs, California, 1996
- *Colposcopy – Certificate,* M.D. Anderson, 1995

PROFESSIONAL EXPERIENCE

NURSE PRACTITIONER, Cancer Outreach and Wellness Coordinator   1990 – Present
Maryvale Hospital, Phoenix, Arizona (full-time)
Responsible for coordinating cancer committee activities and programs. Provide community and staff education. Serve as a nurse consultant for inpatient and outpatient services. Nurse practitioner for the Well Woman Health Check Program and cancer screening and wellness services.

NURSE PRACTITIONER   1999 – present
Metro Tech Vocational High School, Phoenix, Arizona (part-time)
Provide primary care and wellness services to adolescents in a school-based wellness center.

Scannable

**PROFESSIONAL
EXPERIENCE**
(continued)

ONCOLOGY NURSE PRACTITIONER   1995 – 1996
Northern Arizona Hematology and Oncology, Ltd., Sedona and Flagstaff, Arizona (part-time)
Healthcare provider for diverse populations across northern Arizona for oncology, internal medicine, and family practice needs. Provide services in rural clinics and cancer centers. Emphasis on symptom management, wellness, rehabilitation of patient and families. Consultant for home care and hospice organizations.

NURSING FACULTY
University of Phoenix, Phoenix, Arizona   1995 – Present
Professor, BSN, MSN, and NP courses; clinical preceptor
Grand Canyon University, Glendale, Arizona   1995 – Present
Professor, BSN and MSN courses
Arizona State University, Tempe, Arizona   1995 – 1997
Professor, Nurse Practitioner course; clinical preceptor

CONSULTANT (Part-time)   1984 – Present
Medical/Radiation Oncology
Oncology services consultant to hospitals, home health agencies, and private practices.

NURSE/CONSULTANT FOR HOME INFUSION PATIENTS (Part-time)   1993 – 1995
Total Pharmaceutical Care, Inc.
Provided infusion care services to patients in home setting. Functioned as nurse consultant to physicians and staff as needed.

RADIATION ONCOLOGY NURSE AND TECHNOLOGIST   1976 – 1990
Maryvale Samaritan Medical Center
Coordinated and delivered nursing care and radiation therapy to oncology patients. Designed and conducted patient and family education programs and support groups. Designed and implemented community cancer prevention and detection programs. Resource person for oncology unit.

SENIOR CHEMOTHERAPY NURSE (Part-time)   1980 – 1991
Palo Verde Hematology/Oncology
Responsible for mixing and administering chemotherapeutic agents to oncology patients in the office setting. Coordinated overall patient services, education, and counseling. Responsible for initial history on all new patients. Provided in-services for staff on new advances and technology in oncology.

HOME I.V. THERAPY NURSE (Part-time)   1984 – 1985
Home Health Care of America
Provided home I.V. therapy, nutritional therapy, and chemotherapy in the home setting.

CLINIC CHEMOTHERAPY NURSE (Part-time)   1979 – 1980
Dr. Alex Denes
Mixed and administered chemotherapy in a hospital clinic setting. Functioned as research nurse.

STAFF NURSE (Part-time)   1975 – 1976
Nurses Central Registry
Provided nursing care (med/surg) for Phoenix area hospitals.

**AWARDS &
HONORS**

1999	Excellence in Cancer Education Award – Oncology Nursing Society/Ross Products
1998	Susan Baird Writing Award for Nursing Research Writing – Oncology Nursing Society/Chiron Therapeutic
1998	Macy's Heart and Soul Community Service Award for Breast Cancer Awareness
1998	You Make a Difference Award for Community Service and Awareness – Kelloggs Foundation
1994	Helen Misco Scholarship – Ph.D. Studies
1993	Special Volunteer Award, American Cancer Society – Arizona Division
1992	Distinguished Service Award, American Cancer Society – Arizona Division
1991	Lane W. Adams Award, American Cancer Society – National
1990	Special Service Award, American Cancer Society – Arizona Division
1989	Paul Singer Award for Outstanding Community Service – Arizona

Scannable

**AWARDS &
HONORS**
(continued)

1989	Women Helping Women Award, Soroptimist – Golden West Region
1988	Outstanding Achievement Award, American Cancer Society – Arizona Division
1988	Life Saver Award, American Cancer Society – Arizona Division
1987	Distinguished Service Award, American Cancer Society – Arizona Division
1987	Sigma Theta Tau
1987	Life Saver Award, American Cancer Society – Arizona Division
1985	Employee of the Year, Maryvale Samaritan Medical Center
1984	Helen Misko Nursing Scholarship
1973	Raymond Foundation Nursing Scholarship

**RESEARCH
EXPERIENCE**

DATA MANAGER/NURSE/PROVIDER
- SWOG, M.D. Anderson, Zenneca, and Mayo Studies, 1995 – Present
- SWOG, GP-CCOP, and RTOG studies, 1979 – 1994
- Ondansetron study by Glaxo, 1990
- ONS Radiation Therapy Documentation Tool Study, 1992

GRANT WRITING/FUNDING/INVESTIGATOR ROLES
- Ph.D. Dissertation – Cancer Survivorship: The Other Side: The Lived Experience of the Partners of Long-Term Breast Cancer Survivors, principal investigator, 1999
- Cancer Survivorship: The Lived Experience of Long-Term Breast Cancer Survivors, principal investigator, 1997
- Susan G. Koman Foundation – Breast Cancer Screening and Education – Outreach to rural and underserved women, $17,500 grant writer, principal investigator, provider, 1996
- Susan G. Koman Foundation – Addressing Lymphedema: An Aquatic Therapy Approach Study, $5,000 grant writer, principal investigator, 1996
- Avon Breast Health Awareness Project – Blind and Deaf Population, $20,000, principal investigator, project coordinator, and provider, 1995
- The Breast Cancer Experience – Quantitative Study, principal investigator, 1994
- Post-Breast Cancer: A Woman's Lived Experience – Phenomenological Study, principal investigator, 1993
- The Influence of Educational/Information Support Groups on the Quality of Life Scores of Cancer Caregivers – Master's Thesis, principal investigator, 1990

GRANT FUNDING AND PARTICIPATION

1997	**Susan G. Koman Foundation, Breast and Cervical Cancer Screening Program** $20,000 – Treatment support, provider
1997	**Susan G. Koman Foundation, Breast Cancer Screening Program** $15,000 – Provider
1997	**Samaritan Charitable Trust Foundation, Quality of Life Program** $5,000
1997	**Samaritan Charitable Trust Foundation, Oncology Nursing Education Program** $10,000
1997	**Samaritan Charitable Trust Foundation, Cancer Screening/Rural Outreach** $20,000
1996	**Oncology Nursing Education Program** $10,000
1996	**Cancer Screening/Rural Outreach** $25,000
1995	**Oncology Nursing Education Program** $10,000
1995	**Cancer Screening/Rural Outreach** $25,000
1994	**MSMC Education Grant, Mead Johnson** $1,500 – Education grant
1993	**Cancer Care Grant, Samaritan Health Services** $350,000 – Project coordinator for mobile service portion of grant
1993	**Victories in Cancer Care Grant, Samaritan Health Services** $300,000 – Samaritan Charitable Trust (SCT). Project coordinator for cancer mobile services and oncology education (portion of grant)

Scannable

RESEARCH EXPERIENCE
(continued)

1992 **Cancer Care Grant, Samaritan Health Services**
$450,000 Total – Project coordinator for caregivers program and prevention and detection program portion of grant

1992 **Arizona Breast and Cervical Cancer Study, DHS**
$270,000 Total – CDC. Patient and Family Support Committee chairperson, Executive Committee member

1991 **Mobile Cancer Program Study, Samaritan Health Services**
$100,000 – SCT. PI and clinical coordinator/practitioner

1991 **Oncology Education Grant, Samaritan Health Services**
$25,000 – SCT. Clinical coordinator/educator

1990 **Cancer Program Development Grant, Maryvale Samaritan Medical Center**
$10,800 – SCT. Program coordinator

1990 **Cancer Prevention and Detection Grant, MSMC**
$35,980 – SCT. Program coordinator

1989 **Breast Cancer Awareness/Detection Grant, MSMC**
$90,000 – SCT. Program coordinator

1988 **Fighting Cancer in Our Schools, MSMC**
$2,000 – SCT. Program coordinator/educator

1988 **Oncology Education – Teleconference Grant, MSMC**
$7,500 – SCT. Program coordinator/educator

1988 **Cancer Prevention and Detection Grant, MSMC**
$4,000 – SCT. Program coordinator

1988 **Oncology Advancement Grant, MSMC**
$6,500 – SCT. Program consultant

1988 **Community Cancer Education Grant, MSMC**
$1,000 – SCT. Program coordinator/educator

1987 **Kids Can Cope Grant, MSMC**
$1,400 – SCT. Program coordinator/educator

1987 **Community School Education Grant, MSMC**
$1,500 – SCT. Program coordinator/educator

ASSOCIATION MEMBERSHIPS

• **Oncology Nursing Society**, 1978 – Present
  - Steering Council, 1997 – 1998
  - Board of Directors Director at Large, 1994 – 1997
  - Unlicensed Assisted Personnel Committee, 1994 – Present
  - Multicultural Advisory Committee, 1994 – Present
  - Transcultural Nursing SIG, 1994 – Present
  - Cancer Rehabilitation SIG, 1992 – Present
  - Multicultural Task Force, 1992 – 1993
• **Oncology Nursing Society**, 1978 – Present
  - Radiation Safety Committee, 1992 – 1993
  - Radiation Therapy SIG Editor, 1989 – 1991
  - ONC Test Development Task Force, 1990
  - Role Definition Task Force, 1989
• **Phoenix Oncology Nursing Society**, 1977 – Present
  - Annual Conference Chairman, 1989, 1990, 1991, 1995
  - Special Project Chairman, 1990 – 1993
  - President, 1986 – 1990
  - Newsletter Editor, 1984 – 1988
• **Arizona Society of Radiologic Technologist Member**, 1976 – Present
• **American Society of Radiologic Technologist**, 1967 – Present
• **Intercultural Cancer Council**, 1998 – Present
• **International Society of Nurses in Cancer Care Member**, 1986 – 1990
• **Arizona Nursing Network**, 1985 – 1990
  - Secretary, 1986 – 1988
• **Sigma Theta Tau Member**, 1987 – Present
• **National Rural Health Association**, 1995 – Present
• **Southwest Oncology Group**, 1979 – Present
  - Breast Cancer/Radiation Committee, 1990 – 1994
  - Nursing Committee, 1988 – 1994

Scannable

**VOLUNTEER
ACTIVITIES**

- *Arizona Women's Cancer Network*, 1992 – Present
  - Service Delivery Committee Chairman, 1993 – Present
  - Patient and Family Support Committee Chairperson, 1992 – 1993
- *American Cancer Society – Arizona*, 1970 – Present
  - Breast Cancer Core Team Chairman, 1994 – Present
  - Vice President, Maricopa County, 1992 – Present
  - Medical Director and Practitioner – childhood cancer programs and women's cancer program, 1985 – Present
  - Board of Directors, Division, 1988 – 1995
  - Committee membership (Service/Rehabilitation, Professional Education, Public Issues, Development, Field Services), 1990 – 1995
  - Board of Director, Unit (G/P/M), 1986 – 1995
  - Service/Rehabilitation Chairperson, Division, 1989 – 1992
  - ONCOPA Chairperson, 1987, 1988, 1989
  - Medical Director and Practitioner – Childhood Cancer Programs and Women's Cancer Program, 1985 – Present
  - Service and Rehabilitation State Chairman, 1989 – 1991 (have served on unit committees during last 24 years)
- *City of Phoenix Parks and Recreation – Special Population*, 1991 – 1993
  - Nursing Director for White Water Raft Trip through the Grand Canyon for people with disabilities, 1992, 1993, and 1994
- *Kids Can Cope*, 1985 – 1988
  - Board of Directors
- *Our Lady of Perpetual Help Catholic Church*, 1975 – Present
  - Home Eucharist Minister, 1983 – Present
  - Lay Eucharist Minister, 1983 – Present
  - Religious Education Teacher, 1975 – 1990
  - Parish Council, 1984 – 1988
  - Teen Advisor, 1978 – 1984

**CURRENT
HOSPITAL
SERVICES**

- Oncology Service Line, 1994 – Present
- SHS Pain Committee, 1994 – Present
- TSMC Cancer Committee Coordinator, 1994 – Present
- SHS Steering Committee, 1992 – Present
- SHS Wellness Committee, 1993 – Present
- Oncology Clinical Nursing Council Chairperson, 1991 – Present
- Samaritan Oncology Education Committee Chairperson, 1991 – Present
- Samaritan Screening/Detection Committee Chairperson, 1990 – Present
- MSMC Cancer Committee Coordinator, 1989 – Present
- MSMC Tumor Board Coordinator, 1976 – Present
- Samaritan Mobile Cancer Services Coordinator, 1992 – Present
- Samaritan Outreach Committee, 1991 – Present
- Samaritan Oncology Subcommittee, 1990 – Present
- Samaritan Research Committee, 1987 – 1993
- MSMC Radiation Safety Committee, 1976 – 1993
- MSMC Radiology Committee, 1976 – 1993

**PRODUCTIONS &
PUBLICATIONS**

- Family Practice and Geriatrics Series Contributor, *Women's Health Nurse Practitioner Certification Review Book,* JoAnn Zerwerkh, Jo Carol Warren (Eds.), W.B. Saunders, 1999.
- Cancer Screening and Detection in the Home, *Oncology Home Care,* Vicky Filler (Ed.), pending publication, ONS Press, Pittsburgh, Pennsylvania.
- Breast Cancer Screening and Detection in Rural Communities, *Innovations in Breast Cancer Care,* Vol. 1, No. 3, April 1996, Jody Pelusi, p. 52–54, 67.
- Assistive Personnel: Their Use in Cancer Care – An Oncology Nursing Society Position Statement, *Oncology Nursing Forum,* Vol. 23, No. 4, May 1996, Barbara R. Medvec, Jody L. Pelusi, Dawn Camp-Sorrell, Paula Kleinschmidt, Linda Krebs, and Kathy Moomey, p. 647–651.

**PRODUCTIONS &
PUBLICATIONS
(continued)**

- *What Every Man Should Know About Cancer – Addressing Men's Wellness*, Glaxo Video, April 1996.
- *On the Frontier: The Challenges and Rewards of Rural Nursing*, Glaxo Video, 1995.
- Case Study – Cancer Practice, June 1994.
- Treating Breast Cancer in the Native American Population, *Innovations in Oncology*, December 1994.
- Editor, *1992 and 1993 Annual Cancer Report, Maryvale Samaritan Medical Center,* Samaritan Health Services, 1994.
- Contributing Editor, "Handbook of Therapeutic Interventions," *Chemotherapy*. Springhouse, PA: Springhouse Corporation, 1993, pp. 170–176.
- Editor, "3rd Annual Cancer Report," Maryvale Samaritan Medical Center, Phoenix, AZ: Samaritan Health Systems, 1993.
- Contributing Editor, "Radiation Therapy," *Nursing Procedures*. Springhouse, PA: Springhouse Corporation, 1992, pp. 205–210.
- Editor, *Second Annual Cancer Report, Maryvale Samaritan Medical Center*. Phoenix, AZ: Samaritan Health System, 1990 – 1991.
- Editor, *First Annual Cancer Report, Maryvale Samaritan Medical Center*. Phoenix, AZ: Samaritan Health System, 1989.
- Levine, Pelusi, and Steinway, *Kids Can Cope Manual*. Phoenix, AZ: Kids Can Cope Foundation, 1989.
- Editor, *The Boost* [Newsletter of the National Radiation Oncology Special Interest Group, Oncology Nursing Society] (1988 – 1990).
- Pelusi, Pinckard, and Hilger, "Radiation Therapy and You," [a patient education video]. Phoenix, AZ: Samaritan Health Services Publication, 1987.
- Haber, B., and Pelusi, J. "Cancer is a Scary Word" [a patient education pamphlet for children whose parents have cancer]. Phoenix, AZ: Samaritan Health Services Publication, 1987.

ACCOMPLISHMENTS

- American Cancer Society – National Advisory Committee – Primary Care, 1995 – Present
- Panelist, "Reduce Your Risk" (television special on cancer prevention), 1993
- Panelist, "Samaritan Presents – Taking Control" (television special on cancer prevention and early detection), 1992
- Panelist, television interview on cancer-related issues, 1996 (3), 1995 (3), 1994 (6), 1993 (5), 1992 (3), 1991 (2), 1991 (1)
- Panelist, radio talk show related to cancer issues, 1996 (4), 1995 (5), 1994 (10), 1993 (6), 1992 (6), 1991 (2), 1990 (2)
- Development of Arizona ONCC Review Program, 1988
- Development of Oncology Nurses Bed/Breakfast Program – Arizona
- Development of "Because We Care For You" – program and support for in-home caregivers
- Development of "Upbeat Retreat" – retreat for women with cancer
- Development of "New Beginnings" – support group for women with cancer
- Development of "A Time for Survivors" – support group for cancer survivors
- Development of SHS Oncology Education Programs (Chemotherapy Validation Courses – Basic, Revalidation, and Home Health)
- Development of SHS Prevention and Detection Program for Nurses

PRESENTATIONS

INTERNATIONAL:

1999   ***Cervical Cancer: The Cancer that Should Have No Statistics***, ONS International Symposium, conductor and presenter

1997   ***Nurse's Role in Cancer Prevention and Detection***, Keynote Address, Poland Oncology Nursing Society, Warsaw, Poland

5/1994   ***Because We Care For You – Addressing the Needs of Caregivers***, 2nd Annual International Patient Education Conference, Tempe, Arizona

6/1994   ***Women's Stories of Struggle: Post Breast Cancer Treatment***, 2nd Annual International Quantitative Research Conference, Hershey, Pennsylvania

NATIONAL:

9/1996   ***Breast Cancer Update and Cancer Survivor Issues***, United States Air Force Medical Team, Scottsdale, Arizona

PRESENTATIONS
(continued)

5/1996	**Tribulations and Triumphs of Rural Oncology Nursing**, Oncology Nursing Society, Philadelphia, Pennsylvania
3/1996	**Setting Up Smoking Cessations in Your Private Practice**, American Cancer Society, Washington, DC
11/1995	**Psychoneuro Immunology in Oncology Practice**, Oncology Nursing Society, Nashville, Tennessee
7/1995	**Rural Oncology Nursing**, National Rural Health Association Nursing Conference, Boseman, Montana
9/1994	**Caregivers**, Veterans Administration's Patient Health Education, "Patient Centered and Health Care Reform", Las Vegas, Nevada
5/1994	**Changing Paradigms in Oncologic Urology Nursing**, American Urology Association, San Francisco, California
5/1994	**Cultural Competence: Facing the Challenges of Our Changing World**, Oncology Nursing Society 19th Annual Congress, Cincinnati, Ohio
5/1993	**Radiation Therapy – Transcultural Issues for the Native American**, Oncology Nursing Society Congress, Orlando, Florida
4/1993	**Sexuality: A Forgotten Dimension of Transcultural Patient Education**, National Cancer Institute, Pasadena, California
5/1992	**The Silent Attacker of Men: Prostate Cancer**, Oncology Nursing Society, San Diego, California
5/1991	**When a Parent Has Cancer**, Oncology Nursing Society, Washington, D.C.
5/1990	**Role of the Radiation Oncology Nurse**, Oncology Nursing Society, San Antonio, Texas
5/1990	**Influence of Informational/Education Support Group on Quality of Life Scores of Cancer Caregivers**, WSRN, Albuquerque, New Mexico

REGIONAL:

4/1997	**Pain Management Across Settings**, Premier Health Care, Las Vegas, Nevada
4/1997	**Breast Cancer Update for Physicians and Nurse Practitioners**, Luke Air Force Base, Arizona
4/1997	**Multiple Myeloma**, The Grand Canyon ONS-CHIP, Sedona, Arizona
4/1997	**Cultural Diversity in Pain Management**, Arizona Hospice Association, Phoenix, Arizona
3/1997	**Pain Management**, Nurse Practitioner's Pharmacology Update, Phoenix, Arizona
2/1997	**Women and Wellness**, Federally Employed Women's Association, Phoenix, Arizona
9/1996	**Management of Breast Cancer**, United States Air Force Medical Teams, Arizona, New Mexico, and Nevada
8/1996	**Women, Wellness, and Cancer**, Women's Health Conference of Northern Arizona, Showlow, Arizona
6/1996	**Breast Cancer – What Women Need to Know**, Association of Retired Teachers of Arizona, Annual Conference
3/1996	**Survivorship**, New York
11/1995	**When a Parent Has Cancer**, New York (2 times)
3/1995	**Cancer Prevention – Putting Wellness into Your Practice**, American Association of Office Nurses, Tempe, Arizona
3/1995	**Women's Wellness – Facing the Facts**, Association of Retired Teachers, Scottsdale, Arizona
11/1994	**Leukemia and Its Treatment**, Phoenix Oncology Nursing Society
10/1994	**Addressing CLL and Its Treatment**, Boston, Massachusetts
9/1994	**The Impact of Cancer and Its Treatment on Sexuality**, American Oncology Nursing Society/ACS
9/1994	**Cancer Survivorship**, Cancer Registry Association of Arizona, State Meeting, Phoenix, Arizona
9/1994	**What Every Woman Should Know About Cancer: A Wellness Approach**, Phoenix, Arizona
7/1994	**Circle of Life – Breast Cancer Education for Native Americans**, Scottsdale, Arizona

Scannable

PRESENTATIONS
(continued)

6/1994	***Chronic Lymphocytic Leukemia and Its Treatment***, Boise, Idaho.
4/1994	***Chemotherapy: What to Know about Patients On and Off Treatment***, Arizona Family Planning Council – 1994 Spring Pharmacology Update for Nurse Practitioners, Phoenix, Arizona
4/1994	***Breast Cancer Update***, Arizona Operating Room Nursing Society Annual Meeting, Tempe, Arizona
10/1993	***Women's Health Issues and Breast Cancer***, YWCA State Meeting, Phoenix, Arizona
9/1993	***Men's Health Issues – Prostate Cancer (Keynote)***, Mercy Care Cancer Symposium, Cedar Rapids, Iowa
8/1993	***Rehabilitation and Long-term Survivorship Issues***, St. Patrick's Hospital Symposium, Lake Charles, Louisiana
6/1993	***Childhood Cancer***, American Cancer Society, Phoenix, Arizona
6/1993	***Understanding Sexual Changes Caused By Cancer and Its Treatment***, Visiting Nurse Service, Yuma, Arizona
5/1993	***Behavioral Approach to Cancer Pain Management***, Hospice, Phoenix, Arizona
5/1993	***Breast Cancer – From Prevention to Long-term Follow-up***, Arizona Family Planning Counsel, Phoenix, Arizona
4/1993	***Changing Paradigms in Oncology Care***, Mission Cancer Symposium, Ashville, North Carolina
4/1993	***The Role of the Operating Room Nurse in Cancer Care***, Arizona Association of Operating Room Nurses, Phoenix, Arizona
2/1993	***Because I am the Man: Sexuality Issues for the Individual with Cancer and their Partner***, Fifth Annual Southwest Oncology Symposium, Phoenix
10/1991	***The Challenge of Long-Range Planning: Cancer Survivorship***, Phoenix Oncology Nursing Society and Arizona State University Annual Conference, Phoenix, Arizona
10/1992	***Cancer: What It Means to You***, Arizona Society of Radiologic Technologists, Flagstaff, Arizona
9/1992	***Sexuality in the Ostomate***, Five-State Regional Ostomy Association, Phoenix, Arizona
3/1992	***The Forgotten Priority: Cancer In the Elderly***, Boswell Hospital Symposiums, Sun City, Arizona
3/1992	***The Impact of Cancer and Its Treatment on Sexuality***, Sixth Annual Southern Arizona Oncology Nursing Society Conference, Tucson, Arizona
2/1992	***Family Rehabilitation in Cancer Care***, Fourth Annual Southwest Oncology Symposium, Phoenix, Arizona
10/199	***Cancer: It's a Family Disease***, Arizona State University and Phoenix Oncology Nursing Society Conference, Scottsdale, Arizona
9/1991	***La Paz County Health Assessment Project***, Rural Health Conference, Phoenix, Arizona
8/1991	***Cancer Caregiver: Intervention Study Review***, Phoenix Oncology Nursing Society Conference, Phoenix, Arizona
7/1991	***Overview: Cancer and Young Adults***, City Street Teen Program, Phoenix, Arizona
6/1991	***Cancer Rehabilitation***, Arizona Physical Therapist Conference, Phoenix, Arizona
5/1990	***Cancer in the Elderly***, Maricopa County Long-term Care (Director of Nurses) Conference, Phoenix, Arizona
5/1990	***Overview of Inpatient Cancer Chemotherapy***, Health Service Advisory Group, Scottsdale, Arizona
4/1990	***Prevention and Detection: The Role of the Nurse***, American Cancer Society Conference, Tempe, Arizona

POSTERS:

4/1994	***Because We Care for You*** and ***Breast Cancer Clinical Pathway***, 2nd Annual International Patient Education Conference, Tempe, Arizona
4/1994	***Cancer Prevention and Detection Program for Nurses***, National Nursing Staff Education Conference, Scottsdale, Arizona

Scannable

PRESENTATIONS
(continued)

LOCAL: *The Many Faces of Pain: A Multicultural Approach to Pain Management*, Scottsdale Health Care Conference, Scottsdale, Arizona
Provided numerous lectures to community and health care professionals on cancer-related topics. List furnished upon request.

COURSES DEVELOPED & TAUGHT

1996 – Present	*Nursing Pathophysiology*. Six-week course focusing on the pathophysiology of illness, disease and wellness, University of Phoenix, Phoenix, Arizona. Enrollment = 20.
1996 – Present	*Physical Assessment*. Thirteen-week course for nurse practitioner students with a clinical component, University of Phoenix, Phoenix, Arizona. Enrollment = 15.
1996 – Present	*Health Policy*. Six-week graduate course, exploring financial regulatory and policy issues related to health care, University of Phoenix, Phoenix, Arizona. Enrollment = 20–30.
1996 – Present	*Infra Structure*. Six-week graduate course looking at the infrastructure of the health care system, University of Phoenix, Phoenix, Arizona. Enrollment = 15–20.
1995 – Present	*Nursing Research*. Six-week graduate course, University of Phoenix, Phoenix, Arizona. Enrollment = 15–20.
1996	*Pathophysiology and Assessment*. Nine-week course devoted to the pathophysiology of disease and wellness process with an emphasis on the assessment for each nursing N.P. program, University of Phoenix.
1995 – Present	*Health Care Policy and Economics*. A five-week course focusing on the changing health care environment with emphasis on policy and economics (graduate), University of Phoenix. Enrollment = 12–15.
1995	*Advanced Health Assessment*. Arizona State University, Tempe, Arizona. Enrollment = 50–85.
1995 – Present	*Community Health Promotion to High-Risk Groups*. A nine-week course focusing on the role of health promotion to high-risk populations and the role of community health assessments. University of Phoenix, Phoenix, Arizona. Enrollment = 15–20.
1995 – Present	*Community Health Nursing*. A five-week course focusing on the role of the nurse within varied community settings. University of Phoenix, Phoenix, Arizona. Enrollment = 15–20.
1993 – 1994	*Breast Cancer* education course. An eight-week course focusing on prevention and detection, disease trajectory, treatment options, long-term survivorship issues, family assessment, patient and family education, spirituality, sexuality, nutritional and concerns. Phoenix, Arizona. Enrollment = 25.
1993 – Present	*Cancer Prevention and Detection Course for Nurses*. A one-day course focusing on educating nurses about risk factors, warning signs, and screening techniques for common cancers as well as issues related to prevention and detection. Phoenix, Arizona. Enrollment = 50.
1993 – Present	*Group Facilitation Course*. A one-day course focusing on group facilitation techniques and strategies related to support groups. Phoenix, Arizona. Enrollment = 45.
1990 – Present	*Cancer Core Course*, a three-day course. Phoenix, Arizona. Enrollment = 35. (offered twice a year)
1987 – Present	*ONCC Review Course*, a five-day course reviewing basic oncology issues by ONS guidelines. Phoenix, Arizona. Enrollment = 30. (offered once a year)
*1987 – Present	*Chemotherapy Revalidation Course*, a six hour course. Phoenix, Arizona (and other regional sites). Enrollment = 50. (offered five times a year)
*1986 – Present	*Chemotherapy Validation Home Health Course*, an eight-hour course. Phoenix, Arizona (and other regional sites). Enrollment = 40. (offered three times a year)
*1984 – Present	*Chemotherapy Validation Course*, a three-day course. Phoenix, Arizona (and other regional sites). Enrollment = 45. (offered five times a year)

Scannable

17 | Creative Résumés

What fun to be in an industry where almost anything goes! In advertising and the arts, you have a license to be creative with your résumé. After all, creativity is one of your strongest qualifications for the job. It is the need for this creativity that determines when résumés like the ones in this chapter are appropriate. Using a creative résumé takes a very special type of person. They are not for accountants, bankers, and executives.

Needless to say, these résumés are not scannable, but the chances of a gallery, museum, graphic art firm, or ad agency scanning your résumé are almost non-existent. Scannability in creative industries is not an issue in almost all cases. When scannability is an issue, simply create an ASCII text file résumé and send it along with your creative version (see Chapter 3).

No matter how creative you want to be, you must still keep readability in mind. If your audience can't read your résumé, what good is it? The résumés on pages 264 and 268–270 push the envelope. They are still readable . . . but just barely!

Here I most gratefully acknowledge the work of Gregg Berryman. I have in my library a copy of his book, *Designing Creative Résumés* (Menlo Park, CA: Crisp Publications, Inc., 1985). The clients on pages 268–270 chose their styles from his examples and my staff re-created them. His book is a great resource for creative résumé ideas and, although it is out of print at this writing, it can be found in many city libraries.

Mason Michael Brooklyn

Experience

6/00 – 8/00
adidas, AG
Marketing Racketsport Germany
Herzogenaurach, Germany
Marketing Associate (Intern)
- *collected, analyzed, and disseminated information to the German sales force concerning rollout of the 2000 Racketsport collections*
- *translated and proofread promotional and company material including the 2000 textile catalog*

8/97 – 4/98
William R. Biggs/Gilmore Assoc.
Advertising Associate (Intern)
- *supervised company promotional material through all phases of development*
- *coordinated the redevelopment of the traffic function*
- *placed print media*

1/97 – 4/98
University Theatre, WMU
Assistant to the Publicist
- *supervised "front of house," i.e., ticket audits and sales receipts*
- *trained and managed usher corps*
- *coordinated maintenance of master mailing list*
- *created and developed promotional materials*

1/98 – 4/98
Department of Fine Arts, WMU
Student Coordinator
Michigan Youth Arts Festival
- *promoted MYAF working with various university, local, and state media*
- *assembled and managed student staff (two previous years on student staff)*

4/97 – 12/97
WMU, Dept. of Student Services
Orientation Leader
- *oriented the WMU freshman class using a working knowledge of all areas of the university*
- *organized, wrote, and directed skit as a part of the program*
- *conducted follow-up interviews to monitor progress and advice*

Education

December 2000, with honors
Master of International Management
American Graduate School of International Management, Glendale, Arizona
- *Includes semester at the European Business School, Schloss Reichhartshausen, Germany (conducted in German)*

April 1999, magna cum laude
Bachelor of Business Administration
Western Michigan University, Kalamazoo, Michigan
- *Major: Advertising*
- *Minor: German, General Business*
- *1999 Michigan Association of Governing Boards of State Colleges and Universities Outstanding Student*
- *1999 WMU, AMA Chapter, and Detroit Ad Club Outstanding Student*
- *Board of Trustees Scholarship*

Languages

Native in English
Highly proficient in German
Working knowledge of Spanish
Computers: Apple, IBM, Wang

Activities & Awards

- *Phi Sigma Kappa, 4 years*
  Offices: Pres., Secr., Social
  Terrill Graduate Fellowship
  1997 Brother of the Year
- *1997 WMU Homecoming Co-Chair*
- *Advertising Club, Secr./Treas.*
- *Advertising Explorer Outpost Leader*

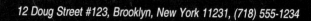

RCH

Robert C. Hollywood
2nd Assistant Cameraman
1234 North 50th Place
Phoenix, Arizona 85014
(602) 555-1234

EMPLOYMENT HISTORY

1995 – Present — *Free-Lance Camera Assistant* — *Hollywood, CA*
Cinematography Camera Assistant

1995 – 1996 — Sunrise Sets, *Scenery Designer* — *N. Hollywood, CA*

1993 – 1995 — Clairmont Camera, Inc. — *Studio City, CA*
Operations
- Personally assisted production companies on nationwide and international film projects
- Position required complete knowledge of all equipment on premise, which included: Arriflex • Fries • Stedicam • Norris • MovieCam • Mitchell • Zeiss • Cooke • Angenieux
- Prepared over 1,000 commercial packages and 150 feature film units
- Inspected and evaluated all equipment on a continual basis
- Shipping and receiving

1992 – 1993 — Setefex, Inc. — *Hollywood, CA*
Shop Foreman
- Promoted to supervise building crews for commercial and theatrical scenery company
- Responsible for hiring, training, and directing an average crew of 25 carpenters, painters, welders, and drivers
- Estimated costs and prepared bids on potential projects
- Acquired and completed over 100 sets and special effects for film, television, and theater
- Established a 38% profit margin, which exceeded all previous years

1991 – 1992 — KNAZ-TV — *Flagstaff, AZ*
Production Department/News/Commercial
- Technical Director News 2Night Productions
- News and Sports Photographer
- Package Editor
- Master Control Operator

EDUCATION

1987 – 1991 — Northern Arizona University — *Flagstaff, AZ*
Degree: B.S. of Telecommunications
- Film/T.V. emphasized

Christine Lynn Hightower

OBJECTIVE

A responsible position within the marketing/consulting industry that requires utilization of research, problem solving and presentation skills, and a knowledge of foreign markets

EDUCATION
May 1999

MASTER OF INTERNATIONAL MANAGEMENT
American Graduate School of International Management
Thunderbird Campus, Glendale, Arizona
Emphasis on International Marketing
• Researched, coordinated, and presented marketing feasibility study for frozen yogurt in Germany
• Created a marketing plan for Virginia Kitchens entry into Canadian markets

May 1998

Autónoma Universidad de Guadalajara, Mexico
• Studied Mexican political system and country risk
• Extensive travel throughout Mexico

May 1996

BACHELOR OF SCIENCE BUSINESS ADMINISTRATION
Loyola University of Chicago Watertower Campus, Chicago, Illinois
Marketing Specialization

January 1995

Loyola University, Rome Center, Italy
• Accepted into International Studies Program
• Extensive travel throughout Western Europe

EXPERIENCE
1998

GRADUATE ASSISTANTSHIP IN MARKETING
American Graduate School of International Management
• Coordinated logistics for visiting presenters
• Publicized upcoming presentations in campus newspaper
• Performed administrative duties

1997

ASSISTANT STORE MANAGER, Wohl Shoe Company
Carson Pirie Scott, Mount Prospect, Illinois
• Trained and supervised personnel
• Motivated staff through sales contests
• Participated in managerial training program

ADMINISTRATIVE ASSISTANT, Fasco Industries, Inc.
North American Headquarters, Lake Forest, Illinois
• Developed computerized indexing system
• Assisted in the creation of in-house tax department
• Planned full company convention

1997

SALES OFFICER, Scentura Creations
Perfume Sales, Elk Grove, Illinois
• Demonstrated success in cold call selling
• Trained sales personnel

INTERNSHIP, August, Bishop, & Meier, Inc.
Sales Promotion Agency, Chicago, Illinois
• Assisted Account Supervisor in account service
• Participated in establishment of print media placement department

LANGUAGE & COMPUTER SKILLS
• Proficient in Spanish, knowledge of Italian
• Skilled in WordPerfect and Lotus 1-2-3
• Experience with Macintosh SE

ACTIVITIES & INTERESTS
• Active member of Hopology Club
• Active member of International Hash House Harriers Club

Current Address: Box 1234, 12345 N. 59th Ave., Glendale, Arizona 85306, (602) 555-1234
Permanent Address: 1234 RFD, Long Grove, Illinois 60047, (708) 555-1234

266

Cynthia Claremont

OBJECTIVE

A responsible position as an Administrative Assistant or Secretary that will utilize my training and experience.

QUALIFICATIONS

Enthusiastic administrative assistant with an Associate Degree and experience in:
- Desktop publishing, office management, principles of accounting, research, and filing
- WordPerfect, MS Word, MS Office, Lotus 1-2-3, Excel, and other PC software
- Typing 60 wpm, facsimile, 10-key calculators, multi-line telephones, and most office machines

PROFILE

- Quality-conscious professional with a dedication to precision.
- Background includes customer service, public relations, and collections.
- Effective team player with strong interpersonal and communication skills.
- Detail oriented and organized.
- Comfortable taking the initiative and working independently.
- Adept at working under pressure to meet time-sensitive deadlines.

EDUCATION

ASSOCIATE OF APPLIED SCIENCE (1996)
Blair Junior College
Colorado Springs, Colorado
- Administrative Assistant major
- GPA 3.75
- Director's List for achieving 4.0 GPA
- Dean's List
- Student of the Month, August 1995

ADDRESS

1234 Basketring Road #2
Columbia, Maryland 21045
(410) 555-1234

EMPLOYMENT HISTORY

RIVERWOOD MENTAL HEALTH CENTER, Columbia, Maryland
Temporary through TAD Staffing Services (1997 – present)
Administrative Assistant/Receptionist
- Greeted customers and answered five-line telephone, directing calls to their appropriate parties.
- Scheduled and cancelled appointments for the doctors.
- Updated and filed medical records.

ZURICH INSURANCE COMPANY, Colorado Springs, Colorado
Temporary through ADD Staff (1997)
Administrative Assistant
- Performed data entry using AmiPro database software.
- Sent faxes, made copies, and performed other office tasks.

NORWEST DIRECT, Colorado Springs, CO
Temporary through Western Staff Services (1996)
Administrative Assistant
- Secretary for the Adverse Actions Division of a direct marketing mortgage lending company.
- Responsible for typing and proofreading of loan denials using a Windows-based proprietary computer software.
- Interfaced closely with loan closers.
- As the first person hired in the department, trained all other administrative assistants.

ALCO DEPARTMENT STORE, Colorado Springs, CO (1983 – 1986)
Cashier
- Acquired cash control and customer relations skills by computing sales on a cash register and receiving money.
- Executed markdowns and markups on inventory.
- Performed end-of-shift closeouts and cleanup of the store.

Resume

Education

Employment History

Personal

Dianne D. Quad

12345 North 61st Drive
Glendale, Arizona 85304

(602) 555-1234

1994
Bachelor of Arts
Communications and English
Rutgers University
New Jersey

Continuing education classes at UCLA

2000
Advertising Sales Representative
Scottsdale Progress
Scottsdale, Arizona

1998 – 2000
Account Executive
KC Design, Advertising and Promotion
Phoenix, Arizona

1994 – 1998
Customer Sales and Service
Representative
Quad/Marketing, Inc.
Los Angeles & New York

1993 – 1994
Marketing Assistant
BBDO Advertising
New York

Qualifications

- Excellent oral and written communication skills
- Creative
- Problem solver
- Self-starter
- Strong organizational and coordinating skills

Goals

To join energy and insight with business experience to be part of a productive work environment

Interests

Reading, athletics, family, social well-being

Reference available upon request

Dianne D. Rutgers
12345 North 61st Drive
Glendale, Arizona 85304
(602) 555-1234

Education

1994
Bachelor of Arts
Communications and English
Rutgers University
New Jersey

Continuing education classes at
UCLA

Employment History

2000
Advertising Sales
Representative
Scottsdale Progress
Scottsdale, Arizona

1998 – 2000
Account Executive
KC Design
Advertising and Promotion
Phoenix, Arizona

1994 – 1998
Customer Sales and Service
Representative
Quad/Marketing, Inc.
Los Angeles and New York

1993 – 1994
Marketing Assistant
BBDO Advertising
New York

Qualifications

- *Excellent oral and written communication skills*
- *Creative*
- *Problem solver*
- *Self-starter*
- *Strong organizational and coordinating skills*
- *Strategic thinker*

Goals

To join energy and insight with business experience to be part of a productive work environment

Interests

Reading, athletics, family, social well-being

References available upon request

Elena Valerie Latis
1234 W. Olive Avenue #123
Glendale, Arizona 85302
(602) 555-1234

OBJECTIVE

A position with a multinational firm in the field of marketing/advertising

EDUCATION

MASTER OF INTERNATIONAL MANAGEMENT, MIM *(5/00)*
The American Graduate School of International Management
THUNDERBIRD Campus, Glendale, Arizona

INTERNATIONAL ADVERTISING (INTERAD) SEMINAR,
Thunderbird, Account Executive *(9/99–12/99)*
Served as a liaison between Kellogg's Corporation and 7-member marketing team. Developed advertising strategy for Kellogg's Corn Flakes in Russia.

BACHELOR OF ARTS, Indiana University, *Bloomington, IN (8/98)*
Majors: Journalism and Slavic Studies
Minors: German and Spanish Languages and Culture
International Media Law Graduate Seminar – Emphasis on GATT, constitutional rights, political barriers to media

FOREIGN STUDY
Barcelona, Spain *– Thunderbird (1999–2000)*
Graz, Austria *– Indiana/Graz University Exchange Program (1997)*
Thessaloniki, Greece *– Study Abroad Program (1993, 1996)*

PROFESSIONAL EXPERIENCE

RUSSIAN ECONOMIC COUNCIL, *Thunderbird Convention (5/99)*
Translated for city councilmen from Moscow, Leningrad, and Novgorod on the subjects of local government reforms, decision making, and conflict resolution between ethnic and racial groups.

MANACO SYSTEMS INTERNATIONAL, LTD., *Northfield, IL*
Account Executive *(8/98–1/99)*
Intern, Assistant Account Executive *(5/98–8/98)*
Presented products to prospective clients from Argentina, Chile, Mexico, and Turkey via news releases, brochures, advertisements, and public speaking. Assisted in preparing trade agreements. Created and coordinated exhibit booths at trade shows. Selected and purchased garment lines and gift items; budget of $750,000.

M & N TRANSPORTATION, INC., *Morton Grove, IL*
Intern, Administrative Assistant *(5/96–8/96)*
Wrote copy and laid out of brochures for prospective clients. Solicited business; assisted dispatcher; computerized filing systems (database)

NEW LIFE BROADCASTING CO., WVVX FM
Highland Park, IL
Copy Editor *(5/95–8/95)*
Wrote commercials in English and Russian; edited copy. Solicited air time advertisements.

LANGUAGES

Fluent *in Russian, German, Spanish, and English*
Conversational *in Greek, Czechoslovakian, and Polish*

Diane W. Tomball

1234 Del Paz Drive • Colorado Springs, CO 80918 • Home Phone: (719) 555-1234

PROFILE

- Experienced painter and art educator with diverse background in:
  - ▸ Color theory
  - ▸ Presentation
  - ▸ Art therapy
  - ▸ Design
  - ▸ Drawing
  - ▸ Watercolors
  - ▸ Oil painting
  - ▸ Sculpture
  - ▸ Teaching
  - ▸ Administration
  - ▸ Marketing
  - ▸ Promotion

EXPERIENCE

Teaching

- Creative teacher with an interactive, hands-on teaching style; never found a student who was not teachable.
- Experienced in the instruction of student populations from diverse economic backgrounds, ages, and talent levels.
- Developed curriculum for art and art appreciation classes; committed to excellence in education.
- Taught in college, workshop, and nonacademic settings, including Michael's, Hobby Lobby, retirement centers.
- Helped students appreciate how people have used art to express ideas throughout history.
- Guided students in evaluating and critiquing 20th century art.
- Coordinated and conducted a teaching tour of Europe for 15 art students from Tomball College (1992).
- Visited the great museums of Europe, including The Louvre, The British Museum, The Vatican, and museums in Amsterdam, Florence, and Venice.
- Traveled extensively, studying the great masters in such museums as the Guggenheim and National Art Gallery (New York), The High Museum (Atlanta), The Art Institute of Chicago, and the Mexico Museum of Anthropology.

Art and Exhibits

- Skilled in the creative use of oils, acrylics, pen/ink, pencil, Prisma color, watercolors, and pastels.
- Two pieces of art work selected for the juried Cook Communications Art Show (1997).
- One of 20 chosen from 400 artists for the Alternative Arts Alliance road show in Denver (1996).
- Exhibited at the Arvada Arts Center (Denver), Cañon Arts Center (Cañon City), corporate offices, and others.
- Awarded the Lone Star Art Guild State Best of Show for an oil painting (Houston, 1990).
- Received the Artcetera Artist's Award from one of the largest Houston art leagues (1988).
- Honored with numerous awards and ribbons from local and state art shows (1985 – 1994).
- Recipient of a full art scholarship from North Harris County College based on juried works of art, including oils, watercolors, pastels, portraits, clay sculptures, and acrylics.

Administration

- Developed marketing strategies to place art classes in innovative business settings, including Compaq Corp.
- Organized and promoted art shows, exhibits, and classes, including the first annual Tomball College Art Show.
- Efficiently managed department and classroom budgets, ensuring profitability.
- Recruited guest speakers and volunteer workers from the community and academia.
- Juried the Northwest Art League's Lone Star State Art Show with more than 500 works of art.
- Coordinated the yearbook as President of the Northwest Art League.

HISTORY

Art Instructor, Hobby Lobby, Michael's, The Bridge, Crossings, Colorado Springs, Colorado	1995 – present
Art Teacher, Compaq Computer Corporation, galleries, and stores, Houston, Texas	1984 – 1994
Art Instructor, Tomball College, Tomball, Texas	1991 – 1992
Substitute Teacher (all levels and subjects), Cypress Fairbanks School District, Houston, Texas	1980 – 1984
Family Relations Teacher, Everman High School, Everman, Texas	1967 – 1969
Child Development Teacher, Ft. Worth Public School System, Ft. Worth, Texas	1966 – 1967
Home Economics Teacher, Gordon High School, Gordon, Texas	1965 – 1966

EDUCATION

Master of Art Education, University of Houston, Texas	1989 – 1991
Art Curriculum (29 hours), North Harris County College, Houston, Texas	1988 – 1989
Private Art Instruction under nationally known artists, including Dick Turner (portraiture), Buck Paulson (land/seascapes), and Efime Fruman (old master's techniques)	1979 – 1988
Bachelor of Science in Home Economics, Abilene Christian College, Abilene, Texas	1961 – 1965

RUSS MARTIN

STRENGTHS

- Talented actor with strong stage instincts and formal training.
- Varied background that includes directing and technical work.
- Experienced in set and stage construction, lighting, and sound.
- Height: 6 feet, 0 inches – Weight: 190 lbs. – Hair: Dark Brown – Eyes: Green.

THEATRE

Cyrano de Bergerac	Cyrano	Colorado State University, Ft. Collins, CO
Boardwalk Melody Murders	Guido	Masqued Dinner Theatre, Colorado Springs, CO
Romeo and Juliet	Mercutio	Longmont Theatre Company, Longmont, CO
The Glass Menagerie	Tom	Colorado State University, Ft. Collins, CO
Hamlet	Horatio	Longmont Theatre Company, Longmont, CO
No Exit	Valet	Colorado State University, Ft. Collins, CO
The Bald Soprano	Mr. Martin	Colorado State University, Ft. Collins, CO
Midsummer Night's Dream	The Moon	Longmont Theatre Company, Longmont, CO
Black Comedy	Mr. Bamburger	Hamilton Southeastern, Fishers, IN
Bent	Max	Colorado State University, Ft. Collins, CO
The Elephant Man	Freak Handler	Colorado State University, Ft. Collins, CO
The Secret	Sam Connor	Hamilton Southeastern, Fishers, IN
Our Town	Howie Newsome	Hamilton Southeastern, Fishers, IN
Who's on First	Lou Abbott	Colorado State University, Ft. Collins, CO
Bent	SS Guard	Colorado State University, Ft. Collins, CO
The Elephant Man	Constable	Longmont Theatre Company, Longmont, CO
Other People's Money	President	Colorado State University, Ft. Collins, CO

MUSICAL THEATRE

Man of La Mancha	Padre	Harbor Lights Theatre, Colorado Springs, CO
Fiddler on the Roof	Fyedka	Longmont Theatre Company, Longmont, CO
Damn Yankees	Mr. Applegate	Hamilton Southeastern, Fishers, IN
Anything Goes	Ching/Chorus	Colorado State University, Ft. Collins, CO
Fuente Ovejuna	Devil	Colorado State University, Ft. Collins, CO
Sweet Charity	Waiter/Chorus	Longmont Theatre Company, Longmont, CO
Brigadoon	Sandy Dean	Hamilton Southeastern, Fishers, IN
Carousel	Timony/Chorus	Hamilton Southeastern, Fishers, IN
My Fair Lady	Prof. Henry Higgins	Colorado State University, Ft. Collins, CO

EDUCATION

Colorado State University, Fort Collins, CO: Theatre major for four years
Colorado State University, Fort Collins, CO: Tap, jazz, court, and ballroom dance
Colorado State University, Fort Collins, CO: Stage combat (acting and directing)
Vincent Lappas Acting Seminar, Colorado Springs, CO

SPECIAL SKILLS

Singing Voice: Contra-Tenor/Baritone	Weapons handling/maintenance (expert marksman)
Accents: New York, Italian	Veteran motorcyclist
Sword fighting and period fencing (stage and live)	Expert swimmer (formerly competitive)
Performance driving (civilian and military)	Team Sports: volleyball, baseball, bowling, etc.

AWARDS

Best Actor of 1990, Hamilton Southeastern, Fishers, IN
1995 Creative and Performing Arts Award (stipend), Colorado State University, Fort Collins, CO

ADDRESS

1234 Mount Werner Court, Colorado Springs, CO 80906, (719) 555-1234, criscito@aol.com

Trista R. Whittier

12345 Northface Court
Englewood, Colorado 80919
Phone: (719) 555-1234

Education

BACHELOR OF ARTS (1994–1996)
Whittier College, Whittier, California
- Studio arts major
- Emphasis in oil painting

DENMARK INTERNATIONAL STUDIES (1995)
Copenhagen, Denmark
- Studied abroad for a semester

UNIVERSITY OF NORTHERN COLORADO (1992–1994)
Greeley, Colorado

SAVANNAH COLLEGE OF ART AND DESIGN (1990–1991)
Savannah, Georgia

Exhibitions

- Two paintings chosen for the Whittier College "Literary Review" (1996)
- Two works selected for display at the Whittier College "Senior Art Exhibit" (1996)
- Abstract oil painting exhibited for two months at Whittier College Library (1996)
- Hired to paint a mural for a Whittier College dormitory (1994)
- Designed a t-shirt print for a fraternity fund raiser (1995)
- Selected to paint a homecoming parade float for the University of Northern Colorado radio station (1992)

Other Experience

RECEPTIONIST (1996), Whittier College Computer Center, Whittier, California
- Provided customer service and answered telephones.

COOK (Summers 1993–1995), Old Chicago's Pizza, Colorado Springs, Colorado
- Prepared food (pizza, pasta, dough).
- Opened and closed the pizza line and pasta bar.

CUSTOMER SERVICE (1993), Pudge Brothers', Greeley, Colorado
- Managed the cash register and assisted customers in a newly opened pizza delivery restaurant.

Portfolio

Available upon request

Jefferson Daniel Wood

Graphic Artist Illustrator

~~~~~~~

Pen & Ink Watercolor Oils

1234 S. Euclid Avenue
Boise, Idaho 83706

Phone: 208-555-1234
Fax: 208-555-1234

Profile

▸ Creative graphic artist with experience in pen and ink illustration, watercolor, and oil mediums.
▸ Background in magazine/book, children's book, graphic novel, and comic book illustration.
▸ Hard-working, loyal artist with definitive leadership and sales abilities.
▸ Self-starter; able to motivate others to perform to their maximum potential.

Education

Bachelor of Fine Arts, Savannah College of Art and Design, Savannah, Georgia, 1995
▸ Department of Sequential Art
▸ Awarded McCammon $10,000 Scholarship
▸ Three-week watercolor workshop in the Greek islands
▸ Trained under Bo Hampton, a pupil of Will Eisner and Al Williamson, two comic book greats.

Art Experience

▸ Completed 10 illustrations for *Resumes in Cyberspace: Your Complete Guide to a Computerized Job Search* by Pat Criscito, CPS, CPRW, published by Barron's Educational Series, Inc., Hauppauge, New York, 1997 (two of the illustrations appear on this resume).
▸ Painted three watercolor poetry prints for *Soul Lights, Inc.,* by Mary S. Humble, Cramerton, North Carolina, self-published and distributed to Deseret Books and other LDS bookstores.
▸ Created a weekly adventure comic strip called *The Mosquito* for the *Georgia Guardian*, a college newspaper, September 1991 – May 1992.
▸ Selected to show an oil painting in the Savannah College Graduation Exhibit, May 1995.
▸ Painted a series of nine watercolors while in the Greek islands.
▸ Completed numerous private works that hang in homes and offices in several states.

Other Experience

▸ Assistant Manager, Chatham Apartments, Savannah, Georgia, 1991 – 1994; helped manage more than 200 rental units in a 15-story apartment complex.
▸ Waiter, Bobbie's Diner, Savannah, Georgia, 1991 – 1994.
▸ Completed a two-year mission for the LDS Church, 1994 – 1995.

Skills

▸ Computer experience: Macintosh, Adobe Illustrator, Adobe Photoshop, Quark Express, IBM PC, Windows 95, WordPerfect, Microsoft Publishing
▸ Languages: Knowledge of Hebrew

18 Cover Letters, Letterheads, and Paper Colors

The first rule of cover letters: Never use a generic cover letter with only "To Whom It May Concern." With tons of work on your desk, would you be interested in such a mass mailing? You would probably consider it junk mail, right? You would be much more likely to read a letter that was directed to you personally and so would human resources professionals.

The second rule: Every résumé sent by mail or fax needs a personalized cover letter even if the advertisement didn't request a cover letter.

The third rule: Résumés sent by e-mail don't need a cover letter. Use only a quick paragraph with three to five sentences telling your reader where you heard about the position and why your qualifications are a perfect fit for the position's requirements. E-mail is intended to be short, sweet, and to the point. Then, cut and paste your ASCII text résumé into the e-mail message screen instead of just attaching your MS Word or WordPerfect file (see page 30 for an example of an ASCII text file or find a copy of Barron's *Résumés in Cyberspace* for detailed instructions on how to create and use an electronic résumé).

This chapter will address several cover letter types. A letter to a recruiter requires different information than a letter in answer to an advertisement. A targeted cover letter that tells a story and captures your reader's attention is ideal when possible, but such letters aren't always practical. Not everyone has the writing skills to produce an effective story, and the time involved in researching and writing the story would be impractical for mass mailings. A hard-hitting salesperson can write a dynamic cover letter, but not everyone is comfortable with that style and a good cover letter doesn't have to be "pushy."

Before we get into specific styles, let's cover some general rules that apply to most cover letters. The letters on pages 279–286 are general cover letters following these rules.

1. Customize each cover letter with an inside address (do not use "to whom it may concern").

2. Personalize the greeting (Dear Ms. Smith). Try to get the name of a person whenever possible. A blind advertisement makes that impossible, but in other cases a quick telephone call can often result in a name and sometimes a valuable telephone conversation. When you can't get a name, use Dear Recruiter, Dear Hiring Manager, Dear Search Committee, or Dear Sir/Madam.

3. Mention where you heard about the position so your reader knows where to direct your résumé and letter. The first paragraph of your cover letter is a great place to state (or restate) your objective. Since you know the specific job being offered, you can tailor your objective to suit the position.

4. Drop names in the first paragraph if you know someone in the company. Hiring managers take unsolicited résumés more seriously when they assume you were referred by one of their employees or customers.

5. The second paragraph (or two) is the perfect place to mention specific experience that is targeted to the job opening. This is your "I'm super great because" information. Here is where you summarize why you are absolutely perfect for the position. Really sell yourself. Pick and choose some of your experience and/or education that is specifically related to the company's requirements, or elaborate on qualifications that are not in your résumé but apply to this particular job. If you make mention of the company and its needs, it becomes immediately obvious that your cover letter is not generic. Entice the reader to find out more about you in your résumé. Don't make this section too long or you will quickly lose the reader's interest.

6. The closing should be concise. Let the reader know what you want (an application, an interview, an opportunity to call). If you are planning to call the person on a certain day, you could close by saying, "I will contact you next Tuesday to set up a mutually convenient time to meet." Don't call on Mondays or Fridays if you can help it. If you aren't comfortable making these cold calls, then close your letter with something like: "I look forward to hearing from you soon." And remember to say, "Thank you for your consideration" or something to that effect (but don't be obsequious, please!).

❑ Story Letters

If you are planning a direct mail campaign to 50 or 100 or 400 companies, this type of letter is not for you. It just isn't practical. However, you will have to admit that the letters on pages 287–290 are great attention getters. For those dream jobs that require something special, this is the way to go. In a story cover letter, you must be able to tell a good story and write it well. If writing is not your forté, you can hire someone to write the letter, but you must still do the research and have a general outline of the story.

❑ Letters to Headhunters

There are two types of recruiters (or headhunters): retained and contingency. The difference is that retained recruiters are hired by a company and are then paid by that company whether they ever find the right employee for the position or not.

Contingency firms are also paid by the company but only when they find a good match and the job seeker is hired. Legitimate recruiting firms don't charge the job seeker, which means they are working for their client companies and not *you*.

Because their mission is not to find the perfect job for you but to find the perfect employee for their client, they have little interest in communicating with you unless you are a prime candidate for a position they are seeking to fill *now*. Don't call recruiters; they will call you if they are interested. This affects both the beginning and ending of your cover letter. If you don't have a person's name, use Dear Recruiter. You should resign yourself to waiting for the recruiter to call you, so "I look forward to hearing from you soon" is an appropriate closing for a recruiter cover letter.

In addition to the "I'm super great because" paragraph(s), you need to add another paragraph just before the closing that tells the recruiter your ideal position title, industry, salary, and geographic preferences. Check the cover letters on pages 291–294 for examples.

❏ Dynamic Letters

Job openings that require a certain amount of dynamic spirit—like sales—deserve a more dynamic letter. This can be accomplished in the opening paragraph. The rest of the letter is written like a standard cover letter but with a little more energy than usual. The last paragraph can be a bit more aggressive—you call the hiring manager instead of waiting for him/her to call you. See pages 295–298 for examples of cover letters that exude confidence and power.

❏ Thank You Letters

According to a recent survey, less than 20% of applicants write a thank you note after an interview. Of the recruiters surveyed, 94% said that a thank you letter would increase the applicant's chances of getting the job, or at least help him/her stay in the running, provided the applicant is otherwise qualified. Fifteen minutes of your time and a first class postage stamp are very inexpensive investments in your career!

Thank you letters simply thank the interviewer for his or her time and reiterate some of the important things you learned about the company in the interview. Add some key qualifications that you forgot to mention in the interview, or emphasize some of the more important things you discussed. If the interviewer shared some information that gave you an insight into the company and its culture, mention how much you appreciated it.

A thank you letter should be short—three paragraphs at the most. Don't try for the hard sell. You had your chance in the interview. The thank you letter just reinforces what you have already said. See the examples on pages 299–304.

❏ Letterheads

It is so easy to create a letterhead all your own and to make it match your résumé. Just copy into a new document the name and address you have already created for your résumé. It couldn't be simpler! It makes a very sharp impression when your cover letter and résumé match in every respect from paper color to font to letterhead.

❏ Paper Colors

Color, like music, creates an atmosphere. Everyone knows that different colors evoke different feelings. Red can make a person feel warm, whereas blue does just the opposite.

Of course, you wouldn't want to use red in a résumé! . . . although an artist could get away with just about any color. As a general rule, résumé papers should be neutral or light in color. After 20 years in the résumé business, I have discovered that brilliant white linen paper is still the most popular, followed closely by a slightly off-white and then by shades of light gray.

Just make sure that the color of the paper you choose is representative of your personality and industry and that it doesn't detract from your message. For instance, a dark paper color makes your résumé hard to read.

In a scannable résumé, never use papers with a background (pictures, marble shades, or speckles). A scanner tries to interpret the patterns and dots as letters. This is a good rule to follow even for paper résumés that will never be scanned. Often companies will photocopy résumés for hiring managers, and dark colors or patterns will simply turn into dark masses that make your résumé difficult to read. If a company has multiple locations, the original résumé may even get faxed from one site to another and the same thing happens.

The type of paper (bond, linen, laid, cover stock, or coated) isn't as important, although it also projects an image. Uncoated paper (bond, linen, laid) makes a classic statement. It feels rich and makes people think of corporate stationery and important documents. Coated stock recalls memories of magazines, brochures, and annual reports. Heavy cover stock and laid paper can't be successfully folded and don't hold the ink from a laser printer or copier very well, so they must be handled gently. All of these factors play a part in your paper choice.

Regardless of the paper you choose, mail your résumé flat instead of folded. It costs a few extra cents in postage and a little more for the 9 × 12 envelope, but the impression it makes is well worth the extra cost. It also helps with the scannability of your résumé. Thank you letters and other follow-up letters can be folded in standard No. 10 business envelopes.

John Q. Carter

1234 50th Street
Lubbock, Texas 79416
(806) 555-1234

June 10, 1999

Letter answering
an advertisement.

Mr. John Q. Smith
Director of Human Resources
Continental Grain Company
123 Park Avenue
New York, New York 10172

Dear Mr. Smith:

I am very interested in the financial analysis position that you advertised in *The New York Times,* and would like the opportunity to discuss the possibility of working for your company.

I believe my experience in financial analysis, coupled with a strong quantitative and analytical background from my MBA and engineering degrees, makes me an excellent candidate. As you will notice in the enclosed résumé, I have spent more than three years working in various Latin American countries gaining experience with international markets and different cultures. I have also acquired an extensive knowledge of computer systems through my work experience and education.

I look forward to speaking with you soon. Please feel free to contact me if you have any questions or would like to discuss my qualifications further.

Sincerely,

John Q. Carter

Enclosure

MARCUS BAILEY

1234 Vondelpark Drive ▸ Colorado Springs, Colorado 80907
Phone: (719) 555-1234 ▸ E-mail: criscito@aol.com

June 24, 1999

Letter answering an advertisement
that requested salary requirements.

Director of WW Infrastructure Service Delivery
1234 South Yosemite Street, Suite 470
Englewood, Colorado 80111

Dear Recruiter:

I am very interested in the position you advertised in *The Denver Post* for a Director of Worldwide Infrastructure Service Delivery Growth. My background and qualifications are an excellent match with your requirements.

My twelve years of experience in information systems engineering and management have focused on integration and organizational process improvement. During this period, I have developed outstanding leadership and management skills, compiled an excellent knowledge base of all phases of system and software engineering, and provided the vision for integrating future information technology into critical computer and telecommunication systems. Currently, I am responsible for infrastructure management valued at $10 million, including hardware, software, and networking systems with wireless and web technologies. The systems are geographically distributed, which poses service delivery challenges. I have also managed the development of $8+ million training systems and support tools for various clients. My primary focus is now on reducing the resource conflicts associated with the performance, costs, and schedules of 15 projects throughout their life cycles.

Education in mathematics, as well as an MBA and a second graduate degree in operations research, combined with my extensive computer science experience, enables me to move easily between different industries that use information technology. This would be a tremendous benefit to your organization, providing more flexibility and proven technical leadership.

As a results-oriented person, I do not wait for things to happen. I set the standards for customer service and quality. I am a team builder, motivator, and producer with a keen eye for operational deficiency and the ability to respond with creative and effective solutions. I am well known for my ability to ensure that the project team is process-oriented, creative, motivated, and challenged.

The travel required in this position would not be problem. I am an experienced international traveler and would be willing to travel up to 40 percent of the time. My salary requirements are negotiable.

More details of my accomplishments are provided in the attached résumé. There you will see how my technical background and thorough understanding of information technology have been used to mitigate risks, improve competitive advantage and profitability, achieve corporate strategic objectives, and satisfy our quality service delivery goals. If your company could use these skills in this position, don't hesitate to call. I will look forward to hearing from you soon.

Sincerely,

Marcus Bailey

Enclosures

P. O. Box 1234
Phoenix, Arizona 85123
(602) 555-1234

August 1, 1999

Ms. Marilyn Smith
Dallas Partnership
1234 Elm Street, Suite 12
Dallas, Texas 75270

Letter sent at the recommendation of a mutual friend asking for an informational interview.

Dear Ms. Smith:

I am writing you at the recommendation of Mr. Bill Smith of the Arizona Economic Council in Phoenix. I developed a very amicable working relationship with Bill and the rest of the AEC staff during the short time I was there. As of September 1, however, I will be establishing permanent residency in the Dallas area and am seeking employment in the field of international marketing/management. Bill believed you would be a good person to talk with about the Dallas business scene and where the best employment opportunities in my field are to be found. Please note my qualifications:

- **Advanced Education – Master of International Management**: Graduated from "Thunderbird" graduate school, devoted exclusively to international business. Performed extensive graduate research and writing projects demonstrating my understanding of management, marketing, and finance on the international level.

- **Unique International Business Skills – Proficient in German**: Earned an undergraduate degree in German. Spent one year living in Freiburg, Germany, while studying German at Albert Ludwigs Universität.

- **Demonstrated Organizational Skills, Technical Competency**: I have a consistent record of achievements and honors. In academics, nonprofit organizations, and employment, I have always taken, or been asked to accept, additional responsibilities, thus reflecting my honest work ethic, skill in organizing work for expeditious completion, and ability to work under pressure.

Enclosed is my résumé for your review. Perhaps you may have a suggestion or two of whom to contact or where to look. Aside from my search for employment, I would genuinely enjoy meeting you, as Bill has spoken so highly of you. Since I plan to make Dallas my permanent home, I am interested in developing a relationship with the city and its people for reasons beyond employment. I will call your office next week to see if you may have 5 or 10 minutes to meet with me sometime in the near future.

Sincerely,

John R. Wright

Enclosure

JAMES A. CLEMENS, Ed.D.

1234 Country Club Drive • Colorado Springs, Colorado 80909 • Home: (719) 555-1234

March 26, 2000

Letter for a position in education.

Hazard, Young, Attea & Associates
1234 Waukegan Road
Glenview, Illinois 60025

Dear Recruiter:

Please accept this letter and résumé in application for the position of Superintendent of Sarasota County School District.

I recently completed my eighth year as Deputy Superintendent in Colorado Springs School District 11. My assignments and responsibilities have touched virtually every aspect of curriculum, instruction, finance, administration, personnel, training, planning, and development. I have now chosen to pursue a superintendent's position in a school district such as yours that can utilize this combination of experience, energy, enthusiasm, education, and expertise.

It is my belief that, more than anything else, public education is in need of leadership and not simply administration. I have demonstrated the ability to bring diverse groups together, motivating them to define strategically the community's views of the future of our school system. Under my leadership, School District 11—with 33,000 students and 3,500 employees—achieved increased student test scores within a short period of time and under severe financial constraints. My philosophy is simple and stems from this student-centered doctrine: ***All students can learn. All students want to learn. Success breeds success.***

Over recent years, the changes in public education have been sweeping, and there are more changes to come. As an educational professional, I believe that I bring a unique set of skills, interests, and abilities to lead your school district into the future.

The enclosed résumé and letters of recommendation provide additional information on my credentials and accomplishments. I appreciate your consideration and look forward to meeting with you to discuss a mutually rewarding relationship.

Very truly yours,

James A. Clemens, Ed.D.

Enclosures

KITTY KOCHER

1234 N. Grand Avenue • Pueblo, Colorado 81003 • (719) 555-1234 • E-mail: criscito@aol.com

July 21, 1999

Business and Technology Center
1234 N. Main Street
Pueblo, Colorado 81003

Dear Sir/Madam:

Leadership, strategic planning, market analysis, marketing, and business development skills are inherent traits that are fine-tuned through hands-on experience. For the past nine years, I have been using my business talents to help small business owners with marketing, labor issues, and legislative affairs.

As you will notice in the enclosed résumé, I have an extensive business development, marketing, and advertising background. I am currently the director of a destination marketing organization located in Manitou Springs. The advertising agency I operate provides media buying services, printing, creative services, and marketing research programs. The Internet service provider program I started has led to the development of a web site with more than 5 million visitors in 1997, and the traffic is growing. From 1998 to date, the site has had nearly 8 million visitors. Nearly $500,000 in sales was attributed to the web site 1997. We tracked a $115 ROI for every dollar spent by our clients since 1994.

My diverse business experience has helped me develop strong skills in verbal presentations, meeting planning, financial management, community relations, data analysis, and special events. As with all successful small businesspeople, I can be "the chief cook and bottle washer."

I would welcome the opportunity to discuss how my skills would benefit your organization. You can reach me to schedule a personal interview by calling after 6:30 PM or by e-mail. I look forward to hearing from you in the near future. Thank you for your consideration.

Sincerely,

Kitty Kocher

Enclosure

Pamela Camp, CRCST

1234 Silver Drive • Colorado Springs, Colorado 80918 • (719) 555-1234

November 11, 1999

Networking letter for an industry with limited openings.

Human Resources
Overland Park Regional Medical Center
1234 Quivira Road
Overland Park, Kansas 66215

Dear Recruiter:

I picked up a back issue of *The Kansas City Star* on my last visit to the city and noticed your advertisement for a Sterile Services Technician. Even though this position is probably filled by now, I wanted you to have a copy of my résumé should another such opening become available. My family and I will be moving back to the Kansas City area in January, but I could be available with as little as two weeks notice.

As you will see in my résumé, I have spent the last nine years as an Instrument Technician in a community hospital here in Colorado Springs. I have been totally responsible for the sterilization of surgical instruments and equipment for six operating rooms. In 1994, I completed the Purdue University Certified Registered Central Service Technician course and passed the national exams. Since then, I have kept my certification up to date with 12 CEUs per year.

The enclosed résumé will provide you with more information regarding my experience and accomplishments. I would welcome the opportunity to speak with you in person or over the phone to further discuss how my skills could meet your needs. I look forward to hearing from you soon.

Sincerely,

Pamela Camp

Enclosure

KEISHA CHAMBER

July 12, 1999

> Networking letter requesting an internship or informational interview.

Stephen Smith
P.O Box 1234
LaJunta, Colorado 81050

Dear Mr. Smith:

John Smith, Professor at UCCS, recommended that I contact you. I have just graduated from the University of Colorado at Colorado Springs with an undergraduate degree in geography and environmental sciences. I have spent the past few years in residence at the Olympic Training Center and have had little time for anything besides training for my sport and working on my degree. Because of my schedule, I have not been able to take advantage of any internships in my field of study. Now that I have graduated, I would like to spend the next year working for a company like yours and learning all there is to know about the GIS industry. I am available full time in whatever capacity you need.

The opportunity to work for your company would be a real asset to my career, and I would appreciate your serious consideration of my qualifications. If you don't see a fit with your organization at the present time, I would still like to have the opportunity to meet with you or someone in your company who could take a few minutes to provide me with some ideas for how I might break into and succeed in this industry. Thank you for your consideration, and I look forward to hearing from you soon.

Sincerely,

Keisha Chamber

Enclosure

1234 San Juan Road, Apt. 12 • Sacramento, California 95833 • (916) 555-1234

facsimile
TRANSMITTAL

To: *Kaiser Permanente*

Fax: *1-916-555-1234*

From: *Patti Kuharski*

Re: *Security Services Manager Position*

Date: *January 12, 2000*

Pages: *2*

Message: *I am very interested in the Security Services Manager position that you advertised in yesterday's <u>Sacramento Bee</u>. I am seeking new opportunities in a more dynamic environment that could use my skills in facilities and security management.*

As you will notice in the enclosed résumé, I have more than fifteen years of experience managing security/safety programs with high-profile defense contractors. I am a recognized expert in program management and have a strong background in facilities management. My experience has also included supervision of personnel and I am skilled in team concepts and effective communication.

The enclosed résumé provides additional information on my work experience and accomplishments. I would appreciate the opportunity to meet with you to discuss the possibility of becoming part of this security services team. Thank you for your consideration. I look forward to hearing from you soon.

> Always follow up a fax with a
> mailed copy of the cover letter
> and résumé to ensure scannability.

JOSE CASTELLANOS

P.O. Box 1234 • Phoenix, Arizona 85123 • (602) 555-1234

June 26, 1999

Ms. Cindy Smith
College Relations Manager
Hallmark Cards, Inc.
P.O. Box 123456
Kansas City, Missouri 64141

Dear Ms. Smith:

It was in my hometown of Bogotá, Colombia, that as a teenager I came into contact with Hallmark for the first time. Even though I was not aware of the vision, effort, and commitment of resources that had gone into the Mother's Day card I had purchased, I was a happy customer. I never thought to wonder about the logistics of how that card had gotten to that small store or why a company more than 3,000 miles away was able to appeal to me, a kid from another country, culture, and language.

Hallmark's aggressive market penetration in more than 100 countries and its striving to provide employees with a supportive and challenging environment to best develop and apply their individual skills demonstrate to me that Hallmark is a company well worth entrusting with my career. In addition, I am impressed and attracted by Hallmark's commitment to supporting the communities in which it operates.

In light of Hallmark's international interest, you may be interested in my background. I started a small business in Colombia, which tested my energy, creativity, and initiative. The business quickly grew to be competitive as a result of innovative marketing and operation strategies. I have since learned to speak English, obtained a Bachelor of Business Administration from a U.S. university, and worked in several countries in varied positions, successfully adapting to both the people and management styles of these countries. Furthermore, in order to be better prepared for today's complex business environment, I am pursuing a Master of International Management degree, which I will complete in December.

It is my hope that my solid academic and cultural backgrounds, business experience, and interest in the international arena will convey to you that I have the qualifications to make a valuable contribution to Hallmark's efforts to remain the worldwide leader of the social expression industry.

I would like to be part of the Hallmark team that once helped me express myself through that card I gave my mother, and to take part in expanding the company to reach even more people all over the world. I would appreciate the opportunity to interview with you during your upcoming visit to Phoenix and hope that you will give the enclosed résumé favorable consideration. Thank you for your attention.

Sincerely,

Jose Castellanos

Enclosure

KATHLEEN A. SWIFT

Phone: (719) 555-1234 ▪ Fax: (719) 555-1234 ▪ E-mail: criscito@aol.com
1234 Pejn Avenue ▪ Colorado Springs, Colorado 80904

December 23, 1999

A story letter asking for a promotion.

Mr. John Smith
Sai Software Consultants, Inc.
1234 Lehman Drive, Suite 201
Colorado Springs, CO 80918

Dear Mr. Smith:

Monday is my favorite day of the week! Since I began working with Sai, mornings can't come fast enough. Every day presents another opportunity to make connections for our clients and candidates. Recruiting is creating new lives for people, finding ways for them to advance their careers. The opportunity to work with so many people and to delve into the revolution of technology are two of the most intriguing aspects of my job.

Because Sai is committed to being the best, I am anxious to continue being a part of that promise to our customers. I want to do my part in the continued growth of the company and would appreciate your consideration of my qualifications for a promotion to Account Executive in the Colorado Springs branch. I understand the importance of this role and realize, too, that timing is the key to assuring exceptional customer service. With that in mind, please know that I am ready to make the transition as soon as possible.

I will do my utmost to be an asset to Sai. Thank you for your consideration. I look forward to speaking with you in depth about this position and my proposed contributions during our meeting on Friday. In the meantime, if you have any questions, feel free to call me at extension 123.

Regards,

Kathleen A. Swift

Enclosure

Gloria R. Clawson

1234 Queen Anne Way • Colorado Springs, Colorado 80917 • (719) 555-1234

July 21, 1999

> **A dream job with little relevant experience.**

United Airlines (AFA)
Attn: F/A Employment
Box 66100
Chicago, Illinois 60666

Dear Sir/Madam:

I have dreamed of being a flight attendant since I was sixteen, but something has always prevented me from fulfilling that dream. Now that I've had previous experience with Western Pacific Airlines, I'm confident that I qualify for such a position. I would very much like to continue my career as a flight attendant, and work for United Airlines, which I feel is a well established and reputable organization.

With my twenty years of public relations experience, I would be an asset to United. I am a highly qualified individual who is ready to move forward into a more professional career. As you will see from the enclosed letters of recommendation, I am a very efficient and conscientious worker. I have a particularly strong desire to travel and work with people. With my outgoing personality and infectious smile, I know I would make a great addition to your team.

My résumé can only highlight my qualifications. A personal interview will assure you of my potential value to your company. I look forward to hearing from you so we may take the discussions of this challenging position one step further.

Sincerely,

Gloria R. Clawson

Enclosure

LORNA HURLEY

1234 Saturn Drive #123 • Colorado Springs, Colorado 80906 • (719) 555-1234

October 19, 1999

Making connections with the feelings of the reader and explaining too many qualifications for the job.

Human Resources
USAA
1234 Telstar Drive
Colorado Springs, CO 80920

Ref Code: PC-COS-1234

Dear Recruiter:

I have long been a satisfied customer of USAA, as was my father before me, so when I noticed your advertisement for Customer Account Professionals in a recent edition of <u>The Gazette</u>, I was immediately attracted to the possibility of working for USAA again. I was a supervisor in the Communications Center in your San Antonio headquarters for two years before returning to Colorado Springs for family reasons.

I know you aren't presently looking for a customer service supervisor, but I was a supervisor at Allstate insurance in the customer and agency service department. In fact all of my positions have involved a high level of customer service for both internal and external clients. At Allstate, I reviewed detailed policy information and relayed that information to both the insureds and their agents. I am accustomed to working in a fast-paced team environment with conflicting deadlines and have good computer skills. My college degrees and continuing professional development have prepared me for success within your customer service department.

Even though you might consider my qualifications too strong for this position, I want to assure you that I would enjoy the opportunity to learn USAA's Colorado Springs business from the ground up. I would welcome the opportunity for an interview to further discuss how my unique skills could benefit USAA. Thank you for your consideration, and I look forward to hearing from you soon.

Sincerely,

Lorna Hurley

Enclosure

1234 Bridle Trail
Pueblo, Colorado 81005

Phone: (719) 555-1234
E-mail: criscito@aol.com

November 17, 1999

> Letter to a recruiter. Note the third paragraph that is unique in letters to headhunters.

Mr. Stefan Smith
President
Management Search, Inc.
1234 S. Cook St., Suite 12
Barrington, IL 60010

Dear Mr. Smith:

Is one of your clients looking for a Human Resources or Labor Relations Manager with a proven track record of success in both manufacturing and high-tech services industries? Then you will want to review my qualifications.

As a successful human resource generalist with extensive labor relations experience, I have become well known for my ability to improve employee morale and increase trust between unions and management. I have negotiated and administered several collective bargaining agreements and was often called in to diffuse stalled bargaining processes. My dynamic leadership style motivates change within the corporate culture and builds support from within the ranks. These skills, plus many more, would be true assets to any company whether they are unionized or not.

My target job is at the middle-management level with an innovative company that could challenge my skills in human resource management, employee relations, and compensation and benefit administration. I have no geographic preferences and would be open to relocation. My salary requirements would of course depend on the city, but I would anticipate a base salary in the area of $60,000.

Should one of your clients have a current or emerging need for a member of their human resource management team, I would appreciate your serious consideration of my qualifications as outlined in the enclosed résumé. I am free to meet with you at your convenience and look forward to hearing from you soon.

Sincerely,

Tony Polacek

Enclosure

LEE DAVID MILLER

1234 Amstel Drive • Colorado Springs, Colorado 80907 • (719) 555-1234 • E-mail: criscito@aol.com

August 13, 1999

Letter to a recruiter.

Mr. Scott Smith
Office Manager
Korn/Ferry International
1234 S. Wacker Drive, Ste. 12
Sears Tower
Chicago, IL 60606

Dear Mr. Smith:

After a 25-year career in a number of senior management positions with high-tech computer/ communications companies in the Silicon Valley (and a short stint owning my own consulting company), I have seen many examples of great leadership and a few that were less than that. What seems to separate the truly successful senior executive from the mediocre is the degree of commitment he is able to instill in his people. I have been successful in building strong teams of productive professionals by creating comfortable, yet challenging environments that are stimulating and satisfying. Having participated in changes that have transformed the industry, I want to continue to be a part of this challenge in a senior leadership position that can take advantage of my in-depth knowledge of current technologies.

If one of your clients is looking for an experienced vice president or director who can motivate a team not only to meet but to exceed growth and financial goals, I am the person who can deliver those expectations and more. I am looking for a position that will continue to challenge me and give me the opportunity to lead a company into the 21st century. I have no geographic preferences and would expect compensation in the $130–175,000 range, exclusive of benefits.

The enclosed résumé will provide you with the details of my experience and accomplishments. I would welcome the opportunity for an interview to discuss how my skills and experience can meet your needs. Thank you for your consideration.

Sincerely,

Lee David Miller

Enclosure

HAROLD LITKE

123 East Oak Knoll, #12 • *Lewisville, Texas 75067* • *(972) 555-1234* • *criscito@aol.com*

January 11, 2000

Letter to a recruiter.

Ms. Sara Smith
Regional Vice President
Accountants On Call
1234 17th St., Suite 123
Denver, CO 80202

Dear Ms. Smith:

In today's tight job market, you undoubtedly receive hundreds of résumés every week from people seeking employment. However, you have a reputation for being able to recognize marketable talents, such as the ones I possess: diverse management expertise, a background in finance and collections, flexibility, commitment, and a highly effective management style.

I am a responsible leader with more than nine years of successful financial management experience. In my current position as the Investment Control Unit Manager for a multi-billion-dollar home equity services corporation, I manage $750 million in accounts receivable and nine employees. In addition to collections, I have experience in the banking, financial services, and home construction industries.

If one of your clients needs these skills and much more, please consider me as a candidate. I would like to live somewhere on the Front Range of Colorado. My minimum salary requirements are $60,000, exclusive of a bonus plan and company stock program.

Enclosed is a copy of my résumé, which provides more details regarding my experience and accomplishments. I am available to meet with you at your convenience to answer any questions you might have. I am in Colorado Springs until January 23rd, so please feel free to contact me locally at (719) 555-1234 or by e-mail at criscito@aol.com. I look forward to speaking with you soon.

Sincerely,

Harold Litke

Enclosure

August 16, 1999

Letter to a recruiter.

Mr. Thomas Smith
Executive Vice President
Anderson & Schwab, Inc.
1234 Seventeenth St., 2nd Floor
Denver, CO 80202

Dear Mr. Smith:

Are you searching for a goal-oriented sales manager with a reputation for building territories by as much as 40 percent per year? Then you've found him. I have been in sales management positions for the past eighteen years and would like to continue my career in a regional sales management position somewhere in the Rocky Mountain states.

As you can see in my résumé, I have experience in the sale of chemicals, equipment, and instrumentation to the life science, research, and medical markets. My background in international biotechnology and medical research would be an asset to any company in the industry. I have consistently exceeded sales goals during all of my career and could bring this track record of success to a sales management position. My education includes an undergraduate degree in biological sciences and education, as well as continuing professional development that has included the Tom Hopkins Boot Camp, Systems on Consultative Selling, Mercury International Selling Seminar, and Anthony Robbins on Unlimited Power, among others.

My target job is at the regional sales management level in Colorado, New Mexico, Arizona, Texas, or Utah. My salary requirements would depend on the city, of course, but I would anticipate a base salary in the area of $80,000 plus benefits and bonus.

Should one of your clients have a current or emerging need for a member of their sales management team, I would appreciate your serious consideration of my qualifications as outlined in the enclosed résumé. I am free to meet with your at your convenience and look forward to hearing from you soon.

Sincerely,

David F. Kovach

Enclosure

JOHN M. DELL

1234 West Athens Street
Phoenix, Arizona 85123

Telephone: (602) 555-1234
E-mail: criscito@aol.com

May 11, 1999

Dynamic cover letter.

Human Resources Department
Conservation International
1234 50th Street, N.W.
Washington, D.C. 20036

Dear Recruiter:

I am a graduate student at Arizona State University. In the past week at school, at least five people have approached me to let me know that "the perfect job for me" was advertised in the Career Services Center. As I read over your job description for the Tagua Product Manager, I couldn't help but agree.

Your needs and my skills and experience are a perfect match. In fact, just two weeks ago I met with Coopena, a native Brazilian company operating within the Amazon rain forest to market locally made products in harmony with the environment. "Cause marketing" and international market development are my areas of interest.

My entrepreneurial experience and education are tailored to your needs. I have run my own business for the past four years. I create and market artwear with ethnic and environmental themes. My marketing is primarily through sales representatives and trade shows, which has resulted in sales to most major department stores (including Nordstrom, Marshall Field, and Macy's) as well as to more than 500 other accounts. In addition, my cross-cultural and interpersonal skills are conducive to effective teamwork within a multicultural environment.

My education at ASU has included emphasis on marketing and international market development. Often, my studies have centered on environmental issues. I authored an ethics paper on the *Exxon Valdez* oil spill. Currently, I am conducting an extensive market research project for a company selling food products for emergency aid relief to private voluntary organizations. My language skills include a proficiency in Spanish. In addition, this semester I have continued to work on market development for Tenneco to sell used equipment in Third World countries.

It is important to me to believe in what a company does. I plan to apply my skills and interests in assisting a company like Conservation International achieve its objectives. In addition, I can offer Conservation International the benefit of my creative and innovative thinking.

I look forward to the opportunity to discuss how my skills and education fit into your needs and objectives. Please feel free to call if you have any questions.

Regards,

John M. Dell

Enclosure

Michael C. DeWitt

Permanent Address: 1234 Edgepark Road ♦ Vienna, Virginia 22182 ♦ Message: (703) 555-1234
Present Address: Jan Luykenstraat 1234 ♦ 1071 CR Amsterdam ♦ The Netherlands
Home: (+31) 20-555-1234 ♦ Work: (+31) 20-555-1234 ♦ E-mail: criscito@aol.com

February 17, 2000

Dynamic cover letter.

Mr. Mike Smith
Vice President, Sales
BT North America
1234 East 52nd Street
New York, NY 10022

Dear Mr. Smith:

Would you have an interest in an individual who has generated over $50 million in global account revenues for MCI, and who recently played a key role in the success of a new BT European joint venture? If so, I'd like to speak with you about how I can employ these skills and my knowledge of MCI/WorldCom to help BT North America achieve its revenue and business objectives in the new global marketplace.

As a successful sales and business development manager with MCI, I have a proven track record of delivering significant revenue and profit growth by building value propositions for advanced voice, data, and Internet applications. These skills have placed me within the top one percent of MCI's global sales force on three separate occasions.

In my current assignment as a member of the senior management team for Telfort in The Netherlands, I direct a group that, in just six months time, has been instrumental in contributing over $10 million in revenue to this successful startup.

With my overseas assignment drawing to a close in April 2000, I have a strong interest in pursuing opportunities within BT North America. Should you have a current or emerging need for a proven contributor to your management team, I would appreciate your serious consideration of my qualifications outlined in the enclosed résumé.

My present travel plans call for me to be in the United States from 2/20 through 3/2. I would welcome the opportunity to meet with you in person and will contact you shortly to determine if this is convenient for you. I look forward to hearing from you soon.

Sincerely,

Michael C. DeWitt

Enclosure

DETLEF E. SAPETA

1234 Gilcrest Road ▸ Colorado Springs, CO 80906 ▸ (719) 555-1234 ▸ E-mail: criscito@aol.com

March 4, 1999

Dynamic cover letter.

Ms. Cherlynn M. Smith
Staff Recruiter
A la Carte International, West
1234 E. Girard Drive
Aurora, CO 80013

Dear Ms. Smith:

Are you in need of a catalyst for change . . . someone who can turn around unprofitable operations and generate guest and employee loyalty? Then you have found him! I am ready to bring my considerable experience in hotel management to A la Carte International and would appreciate your serious consideration of my qualifications:

- High-level hotel management experience, broad operational knowledge, flexibility, commitment, and a dynamic, innovative leadership style.
- More than 20 years of successful experience at both the General Manager and District Manager levels.
- Background in multi-property management—I was the Managing Director of four hotels with more than 700 rooms, including one 4-star, 4-diamond property.
- Experience in managing budgets of up to $50 million and operations generating 32–37% in gross profits annually.
- Very persuasive speaker and business negotiator who routinely makes presentations at the highest levels of management.

If A la Carte could use these skills and much more, please consider me as a candidate. I have spent the last two years managing a family business and doing some hotel consulting work, but I have hotel management in my blood and I want to get back to work **now**! I have no real geographic preferences and am very flexible. I have lived and traveled all over the world and find that every location has its own unique charm.

Enclosed is a copy of my résumé that provides more details regarding my experience and accomplishments. I am available to meet with you at your convenience to answer any questions you might have and look forward to speaking with you soon.

Sincerely,

Detlef E. Sapeta

Enclosure

Deborah F. Buehler

1234 Lexington Park Drive • Colorado Springs, CO 80920
Phone: (719) 555-1234 • E-mail: criscito@aol.com

January 31, 2000

KVUU 99.9 Radio
Citadel Radio Center
Tiffany Square
1234 Corporate Drive, Suite 123
Colorado Springs, CO 80919

Dear Recruiter:

I heard on one of your radio shows today that you are searching for a goal-oriented Account Executive. You've found her.

After fourteen years in the sale of educational services, I have a proven track record of exceeding sales goals and generating profits for my employer. I am especially adept at making sales presentations and enjoy the one-on-one interaction of working directly with the customer. Besides my sales experience, I have a strong background in management and administration. That experience helps me to organize territories and supervise other sales representatives.

The enclosed résumé will give you more information on my experience and accomplishments. I would welcome the opportunity for an interview to further explore how my skills and experience could benefit KVUU. I look forward to hearing from you soon.

Sincerely,

Deborah F. Buehler

Enclosure

Liz Steele

1234 Ashwood Circle
Colorado Springs, CO 80906
Phone: (719) 555-1234
E-mail: criscito@aol.com

June 7, 1999

> Thank you letter that drops the name of the recipient's manager.

Ms. Jeanine Smith
Director of Sales and Marketing
The Cliff House
1234 Canon Avenue
Manitou Springs, Colorado 80829

Dear Ms. Smith:

Thank you for taking the time to interview me for the Sales Manager position at The Cliff House. As we discussed, I have built two successful businesses from the ground up and am very comfortable making cold calls, networking, and building a clientele from scratch. One of those businesses was a travel agency, where I worked closely with my counterparts in the hospitality industry and made high-level presentations to corporate prospects. This experience would translate well into the hotel industry here in the Colorado Springs area.

I had the unexpected pleasure of speaking with Craig Hartman on Friday, May 28, and got a positive feeling for the management culture at The Cliff House even before meeting you. I know that I would be a good fit in the Sales Manager position. Enclosed is a copy of my reference list, as you requested. If you have any further questions, feel free to give me a call. I look forward to hearing from you soon.

Sincerely,

Liz Steele

Enclosure

Regina M. Contrell

1234 Blodgett Drive
Colorado Springs, CO 80919

E-mail: criscito@aol.com

Phone (719) 555-1234
Fax (719) 555-1234

February 1, 2000

> Thank you letter for an interview
> and expression of continued interest.

Ms. Joan C. Smith
Assistant Superintendent
Elementary School Education
Virginia Beach City Public Schools
1234 George Mason Drive
Virginia Beach, Virginia 23456-0038

Dear Ms. Smith:

Thank you so much for considering my application for the Principal position at New Castle Elementary School. I was excited about our interview and the quality of your district, and I understand completely your choice of an existing principal within your district for this position. I wanted to let you know that I am still very much interested in a position in the Virginia Beach City Public Schools and would appreciate your consideration of my qualifications for the other Principal positions you are advertising on your web site.

As we discussed in my interview, I lived for twenty years in the Virginia Beach area and served as an administrator in the Norfolk Public Schools for thirteen years. My husband's business interests are bringing us back to Virginia soon, and I can be available with little notice. I appreciate your consideration of my qualifications and look forward to hearing from you soon.

Sincerely,

Regina M. Contrell

Enclosure

MICHAEL A. STEVENS

1234 Plainview Place • Manitou Springs, Colorado 80829 • (719) 555-1234

November 3, 1999

Thank you letter for an interview.

Mr. Tom Smith
Volt Services Group
1234 South Tejon, Suite 12
Colorado Springs, Colorado 80903

Dear Tom:

I wanted to thank you for the opportunity to meet with you last Thursday to discuss sales opportunities with your company. I hope our meeting went well enough for us to move forward in the process. I know you have interviewed many qualified candidates, but I wanted to let you know that I am the best candidate for the position. After more than ten years in sales, I would bring to Volt a proven record of success that helped me to achieve the top 10 percent of sales representatives for both MCI and California Casualty Insurance.

Thank you again for your time and consideration. I look forward to hearing from you soon.

Sincerely,

Michael A. Stevens

BEN VISCON

1234 42nd Avenue, S.W., Seattle, Washington 98136
Telephone: (206) 555-1234

November 16, 1999

Thank you letter for an interview.

Ms. Janet Smith
REI
P.O. Box 1234
Sumner, Washington 98390

Dear Janet:

It was a pleasure meeting you today, and I appreciate your taking the time to discuss career opportunities at rei.com with me. The growth of your company in the past few years is very exciting and I would very much like to become part of that success.

As we discussed, I would welcome the opportunity to take my eleven years of retail buying, planning, and management to the next level with e-commerce. I have a proven background in operations management, planning, and product management and could bring that experience to rei.com.

Thank you again for your consideration, and I look forward to hearing from you soon.

Sincerely,

Ben Viscon

Anne K. Mori

1234 Camfield Circle ▸ Colorado Springs, Colorado 80920 ▸ (719) 555-1234

January 17, 2000

Thank you letter for a tour and to request an interview.

Ms. Dana Smith
Administrator
Laurel Manor Care Center
1234 S. Chelton Road
Colorado Springs, Colorado 80910

Dear Dana:

I very much enjoyed having the opportunity to meet you and to tour Laurel Manor recently. I would like to thank you for taking the time to show me around and answer a few questions. Your facility impressed me as a warm, caring place for families to bring their loved ones and a pleasant working environment for employees.

I am very interested in interviewing for the Rehab Manager position you have advertised. I have had more than 12 years of experience as a speech–language pathologist and have spent the past year working in long-term care. I have worked very closely with our rehab director and have a working knowledge of OBRA, Medicare guidelines, and documentation, as well as managed care contracts, which greatly affect how and what we do in therapy!

Enclosed is a copy of my résumé, which should give you a broader picture of my clinical and supervisory experience. I look forward to hearing from you.

Sincerely,

Anne K. Mori

Enclosure

Betty Wesson

1234 Capella Drive • Monument, Colorado 80132 • Phone & Fax: (719) 555-1234

December 2, 1999

Thank you letter for
an informational interview.

Mr. George Smith
PRACO Advertising
1234 N. Tejon Street
Colorado Springs, CO 80903

Dear George:

I sincerely enjoyed our conversation last week. You answered so many of my questions and provided me with incredibly valuable information. I understand how difficult it is to break into the business of television production, but I am hopeful that my organizational background will allow me an opportunity.

Thank you for contacting Ms. Scott on my behalf. I will call you on Friday to follow up on that meeting. I know your time is valuable, but if you know of anyone in Colorado Springs whom I might contact, I would appreciate your letting me know.

Thank you for giving me so much of your time. I look forward to speaking with you on Friday.

Sincerely,

Betty Wesson

19 Index of Job Titles

How many times have you wished for a line or two to describe something you did in a job long ago or even just yesterday? If you are like me, it happens all the time. Unless you can get your hands on the actual job description for your position, finding the words to tell someone in a few short sentences what your duties were or what you accomplished is one of the hardest parts of writing a résumé.

That is what makes this index different from other résumé books. Instead of listing only the titles from the objectives of all the résumés in this book, it lists every job that every résumé mentions. That means you can turn to a page that has been referenced in the index and find wording somewhere in that résumé that applies to a specific job title. Sometimes it will be only one or two lines. Other times the entire résumé will be devoted to it. This should assist you in coming up with words to describe the various jobs you have performed in the past.

313